Teaching Problems and the Problems of Teaching

Teaching Problems and the Problems of Teaching

Magdalene Lampert

Yale University Press   New Haven & London

Designed and typeset in Adobe Minion by Mary Cronin.
Printed in the United States of America.

Library of Congress Cataloging-in-Publication Data

Lampert, Magdalene.
   Teaching problems and the problems of teaching / Magdalene Lampert.
      p. cm.
Includes bibliographical references.
ISBN 978-0-300-08973-8 (cloth.: alk. paper)
ISBN 978-0-300-09947-8 (pbk.: alk. paper)
1. Mathematics—Study and teaching (Elementary)—United States—Case
studies. 2. Effective teaching—United States—Case studies. I. Title

   QA135.6.L36 2001
   372.7—dc21
                        2001002322

A catalogue record for this book is available from the British Library.

The paper in this book meets the guidelines for permanence and durability of
the Committee on Production Guidelines for Book Longevity of the Council
on Library Resources.

10 9 8 7 6

This book is dedicated to the Lampert Family, whose tradition of adventure I hope it continues

Contents

Acknowledgments

The teaching I write about in this book is not mine alone; it owes its construction to many teachers with whom I have worked in many schools: in the BLOCKS Project in Philadelphia, Pennsylvania; at A. D. Eisenhower High School in Norristown, Pennsylvania; at Holy Spirit High School in Absecon, New Jersey; at the Prospect School in North Bennington, Vermont; at the Harrisville School in Harrisville, New Hampshire; at Buckingham, Browne, and Nichols School in Cambridge, Massachusetts; and most recently, at Spartan Village School in East Lansing, Michigan.

At Spartan Village School, I was able to teach fifth-grade mathematics for an hour a day for eight years while on the faculty of Michigan State University through the generous collaboration of my co-teacher, Thom Dye. We were able to work as we did with the support of our principal, Jessie Fry; my department chair, Henrietta Barnes; and my dean, Judith Lanier. Michigan State also made it possible for me to belong to and learn from a group of fellow teacher-researchers: Deborah Ball, Dan Chazan, Ruth Heaton, Suzanne Wilson, and David Wong. My current colleagues at the University of Michigan, in the School of Education, the School of Information, and the School of Business, have provided me with the time and the distance to reflect on what it is I know about teaching and with a lively audience for trying out my ideas about how to represent it. Discussions with my Dutch colleagues, especially Wil Oonk, Fred Goffree, and Leen Streefland during a semester in residence at the Freudenthal Institute in Utrecht, the Netherlands, helped me to refine my conceptual framework for representing the complications in the work of teaching with problems.

The analysis of the mountains of data that were collected to document the teaching analyzed in this book would not have been possible without the technical and conceptual assistance of Merrie Blunk, Carol Crumbaugh, Mike Goldenberg, Pam Hayes, Alice Horton-Merz, Nan Jackson, Peggy Kearns, Ginny Keen, Angia Macomber, Jim Merz, Peggy Rittenhouse, Mark Rosenberg, Sarah Theule-Lubienski, and Peri Weingrad. My colleagues Susan Florio-Ruane, Penelope Peterson, and Ralph Putnam assisted in the training of the research staff. The research would not have been possible without the generous support of the Spencer Foundation and the National Science Foundation.

For help in editing and designing the book, I thank Kathy Morris, Susan Arellano, Joyce Ippolito, Susan Laity, and Mary Cronin.

For keeping my writing connected to the immediacy of problems in teaching, I thank my teacher-readers, Ann Weber and Michael Gordon, and I thank my most recent teacher, Filippo Graziani, for giving me the opportunity to investigate the themes in this book from a very different point of view as I was completing my work on the project.

Finally, for both reading too many drafts and repeatedly convincing me over too much time that this project was worth continuing, I thank Deborah Ball, Gary Fenstermacher, Mary Catherine O'Connor, Raven Wallace, and especially my husband, David Cohen. I try to acknowledge their particular contributions at specific places throughout the book, but I am sure I cannot adequately represent the boundaries between their thinking and mine.

1

Understanding Teaching:
Why Is It So Hard?

This book is about teaching with problems and the problems in teaching. By taking a close look at the actions of a single teacher, teaching a single subject to a whole class over an entire academic year, I attempt to identify the problems that must be addressed in the work of teaching. Considering the nature of a teacher's actions as she addresses these problems, I try to explain what it is that is so hard about the work of teaching and what we might mean when we call this practice "complex." The single teacher I study here is myself. Like all teachers, I take a particular approach to teaching, and this book is also a study of that approach. I teach by engaging my students with the big ideas of the discipline as they work on problems and discuss the reasonableness of their strategies and solutions. Using problems, I teach them that they all can learn and that they can do it in school. But I do not attempt to prove that teaching with problems "works." I explain what kind of work is involved in doing it in an ordinary classroom in relations with students and subject matter.

The Problems in Teaching

The problems in teaching are many. Teachers face some students who do not want to learn what they want to teach, some who already know it, or think they do, and some who are poorly prepared to study what is taught. They must figure out how to teach each student, while working with a class of students who are all different from one another. They must respond to the many authorities who tell them what to teach. They have a limited amount of time to teach what needs to be taught, and they are interrupted often. The litany is so familiar. Why is the work teachers must do to address these problems so difficult for others to appreciate?

The fundamental structure of activity in the practice of teaching involves a teacher doing something with students around something to be learned. The fundamental problem of teaching practice is being able to do the things that will enable students to learn the things under study. I am being deliberately vague here in using words like "something" and "thing." The things a teacher and students can do are numerous, as are the things that can be taught and studied.

One reason teaching is a complex practice is that many of the problems a teacher must address to get students to learn occur simultaneously, not one after another. Because of this simultaneity, several different problems must be addressed by a single action. And a teacher's actions are not taken independently; they are inter-actions with students, individually and as a group. A teacher acts in different social arrangements in the same time frame. A teacher also acts in different time frames and at different levels of ideas with individuals, groups, and the class to make each lesson coherent, to link one lesson to another, and to cover a curriculum over the course of a year. Problems exist across social, temporal, and intellectual domains, and often the actions that need to be taken to solve problems are different in different domains.

When I am teaching fifth-grade mathematics, for example, I teach a mathematical idea or procedure to a student while also teaching that student to be civil to classmates and to me, to complete the tasks assigned, and to think of herself or himself and everyone else in the class as capable of learning, no matter what their gender, race, or parents' income. As I work to get students to learn something like "improper fractions," I know I will also need to be teaching them the meaning of division, how division relates to other operations, and the nature of our number system. While I take action to get some particular content to be studied by a particular student in a particular moment, I simultaneously have to do the work of engaging all of the students in my class in the lesson as a whole, even as I am paying different kinds of attention to groups of students with diverse characteristics. And I need to act in a way that preserves my potential to keep acting productively, day after day, throughout the year. This means making and maintaining relationships with students and relationships among ideas, as both students and ideas are continuous from one lesson to another. As I teach moment by moment across the school year, I enact my practice to reverberate through time, through relationships, and through fields of learning. As I act, I am shaping and being shaped by the evolving intellectual and social networks in which I am acting.

Pointing out the complexities of school teaching has led some to the conclusion that it may be an "impossible" practice. That is not my argument. It is possible to teach students and subjects in a classroom, and even to teach well and elegantly. How a teacher manages the complexity is what we need to understand. To study teaching practice as it is enacted in school classrooms we need an approach to analysis that can focus on the many levels in action at once, integrating the investigation of the problems of practice that a teacher needs to work on in a particular moment with the investigation of problems of practice that are addressed in teaching a lesson or a unit or a year. The study of the practical problems a teacher works on to teach each individual student can not be separate from the study of the practical problems of teaching different kinds of groups or teaching the class as a whole, as all of these elements of the work occur simultaneously in the public space of the classroom. These problems are tackled all at once, by the same person. The work aimed toward accomplishing any single goal of teaching needs to be examined in concert with examining concurrent work, perhaps aimed toward other goals, even toward conflicting goals across the temporal, social, and intellectual problem space in which practice occurs.

Teaching with Problems

Teaching with problems is an approach to instruction that has gone in and out of favor with educational reformers.[1] Using problems during school lessons is widely recommended today as a solution to the challenges faced by contemporary educators. Problem-based instruction is supposed to improve students' performance and increase their motivation to learn. It is supposed to make school more relevant and understanding more solid. In reading and writing, science and mathematics, art and history, new curricula are being adopted that present the material to be studied in the form of activities that problem-solvers in these fields need to know how to do. In order to learn, students are supposed to be doing things like writing essays to convince their classmates to vote one way or another in a school election, designing an appealing layout and color scheme for a new playground, figuring out just how polluted their local rivers are, and conducting surveys to study community demographics. Some reformers believe that such activities will prepare students for the work world; others, that they will increase students' capacity to think strategically or improve their ability to communicate about ideas; still others promote problem work on the assumption that it will make academics more accessible to a broader population of learners. But whatever its goal, the implications of this kind of student activity for the work of teaching are not obvious. What is to be taught as students work on such problems—and more importantly how it is to be taught—usually remains vaguely articulated.

Teaching with problems is a particular kind of teaching, and it is a kind that is not well understood. This is not to say that no one knows how to do it. We know that there are teachers who are accomplished at this kind of work and students who know how to learn from it.[2] But we know little about what the work entails. We certainly need to know more about the elements of such work if more teachers are to learn how to do it and if reformers are to make thoughtful judgments about how, or even whether, such an approach to curriculum and instruction can be successfully implemented on a broad scale.[3]

Why Teach with Problems?

I came to doing this kind of teaching and to the teaching of elementary mathematics through an unusual route. Unlike most elementary school teachers and many who work in the field of elementary mathematics education, I began by studying mathematics and later moved to trying to figure out how to teach it to elementary school children. And my mathematical genealogy was mixed.

On one side of the intellectual bloodline was my family, where practical uses of mathematics complemented a healthy respect for whatever could be learned in school. Early in my life, I was exposed to creating "alternative algorithms" by my father, who ran a small dairy business.[4] My work on the practical problems that arose in our dairy business went hand in hand with learning conventional arithmetic skills in school. I was made to practice my "times tables" in the car on family outings and do pages and pages of homework every night, and I could use what I learned in school to help in the business. The mathematics education I experienced as a child set me up to see the subject as one that fit together in a coherent whole, with home and school as complementary occasions to learn and use its tools and ideas.

On the other side of my intellectual bloodline was an academic interest in the foundations of the discipline. As a college student, I began to investigate in a formal way what it means to know something mathematically. I read several histories of mathematics and investigated the relationship between the development of mathematical knowledge and the kinds of problems that mathematicians were trying to solve. I chose to do a senior thesis in the philosophy of mathematics and began to listen in on the centuries-long argument about what it means to know that a mathematical statement is true. I focused my studies on a particular view of mathematical truth expounded by a group of mathematical scholars who referred to themselves as "intuitionists." Intuitionism was established as a school of thought in the 1930s when argument about the nature of mathematical truth was rampant. Intuitionists countered the absolutism of the formalists and the logicists with the notion that mathematics is what is known by persons and it is invented out of their ideas about quantity and shape.[5] Perhaps the most significant thing I learned from this work is that there are several different ways of thinking about why a mathematical statement is true, all reasoned and warranted. I observed that what it means to know something is a question that twentieth-century scholars can and do argue about.

Entering mathematics teaching with such a mixed and unusual ancestry gave me an interesting perspective on what I should be teaching and how to teach it. My experience turned me away from the familiar idea that for my students to know mathematics they would simply have to memorize the rules and then study examples of how to apply them. I assumed that understanding mathematics, or, in more common parlance, "getting it," would have to be a matter of reasoning from assumptions to their implied conclusions while learning to use the tools and concepts that had already been developed in the field. At the same time, I recognized that such reasoning would only be possible if students had a firm grasp of basic arithmetic procedures. This combination of perspectives led me to believe that teaching mathematics would have to engage students in doing mathematics as they were learning it.[6] Given how I learned mathematics, it followed that my goals for my students would include learning to use the familiar ideas and rules of arithmetic, as well as learning how to talk about mathematics and learning that they were capable of reasoning their way through a mathematical problem.

What I Teach with Problems

For eight years, I taught fifth-grade mathematics; for six of those years, I worked in the same school. What I was teaching might not seem very different from what a lot of fifth grade teachers would claim as their territory. Under headings used by most curriculum guides and textbooks, it included multiplication and division with "big numbers," division with numbers that "don't come out even," fractions beyond a half and a quarter—including comparing, adding, and subtracting them—fractions written as decimals, properties of basic geometric shapes, area and perimeter, averages. But the way my students studied these topics was not at all typical. They worked on problems. The problems came from many sources: textbooks, supplementary materials, alternative curricula, and issues that arose in our classroom that required mathematical thinking. In the course of working on problems, they investigated different solution strategies. They represented patterns and relationships graphically and symbolically. They disagreed and defended their approaches and clarified their assumptions. And they studied fractions and decimals, multiplication and division, and several other familiar topics as these topics came up in their journey through the mathematics that the problems brought to their attention.

Learning in my class was a matter of becoming convinced that your strategy and your answer are mathematically legitimate. In mathematics, knowing that something is true requires reasoning from agreed-upon assumptions to their logical conclusions in the context of some given conditions, practical or theoretical. Studying mathematics this way involves my students in finding out what kind of activity mathematics is; it provides them an opportunity to learn and use the concepts, tools, and procedures that the field has developed. The problems students work on are both practical ones, like figuring out prices and schedules and the like, and intellectual ones, like identifying the conditions that make it necessary to conclude that all of the numbers that are divisible by twenty-one are also divisible by seven, and that twenty-one is not divisible by two.

A Case of Teaching

This book is a large case study of a large territory. As a case study, it covers the territory in considerable depth. But readers will wonder what it represents, or how it is applicable. Part of the answer is informed by who I am and where I have taught. Although I did an unusual kind of teaching, the classrooms and the schools where I have taught are ordinary in the context of American public schools.[7] I taught a particular subject—mathematics—and for most of my career, I taught it to ten-year-olds. From the particular perspective of this teaching, supplemented by additional experience teaching at other grade levels, teaching other subjects to other kinds of students, and observing the work of many teachers in all kinds of classrooms, I am secure in the assertion that there are problems of teaching practice that are common across differences in schools, subjects, and age groups.

To investigate these problems, I first describe what I did to teach a particular subject with a particular class in a particular year. From an analysis of that "doing" I have distilled some ideas about domains of practice in which schoolteachers do their work. Different teachers, in different kinds of communities, with students of different ages, teaching different subjects, work on the same kinds of problems, although the problems themselves, and certainly their solutions, will be different. I do not claim to have exhausted the potential list of domains with my analysis. I have intentionally limited my research to the work of teaching that occurs in interaction with students and subject matter, and even there, one can probably find domains I have not investigated. Whether I have identified the right domains, or enough of them, and what the exceptions are to my assertion, I leave to future inquiry. Certainly, much important work in teaching occurs outside of interactions with students in professional exchanges among teachers, and between teachers, principals, parents, and others in the community. The analysis of that work is also crucial to understanding teaching practice, but it is beyond the scope of this book.

My intention in writing this book is not to argue in favor of a particular approach to teaching or to have the last word on the nature of teaching practice, but to contribute to a conversation about the nature of the work that schoolteachers do. I enter that conversation as both a teacher and a researcher. I am not a typical teacher. I was not teaching all day during the period of this study, nor was I teaching all subjects. I bring more in the way of experience and education to my daily lessons than most elementary schoolteachers. Precisely because I did not teach all day, I was able to keep extensive records on my daily practice. Because I have had the benefit of being both a teacher and a researcher, I have been able to bring unusual resources to the analysis of those records to improve our knowledge of teaching. To be an effective and responsible teacher, I tried to do what I believed was right in my interactions with students and with the mathematics under study. My task as a researcher is to do the best job I can to represent the work of teaching using the extensive records of practice collected in my classroom. As a responsible researcher, I recognize that I do not have the evidence to claim that what I did would be always be the right thing to do in other classroom situations.

In the lessons that I analyze, I was teaching mathematics to fifth-grade students. I have tried to write this book so that the mathematics does not get in the way of the study of teaching, while at the same time explicating how I relate to my subject as I work. I hope that teachers and researchers interested in other subjects will find something of value here. At the same time, I have made an effort to portray what it looks like to do serious mathematics with ten-year-olds. Mathematicians will probably be unhappy with some of the imprecision of my language, but I hope they can get beyond the classroom colloquialisms to investigate what it takes to teach the ideas they hold so dear in an ordinary school classroom.

There is no shortage of reformers who claim to know how teaching should be done. All teachers have been subject to a plethora of panaceas: individualized curriculum, small-group collaboration, daily silent study time, just to name a few that have been recently promoted. Teaching with problems certainly needs to be on the list. Such reforms are often grounded in research and many of them have value. But the implications of any of them for coordinating teaching actions over time and across a whole class are rarely spelled out. In many ways, this coordination is the essence of the practice of teaching. My analysis of what is involved in doing this work does not lead to obvious implications about how to improve teaching, nor does it provide answers to the currently burning questions in the policy world about tracking, or curriculum standards, or what teachers need to know. My hope is that it can inform debates about these issues with a more adequate understanding of the problems in practice that teachers need to manage in order to teach productively.

2

An Instance of Teaching Practice

I begin the investigation of practice, introduce my school, my students, and my classroom, and frame the questions that have guided my inquiry with a description of a bit of my teaching. In this teaching, I used students' work on a problem to direct their studies of important mathematical skills and ideas. There is nothing particularly special about the lesson I describe here—I could have started anywhere.

The Big Picture

In the room where I teach, the desks and chairs are usually arranged in groups of four or six, making "tables" at which students face one another. As the students sit in their assigned places, they can look toward other members of their class, toward the "front" (where a teacher is likely to be standing when addressing the class as a whole), or toward the "back" (where there are displays of student work and a couch where students sometimes sit to read or talk). Even though the room contains little furniture besides the desks and chairs, it is crowded. It was designed for a smaller group of younger students. But for the past few years, all of the fifth graders in the school—between twenty-five and thirty students—have been taught in this room.

Each day, at the beginning of the afternoon, the fifth graders return from the playground, where they have been running around during recess, playing games, whispering with their friends, and teasing each other. They come in through the coat room, giving them a transition space to adjust their clothes and get in their parting shots before entering the classroom, where they know I am waiting for them. On top of most of the students' desks are the bound notebook and the black felt-tip pen that I have given them for their math work. By this time of year, mid-November, the notebooks are beginning to look worn from daily use. Many are personalized with Magic Marker graffiti on the cover.

Our school is small: only one or two classes for each grade. It was built in the 1960s and recently renovated. All of the rooms open both to a central hall and to the outside. The families who send their children to this school all live in the neighborhood, all in small, two-bedroom apartments in two-story brick buildings. The neighborhood is isolated from the more affluent parts of town, with a train track on one side, a highway on another, and a large public university the rest of the way around. Despite the similarities in families' living arrangements, the members of the school community are more different from one another than is typically the case in such neighborhoods. Some parents are established professionals with stable families, working at the university toward an advanced degree, while others are just beginning as college freshmen, with no local social networks, struggling to be the first in their families to get an education beyond high school. Some have lived here for many years, others have just come to the neighborhood, some from large urban areas, some from Midwestern farms, others from faraway lands. Some of the families of my students do not speak English as their native language. Some do not speak English at all at the beginning of the year.

In the morning another teacher, Thom Dye, teaches language arts to the same class. He and I have been working together almost daily for five years. He typically begins the day with reading, writing, and spelling. Then I come in and teach math. In the afternoons, Thom teaches social studies and science, and once or twice a week, other teachers teach fifth-grade music, physical education, and art. For the first few years that we worked together, Thom sat in on some of my math classes, I sometimes watched while he taught reading and writing, science and social studies, and we talked a lot about our teaching. We regularly interact with our class as a team, especially in the transition from one subject to another. By this time in our collaboration, we can finish one another's sentences, and often have to.

Zooming in to a Lesson on Rate

When the math lesson begins, the chalkboard on the front wall of the room is covered, as usual, with assignments and student work in different subjects, left over from the morning's lessons. On the right side of the board, the date and the schedule for the day are written as usual. Next to that, more or less in the middle of the board, is the math Problem of the Day, which I had written there while the class was at recess.

> Monday, November 20
>
> *Condition: A car is going 55 mph. Make a diagram to show where it will be*
>
> *A. after an hour*
> *B. after two hours*
> *C. after half an hour*
> *D. after 15 minutes*

As the students come in from recess and part from their playground buddies, some snatch a quick drink from the water fountain; they sit down, look at the chalkboard, and start writing in their notebooks, dating the page and copying the problems that are there. As I knew by now they would be, some were quick, some were slow, some were writing in careful cursive, others producing idiosyncratically mangled printing. Most did something in between. The students in front of me spanned the spectrum of ten-year-olds in every way you can imagine—from Catherine, a studious girl who read at the twelfth-grade level and wore braids, to Tyrone, a new boy in the school who came from South Carolina in the middle of September and had a great deal of difficulty focusing on anything for more than a minute; from Giyoo, a Japanese boy who was four feet tall, thin as a rail, and very quiet, to Eddie, an impish little boy with bushy blond hair, hyperactive, talkative, and freckle-faced; from Varouna, a dark, black Kenyan girl who was large and chatty, to Donna Ruth, a statuesque African American girl from Detroit whose social sophistication matched her adolescent appearance. As in all of the previous five years I had taught fifth-grade math in this school, the students are of widely mixed abilities, ethnicities, and economic circumstances.

Following the typical schedule for our daily math lessons, the students begin to work in their small groups after they copy the problem, talking and figuring and diagramming and calculating. Some work alone, and even though they are next to classmates, they don't share in the conversation. All of the students work on the problem for the first half hour of class while I walk around the room, watching what they are doing, listening to what they are saying, sometimes talking with them. They know by now that in the second half of class, we will be discussing their approaches to the problem and its solution, and that they will be expected to talk about their work on the problem.

Most of the students are creating some kind of diagram in their notebooks while working on the problem, following a pattern that has characterized their work for several days. The diagrams have some elements in common, but I have encouraged students to make them in ways that make sense to them. For example, Ellie's diagram is a line marked at regular intervals, showing "time" above the line and "miles" below:

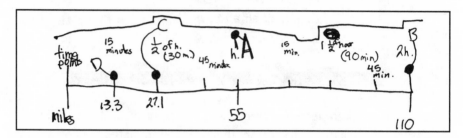

Yasu has "miles" on top and "min" under the line, and indicates that the intervals represent ten minutes:

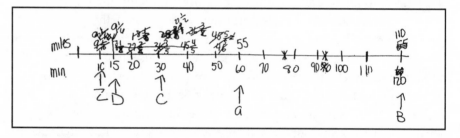

Sam marks only those points on the line that correspond to the problem conditions:

These examples represent the major variations in students' solutions, but there are others as well; some students have no diagram at all in their notebooks.

About halfway through the hour, I walk to the front of the room and ring a small bell—a signal that the other teachers and I use to communicate that we would like everyone to be quiet. Then, as we do every day, the class and I spend the second half hour together analyzing the problem, and strategies for solving it, in a public discussion. On this day, we begin by talking about "part A" of the problem and proceed through the next three parts. We first establish that the conditions of the problem in which the speed is given as 55 miles per hour could be taken to mean that after 1 hour, the car would have gone 55 miles (part A). I erase the problem and draw a diagram on the board that records this information, leaving room to represent other parts of the work.

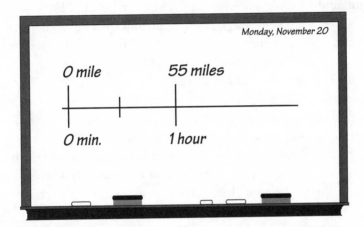

I invite students to reason about how 2 hours is twice as long as 1 hour, and about how this would imply that the car would travel twice as far in that time (part B). I represent a summary of our discussion on the diagram. We then talk about part C, reasoning that if the journey were shorter than an hour by half, the distance covered would be half of what it would be for an hour. No one disagrees and both of these conclusions are registered on the diagram. The chalkboard at the front of the room now looks like this:

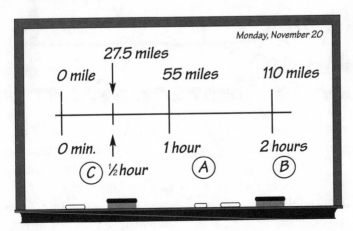

Zooming Further In: Teaching Richard, Catherine, and Awad

About ten minutes before the end of class, I point to the diagram on the board, showing solutions to parts A, B, and C of the problem. I ask if someone could show where the solution to part D (how far the car would go in fifteen minutes) would appear on the diagram. Several students raise their hands, including Richard, who is sitting near the front of the room. Richard does not often volunteer to say something in whole-class discussions. He is always friendly and cooperative in his small group, but he does not contribute much in the way of mathematical assertions to his classmates' conversation, and he does not write much in his notebook. He is new to the school this year, and I am still trying to figure out what he can do. I can never look at him without remembering that on the first day of school, when he introduced himself to the class, he said math was his "worse subject." I cannot predict precisely what he will do with this problem or know exactly what it will mean to him socially to come up to the board. But because it is my aim that all students understand mathematics, I call on him to show us on the diagram how far the car will go in fifteen minutes.

Richard stands up, turns his notebook so he can look at what he has written, and makes his way slowly to the front of the room, while everyone waits silently. At the chalkboard, he makes a mark on the line about halfway between "0 miles" and "27.5 miles" and writes "15 minutes" above it and "18" below it, saying, "Ummm. Eighteen." The diagram now looks like this:

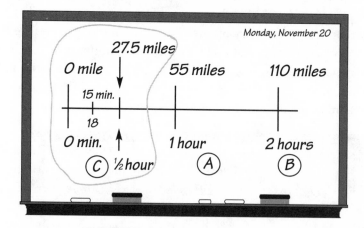

I don't respond immediately. Richard's solution is located in roughly the right region of the line, but I don't recognize what computation or reasoning could have led him to the number "18." I want to be encouraging and supportive. Richard could have just been careless in where he put the numbers. I could simply pass over his placement of the numbers as an error and correct the diagram, or ask another student to do so, but instead, I treat

Richard as if he had been deliberate. I also wonder if he is confusing the numbers associated with distance and time, possibly because he has carried out a procedure and lost track of what the problem was he was trying to solve. I ask him, as he is sitting down, "Eighteen miles or eighteen minutes?" He looks back at the diagram and responds in a few seconds, "Eighteen minutes."

Leaving aside my puzzle about where the number "eighteen" came from, I focus on its placement on the diagram. I remember that when I had looked at some students' diagrams earlier I had seen that some of them had put the time on top of the line and the corresponding miles on the bottom, the other way around from how I had represented the relationship in the diagram I made on the board. I had encouraged these idiosyncratic approaches, and I thought this might have something to do with what Richard had said. I tell the class about the differences I had observed in students' diagrams as Richard stands again at the board, asking him in front of the class whether he might have had the diagram in his notebook "the other way around." I put his answer of "eighteen" in the context of the problem as I comment on his placement of the number on the diagram, saying: "You wrote the eighteen down next to minutes. Did you mean eighteen miles and fifteen minutes? 'Cause that is what the question was: How far does it go in fifteen minutes?"

Richard nods his head "yes," indicating that he meant eighteen *miles* and fifteen *minutes*. He comes back to the board and erases what he had done and rewrites it like this:

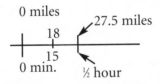

Still puzzled about where "eighteen" came from, I ask the class if "anybody" can "explain what Richard was thinking." This was something I had by now done several times this year in response to a student's answer, and I had done it in almost every lesson. It often gives me an insight about how to proceed when I cannot explain the student's answer to myself. And it draws more students into practicing how to talk about mathematics.

Several hands go up. I look around and take note of who wants to say something, checking on who seems to be paying attention to the discussion at this point. It is a few minutes from the end of class, and we are working on the most complex part of today's work. I wonder if we should just hold off until the next day to continue the discussion. I call on Catherine. My experience with her contributions to class discussions so far leads me to expect that she will be polite and articulate, whatever she says, possibly helping me out of the impasse with Richard. But instead of trying to explain Richard's thinking, she says, hestitatingly, "Ummmm, I disagree with that." She pauses for a moment, looks at me, and begins again, "Ummmm…" indicating that she is getting ready to tell us why she disagrees. Do I let her continue? She announced that she was not going to do what I had asked; she was not going to explain why Richard could think that it was reasonable to conclude that the car went 18 miles in 15 minutes. Or even why what Richard said was not reasonable. Instead, she wants to tell me, and the class, what she is thinking about the problem. I take note of the fact that she doesn't just blurt out what she wants to say when I give her the floor. She seems to be waiting for me to indicate that she should continue, wondering if it would be appropriate for her not to comment on Richard's solution. I had seen enough of Catherine's performance since September to imagine that if I did tell her to continue, she would provide not only the correct solution but also a clear and correct explanation of why her solution made sense. But what effect would that have on Richard? How would it affect Catherine if I did not let her continue? What effect would either course of action have on what the rest of the class could learn about the math, as well as what they could learn about Richard and about Catherine or about the racial and gender groups to which these students—an African American boy and a Caucasian girl—belonged? I would need to act without knowing the answers to these questions, but I might learn something from what I do.

Instead of indicating to Catherine that she should continue, I ask, pointing to Richard's "18" on the board, "Does anyone agree with this answer?" putting a lot of emphasis on the word "agree."

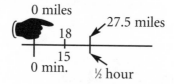

In asking this, I indicate that agreeing with Richard, that is, doing the problem the way he did it, is a possibility. No hands go up. I then turn back to Richard and ask him if he can explain what he was thinking. He first says "no" and then he asks if he can "change his mind" and "put thirteen and a half or thirteen point five." I had been working on this aspect of "classroom culture"; I did not want students to be embarrassed to try out ideas in front of their peers and then change their minds. I look around the room to see who still has a hand up, who is watching me or Richard, what Catherine is doing.

I did not see or hear whatever it was that led Richard to change his mind. I ask him why he changed his mind, pointing to the place on the chalkboard diagram that would represent how far the car would go in 15 minutes, where Richard had written "18." Richard then explains why he changed his mind: "Because eighteen plus eighteen isn't twenty-seven." He seems to have recognized, possibly following on the earlier part of the discussion (of problem-parts B and C), that a car traveling at a constant speed would have to go twice as far in 30 minutes as it goes 15 minutes. I respond with an "Ah hah!" and then quickly pick up on and publicly expand his reasoning. I say to him and to the class, still pointing to the place midway between 0 miles and 27.5 miles, but covering his "18," that whatever went in that spot had to be a number which, when doubled, would have to "come close to twenty-seven."

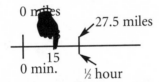

Even though we had earlier concluded (and it was recorded on the diagram) that the car goes 27.5 miles in half an hour, I repeat Richard's "twenty-seven" because he has appropriately used estimation.

I see several students raise their hands while I am talking. Some are murmuring, and I can hear that there is some concern about the difference between "close" and "exact." Should I ask for someone else to assert and explain in relation to part D of the problem at this point? Do those who are murmuring want to teach Richard that he must have a more exact answer? I do not call on another student at this point, but I tell Richard that what he had said was "good reasoning" and I ask him what "coming close" would mean. While other students are talking in the background and someone calls out, "Not close!" Richard responds, "Thirteen point five or thirteen and a half." I erase Richard's earlier answer of "18" written on the diagram, and replace it with "13.5."

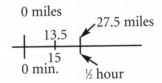

With my next comment, I simultaneously accept and ask for revisions in Richard's thinking, asserting that doubling "thirteen point five" would only get us "twenty-seven" not "twenty-seven and a half," noting that it is "very close." In terms of what I knew about Richard's capacity to work with numbers, I consider it an accomplishment for him to have figured out half of a number that was not evenly divisible by two. I look around at who has a hand raised. Whom could I call on to continue the discussion in this ambiguous tone, accepting Richard's reasoning as legitimate, but refining his conclusion? I choose Awad, and he speaks with careful, quiet reserve, saying, "Ummm. I think it's thirteen point seventy-five." There is a pause in the talk while I add this number above the "13.5" that I had heard from Richard. The diagram on the chalkboard now looks like this:

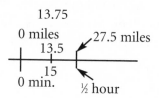

I repeat Awad's answer with a questioning tone ("Thirteen point seventy-five?") as I write, indicating that both Richard's and Awad's solutions are up for discussion.

Anthony, a small boy whom I know by now likes to talk at length to the whole class about his ideas, was shaking his head "yes" vigorously, and waving his hand. What effect would his public display of interest and assent here have on Awad, a much quieter but solid student? And on Richard? How would whatever Anthony might be wanting to say affect Richard's sense of mathematical competence? And how would it affect the other students in the class? Would they let Anthony have the "last word"? Would anyone else in the class be able to make sense of whatever he was going to say? Would I? In terms of teaching the class about mathematical efficacy, what would anyone be making of the fact that these were three boys, or that they were all "students of color"?

Richard had made an impressive performance, both in having the courage to revise his first answer and in explaining why the first answer did not make sense. He had successfully divided an odd number (27) in half, and represented the answer in decimal terms (13.5). But some students were obviously troubled that his answer was not an exact answer to the question in the problem. I knew that if we were talking about a real car, on a real journey, it might not make that much difference if we said it went thirteen and a half miles or thirteen and three-quarter miles. It would depend on why we were figuring out the distance traveled in the first place. Should I move the discussion in that direction, giving Richard what might be perceived as undeserved "credit" by those who were ready to tell us more accurately what distance had been traveled in fifteen minutes? Or would working toward the exact answer get us working on some of the particular mathematics I had hoped to bring up with this problem, that is, extending the halving process with odd numbers to finding fourths? Letting Anthony into the discussion would increase the number of talking participants. What would be fair in this case? What effect would it have on Richard for Anthony and Awad to agree on an answer that was different from the one he had given? And how would Catherine feel about Anthony getting to explain when she had not? What would be most mathematically appropriate thing to do? What would move the lesson along? What would bring more students into the discussion?

I was conscious of having spent several minutes with Richard, and now moved to give Anthony the floor. My questions at this point are not the thought experiments of the academic. They had to be answered with action.

Changing Focus: Teaching Anthony and Tyrone

When Awad said "I think it's thirteen point seventy five," I had responded with a question, not committing myself to his assertion, but asking, "Thirteen point seven five?" That was when Anthony started aggressively bidding for a chance to speak, responding to my question about Awad's answer. At this point, I say to Anthony, "Anthony, you think that too?" He does not answer yes or no, but immediately launches into a long description of how he arrived at "thirteen point seven five" by taking 27.5 apart, dividing each of its parts in two, and then putting them back together again.

Anthony: I did twenty-seven five divided by two.

So it was hard but I just, I divided five divided by two, which gave me, no that's point five divided by two. It's point two five.

Then I divided twenty-seven into two pieces.

First I did twenty-six divided by two pieces equals thirteen. So there is an extra one.

Yeah, so I divided one divided by two

Plus twenty-five.

So I added the five to the twenty-five I had.

As he talks, I try to follow what Anthony is talking about and judge whether his procedure makes sense. I wonder if anyone else can follow. I also wonder if they are learning something from Anthony that will get them into trouble later on. What Anthony says is confusing because he often leaves out the word "point," which would indicate when he is talking about decimal numbers. What he did before he started halving was to take 27.5 apart into two parts: 27 and .5. Then he takes half of .5 to get .25. He then takes 27 apart into two pieces: 26 and 1. He cuts each of those components in half to get

13 and .5, respectively, and then adds the .5 together with the .25 from earlier. Although he does not describe this step, he would then add the halves of each of the parts back together again: 13, plus .5, plus .25, to get 13.75. Anthony's explanation is also confusing because sometimes when he "divides" a number into pieces, he is "decomposing," as when he "divides twenty-seven in two pieces" and gets 26 and 1. At other points in the explanation, he uses the word "divide" more conventionally to mean that the resulting two pieces have to be the same, as when he says "twenty-six divided by two pieces equals thirteen." From a formal mathematical perspective, there is much that could be corrected in Anthony's locution. But I conclude that his reasoning is nonetheless sound.

This is a schematic of what I hear Anthony doing:

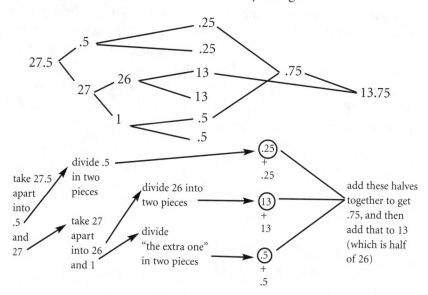

Anthony observes that what he did to figure out how far the car would go in fifteen minutes is "hard," but he recounts the process he went through, step by step. I can follow what he says because I have thought a lot about "decomposition/recomposition" as a strategy for multiplying and dividing numbers larger than ten, and I have worked on this procedure with students in previous years. But we had not yet talked much in this class this year about that way of working with numbers larger than ten. I would be surprised if anyone else could understand enough of what Anthony was saying to judge whether it made sense. Anthony did not use the language of "halving" that Richard had used. Was he making the connection? Was Richard? Or anyone else? Had I wasted time by letting Anthony say all that? Again, the answers to these questions would need to be expressed in the teaching action I would take next.

Anthony could have been building on what he heard Richard say; that is, he could have been recognizing that the number of miles associated with thirty minutes (27.5) had to be double the number of miles associated with fifteen minutes, assuming the speed stayed constant. If so, he made the connection between doubling and halving, and then between halving and dividing by two. He was using a key set of mathematical relationships, useful not only in thinking about the meaning of division by two and how to accomplish it with numbers, but also in thinking about division by any number. The decomposition strategy that Anthony used also brought a big mathematical idea to my attention that had not been part of any lesson so far that year and I knew it was something I wanted to teach. Should I follow up on any of these ideas? How would following up or not affect Anthony's sense of competence? Or Richard's? Or anyone else's? How would it change the judgments of other students in the class about who was "smart at math" and their subsequent interest in paying attention to what anyone did or said? Where was Catherine at this point, personally and mathematically? She had wanted to be the one who explained all this to the class and I had cut her off. Should I go back to her at this point? She was the only girl who had spoken in the last few minutes. Would other students be interpreting this as domination of mathematical discussions by boys? What about all the students who had not yet had anything to say in this discussion? And what time was it, anyway?

Whatever action I would have taken to answer these questions is subverted because Tyrone, who is sitting next to Anthony, immediately turns to him and asks, not in a public tone meant to address the whole class, but just loudly enough for everyone including me to hear him, "Why do you divide?" Tyrone's question catches my attention because it is exactly the sort of question I always hope for but rarely hear from a student. Like most fifth graders, my students typically proceed through computations and lose track of why they are doing them in the first place. Tyrone creates an opening for me to turn to the very basic questions that underlie the mathematical relationships Anthony had used to relate time and distance in the problem. So I reiterate Tyrone's question to Anthony, "Why do you divide?" And Anthony answers, "To know what's half of it." Anthony does not explain why "knowing what's half of it" is relevant to solving this problem, but he does assert the connection between halving and dividing (by two), which was one of the things that this class needed to study this year.

Following on this exchange between Tyrone and Anthony, I give a relatively long "speech." Some of what I say is addressed to individuals, some to this pair of students, and some to the whole class.

Lampert: [to Tyrone] Does that make sense to you Tyrone, why we divide?

[to the class] Because we started out with twenty-seven, and fifteen minutes is half of thirty minutes, so we divided by two, so we have to divide this [pointing to 27.5 minutes on the chalkboard diagram] by two.

[to Tyrone and Anthony] That was a very good exchange.

[to Tyrone] I like the way you asked that question.

[to the class, while facing Anthony] And I think people need to do more of that in this class. Asking questions when they don't know why you divide or why you multiply or something like that and Anthony you did a good job of explaining. You divide because you want to find half.

In this string of comments I am trying to accomplish several goals while speaking coherently about the mathematics at hand. I incorporate Richard's idea in what I say by focusing on fifteen minutes being half of thirty minutes, hoping he will recognize the connection between what he did and what Anthony did. I link what Anthony did to earlier work by referring to the diagram on the board and to the problem context. I explicate the idea that we are halving the "minutes" as I talk about the computation on the numbers associated with miles. I speak in a way that attempts to communicate to both Anthony and Tyrone, as well as to the rest of the class, that what people say in discussions is supposed to "make sense" to whoever is listening. And when I turn to Tyrone, I say to him and the whole class that I consider the kind of question he asked to be an important contribution. I classify what he said as a question about "not knowing why" and I name what Anthony did when he said "to know what's half of it" as "explaining," publicly judging it to be a "good job." Although parts of this statement are addressed to particular students, all of what I say is within the hearing of the whole class.

After a pause of a few seconds, I change the focus again, moving my attention away from Anthony and Tyrone to check on who might be following what is going on. I ask the class, "What do you divide by to find half?" Several hands go up. After someone who had not spoken recently says "Two," I ask several more questions of the same form in quick succession: "What do you divide by to find a quarter?" "A sixth?" "A third?" Each time, I watch whose hands go up, and I call on a student who has not spoken for a while. The answers are given swiftly and not discussed. I am using this as an opportunity to practice the language of fractions and relate it to division, and I am looking for whether particular students can use that language appropriately.

Changing Focus Again: Teaching Ellie, Sam, and Yasu

Ellie keeps her hand raised after the last of these questions has been answered, signaling that she wants to say something else besides what you divide by to find a third. I call on her and she asks, pointing at the diagram on the board, "Can I say another thing for that?" She has not spoken in a while and looks eager. With the analysis of Richard and Anthony's ideas, we had come to a conceptual plateau. We had examined strategies using both common fractions and decimal representations to find the solution. What might she want to add? I give my assent to Ellie to speak while looking at the clock. It is time for this lesson to be over. When she has the floor, Ellie asserts, "I think it's thirteen point three." In response to her assertion I ask, simply "Why?" Ellie answers, "Because, when I divided fifty-five divided by four I got thirteen remainder three." She converted "13 R.3" into "thirteen point three" when she said her answer to the division. I imagine that what Ellie has done in her notebook was something like this:

$$\begin{array}{r} 13.3 \\ 4\overline{)55} \\ -\underline{4} \\ 15 \\ -\underline{12} \\ 3 \end{array}$$

I had seen other students do similar things in the past few days, but we had not talked about what the answer to such a division might mean. Ellie's assertion and the description of the process she used to arrive at "thirteen point three" touches on several of the topics I knew I needed to teach to her and to most of the students in this class this year.

Ellie's bid to make a contribution at this point helps me solve a teaching problem I had been worrying about for the last few minutes. With her entry into the discussion, another girl besides Catherine is verbally participating. But her procedure and her interpretation of the results as "thirteen point three" raise several new teaching problems for me. She brings a new idea to the attention of the class by taking a fourth of 55 to get the miles associated with 15 minutes instead of doing it by taking half of 27.5 as Richard, Anthony, and Awad had done. The equivalence of those two calculations (the boys' "27.5 divided by 2" and Ellie's "55 divided by 4") is something worth bringing to everyone's attention in the context of work on the concept of rate and its relationship to ratio. I also think Ellie needs to be acknowledged for doing most of the "long division algorithm" correctly. But the way she interpreted the remainder indicated that she didn't understand at least this part of what she was doing. Another problem I have is that I am out of time for today. I see that the teacher of the next lesson is now in the room and looking anxious for me to wrap up this lesson.

I must address all of these problems simultaneously with my next action, or choose to ignore some of them for the moment and solve others. As I had done in response to Awad's assertion of "Thirteen point seven five," I repeat what Ellie says with a questioning tone, "Thirteen point three?" and I write it on the board next to the other assertions associated with a journey of fifteen minutes.

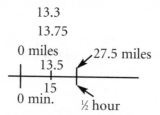

I cannot stop without recognizing that Ellie has a way of thinking about this problem that is different from the one we have been talking about and mathematically notable, given what I wanted to be teaching. I want to acknowledge that she has made a new kind of contribution. She had carried out what is conventionally called a "long division" and she was trying to make sense of the remainder. I tell the class that "that's another way to do this." Clearly attributing "thirteen point three" to Ellie, I again both accept a student's answer and leave it open for discussion:

> Lampert: Okay, so that's another way to do this, to think about fifteen minutes as one-fourth of a whole hour [pointing to one hour on the chalkboard diagram].
>
> If you divide the minutes by four you get fifteen minutes. If you divide the hours, I mean the miles [pointing to 55 miles on the chalkboard diagram], by four Ellie says you get thirteen point three [pointing to the place on the diagram that represents one-fourth of an hour/one-fourth of fifty-five miles].

Sam, sitting near the back of the room, has been trying to get my attention ever since I let Ellie into the discussion, not only raising his hand, but raising his body up off of his chair seat. I call on him. He doesn't follow on Ellie's line of thinking by talking about fourths or division by 4, but instead returns to the halving strategy used by the other boys, adding another new and mathematically notable dimension to the discussion by stating his solution with a whole number (13) and a fraction (¾) rather than in decimal form (13.75). Sam says, "I divided the twenty-seven in half but I kind of agree with the thirteen point seventy-five and I wrote thirteen and three-fourths."

I add Sam's assertion to what is on the board and look with frustration and empathy toward the teacher of the next lesson. What is on the board now is this:

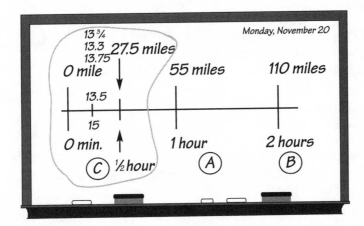

I do not comment on Sam's use of a common fraction and his assertion about the decimal equivalent.

I really wanted to get to the point Sam brought up, but now it is past the time when my lesson needs to be over, and there is still Ellie's assertion to be analyzed. Yasu raises her hand. Here is another girl who wants to say something, an Asian female who is quiet most of the time. I call on her and she says, "I don't agree with Ellie's answer." Like Richard, Yasu is new to our school this year. Even though she doesn't say much in either small-group or large-group settings, her written work has been conceptually and procedurally flawless since the beginning of the year. I don't yet have a good sense of the limits of her competence to do fifth-grade mathematics work. I don't have a clear idea of how sophisticated her use of English is, either. Now I have a student who is maybe going to help me teach Ellie and the rest of the class about remainders in division. We still have not gone very far with the relationship between dividing 27.5 in half and dividing 55 by 4. I wonder how many students even noticed that switch. They are surprisingly quiet, given that we can all see what time it is.

Despite knowing I am out of time, I take the risk of asking Yasu why she disagrees with Ellie. Her answer could not be mathematically more reasonable or linguistically more clear. She explains that the distance traveled in 15 minutes at a rate of 55 mph cannot be 13.3, "Because if you double that you'll get twenty-six point six." What she is saying harkens back conceptually to the same strategy Richard used to disprove his first assertion: I am bowled over. This is the kind of argument that I have been hoping my students would learn to do. What Yasu has done here is a sophisticated bit of logic for a ten-year-old. And in the school context, what she has done is crucially important to learning to do mathematics: she has proven that Ellie's answer cannot make mathematical sense by piecing together the following argument:

Ellie's claim:	13.3 is one-fourth of 55
Richard's, Awad's, Anthony's, and Sam's claim:	27.5 is one-half of 55
Unspoken assumption:	one-fourth + one-fourth = one-half
Yasu's counterclaim:	13.3 + 13.3 = 26.6
Therefore:	13.3 cannot be one-fourth of 55

Logical proof of this form is a fundamental mathematical practice, and in the classroom, it must replace the authority of the teacher in deciding what is right and what is wrong. Ellie's answer is unreasonable, not because "the teacher said so" or because she looked up the answer in a book, but because it does not follow from the assumptions given in the problem. I wonder what Ellie is thinking at this point, as she is looking at me and Yasu with rapt attention.

I respond to Yasu somewhat flatly, worried about Ellie's response: "Uh huh. That's interesting. And twenty-six point six isn't twenty-seven point five [pointing to 27.5 on the chalkboard diagram]. That's an interesting comment." I wonder what I have to teach Yasu at this point. Yasu did not talk about fourths. (She could have said that if you multiply 13.3 by 4, you get 53.2, not 55.) Does she recognize that Ellie came up with a different way of working on this problem? (That she divided by 4 whereas what the boys had done was to take half of a half?)

I ask Ellie what she thinks about what Yasu said. She looks up, says "Mmmmmm," looks to her notebook, and looks up again. After what feels to me like a long period of wait time, I draw the lesson to a close, promising a return to these ideas. I say to the class: "You know what I think? I think that we are going to schedule a little time on remainders and division. 'Cause I think we are getting a little mix—mixing up a lot of ideas here and we don't have time to go into them today. Okay?"

The quizzical "Okay?" at the end here leaves the door open just a crack for anyone who needs to make one last comment. No one raises a hand.

Referring to the chalkboard representation of our discussion of part D, I then close the lesson by pointing to all the answers on the diagram (13.5, 13.75, 13.3, 13 ¾) that indicate speculations about how far the car will go in 15 minutes at 55 miles per hour. I say, "These answers that people have here are all around 13. And that is a region of making sense." As I drop my voice in conclusion, the teacher of the next lesson comes anxiously up to the front of the room, and tells students to put away their math notebooks and take out their social studies textbooks.

From Narrative to Analysis

Where might we begin to identify the elements of practice that need to be included in an analysis of this teaching? How can these elements be related in a way that captures the complexity of the work? How can we analyze practice in a way that will improve our understanding of the problems involved in doing teaching, of the resources teachers can use to address those problems, and of the work entailed in using those resources?

In the example recounted here, teaching occurs in many single exchanges and in crafting the lesson as a whole; it occurs in the terrain of division, in the relationship between division and fractions, and in the larger domain of what mathematicians might call "multiplicative structures" where rate, ratio, functions, and other big, related ideas reside. It occurs in my interacting with individuals and in their interactions with one another. It occurs as I attempt to modulate the aggressive boys and encourage the quiet girls, and as I work to bring the whole class along while attending to each individual's understanding and self-image. It occurs in my using words that keep the concrete context of time, speed, and distance in the conversation and in connecting this context to the mathematical terrain of rate and ratio. It occurs in rehearsing familiar number facts and in encouraging reasoning about when assertions make sense. It occurs in the spontaneous construction of idiosyncratic improvisations and in maintaining the daily task-related routines that are consistent across the year, like the use of notebooks and the small- and large-group participation structures. It occurs as I build on what I have learned since the beginning of September about Richard and Catherine and Anthony and the others to bring them each one more step along the road toward mathematical competence and as I anticipate what I will be able to do with them tomorrow and next week and after winter vacation.

Practitioners and scholars are beginning to accumulate a corpus of first-person narrative descriptions like the one above, portraying the complexities of teaching from the teachers' point of view.[1] Some researchers argue that such teacher-narratives represent practice more adequately than other genres.[2] But there is as yet no coherent tradition of scholarship whose purpose is to look across stories and identify the complexities of practice in a way that is as multifocal as the work itself; nor is there a professional language that goes very far beyond the anecdote or "case" for talking about practice in a way that captures the multiple ways in which any teaching action may be working to link students and content.[3] Not only do we lack shared understandings of the terms and ideas that might be used to understand what is going on in the work of teaching, but we also lack agreement about rules of discourse for constructing knowledge about the practice: for warranting the claims that might be made about teaching, for disagreeing with a particular interpretation of a teaching act, for reasoning from assumptions to conclusions about the teaching we observe.[4]

In order to understand the practice described in the story above, and to understand the work of teaching in general, we need to examine the many elements of a teacher's work as well as how they are coordinated in the actions taken to get fifth-grade mathematics studied by all of the students. Conventional academic categories would have me limit a scholarly investigation of this work either to an analysis of the curriculum or to a study of the instructional methods. Or they would have me examining my interactions with students, or observing the ways in which the content was portrayed. Decomposing the practice of teaching into curriculum, instruction, students, and content leaves troublesome gaps, rendering the most fundamental aspects of the work invisible. The gaps between these conventional analytic frames appear precisely where the important aspects of the work of teaching are to be found. In order to go beyond compelling narratives toward a better understanding of the practice of teaching, we need a representation of the multiple levels of teaching action as they occur in different social relationships over time to accomplish multiple goals simultaneously.

3

Why I Wrote This Book—and How

We would like to imagine that someone could "know teaching"—or at least know my teaching—by observing a series of interactions like the ones described in chapter 2 or by reading a narrative account of such actions. But from inside the practice, I have come to realize the shortcomings of such representations as I have listened to conversations among observers of my teaching. Such conversations often begin with an observer saying something general about the teaching; usually, "It was terrific" or "It was confusing." These general comments might be followed by more focused statements like, "You let the boys talk all the time," "The kind of problem you presented was not realistic," or "You got into math that was much too complicated for most of the students in the class." An observer might pick out a particular move I made, noting how I "passed over" Catherine's disagreement with Richard, how I "diverged from the mathematics" to comment on the socially appropriate nature of the exchange between Anthony and Tyrone, how I "imposed" my own interpretation of Anthony's strategy, or how I let the lesson end without "correcting" Ellie's assertion that 55 divided by 4 was "thirteen point three." These "descriptions" of what people see in my teaching capture so little of the work as I experience it from inside the role. They judge the practice without analyzing it. And I think, "They just don't understand."

Isolation Versus Communication

As the teacher being observed, it is tempting to respond to comments like these defensively by asserting that "you had to have been there" to understand what I was doing. You would have had to have been in the room with me not only on the occasion when I did these things but also from the first day of school, when I began to teach this group of students about this mathematics. And you would have had to have known my students as I knew them, over time, and you would have had to have followed our meandering through a broad swath of mathematics. On the many occasions when someone has observed a small slice of my practice and questioned something I did, I have felt a great deal of sympathy for those teaching practitioners who respond to an observer's comments by closing down the possibility of further conversation with responses like: "This is just my way of doing things" or "Your way of thinking about what happened does not apply to my students." But I also recoil from such statements for what they suggest about the nature and limits of professional knowledge building.

Turning such a cold shoulder to observers' interpretations and questions means that each teacher must identify and solve the problems of teaching in isolation, making the deliberate improvement of practice a private undertaking. Working in this kind of intellectual isolation is common in American schools.[1] It means that the hard parts of teaching—elements of the work that are felt to be hard by the teacher—are not communicated to others. It means that analyses of teaching problems by observers, and the solutions they propose, will continue to be generated without an appreciation of the complexities of the practice being observed, and thus have little chance of being accepted by the practitioner. It shuts out the possibility of practitioners improving practice through collaborative analysis and design.[2] Without a professional discourse about classroom practice, education is in a weak position to improve itself. Even though I am frustrated when I try to analyze my practice with someone who has observed just a piece of it, such analysis seems essential to figuring out what can be done in classrooms to improve student learning.

As the nature of teaching practice is made more explicit, it should be easier to teach well and to learn what good teachers know how to do. It should be easier for teachers to work together on improving what they do. And it should be easier to make the changes in teaching practice that are needed if we are to produce better learning outcomes for students, more uniformly. Teachers do not need to do this all by themselves. There are multiple ways in which practitioners can be helped to solve the problems of practice once those problems are better understood. The articulation of the complications in practice could enable problem-solving collaborations between practitioners and researchers, practitioners and policy makers, and practitioners and curriculum developers because there will be a language for getting at the nature of the problems to be solved. As we describe the work of teaching more clearly, we might better judge the value and impact of resources provided to teachers, like curriculum guides, teacher development programs, assessment tools, planning strategies, class size, homogeneous or heterogeneous classes, and the like.[3] As we will see, the usefulness of these kinds of resources expands and contracts with the social and intellectual relationships that a teacher makes with learners to support their study of content.

Teaching as Working in Relationships: A Basic Model of Practice

My purpose is to develop a more comprehensive representation of the work of teaching: one that could be useful to both practitioners and those who take an interest in their work. Such a representation must go beyond

narratives and develop a language of analysis. An analytic frame for understanding classroom teaching will only be useful if it captures the complexity
of practice in terms of what teachers can do to address the fundamental
problems in teaching.

To begin with, addressing any problem in classroom teaching involves
action by at least two people: a teacher and a learner. Learning can be accomplished without actions taken by teachers, simply by a relationship between
the student and that which is to be learned. But *teaching in school* is the practice we seek to understand, and that involves some kind of collaboration
between teachers and students.[4] Teachers and students have different purposes for their collaboration, but they must work together to accomplish
them.[5]

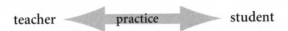

teacher — practice — student

In this diagram, the practice that is entailed in establishing and maintaining
the kind of collaboration that will result in learning occurs where the arrow
is, in the relationship between the teacher and the student. This relationship
is a "problem space" in the work of teaching. Working along the practice-
arrow that connects my work with my students, I can use them as a resource
to solve the problems of my practice. They can also constrain my actions and
hinder my efforts to support their learning.

Just as teaching in school requires working in relationships with students,
it also requires working in relationships with the content of the school curriculum.[6] We need a second practice-arrow in the model to represent this
other problem space where teaching work occurs.

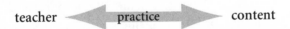

teacher — practice — content

Like teaching actions in relations with students, teaching actions in relations
with content can be seen both as the source of the problems teachers need to
address and as a resource for solving them. And just as students can both
constrain and open up what the teacher can do to teach, the content constrains and opens up possibilities for action.

Teachers act on students and they act on content to solve the problems of
practice. But teaching cannot proceed without some complementary actions
on the part of learners working in relations with the ideas, processes, and
language they are to learn.[7] Teaching can prepare the groundwork for students' actions and influence whether or not they happen, but the work that
will bring about learning is an act of the student in a relationship with the
content. What occurs in this relationship to cause learning could be called

the practice of studying. The work of studying occurs along a third practice-arrow.

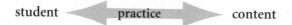

Because learning depends on this relationship, and because the success of teaching depends on learning, we must connect the student-content relationship with the teacher to show a fourth problem space in which practice occurs.

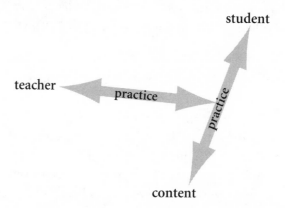

Students must be taught how to study in order for learning to happen.

Unfortunately, the term "studying" has taken on negative connotations when it is connected with schoolwork; we often take it to mean cramming, memorizing, keeping one's nose in the book. In more technical analysis, it is conceived as generic "techniques" or "strategies."[8] I would like to revive a more general and positive interpretation of the term, and use "studying" to mean any practice engaged in by students in school to learn. In relation to teaching with problems, I use it to include activities like inquiring, discussing, thinking, reading carefully, and examining closely.[9] These activities are more like what we have in mind when we say a biologist studies problems of genetic manipulation or an actor studies the role he or she is about to perform. Teaching is the practice of structuring activities of studying in relation to particular content and particular students. If teaching is successful, students study, that is, they "apply their minds purposefully to the acquisition of knowledge or understanding of something."[10]

As a teacher, I take action to make studying happen, and to make it happen in ways that are likely to result in learning. My students take complementary actions to study. I work to establish the social and intellectual conditions for their actions and to respond to what students do. Of course, students have multiple purposes when they interact in school, like making friends, impressing the teacher, and the like, and these purposes can constrain my actions as well as theirs. In order to get students to work with me on their learning, I need to get learning included among their purposes.[11]

By joining the three practice-arrows that model the problem spaces in which teaching occurs, we can see the relationship among the different trajectories along which the practice of teaching plays out: one between the teacher and the student, one between the teacher and the content, and one between the teacher and the student-content relationship.[12]

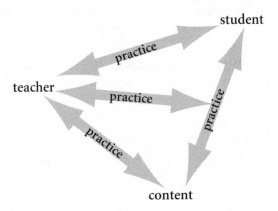

But these three practice-arrows are not separate and distinct sites for a teacher's work. Teaching actions proceed simultaneously in relations with students, with content and with the connection between students and content, in a single three-pronged problem space.

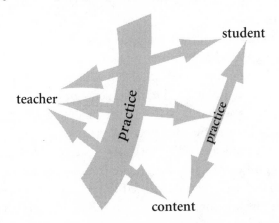

By merging these three problem spaces into one, I do not mean to suggest that performing coordinated actions that take account of all three relationships is a simple matter. Each relationship both limits and expands what the teacher can do to address problems of practice. Interactions with students get in the way of relating to the content, and the content gets in the way of relationships with students. While the teacher is trying something to get students interested in content, she may be doing things that interfere with her own understanding of the content. Such conflicts must be managed in each act of teaching.

The example in chapter 2 can be used to illustrate this overlapping of relationships in the activities of teaching and some of the potential conflicts that arise. We might see the first part of the discussion about how far a car would go if it were traveling at 55 miles per hour for 15 minutes as my effort to teach Richard to exhibit to the class how the operations of addition and multiplication work on fractions written as decimal numbers. Richard's relationship with the content focuses on studying the idea that halving and doubling are sensible strategies to apply to *distance* when halving and doubling are being applied to *time*. As I teach in my relationship with Richard, I build that relationship by expressing my respect and my expectations. By calling him to the board to share his work with the whole class, I communicate my belief that he is trying to be reasonable by asserting "eighteen," I support him by repeating the problem to remind him of the context. I use my relationship with the content when I refer to the diagram that represents the rates and ratios that Richard is studying when I insert the appropriate terminology in the conversation, and when I make the explanation of revision a part of the performance of understanding. I try to enhance Richard's capacity to study the content by constantly referring to the diagram on the board and placing his talk and mine in relation to it. But at the same time, I am putting him at some social risk, and I may be jeopardizing his future participation in the study of mathematics.

In my interaction with Richard, one element of my work was figuring out what he was saying and what it meant in relation to the mathematics I wanted him to learn. To use both my relationship with this student and my relationship with the content, I needed to make sense of what he told me. To do that, I needed to work with him *and* with the mathematics, and I needed to work on supporting his relationship with the mathematics under study. I was challenged to communicate a view of mathematics in my exchange with Richard that was different from the one he initially presented and to have him seriously consider my ideas. I needed to treat him as a reasonable person and listen to his thinking. I could simply have told him that the distance for 15 minutes has to be half the distance for 30 minutes. But he would then have to take what I told him and get into a relationship with it, making sense of what this information would have to do with the problem he has been trying to solve. In other words, he would have to study it.

To analyze the work involved in teaching Richard, we need to examine what I did as a coherent and unified series of actions that are simultaneously social and intellectual. We need to investigate what I did to assess his understanding of division and fractions. We need to figure out what was going on as I created and used the representation on the board to enable Richard to reason about ratio and about the context of the problem, and how I used the class to seek confirmation for his reasoning.[13] These actions are intellectual on my part, but my understanding of Richard and my social connection with him are enriched if I can make use of these exchanges, and my knowledge of the mathematics that we are working on is enhanced. One thing I was doing was finding out whether Richard would be willing to risk giving his solution and then to revise it publicly. I was also trying to find out whether he could use the skill of approximation, and to assess whether he would attend to the numbers in the ratio or whether the quantities represented are miles and minutes. If I did all this, I would be able to use my responses to what he said to strengthen his commitment to knowing, and to knowing this particular material. Over time, after several such encounters, Richard would come to know mathematics by using his relationship with me and with the content. If I structured this relationship appropriately over the months we worked together, he could work at getting to know himself as competent in the domain of mathematics. We could each provide a kind of "feedback loop" for the other in the work we did separately and together. An analytic frame for capturing the work in this piece of teaching needs to identify, label, and conceptualize all of these elements of the work and the connections among them. As we will see, the three-pronged model is only a start on framing the "problem space" in which teachers work in a way that portrays these complexities of practice.

Elaborating the Model: Teaching Across the Year, Across Students, and Across the Curriculum

A piece of a lesson, like my interaction with Richard in the 55-mph-for-15-minutes problem, is often used by analysts of teacher-student-content interaction to understand what is happening in the classroom.[14] Analyzing teaching using such a bounded instance of practice reveals a great deal of its complexity, but it cannot fully capture the nature of the work. What a teacher is doing in any instance of teaching with a particular student and a particular content is part of an ongoing stream of action and interaction set in a wider curriculum and a larger social environment. Teaching the *whole* class the *whole* lesson would be a more meaningful unit of analysis to most teachers, who formally plan and evaluate their actions on this scale.[15] But even a whole lesson represents a small part of the practice to the experienced practitioner.[16] There is so much more work to teaching than walking in, teaching a lesson, and then walking out again. Although there are daily routines, teachers' relationships with students and with the ideas under study must be linked across lessons if those relationships are to be productive and coherent. And so the actions that make the links that lend continuity to intellectual and social relationships must be represented in a comprehensive model of practice.

Understanding the kinds of actions that are taken in a single lesson by a teacher who works with a whole class over a whole school year requires an examination of action patterns in relationships that begin in September and are continually repeated or modified until June. It also requires investigating action patterns that are constructed to teach more than one student at a time as well as those that deliberately teach that the content is a connected web of skills and concepts. My challenge as a scholar and a teacher has been to explicate the specific details of the kind of problem solving I did in my few minutes of interaction with Richard, and at the same time capture the dailiness and indivisibility of what I do across the entire school year with the whole class and the whole curriculum.

Teaching in Time

The different units of time in which teaching happens are one source of its complexity. Teaching problems are solved in particular moments of interaction, and at the larger scale of the lesson as a whole. Problems that arise across groups of events that are perceived to have the same social structure require actions that encompass parts of lessons (such as what the teacher does when students are working independently or when the class is getting ready to start or when only one person is supposed to be addressing the class at a time). These units of work are bigger than single instances of interaction, but smaller than the lesson as a whole. Depending on the teacher's role in the social structure, different kinds of teaching actions are required in different parts of the lesson. Scaling up, the teacher also acts across groups of lessons, ranging from a pair of lessons connected across two days to the totality of all lessons across the year. Still other actions, tasks, or strategies may need to be performed to maintain longer-term connections between students and mathematics. The complexity of teaching in time does not end with considering different units, however, because teaching acts are not uniquely situated in single units of time. Because teachers' relationships with students and with content are ongoing, every teaching act is simultaneously part of an exchange, part of a group of similarly structured exchanges, part of a lesson, part of a unit of lessons, and part of the yearlong relationship between teacher and student. To add to the complexity, there are not clear boundaries to be observed that mark when one time unit stops and the next one begins.

Teaching in Relations with Social Groups

One of the factors that makes the temporal boundaries of teaching events hard to define is that time units overlap with units of social organization. As we have seen, the work of teaching is "located" in relationships with students. But students do not present themselves in the classroom only as individuals. Sometimes the teacher's working relationships are with groups of students, sometimes with the whole class. This complicates where we look for teaching actions. An "event" named according to social structure, like "small-group interaction time," perceived from the perspective of one relationship, does not start and stop simultaneously with the same event perceived from the perspective of another relationship. And like units of time, relationships in the classroom are nested. Students are parts of groups and groups are part of the class. The boundaries of the groups within the class with whom the teacher relates are fluid. Some groups can be relatively stable, like the students who sit together for weeks at a time. Others are continually changing, like the group of students who have their hands raised at any particular moment in the class, or the group of students who have a solid grasp of the particular procedure under discussion. And students, too, are nested. Every single student is simultaneously studying alone, as a member of a group or groups, and as a member of the class as a whole.[17] Moreover, students teach one another in circumstances where that opportunity is made available and encouraged, sometimes communicating mathematics with another individual, sometimes with a small group, and sometimes with the whole class. Relationships in the classroom are sometimes private, sometimes local, and often public, causing communication about content to reverberate through multiple levels of the social structure just as it reverberates through time.

Teaching Connections in Content

When problems are the means for teaching and studying, the intellectual content has complexities of nesting and bounding as well. In creating a solution to a problem or explaining why it makes sense, students need to be able to study how a topic like "decimal numbers" is related to place value and to fractions, and how it connects with the way we do division and multiplication. In working on problems, successful performance and understanding go hand in hand and must be taught simultaneously. The teacher's relationships with content are additionally complicated because they are constructed differently in relationships with different students or different groups of students. Each different kind of social connection (pairs, groups, class) can carry with it different intellectual content as well as different interpersonal content. One individual in a group might be asking the teacher about how to add fractions with unlike denominators while the group is studying what it is about the context of the problem that calls for addition in the first place. The teacher may need to use one action to create intellectual coherence in the content simultaneously with individual students, with dynamically constituted groups of students, and with the class as a whole.

Overlapping Complexities

Like the mathematics, the communication of trust, disapproval, enthusiasm, caring, skepticism, confidence, and the like is both carried in momentary encounters and constructed in relationships over time. Complexities of grouping, complexities of time, and complexities of content interact. In time, in social relationships, and in content, smaller units are encompassed in larger ones, and the problems of productively connecting students with content at different levels can be different. Solving a teaching problem at the lesson level does not take care of subproblems that arise in distinct events involving individuals or groups throughout the lesson. For example, solving the problem of engaging a group of quiet girls in the study of "improper" fractions in a particular mathematics problem does not take care of the problem of engaging a particular girl or the class as a whole in a consideration of that same idea. Neither does it take care of the problem of teaching the class how improper fractions are represented in decimal form.

It is these overlapping complexities that I have set out to investigate and represent in this study of teaching. If teachers are to get over their isolation and be able to communicate about the problems of their practice in ways that lead to realistic solutions, we need to be able to talk about how teaching happens in different kinds of time units, social configurations, and levels of content. We need to be able to portray the simultaneity of the problems that arise and the coherence and continuity of the actions that address them, even when the teacher's goals are in conflict.

An Unusual Research Program

As a teacher and a scholar, my goal has been to use my own teaching to develop a model of the work that can take account of these overlapping temporal, social, and intellectual complexities in the problems of practice. This goal evolved from two kinds of questions that people have asked when they have observed a lesson in my classroom. One is about how the students got to be the way they are at the point in the year they are observing: "Your students are so engaged and so considerate. Did you do something to get them to act that way? Or are they just an especially talented group of ten-year-olds?" The other has to do with covering the curriculum: "You spent so much time on one problem. How did you cover the curriculum? Or don't you have to worry about that?" My students are *not* especially talented, and I *do* need to worry about covering the curriculum. So, I wondered, how could I represent the work involved in producing the kind of social and intellectual performances that people could see going on in my classroom? To do so, it seemed as if I would need a record of what I did with every student every day, all through the year.

I have been fortunate to be able to actually produce such an extensive and unusual record of teaching over time, across the class, and across the curriculum. It forms the basis for the analysis in this book. Some years ago, Sharon Schwille, an experienced teacher and a colleague in the teacher education program at Michigan State University, sensed my frustration in trying to answer those recurring questions about establishing a classroom culture and covering the curriculum. She boldly suggested that I should start to videotape on the first day of school and tape everything I did for a whole year. I had always kept descriptive records of what I did in my teaching for myself in a daily journal.[18] Although my notes were not always as complete as I would have liked, the journal was a start on thinking about what I did to establish and maintain the classroom culture and cover the curriculum. Like acts of teaching, my journal entries moved back and forth in time and across students and content, as I prepared future lessons simultaneously with reflecting on what happened "yesterday," worked on the subject matter that I was trying to teach, and kept track of students' mathematics. Although it seemed like a wild idea, I began to imagine what daily videos could add to my journal records and how they could be used for the study of teaching.

Video technology was getting easier to use, and it would allow me to produce a continuous running record of the teaching and studying that occurred in my classroom from the first day of school to the last. My fifth-grade students were accustomed to keeping records of their work every day in a bound notebook, and that work could be scanned into an electronic database, as could my daily teaching journal. Building computer-controlled access to such records could enable me, or anyone else who wanted to study my teaching, to move around among the records relatively easily, and to connect my journal entries, copies of my students' work, and the video representation in flexible ways.[19] We would not have to segment practice into any kind of rigid units. The video could be used to show a moment or a whole lesson or the flow from one lesson to another.

With the support of the National Science Foundation, Deborah Ball and I began to collect these kinds of daily records of our practice in multiple media over an entire school year and to save and catalogue them in digital format so that we could investigate their usefulness in teacher education.[20] Deborah was also a teacher educator and a researcher, teaching mathematics in the third grade at the same school where I was teaching in the fifth grade. Our aim was to somehow use multimedia technologies to display our work as teachers of elementary school mathematics in a way that would make it possible for others to investigate what we were doing, as well as to further our own studies of teaching.

To supplement the videotaping of daily lessons, we assembled a collection of additional documents in electronic form, including both copies of records produced as a matter of course in everyday teaching and studying and records collected specifically to support the analysis of our practice. The kinds of records we collected are displayed in the following table:

Records Produced as a Regular Part of Everyday Teaching and Studying	Records Produced to Aid in the Analysis of Practice
Teacher journal Student notebooks Teacher comments on student work Student tests Parent reports	Videotape of lessons Audiotape of lessons Structured notes by an observer Seating charts for all lessons Copies of the chalkboard graphics Transcripts

Records in the first category included those that we would routinely keep for planning and reflecting on our teaching and for student assessment: our daily handwritten teaching journals and our students' classwork, tests, and homework as well as reports to students and their parents on students' work. All of these were scanned into a computer database as graphic documents. The journal notes we kept that year were transformed into electronic text documents so that they could be searched using key words.

To complement these ordinary artifacts of teaching and learning in our two classrooms, we collected other records that we thought would be necessary to document our daily practice. Our research team produced two videotapes of most lessons and an audiotape of every lesson. During all of the time we taped, there were many different kinds of activities going on simultaneously. Although we could not realistically capture everything, we did have two cameras running at all times. One videographer would follow the teacher and one would "roam," taking the camera off the tripod during small-group time and filming the whole class from the tripod during large-group time. This allowed us to acquire a continuous record of events while at the same time doing some situated interpretation.[21] While keeping the camera on the tripod was less distracting for students, we wanted close-ups of student work while it was in production as well as documentation of students' talk and body language as they tried to communicate their mathematical ideas to their peers. We decided each day which children to film so as to vary who was being recorded and take advantage of the variety of activity available to record. Much of the time, the cameras captured several small groups seriatim as they worked on a problem. Considering possible types of shooting and editing, we chose neither conventional documentary procedures in which we would collect shots varying greatly in scope and then piece them together in an order different from the original sequence in which they were shot to tell a story,[22] nor the opposite extreme of "locking on" the camera to one perspective and letting it run for the duration of the lesson.[23] Instead, we filmed continuous lesson-long "takes" with the camera zooming in and out and the videographer moving around to focus on details that became salient in the context of each lesson. To capture as much classroom talk as possible, the videotapes of every lesson were supplemented by a continuously running audiotape. Transcripts of verbal interaction were produced from these tapes.[24]

To enable indexing of the video and audio record, trained observers prepared structured field notes on every mathematics lesson we taught during the school year.[25] These field notes described the mathematical content of the whole-class portions of the lessons, pedagogical representations used on the chalkboard to communicate within the class, mathematical problems that arose during small-group work that were distinct from the problems we had set, and particular activities of five focal students in each class, chosen to represent the diversity in the group. In the electronic database, the observers' notes are usable as an index of all of the lessons and student work making possible electronic searches and collections of various kinds of records. In conjunction with the video, they were used to produce seating charts showing who was sitting where every day of the year, as well as graphic reproductions of what was on the chalkboard during different points in lessons. Both the research team and the video and audio equipment were part of the classroom ecology from the first day of school and for every day throughout the year so that we could capture whatever occurred as it transpired over time rather than idiosyncratic "performances" created for the camera or for observers. Taping and observing began each day as students came in from recess and continued for a few minutes after each lesson was over so as to avoid judgments about what constituted a "complete" class period.

Figuring out How to Display the Work of Teaching

Since the original records were collected and catalogued, new technologies have rapidly developed, making it possible to transform all of that material into digital form and put it into a single electronic database.[26] Not only for me, as a teacher-researcher, but for other heretofore intellectually isolated teachers, this kind of multimedia documentation of practice opens up new and exciting possibilities for communication and collaboration. Teachers and teacher developers now commonly use collections of classroom video, children's work, and teachers' records to enrich discussions of problems in practice.[27] But this increase in the use of such materials to study teaching has raised difficult questions about how its use contributes to better communication about the problems of practice.

The Problem of Scale

It was tempting, given the existence of the multimedia documentation of a whole year of teaching in my classroom, to suggest to anyone who wanted to understand my teaching practice that they look at all of the records I have collected. The absurdity of anyone using such a representation to understand *anything* was elegantly captured in a literary essay by Jorge Luis Borges as he played with the idea of constructing a perfectly accurate representation of an imaginary empire in the form of a one-to-one map.[28] Just as I wanted multimedia to display every detail of my teaching for someone who could not be there with me every day, the mapmakers in Borges's imaginary empire wanted to be able to make a map that would be a perfectly accurate reference to the empire. Such a map could then be used to communicate about the empire when the empire itself could not be examined. This quest for accuracy was similar to that of early cartographers who wanted to quell fears of "the unknown" by charting every feature of a newly explored landscape so that people could talk about far-off lands truthfully without having been there.[29]

It soon became clear, in Borges's fable and in early mapmaking, that this would be impossible.[30] Such a map could not be created, and even if it could have been created, it could not have been used. But if we give up this fantasy, we are left with the question of what makes any map an accurate representation of the territory it seeks to portray (or analogously, what makes any portrayal of teaching an "accurate" representation of practice). Current theories of cartography assert that the measure of a map's accuracy is its "workability," i.e., how successful it is in achieving the aims for which it is drawn and its range of application. Through the decisions that are made about inclusion and exclusion, what is actually represented by different maps is not the terrain itself but perspectives on the terrain within which we can locate ourselves for particular purposes. Applying these arguments to the question of representation as it pertains to communication about teaching, Borges's fable focused me on two aspects of the problem: How is a map different from a photograph (or by extension, a multimedia documentation)?

And what can be seen at different scales on a map or at different focal lengths in a photograph or movie? To display practice in a way that would be useful in communications about the work of teaching, I would need to make "maps" of different scales. Representations of practice would need to range from those that could show the small details of work that go on in a single interaction around a single idea with one student, to those that could encompass the work of teaching the whole curriculum to a whole class over a whole year, and everything in between. But the issue was not exactly a question of scale. What would be needed to represent practice in different time frames, social configurations, and intellectual relationships was not just bigger- or smaller-scale maps, but different *kinds of maps* that would show different kinds of information.

The running record of the whole year that had been collected in my classroom was a series of close-ups of teacher-student-content interaction, and like Borges's one-to-one map, unusable. I wondered whether one could make representations of teaching that were more like landscapes or satellite photographs. Such representations would need to show relations among elements of practice that could not be seen in a close-up. If they were to be considered "workable" representations, the test of their accuracy would be whether they could achieve the purpose of representing the complexities of teaching for productive communication about the problems of practice.

Portraying Teaching Using New Technologies

The procedures for collecting records of my practice produced a large file of electronic documents representing teaching practice in multiple media and from multiple perspectives. Taken by themselves these records are unwieldy and practically inaccessible. But using database software, it has become possible to "look at" the teaching that was recorded in ways that are comparable to taking movies with different kinds of lenses. I can bring particular students or mathematical ideas into high relief. I can zoom in on the work I was doing in a single interaction, then zoom out to examine patterns in a collection of all of the verbal and written interactions I had with a single student over the course of a year. I can zoom in to a particular mathematical idea, and then zoom out to look at patterns across actions in all the lessons in which that idea came up and at how I worked to relate that idea to other ideas. With these different views of teaching work in front of me, I have been able to model more of the complex levels at which practice occurs. In the final chapter of this book, after presenting various analytic views of teaching problems, I return to the three-pronged model developed above and revise it to take account of more of the complexity that surfaces in these views.

Although the electronic database has given me (and others who wish to study this practice) a way to access many records of teaching, it does not take the place of analysis that makes visible the domains in which the teacher works. In order to move from the many kinds of collections enabled by the electronic database to a representation of my teaching that would be more accessible than a one-to-one mapping of events, I constructed this book so that the reader could view the multimedia records I have described, not by looking at them all, from beginning to end, but by taking different lenses to them and zooming in and out on the various records of the teaching, studying, and mathematics that occurred over the course of the year. As the unit of time or the unit of interaction or the unit of content in the scope changes, different problems of practice become visible.[31] By using the idea of adjusting a lens to multiple focal lengths while moving it around to look at the terrain of a practice, I have been able to portray the work of teaching in a way that does not fragment action.[32] The reader can look at a particular moment of interaction in relation to an equally vivid image of how this work overlaps with work that happens at the lesson level or larger units of time, social units, and conceptual frames. At each different resolution, you can see a somewhat different image, even as the picture is, at each focal length, a picture of teaching.

By changing the focal length of the lens we train on teaching, zooming in from the scale of lesson or the curricular unit or the year to examine enlarged images of smaller and smaller pieces of work, zooming out again to the year, and then back in again to sharpen our focus on another dimension, we can retain the idea that larger and smaller pieces of work are happening simultaneously and are intricately related, even though we can only "see" at one resolution at a time. Zooming in and out on different parts of the work of teaching, we should be able to develop an understanding of particular exchanges in the context of their multiple frames in somewhat the same way as a teacher does. By representing relationships among elements of practice used by the teacher that might otherwise be perceived as discrete by an observer the complexity of the work becomes more transparent. In the words of Philip and Phyllis Morrison, who used this idea of zooming in and out to represent relationships at larger and larger scales in the work of science, "The unity that arises so clearly out of the diverse scenes will [we] hope, become exciting and perceptible to readers."[33] By zooming out and then zooming in on different related levels, successively enlarging and condensing our field of vision, the Morrisons argued, we could enrich our understanding not only of different levels of phenomena, but of their relationships to one another.

It would be very useful, both for practitioners and for those concerned to understand their practice, to create a technology that would actually be able to zoom in and out on records of practice such as those I was able to collect. Although we are moving in that direction, it is not yet possible. What is technically imaginable remains practically challenging, and it is difficult to represent on the printed page.[34] Perhaps before too long we will have something like telescopic and microscopic video cameras that can be trained on practice over time to enable the kind of examination of the elements of teaching at different levels such as I have described here. Until then, we must rely on imagination, supported by more or less primitive graphics and the logic of text to create a representation.

Where Do Teaching Problems Arise?

In each of the next ten chapters, I use these ideas about representation at different scales to portray the work I did on common problems of practice in teaching. I set up the room and the schedule. I plan lessons. I work with students while students work independently or in small groups. I instruct the whole class at once. I link lessons over time. I cover the curriculum. I motivate students to do what needs to be done to learn. I assess whether progress is being made. I manage diversity of all sorts. And finally, I bring the year to a close. Each of these activities presents me with problems that need to be addressed in my relationships with students, with curriculum content, and in the effort to productively connect students with content. Practice in all of these domains can be done well or badly, it can be done as teacher-centered or student-centered, conservative or adventurous. But work must be done in each of these domains by teachers of different subjects in different grades, in city schools, in rural schools, and in the suburbs. In each chapter, I set out a frame for communicating about the kinds of work that can be done in each domain in a classroom where problems are used to engage students in learning. The chapters are organized to describe and investigate the set of actions that constitute the work of teaching while maintaining the multiple and integrated quality of those actions over time. The actions I have chosen as the focus of my analysis address problems common to all teaching, although I did a particular kind of teaching (teaching with problems) in a particular subject (mathematics) with a particular age of students (ten-year-olds). These characteristics of my situation, and others, shaped the particular ways in which I solved the problems I faced.

I begin the analysis of practice at the beginning of the year with a look at the work of teaching students ways to study in my classroom (chap. 4). Using excerpts from my journal and transcripts from the first few weeks of September, I investigate the problems of practice involved in identifying and manipulating the resources and constraints of the classroom to enable students to study and to learn, devising and choosing routines, and creating continuous and socially constructed actions that establish and maintain those routines in a school class. Walking into an assigned classroom before the beginning of the school year, every teacher finds a collection of desks and chairs pushed together in a corner, empty chalkboards and bulletin boards, some books, pens and pencils, blank paper, and maybe cupboards for supplies. There might be some computers, a sink, or a rug.

These items provide the canvas on which teaching will be painted over the next nine months. They can be thought of as the resources the teacher will have to work with and the constraints on what she can do. What and who will go where in the room and when, what will be written on chalkboard or paper and who will be able to see it, who will get to talk about what and when, and who is supposed to be listening—these are the yet to be determined but essential elements of the routines that will make it possible for the teacher to teach and the students to study. In planning how to structure available resources within the imposed constraints, the work of teaching begins. Everything must be arranged and then continually rearranged again and again as the teacher observes what students can use, or not. Teaching them to use what is available and how to cope with constraints on time, space, and materials begins at the beginning and continues throughout the year.

Moving from the large-scale work of starting the year to the smaller-scale work of starting a single lesson, I continue to analyze problems of preparation, but in a different dimension (chap. 5). I investigate the work of coordinating prior teaching actions with the actions taken in a new lesson. Using records of my lesson planning and examples of student work, I make explicit the actions entailed in getting ready to teach a lesson on multiplication. I describe the work of figuring out where to begin a lesson, mathematically, and the work of learning about my students and their capacity to study the kind of mathematics that is in the fifth-grade curriculum. I analyze the work of constructing a task for students that will lead to coherent studies of a topic in the curriculum (in this case, multidigit multiplication) and at the same time make it possible for students to use a range of strategies. I draw upon a wealth of resources in choosing tasks for my students. Most teachers' choices will be more limited. But everyone must plan lessons for the particular group of students in front of him or her, depending on what happens from one day to the next.

The next set of teaching problems I investigate arises while students are working independently during a lesson (chap. 6). Students work independently in a classroom as they silently complete a workbook exercise, as they debate among themselves about planning a party, or as they collaborate in a group to edit an essay, without the teacher's direction. In my classroom each day, the problem on the chalkboard set the agenda for the tasks students were to complete independently at the beginning of class. Following the daily routine, they came into the room and worked on a mathematics problem for half an hour or so with the three or four other students seated together in their "group." During this time, I walked around, watching and listening, interacting when I judged that some kind of teaching action was needed to move student work in more productive directions. I investigate the work I did in those actions, supporting the study of mathematical ideas as students tried to figure out the "Problem of the Day." This work includes judging when to intervene and constructing interventions that are both directive and supportive of the development of student efficacy, teaching students how to make use of their peers and how to offer information to their peers in a way that is educative, and observing and analyzing student work so that it can be used as a basis for the teaching that will follow. I zoom in on particular interactions to examine acts of teaching that support the maintenance of the routines, from setting a task in a way that students can work on it independently to constructing an intervention when intervention is appropriate.

Different sorts of teaching problems arise when the teacher interacts with the class as a whole (chap. 7). In my class, I entered into this domain of practice when I brought the class together every day after their period of independent work and led a discussion of the mathematics that was contained in their work. As students explained their solutions to me and to the class, I taught both the student who was explaining and the whole class as I made comments on their explanations. I did this work by responding verbally and by writing and drawing on the chalkboard. To investigate the nature of this work, I analyze a transcript of different parts of a discussion, magnifying the acts of teaching that occur as instructive talk and illustration go on in the presence of the class as a whole. I examine what each piece of talk and illustration does in order to teach, and who is being taught what by my actions. The teaching actions under study here include choosing a question to begin each segment of the discussion, connecting one segment with the next, choosing which student(s) will have the floor, responding to students who bid for attention in ways that connect their comments with the train of the lesson. To teach, I participate in the mathematical activity of student explanation, by listening and by making it obvious that I am listening. I also construct explanations of my own, refer to explanations in texts, and step out of the academic discourse to comment on what we are doing as a way of further teaching students how to study.

Preparing a lesson, guiding students' independent work, and orchestrating a whole-class discussion are elements of practice that occur over and over again every day. Moving to another dimension of practice in the next chapter (8), I widen the angle of my analytic lens to investigate the actions of teaching that link lessons across time, intellectually and socially. First, I investigate how teaching works to develop opportunities for students to study cohesive and related mathematical content over a set of lessons on a single topic. I use two different frames to describe the organization of a cohesive set of lessons: the problem context for the tasks that students are assigned (like time-speed-distance relationships, distributing cakes to bakeries, identifying collections of coins that represent the same amount of money, and so on) and the mathematics that such problem contexts bring into play (like division, fractions, place value in decimal numbers, functional relationships, and so on). Zooming in on an example of teaching as students engage with tasks at the intersection between the problem-context frame and the mathematical topic frame, I draw on records of my planning, student work, and mathematical models created and used continuously throughout a unit I taught in November. In this example, I demonstrate aspects of the work of teaching that connect one lesson to the next and make it possible to portray the ideas under study as a set of conceptual relationships that can be used to understand and solve problems in multiple contexts.

Zooming out again, this time with a lens that can encompass teaching over a whole school year, I next examine the work involved in "covering" the curriculum (chap. 9). Looking directly at the interface between curriculum and instruction, I examine the actions a teacher takes to put temporal boundaries around lessons and groups of lessons, interspersing concerns for subject matter coherence with the realities of the calendar. I describe the work of judging how and when to "go over" something that has already been taught and studied in such a way that constructs an opportunity for students to study the ideas in that material more deeply and broadly as one of the most challenging aspects of teaching from this perspective. Using examples from the fall and winter of the school year, I examine the work of connecting and differentiating content over time. As with other aspects of teaching work, the social and the academic aspects of practice here are deeply intertwined.

Keeping a wide-angle lens, I reposition it somewhat, from a focus on teaching *content* in relationships with students to a focus on teaching *students* in relationships with content (chap. 10). The domain of practice under examination here is something I have named "academic character building." Nothing will be learned in school if students do not regard themselves as the kinds of people who study in school. If they do not choose to pursue knowledge and skills by reading, observing, and researching, they will not learn what I have to teach. If they do not study by paying attention, going over the challenging parts, and memorizing the rules and facts that are used over and over for solving problems, then they will not be successful at school, and I will not be successful at teaching. To investigate the work of making students into the sort of people who will study in school, I analyze the actions I took to establish relationships with two of the students in my fifth-grade classroom toward this end. I zoom in on specific interactions I had with these students and then zoom out to portray the patterns of interaction I constructed over time in an effort to teach them both *how* to study and *that they could* study in school and maintain their personal integrity.

Pulling back from actions taken in relation to particular students, I next look at actions of teaching that communicate with students about the nature of progress in learning (chap. 11). Through investigating the actions of administering formal assessments like tests, grading these assessments, and responding to common errors, I analyze elements of practice that occur in relation to the class as a whole to represent the complexities of acquiring knowledge and skill. I consider the case of a quiz I gave my class in the spring on fractions, how they performed on the quiz, and how I communicated with them about my evaluation of their performance. I look at how students' learning about the qualities of a good mathematical performance can serve as a backdrop for their pursuit of a productive academic identity. Elements of practice that attend to the personal risks entailed in learning (and not learning) in the public forum of the school classroom are the focus of my analysis here.

The fractions quiz was an occasion for me to confront the paradoxes involved in measuring accomplishment in my classroom while teaching my students that knowledge and skill do not simply add up to a larger and larger "sum" over the course of the year. In chapter 12, I analyze the work involved in managing the tension between students' varying levels of competency and organizing a coherent instructional program for the whole class. In the school where I was teaching, there was only one fifth-grade class. I taught all of the fifth graders, from those labeled "educable/trainable" to those labeled "gifted." Over the course of the year, I worked at structuring my actions to take account of their diversity of arithmetic skills and knowledge. Some of them were barely able to add and subtract whole numbers, while others were doing all four operations with fractions and decimals by the middle of the year. I use my journal and transcripts of video records of my interactions with students over the course of the year to portray the work of teaching that addresses this problem of diversity.

I finish my analysis of the year as a case of teaching practice with a look at the work of bringing closure to the school year (chap. 13). I analyze records of the teaching work I did in the last weeks of school to investigate what it might mean to culminate a year of teaching. The teaching problems of the final weeks of school include maintaining consistent task routines while accommodating end-of-the-year rituals and celebrations, organizing both group and individual performances of accomplishment for students, and representing the work of the year for shared appreciation by all participants. In addressing these problems, I continue to use students to teach other students, to use language to name and give meaning to learned skills and understandings, and to orchestrate occasions that bring together social and intellectual activities that integrate multiple levels of knowledge.

With my analysis of teaching and studying across time, content, and students in different domains of practice as a foundation, I return in the last chapter (14) to the further development of a model of the problem space in which teaching practice happens. Beginning with the model of teaching as a three-pronged problem space developed earlier in this chapter, I elaborate the teacher-student-content relationship to include attention to elements of practice that

- occur over time and with groups, including the whole class;

- take account of the connections between ideas and among ideas and skills in teaching content;

- manage conflict at the intersection between social relationships among learners and relationships in the content to be learned; and

- respond to the multiple intentions of the participants and the potential conflicts among them.

Taking all of these elements of practice together, working at teaching turns out to be something like navigating in a multidimensional terrain, getting safely across the street while also crossing the city, sighting one island from another while catching the wind that makes it possible to get around continents and across the ocean.

4

Teaching to Establish
a Classroom Culture

Teaching begins with the problem of how to start the school year with a new group of students, most of whom the teacher has never met, and some of whom have not met one another. Figuring out where to start in the mathematics, getting to know the students, and planning activities are all aspects of this problem. But underlying all of these matters is the work of teaching students how to learn from the kind of teaching that is going to be happening. I call this problem domain "building a classroom culture" because it entails establishing and maintaining norms of action and interaction within which the teacher can teach and students can study. The time frame over which this work plays out is bifocal. Establishing norms happens at the very beginning of the year, but maintaining them must continue on a daily basis until June. In teaching classroom culture, I teach the class as a whole, but maintaining the culture depends on how I structure my interactions with individuals and with groups.

A few days before the first day of school, I wrote an overview in my journal of what I would be teaching to my fifth-grade mathematics class. I include several excerpts constructed from this originally handwritten journal in this book to document my thinking at the time that I did the teaching described. In the following excerpt, I was thinking in three dimensions: first, I listed activities that I might have my students do, then I listed the mathematical topics or content that these activities would give them an opportunity to study, and finally, I wrote a list of mathematical practices that I wanted them to learn. In the first list, I was drawing on the repertoire of activities that I had done before with fifth graders. I was planning to use the ones I thought would be likely to engage students in the mathematics that was conventionally a part of the fifth-grade curriculum, and engage them in a way that would be likely to produce learning. The curriculum list included the topics I knew were standard for American ten-year-olds. The list of practices I would teach came from my studies of what it means to do mathematics and my own experiences doing it.

Monday, September 4

what to teach this year?
I think about repeating a number of things
I've done before:
  fractions of a population
  comparing fractions (+ and −)
  comparing decimals (+ and −)
  Larry's Loot: collecting, categorizing,
    graphing, analyzing data
  the pick-a-number puzzles
  exponents patterns
  how numbers were invented → Mimi II
  time-speed-distance
  (sampling)   } *Mimi I*
  position + direction
  make a circle graph of how you spend your time
  fraction word problems
  the window-washing problem
  graphing functions

This is a list of <u>*activities*</u> *, not* <u>*topics*</u> *or* <u>*content*</u>*.*
There is another way to cut through what
the year will look like: the concept of a fraction
            long division + multiplication
            concept of decimals in relation to
                place value + fractions
            linear functions + cartesian
                graphing
            collecting, sorting, and graphing data

> *area, perimeter, surface area, volume*
> *add + sub. fractions*
> *divisibility rules: factors, primes*
> *intro ratio + proportion*
> *large nos. + exponents*
> *and then there is a third list: learning the*
> *practice of mathematics, things like*
> - *revision*
> - *hypothesizing*
> - *giving evidence, explanation*
> - *representation—words, pictures*
> - *discussion, challenging, responding to challenges*
> - *sense of self as a mathematical knower*
> - *what's a legitimate procedure + why*
>
> *knowledge*
> *"Learning to be a mathematics ^ generator + defender"*

None of these lists is about what work I would need to do to start the year or to teach, once it got started. Simply doing activities would not necessarily involve all of the students in my class in studying the mathematical content and practices I wanted them to learn. To teach, I would need to establish a way for students to work that would make it possible for the activities I planned to be educative.[1] I could not learn for my students; only they could do that. But as the adult in charge, I could structure the environment in which they did their work so that it was more likely to focus their activities on studying and minimize the interference of actions taken to pursue other intentions. I could establish and use my relationship with my students in such a way as to create a productive classroom culture. Establishing some norms for what it would mean for my students and I to "do school" to-gether would be a way to shape the ways in which we would interact, what we would interact about, and what materials we would have available for our work. The establishment of a classroom culture that can support studying is a fundamental element of teaching practice. All teachers do it, to a more or less deliberate extent. It can be done in many ways and with different assumptions about the relationship between routines and what is to be learned, resulting in many different variations on classroom culture.[2] In this chapter, I describe my work in establishing the kind of culture that I antici-pated would support all students' engagement with content in their daily work on problems across the school year. I illustrate what I do to establish physical, social, and linguistic routines to manage my use of students to teach other students in a way that has everyone doing and studying mathematics. I then analyze the problems of teaching that arise in this domain of practice.

Arranging the Physical Environment to Support a Classroom Culture

The first problem I faced was what to do with the room and with the hour that I would have every day with my class. On the day before the first math lesson of the year, I narrowed the scope of my anticipatory reflections and wrote in my journal about what I would need to do about the physical arrangements in the room where I would meet with my class. I would need to make opportunities available for my students to study, and hopefully to learn. I wrote about how I would arrange the furniture, what I would make available to students on their desks to use during the lesson, what I would put on the chalkboard, and when I would have students work alone, in small groups, or together with the whole class during the hour-long period. I thought about how to coordinate what I would do about all this during my mathematics class with what other teachers of my students would be doing.

Sunday, September 10

The desks are not arranged right now in groups of four. Need to talk with Thom about that. I paid attention because I've been trying to decide about how to handle the first day → work individually on a problem coming in from lunch recess for sure, to get <u>that</u> routine in place. Problem needs to be one that can be represented on the board— and it should be a problem that leads to some hypotheses about patterns and relationships, but also one that people can get into at many levels.

Should I go right from individual work to whole-class discussion? I am inclined <u>not</u> to have group work on the first day because there is too much other stuff to initiate them to. And this is where I note that Thom did not arrange the desks in groups

> *of four. I'm sure he has a reason for what*
> *he did—need to ask him.*
>
> *Also, in terms of developing <u>language</u> and*
> *<u>interaction patterns</u> for small-group work*
> *(i.e., what exactly are we supposed to be*
> *talking about + why) I think of the large*
> *group as a place to model that sort of*
> *thing.*

From the very beginning, I wanted the Problem of the Day to have two characteristics: it should lead to work with patterns and relationships about which students would be able to make mathematical hypotheses and it should be "one that people can get into on many levels." I wanted everyone to be able to start work on every problem at whatever level of ability he or she brought to my class. I connected the physical arrangements of students' desks into groups with the development of the language and interaction structures I would need to establish. I would first model these patterns in the large group, in front of the whole class, and then have these models to refer back to in setting norms for small-group work.

I planned to begin the work of "getting routines in place" on day one: I would arrange desks so that students were seated in groups of four and a problem would be on the chalkboard when they came in from recess. I thought that having students sitting in groups of four would enable them to think and work collaboratively, and I wanted to have them do that throughout the year. Although we would start with this seating arrangement, I would not have them work in their groups on the first day "because there was too much other stuff to initiate them to." I would prepare the whole class for the small-group work to come by starting in the first lesson to model methods of studying mathematics which I would then expect them to take up on their own. I recognized that whatever directions for how to work I gave on the first day would "need to be repeated after" and "varied" to fit particular circumstances as they developed. In past years, I had experimented with such arrangements and found these routines to be productive in helping students make the transition from outdoor play to engagement with a mathematical problem. I would no doubt learn more about how these arrangements would work with this new class.

Choosing Mathematical Content to Complement Culture-Building Practices

After working on how I would arrange the furniture and making a schedule of activities for the first lesson, and thinking a bit about how I would work on the problem of establishing new patterns of interaction and language use, the next problem was choosing "the math" I wanted students to learn. I deliberately chose a task for students to do that would involve a kind of arithmetic that was familiar to them. This would make it possible for me to teach and for them to study the social and task routines, as well as the mathematical practices they were intended to support, like generalizing and making hypotheses.[3] I did some mathematics myself in my journal, making a conjecture and then wondering if I could find a counterexample to disprove it. The problem I was thinking about giving the class was to find "additions" whose answers would be between

$$\begin{array}{c} 24 \\ +18 \end{array} \quad \text{and} \quad \begin{array}{c} 37 \\ +15 \end{array}$$

The goal is not to do the two additions, but to focus instead on the kinds of numbers being added and find a third addition whose answer would fall between the two.

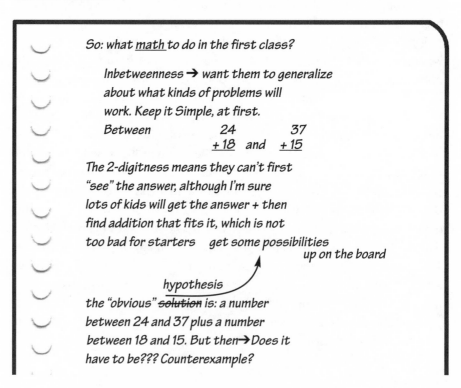

So: what <u>math</u> to do in the first class?

Inbetweenness ➔ want them to generalize about what kinds of problems will work. Keep it Simple, at first.

Between   24   37
         + 18   and   + 15

The 2-digitness means they can't first "see" the answer, although I'm sure lots of kids will get the answer + then find addition that fits it, which is not too bad for starters   get some possibilities up on the board

hypothesis

the "obvious" ~~solution~~ is: a number between 24 and 37 plus a number between 18 and 15. But then➔Does it have to be??? Counterexample?

In planning "what math to do in the first class," I was blending the choice of an activity with the choice of the content I wanted to teach as I would in every lesson to follow. What I wanted to teach as content was not addition of two-digit numbers. As an activity for students to do, working in the realm of addition would be a vehicle for getting to some ideas about how numbers work—what mathematicians would call "number theory" and what mathematics educators call "number sense." At a conference I attended once, I heard Judah Schwartz talk about activities like this one on "inbetweenness" as a way to get students to focus on something other than the answer to a computation. Having chosen this to be the kind of activity we would do on the first day, I also needed to decide on the specific numbers I would use. What students are to study here is not how to solve a particular problem, but the general principles that govern the way numbers are ordered and what can be deduced from the differences in the quantities to be added. The numbers I chose would determine the mathematical trajectory of their work.

I wanted to use two-digit numbers, thinking that maybe this would deter students from working on getting the answers rather than speculating on how to solve the "inbetweenness" problem. I made the problem additionally complicated by using 24 + 18 for the first addition and then using 37 + 15 for the second addition; 37 is larger than 24, but 15 is smaller than 18. As I played with what numbers to use in the problem, I also thought enough about how to solve it to be ready to use it with the class. The tasks of teaching that go into setting the Problem of the Day include choosing the words, the numbers, and the activities students will do. This work, which needs to be done for every problem that is assigned throughout the year, will be analyzed in chapter 5. It can be done by making up a problem, as I did on the first day in my class, or picking one out of a book and using it as is or modifying parts of it. Like making up a problem, choosing an appropriate problem from a book would entail making judgments about the appropriateness of the numbers, the wording, and the activities for teaching particular mathematical content and practices.

Before I finished preparing the problem I would use on the first day, I went on to write in my journal more explicitly about something I would do that I called "routine setting."

"Routine" setting ➔
    have math notebooks + black pen on desk
      when students come into the room from
    recess
    have "Problem of the Day" up on the board
    come in + sit down
    names on front cover
    who thinks they know what to do?
    how many people agree ➔ *emphasize*
      speaking so you can be heard
    similar to morning warm-up ➔ *how?*
    different from morning warm-up ➔ *how?*
    what to do when you have finished the

this will   *problem but others are still working?*
need to   ➔ *look for patterns and*
be repeated   *relationships*
after, varied   ➔ *create other, similar problems*
    why black pens + graph paper?
    page layout ➔ *date*
         ➔ *write the problem*
    erasure? cross out: model on the board
    communication ➔ *to me, to others*

N.B. all this time, the problem will have been
up on the board + many will have already
figured something out.
Maybe have   *part II (subtraction) under*
   a map.   *+ III multiplication*
watch for who had trouble [*writing*] *the problem*
                  [*copying*]

In this journal entry I worked on figuring out how to relate what I would be doing with what I knew students would be expected to do in other subjects, like "morning warm-up." My somewhat cryptic notes show my thinking moving back and forth between what to do and why to do it, as I anticipate and prepare. As I write about the expectation that when students speak they would need to do so in a way that could be heard by everyone, I am working on preparing to teach both something about the task structure (how we would do school) and something about mathematical discourse (how we would do math). No matter how good the problem was that I gave them to work on, students could not have an equal chance to study mathematical argument, nor would they be able to agree or disagree about an assertion and come up with reasons for their judgment unless everyone was able to hear what was being asserted. I knew that for ten-year-olds to make assertions in such a way that they could be heard around the room would take both courage, on their part, and support, on mine. They would need to learn to speak about and listen to mathematics, beginning at the beginning, even though I expected that a lot of what they said would come out sounding like babble at first.

Zooming in on the First Mathematics Lesson of the Year

When my students came into the room for their very first mathematics lesson in September, on the Monday following the first day of school, they each found a bound notebook and a black felt-tip pen on their desks.

Routines with Reasons

Referring to the pens and notebooks on each desk I said:

Lampert: Those two things are tools that are specifically for mathematics. I'd like you to put your name on the front of the notebook. That's going to be your math notebook for this. We'll probably have one for the first part of the year and one for the second half of the year. The purpose of this notebook is for you to write down your thinking.

Now, as Mr. Dye said on Thursday, sometimes when you write down your thinking the idea is to keep track of it for yourself and sometimes when you write down your thinking the idea is to communicate what you're thinking to other people. And we're going to use these notebooks for both of those kinds of recordkeeping.

The reason that you have a black Magic Marker—well, there are three reasons. One reason is because it is easier to see what you write with a black Magic Marker than it is to see what you write with a pen, and so when I'm walking around the room trying to figure out what sort of work people are doing, I like to be able to see it as clearly as possible. And that's one of the uses for your notebook.

> A second reason is because when we copy things that are in your notebook to show people, using black Magic Marker makes it easier to copy than using pencil.

Although "giving reasons" for routines is not a universal feature of putting them in place, I chose to do that during the first lesson in order to integrate teaching routines with teaching students to reason about their actions and mine. I wanted them to know that they could expect explanations from me about why procedures are to be followed, whether they are mathematical procedures or procedures for using materials.

I started the lesson by explaining the purpose of the tools I had distributed and described how they were to be used, making a connection with something their social studies and language arts teacher had said on the first day of school. In terms of the kind of discourse of "sense-making" that I was hoping to establish in this class for all students, it seemed important to explain to the class why we were going to do what I had planned. I would be asking them to "explain why" they did things, and I wanted to begin to model what that sort of talk was like right at the beginning of the year. Explaining would be a consistent part of our relationships. It would be as much a prescribed, regular course of action as using felt-tip pens and bound notebooks to record mathematical work. Besides reasoning, I was teaching students something else, something about myself that I hoped would contribute to building relationships with them, namely, that I planned my work with them in collaboration with the teacher who taught them for most of the day.

Investigating Meaning in Public

As I went on to give the "third reason" for the sort of pens I had given my students, I made a transition from explaining routines to reflecting on the nature of mathematical practice. The next part of the lesson would exemplify a kind of interaction pattern that would also become a routine: namely, discussing the meaning of words to build agreement about how they would be used in this context.

Lampert: The third reason [for writing in notebooks and using black pens] is that we like to know everything that you've been thinking, and, in mathematics, one of the things that is really important to learn about is the process of revision.

Now, you might have talked about revision in writing classes. You might have talked about it in math class. Does anybody think they have an idea to tell the class about what revision might mean? [Students raise hands.]

> OK, Anthony has an idea, and Shahroukh has an idea.
> Charlotte has an idea and Varouna. I'd like to hear all
> those ideas, but it's not only me that you're talking to. It's
> everybody in the class. And if you haven't raised your
> hand with an idea, I want you to listen to the people who
> have an idea and see if you agree or disagree and if you
> have something to add. Okay, Charlotte, what's your idea
> about revision?

I asserted that one kind of work students would be doing to study was an activity we would refer to as "revision"; then, I explicitly structured the discussion to solicit the thinking of several students about what "revision" might be. The meaning would be out there for public consideration by the whole class. I was fortunate to be able to build here on their experience with revising pieces of writing, which I knew they had done in other classes, to introduce this practice. I told students that it was their responsibility to talk in a way that would be heard by everyone and to listen to one another's ideas. This would make it possible for them to think about what another person had said. Before I called on anyone who had a hand raised, I said to the class that having a hand raised meant to me that a person "had an idea." I went on to say that when someone was called on to talk, the idea would be shared with "everybody in the class." I also made it clear that those who had not raised a hand and were not speaking had a job to do beyond simply listening. They were to reflect on what they heard in such a way as to "see if you agree or disagree, and if you have something to add." In subsequent chapters, we will look at the work entailed in supporting students in the practice of "revising their thinking" across the year so that they can use this activity as a means to study mathematics.

On this, the day of the first mathematics lesson, several students had ideas about what it might mean to revise. Their contributions gave me an opportunity to introduce them to the way in which I would behave in relation to their "answers" as well as to add some of my own ideas about the meaning and purpose of revision in a mathematics class. Both the content and the form of this discussion were meant to teach aspects of the practices of mathematics and studying mathematics. The way I conducted this exchange was meant to model a particular kind of interaction that would be used to teach students to engage in mathematical sense-making.

The elements of this form that would repeat themselves throughout the year included:

- soliciting more than one contribution;

- responding to each contribution in a way that communicated my understanding (not necessarily approval) of what the student was saying; and

- asking students to revoice the contributions of other students.

Beginning with an idea from Charlotte about what it means to do "revision," we started the yearlong process of building interactive patterns of communication in an effort to give the words we would use to label our activities a shared meaning. I deliberately and explicitly called on more than one person to give an answer to the question I had posed, and I tried to make it clear that multiple "ideas" would be considered. I was teaching students about the nature of teaching as well as about the nature of studying. Together, we would "do school" in this way on a regular basis.

In the following set of exchanges, I call on Charlotte, and then Shahroukh, Anthony, Varouna, Karim, Eddie, and Richard, asking them all to speak about the meaning of "revision." I was working in my relationships with these individual students to teach them that they could make a useful contribution even if someone else has spoken first. I was also working in my relationship with the whole class to teach everyone that multiple ideas, not right answers, were the "coin of the realm" for buying attention.

Charlotte:	That you write down one idea that you think and then you decide that maybe that's not the right, you don't think that that's the right idea and that you want to change it. And you use revision by writing your other answer instead of erasing your first idea and then using it again, just, it's a second answer.
Lampert:	Okay, that's one good way of explaining revision. Let's see, Shahroukh was another person who had an idea.
Shahroukh:	I think she's got my idea.
Lampert:	Is there anything you would like to add to what Charlotte said?
Shahroukh:	Well, I think revision is, well, it's almost the same, what I'm gonna say, because I think revision is when you have an idea and it's not correct and you don't want to, like,

mess it all up and you don't want to try to erase or cross it out. But, if you write in another line over your revision, rather than your making it all messy.

Lampert: Okay. So part of what we're worried about there is what to do when you change your mind and one thing that people get used to doing when they change their minds is erasing, and what I'm going to ask you to do in math this year is not to erase and that's one reason why we're going to use black magic markers instead of pencils in math. Let's see, Anthony had an idea about revision.

Anthony: Looking over an idea you already had.

Lampert: Okay, looking over an idea you already had. Let's see. Varouna, you had an idea? And then I'll come back to you, Karim.

Varouna: If you have an answer, wrong answer and then somebody has the right answer and you just might try to, like, revision it and get the right answer.

Lampert: Okay, so we have revise and revision. The revision is what you have after you have finished revising something. Those are two. Revision is what you have after you're finished and revise is the act of changing your mind and showing how you changed your mind on paper. Karim?

Karim: Like thinking twice over an answer. Like the first time you thought it was the answer then you thought of it again and it was right.

Lampert: Okay. Thinking twice. That's a good way to think about it and sometimes I think when something is important you might even want to think about it three times or more and go over it a couple times and then revise it. Eddie?

Eddie: When, like, if you wanted to write something down and you forgot it and then you just write down what you thought it was?

Lampert: Okay. So forgetting. The first time you do something there might be some forgetting involved and then as you work along through a problem you might remember some-thing that you didn't remember at first. So, remembering is another part of it. So we have a collection of ideas here about what revision might be. Is there anyone else who would like to say in his or her own words what you do when you revise? You might not have known at the beginning of this lesson, but who would like to summarize all the ideas that they've heard so far? Put it in your own words. Anybody want to try that? Richard, you think you could try that? What do you think revision is after listening to all these people?

Richard: Writing something down and deciding to do it over. Instead of erasing it, just write down on another line or something.

Lampert: Okay, instead of erasing it, just write it down on another line. And sometimes you can, if you just put a straight line right through what you don't want anymore, that's a good indication to me and to other people in the class that you've changed your mind.

Although I respond each time a student speaks, the problems I am addressing are more than the simple evaluation of student assertions. I tell Charlotte (and whoever else is listening) that what she said was "a good way of explaining" revision. I tell Shahroukh that he can "add to what Charlotte said." Implicit in these responses is the message that students can and do give explanations, and can and do build on one another's thinking. I am teaching efficacy: each student needs to learn that his or her contributions will be taken seriously. And I am teaching those students who do not choose to speak what it looks like to use a form they might use to participate in the future. I give Charlotte the opportunity to study the idea that she has not exhausted the topic with her answer. In picking up on Shahroukh's comment about erasing, I am linking a desirable intellectual process with a practical activity that students perceive as undesirable. I suggest that erasing be replaced by crossing out, registering the fact that I will need to be attentive to this connection. I talk about exactly how to cross out, so that students and I will be able to watch the evolution of their thinking. I respond positively to Varouna's notion that you might replace your wrong answer with the right one by "revisioning" it, even as I correct her speech form. I am giving a small grammar lesson, teaching students not only to do revision, but how to speak about what they are doing.

In many of my responses to student contributions, I articulate the process of going over and over and over one's ideas, not stopping when "the answer" appears. Each of these responses gets at a component of revising as a method of studying mathematics. I am teaching both the task structure and the nature of the practice to be studied while engaging in tasks.

Zooming out to the First Week of School: Introducing Conditions, Conjectures, and Revision

Having put some general ideas out on the table about what kind of activity "revising" might be and when it is appropriate to do it, the next step would be to find a way to get students to do revising in a mathematical context. Introducing revising into the study of mathematics would require a change in how I imagined students would typically think about what one does to study mathematics. It would probably also require some changes in what they thought about the roles of "smart" and less smart classmates and about how to interact with them. I did not expect that my students would come to fifth grade knowing how to evaluate their own assertions or those of their peers in order to decide whether or not such assertions needed revising. Nor did I expect that they would see such evaluation and revision as activities that would contribute to their learning.

My goal was to make it possible for everyone in the class, no matter what their capacity for performing calculations or remembering terms and procedures, to study mathematical reasoning and to use mathematical reasoning to study content. In order to do this, I would have to teach them new ways to think about doing mathematics and what it means to be good at mathematics. In order for everyone to have access to mathematical reasoning as a mode of study, students considered by themselves and their peers to be of lower ability would need to be able to disagree with students considered to be "smart" at math. Conversely, students of greater ability would need to respect the thinking of all students, and if they disagreed with someone, be able to explain why. Such behavior is counter to existing action patterns in classrooms, where the students whom everyone agrees are "smart" get to dominate discussions, and others feel incapable of either judging or challenging their assertions. The problem I faced in doing the work I set for myself was something like establishing and maintaining a counterculture in the midst of a conventional school environment.

This "counterculture" needed to be one that would teach students how to study mathematics in my classroom. To begin to establish routines of interaction, I designed and taught a series of lessons during the first week of school whose content would be clearly identifiable as "mathematics," but which would be structured in a way that most students would find to be different from what they had previously learned about how to "do school" in mathematics classes.[4]

In the context of these lessons, I taught my students three new activities and named them as such for public identification:

- finding and articulating the "conditions" or assumptions in problem situations that must be taken into account in making a judgment about whether a solution strategy is appropriate;

- producing "conjectures" about elements of the problem situation including the solution, which would then be subject to reasoned argument;[5] and

- revising conjectures based on mathematical evidence and the identification of conditions.

These activities were important to teach *deliberately*. They represent the essence of mathematical activity in a way that makes it doable by ten-year-olds. They also run directly counter to the usual practices of producing and judging answers in the classroom, thus requiring students to study and learn radically different roles in relation to knowledge use and production. The point here was not to prepare these children to be mathematicians or to teach them to mimic the way mathematicians talk. My purpose was to teach them a method of studying that would make it possible for them to learn both mathematical content and mathematical practices. By reflecting on whether their own assertions and those of their classmates were reasonable, they could engage in an activity that would have them turning over ideas and procedures in their minds, scrutinizing the procedures that were being followed, and investigating alternative interpretations of problems and their solutions. While doing this, they would also be repeating facts and rules, making it more likely that they would remember them when they needed to.

In the first lesson, I put two additions on the chalkboard as planned, and I asked students to come up with other pairs of numbers whose sum was *between* these two sums.

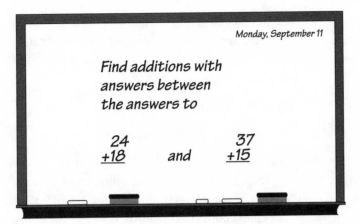

I assessed their responses and saw a paralyzing puzzlement in the eyes of more than a few students. I quickly erased what I had put on the board and changed the two-digit numbers to single-digit numbers.

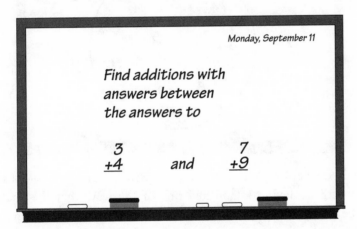

Since my purpose had not been to teach double-digit addition, but to teach students how to study, these simple additions would suffice. They would get us into the activities of finding conditions, conjecturing, and evaluating conjectures without the distraction of computation.

Displaying Alternative Legitimate Responses

I pointed to the two revised additions on the chalkboard, saying:

Lampert: Okay, let me have you look over here.

These are two very easy additions and I bet everybody in the room knows the answer to this one [pointing to 3 + 4] and the answer to this one [pointing to 7 + 9], but I don't want you to tell me the answer. I want you to

tell me another addition problem whose answer is in between the answer to this one [pointing to 3 + 4] and the
answer to this one [pointing to 7 + 9], without saying the
answers.

What do you think? Can you tell me one?

No answers, just an addition problem.

I moved my attention around the class quickly, calling on students who
had raised their hands. Donna Ruth, Leticia, Anthony, Awad, Dorota, Karim,
Varouna, and Charlotte each volunteered "an addition problem," and I put
all the problems on the chalkboard inside a circle between the two sums.

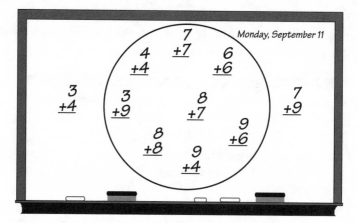

Then, I used what I had displayed to change the nature of the work we were
doing together. Having established one of the ways that the chalkboard
would be used in our work, I moved the class's activity closer to mathematical argument, asking students to generalize about the data they saw in front
of them. This was the first instance of using the chalkboard in this way,
but it was a routine I would use repeatedly throughout the year: putting multiple "conjectures" that were offered as answers to a question on the chalkboard for everyone to see and reflect upon. I did not judge the correctness of
the responses before writing them on this public display. That would be the
work of the class.

Lampert: Now, I want you look at these and see if you can tell me
why all these work.

How could you explain why all of these problems
[pointing inside the circle] have answers in between
these two [pointing to 3 + 4 and 7 + 9]?

The first four students who answered were Ellie, Awad, Yasu, and Shahroukh. None of them responded to the question of "why all" of the problems in the circle have answers between the other two. Instead, they chose a particular sum in the circle and told why its answer was between seven (3 + 4) and sixteen (7 + 9). Yasu, for example, said, "Nine and four is thirteen and thirteen is between the answer of these two problems." And Shahroukh said, "Eight plus seven is fifteen and it's between four plus three and seven plus nine." After a few such contributions, Eddie spoke, excitedly, saying: "I think there's any number below nine times seven it would be lower than that nine times seven."

Eddie changed the way the additions were being spoken about. He also misspoke, using the word "times" where he should have used "plus." I was excited that we were moving into making statements about "any number" and wanted to pursue Eddie's thinking. I knew he was trying to make a generalization, but it was not clear to me yet what he was thinking. I did not have the opportunity to ask Eddie for a clarification because Anthony immediately reacted to Eddie's assertion, registering disagreement and an implied judgment by asking in what I perceived to be a somewhat caustic tone of voice: "Nine *times* seven?" Anthony interrupted the flow of the teaching I was trying to do but he gave me the opportunity to use what he had done as an occasion to teach something I wanted to teach. He had not raised his hand to ask for the floor. My work here was to manage the tension between encouraging Eddie and concurring with Anthony's correction, as well as to acknowledge the correction while maintaining civility in students' interactions with one another. I had to teach not only what a generalization would be, but also how to disagree with another student's assertion.

I saw this as my first opportunity to teach mathematical practice deliberately and to teach students how to use mathematical arguments to study what they needed to learn. I stopped working on the task of leading students through the steps of the activity and started doing another kind of teaching work: commenting on a student's assertion and another student's mode of responding to it. To be able to have this kind of "exchange" in which one student listens to another and challenges the assertion made by the speaker was fundamental to studying mathematics, but it would be counterproductive socially and intellectually if the student who had made the initial assertion perceived that it was his capacity to do mathematics and not the particular assertion he had made that was being challenged. Such a perception would threaten students' relationships not only with one another, but also with me, because I was the adult responsible for keeping them safe.

Modeling Disagreement

In order to manage this dilemma, I repeated what Eddie said, described how Anthony reacted, and then repeated Eddie's response. I then modeled a method of disagreeing that was more respectful of the initiator, while also attributing a capacity for sense-making to Eddie. I made a connection between what these students were doing and what "mathematicians" do, encouraging disagreement, but under the conditions that it be reasonable and polite. Finally, I did the work of bringing attention back to the substance of Eddie's initial assertion.

Lampert: Okay. Now here we have a very interesting exchange, which is something I think is going to happen and hope happens a lot in this class. But we need to have some ways of having this exchange.

Eddie said, I think anything lower than nine times seven is going to have an answer that works. And Anthony said, without raising his hand, nine times seven?

Okay, and then Eddie revised and he said, plus seven. If you disagree, like Anthony just disagreed with Eddie, that's very, very important to do in math class. But, when you disagree or think somebody misspoke, you need to raise your hand and say, I think he must have meant plus, not times.

And then Eddie will probably revise even before you get it out of your mouth. So one thing we have here is how to challenge or disagree with somebody in your class, and that's a very important thing.

Mathematicians do it all the time, but you have to have a good reason and you have to do it with politeness. But the other thing I want to come around to is really what Eddie meant. Eddie, why don't you say again what you're trying to say here.

Eddie then attempted to construct a more elaborate assertion about the conditions under which a sum would be between the two given sums, saying something like that the numbers had to be higher than three or four but lower than seven or nine. We cannot hear very well what he said on the tape. I responded, using somewhat formal terms ("generalization" and "conditions") to name what Eddie had done, and I made an effort to use another student who had asked for the floor to further elaborate:

Lampert:	Okay, so what Eddie is trying to do here is make a generalization about what will always work, and he put a lot of conditions on his statement.
	Let's hear from some other people.
	Awad?

I hinted at a second important element of mathematical practice: putting conditions on an assertion, but I did not elaborate. Awad, Shahroukh, Ivan, Candice, and Charlotte all followed on Eddie's effort to make a general statement about number combinations that would "always work." Other members of the class shook their heads in agreement or disagreement, but did not choose to speak, and it was time for the first lesson to end.

Making and Labeling "Conjectures"

For the rest of the week, we worked in the two related domains of producing particular additions and subtractions that would meet certain conditions, and producing general statements about patterns and relationships in the numbers involved. The new and challenging content that I was introducing was the practice of formulating and asserting general statements about a mathematical relationship and evaluating the reasonability of those statements. In order to study that content, I would need to work at providing a safe environment, not only for students to reconsider their own assertions, but also for them to comment on one another's assertions. Everyone's assertions were to be open to question by everyone else. I was trying to avoid the development of a "pecking order" in the class where some students were known to be always correct and therefore would not be challenged either verbally or in the thinking of others. I was also trying to spread the responsibility beyond the teacher for evaluating anything that was asserted.

For the second Problem of the Day, I moved back to two-digit additions, but I structured the problem as a much more straightforward activity.[6]

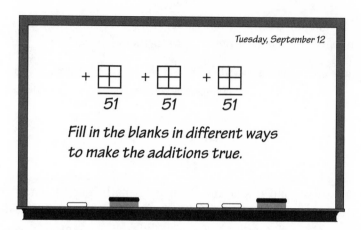

Most students completed the three additions quickly, and I then challenged everyone to see how many more sums to 51 they could make in this form. The nature of this newly assigned activity was mathematically different from the straightforward production of three sums. Informal arguments began among students sitting near one another about how many there could possibly be. Some assertions were based on how many combinations a student had actually produced, and others were based on noticing the patterns in combinations. As I walked around and interacted with individuals and small groups of students, I labeled their assertions as "conjectures." Later, in speaking to the whole class, I explained that a conjecture was a statement that had reasons behind it, but could be revised once it was discussed. I told the students that it was important to formulate a reason for their assertions about the total number of possible sums that would convince their classmates that what they were saying "made sense." What I had done to teach here was to create a situation in which "conjecturing" would be likely to happen, so that I could then label it and students could investigate what this kind of activity was all about.

As students later explained to the whole class how they had come up with their conjectures about the total number of possibilities, I had another opportunity to teach by labeling student activity. Some assumed they could put only one digit in each space in the box, doing additions like:

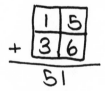

while others put two digits in some of the boxes, for example:

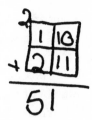

Some students based their assertions about the total number of possibilities on the assumption that they could use negative numbers.[7]

Others made more combinations by using unit fractions, like:

Some students did not use digits at all, but completed the task like this:

using a mathematical shorthand called the "mini-computer" in which the dots in each box have a different value, based on powers of two.[8] They had learned to use the minicomputer in fourth grade, as a tool for creating different compositions of the same quantity. Besides all of these variations on what could be used to make combinations, there was disagreement about whether pairs like:

$$\begin{array}{r} 14 \\ + 37 \\ \hline 51 \end{array} \quad \text{and} \quad \begin{array}{r} 37 \\ + 14 \\ \hline 51 \end{array}$$

should "count" as different.

These multiple interpretations pose a problem for teaching because if all these ways of making combinations are allowed, students will not be able to evaluate the assertions their classmates are making about the total number of possibilities. Unless everyone assumes the same set of conditions on their combinations, there will be many reasonable assertions. If 14 + 37 and 37 + 14 are considered to be two different possibilities, for example, this would lead to a much different conclusion about the total number of possibilities than if these were regarded as two different ways of writing the same combination. Different assumptions would produce different "right" answers to the question of how many combinations were possible. There are many ways this problem could be addressed; my challenge was to find a strategy that was congruent with the kind of classroom culture I was trying to establish.

Noticing the Importance of "Conditions"

The following week, I stated the Problem of the Day in a way that included a statement of the conditions under which everyone would be making their assertions about the total number of possibilities. It was my deliberate intention to teach the place of "conditions" or assumptions in mathematical discourse by making them a more explicit part of students' work.

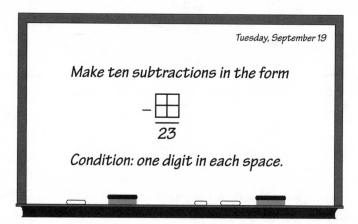

The next step in teaching this element of mathematical practice came the following day when I stated the Problem of the Day in the "if-then" logical form familiar to almost anyone who has studied geometry in high school.

The Problem of the Day was written in this form:

Wednesday, September 20

<u>If</u> you put only one digit in a space and <u>if</u> you only use tens and ones, then I think

there are _____ possibilities for
because _____.

$$-\begin{array}{|c|c|}\hline & \\ \hline & \\ \hline \end{array}$$
14

If you finish, think about how many combinations there would be if you could
use <u>hundreds</u>, tens, and ones.

This way of doing and speaking about mathematics became important because of the kinds of exchanges that I expected students to be having. In the form of these problems, I was teaching them a procedure for investigating disagreements among assertions. When students began working more independently, I could remind them to ask one another what conditions or assumptions led to the differences in their solutions to the problem. We would not simply label an answer "wrong" without examining what the person who produced it was thinking about the problem or the mathematics they used to solve it. In what I wrote on the board on September 20, I was also trying to establish another routine, which I thought would be necessary if students were going to work independently and productively within their small groups by adding directions about what to do "if you finish."

We worked on "making conjectures" in relation to the problem of September 20, and the class ended with students stating a a wide range of assertions about how many possibilities there might be. Following the routine I had initiated a few days before, I put them all on the chalkboard. In both speaking and writing about the assertions on the list, I called them all "conjectures."

The next day, the Problem of the Day that was on the board when students came in the room was:

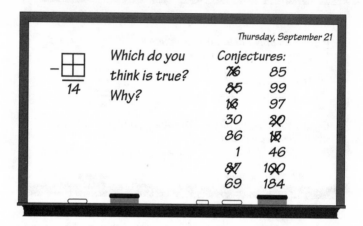

Thursday, September 21

Which do you think is true? Why?

Conjectures:
76 85
85 99
18 97
30 80
86 18
1 46
87 100
69 184

I was demonstrating something else here about how teaching and studying would be happening in this class by continuing to work on a problem from one day into the next. We had discussed some of the conjectures in the list the day before, and I had asked students to "give their reasoning" about why a conjecture did or did not "make sense." The numbers that had been crossed out with an "X" had been rejected with a reasoned argument about how "they could not be true." As we continued to discuss the rest of the conjectures, the talk moved back and forth from evidence to assertions as students began to build on one another's thinking. I wrote in my journal about one example from the discussion on September 21 that particularly pleased me. Yasu was making a general assertion about constraints on the possibilities, and another girl, Charlotte, used Yasu's reasoning to revise her work.

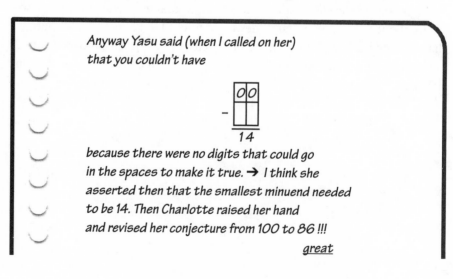

Anyway Yasu said (when I called on her) that you couldn't have

because there were no digits that could go in the spaces to make it true. → I think she asserted then that the smallest minuend needed to be 14. Then Charlotte raised her hand and revised her conjecture from 100 to 86 !!!

great

I had introduced the technical terms "minuend" and "subtrahend" in the discussion the day before to help clear up some communications problems students were having in indicating which part of the subtraction they were talking about.[9]

Developing Norms of Interaction over Time

Like the seating arrangements, the use of the notebook, and the daily appearance of the Problem of the Day on the chalkboard, the linguistic routines that I was working to establish in these lessons took several days to be put in place because they were constructed collaboratively with students' activities. I scaffolded students' use of the terminology of "conditions," "conjectures," and "revisions" by naming these activities whenever I could do so. We used these words throughout the year in place of talking about "answers" and whether they were "right" or "wrong." In the course of the five lessons I have briefly described here, we set down a linguistic and social template for how we would handle almost all problems from this point forward throughout the year. Students would make conjectures, I would put them all on the board, and we would discuss them, clarifying the conditions that the person who made the conjecture was assuming, and figuring out as a class which of the conjectures "made sense." This might all happen in one lesson, or it might happen with the same problem being under consideration for two or more days. I worked at keeping the conversation, both in small groups and in the whole-class discussions, civil in tone and substantive in content. I labeled what students did, and reused those labels often to name mathematical practices. By revisiting a problem to reflect on its possible solutions the day after most students solved the problem itself, I taught my class that such reflection was a way to study mathematics in school.

A search of the lesson transcripts across the year reveals that "conjectures," "conditions," and "revisions" were terms that continued to be used throughout the year to name fundamental practices of teaching and studying. The term "conjecturing," for example, was used to name actions performed by students and teacher variously in classroom conversation for several related purposes:

- as a replacement for the more final word "answer" in exchanges between teacher and students and among students themselves about the solution to a Problem of the Day;

- as a label for student assertions to signal that they are mathematical generalizations of note and open for reasoned discussion;

- to shift the emphasis from the solution of the problem as the goal of a day's work to the defense of the conjecture as the endpoint;

- to raise questions about solutions to problems that are correct and agreed upon but could benefit from some reflection;

- as an indication that like an "answer," a mathematical representation (e.g., the placement of marks along a number line) is an object open to revision;

- to organize a many-faceted discussion, especially as a mechanism for carrying the reflection on a problem over several days;

- as a way to get many possible "solutions" out in public without competition so that students could see where their thinking was in relation to that of their peers;

- to collect assertions about patterns in phenomena going across mathematical domains;

- to highlight what the important assumptions "need to" be if we are to have shared meaning in a conversation (e.g., with area representations of fractions: is a fraction "bigger" if it has more pieces or if it has more area?);

- as a way of pushing toward a refinement in a partially correct idea;

- as an organizer for very open-ended activity (e.g., examining what kinds of linear equations will result in what kinds of graphs, or putting the fraction bars in some kind of "order" and observing their characteristics, or making shapes with different numbers of tangram pieces); and/or

- as a way of refining and clarifying definitions (e.g., the relationships among rectangles, parallelograms, and squares).

Like "conjecturing," "revising" was used consistently throughout the year to name a process that was risky for students and to encourage them to do it. In classroom conversations across the year, it is interesting to note that the words "revise," "revision," or "revising" are used 123 times by the teacher and 145 times by various students, and the words "conjecture" or "conjecturing" are used 198 times by the teacher and 218 times by various students.[10] "Conditions" were brought to the class's attention both by teacher (122 times) and by students (178 times). These figures suggest that these terms were used regularly and not only to teach; students incorporated these terms into their vocabularies to describe what they were doing or seeing others do.

Establishing Structures for Students' Independent and Collaborative Activities

Toward the end of the series of lessons that I have described here, I decided to initiate more formal procedures that were to be followed during small-group work time. I had introduced my class to the process of judging their own work and the work of others to assess what "makes sense." We had talked in whole-class discussions about the procedures involved in making an argument about whether one's assertion is reasonable based on the given conditions in a problem. I demonstrated these procedures in the way I responded to students. Instead of looking to me to judge whether their "answers" were "right," I wanted students to look to themselves and to their conversations with one another, and learn how to shape these interactions into "proofs" of their assertions. Some of the students readily copied what I was doing as they tried to "teach" their peers why their solutions made sense. Others requested more guidance and received more deliberate teaching. I wrote about these variations after the first mathematics lesson, reflecting on how I might communicate with students about their responsibilities for evaluating the legitimacy of their own work.

Tuesday, September 12

Ileana kept checking with me: is this right?
I "went over" what she did with her as follows:
does it seem right to you? Why? And she would
go over the additions + carries. I used the
term "prove" to refer to the process of showing
that it is right.

Awad began using negative numbers
and noticed something which he called to
my attn. , wondering "if this was right" ➔ I'm not
sure he used those words, but that was the flavor of it.

What he was doing was something like this:

$$\begin{array}{ccc} 54 & 55 & 56 \\ +\hat{3} & +\hat{4} & +\hat{5} \\ \hline 51 & 51 & 51 \end{array}$$

and what troubled him was that the
numbers both in some sense
"went up" whereas when he had only

been using counting numbers, when one went "up" the other
went "down"

$$\text{e.g.,} \quad \begin{array}{ccc} 48 & 47 & 46 \\ +3 & +4 & +5 \end{array} \quad \text{etc.}$$

Terrific !

Students Evaluate Their Own Work

Arranging the furniture and the schedule as I had was a structure I deliberately designed to provide students with three different ways to evaluate their own work. One was to work alone. During small-group time, students were not always required to consult with their peers. They could choose to privately reflect on what they were doing and whether it made sense. They could think through silently what they might say if they were called upon to defend their answers. A second way in which they could evaluate their work was to talk about it in the "local" community in which they were sitting. In groups of four to six, they could ask questions of their peers and comment on one another's thinking. The seating arrangements were determined by the teacher, so the people they talked to in this way were as likely to be strangers as they were to be friends. I worked with the other teachers of my class to make the seating assignments based on what we had observed of students in a variety of settings, attempting to balance supportive interaction with social circumstances that would challenge students to clarify their spoken explanations. The third forum for students to assess their own work and that of their classmates was in whole-class discussions under the guidance of the teacher. Participation in these discussions was sometimes voluntary and sometimes required. As we will see in chapter 7, decisions about how to structure participation in these discussions could be used to display the mathematics that was to be taught and studied.

When a diverse class of students is expected to work without constant direction from the teacher, the variability in the pace at which they work and in their levels of confidence in their interpretation of the tasks implied by the problem can lead to unproductive distractions. If some students perceive themselves to be finished working on the Problem of the Day before others, they need to know what to work on next. If students reflect on the problem and do not have an idea about how to begin to work on it, they need a source of inspiration. To anticipate possible difficulties of this sort, I deliberately spoke to my class about the "whole range of people working on these problems" and explicitly created what I referred to as "some organizational rules for coping with what to do when you don't know what to do."

Lampert:	Now as we discussed the other day, when you finish the assigned problem, a very good thing to do is to make up your own conditions and try and solve different problems. And that's what some people did. So, Anthony, if you wanted to go on to decimals or thousands or whatever kinds of numbers, then that's a choice that you can make

after you've finished what's being assigned and I think that's probably what Ivan did, okay.

Now let's see. We still have a few minutes left, so let's talk first, let me have everybody's attention. Dorota, could you close your desk please.

One of the things that we have happening in this class is that we have a whole range of people working on these problems. And different people have, are at a different point in their work. Some people are still experimenting to figure out what kind of problems they can make. And other people are all the way to figuring out what they can do with thousands or ten thousands or decimals.

After setting some expectations for when and how students were to help one another, I talked about the "small-group rules" with the class as a whole. These were rules that Thom Dye and I had found in a book we were using on teaching "problem solving"[11] some years back.

Lampert:	One thing that we haven't talked about in this class is some organizational rules for coping with what to do when you don't know what to do. Now, has Mr. Dye talked to you about small-group rules?
Students:	Yes.
Lampert:	Okay, one of the small-group rules is you are responsible for your own behavior as the first rule. So what that means is you can't say, well, he's bugging me or you know, he's distracting or she told me to get a drink. You are responsible for your own behavior.
	The second small-group rule is you must be willing to help anyone in your group who asks and your group is the people at your table.
	And the third rule is you may not ask the teacher for help unless everyone in your group has the same question.

We had tried these as a way to organize students' independent work in a way that was congruent with our intellectual goals, and we were pleased with the results. The rules had been written out and posted on the wall in September every year since.

SMALL-GROUP RULES

1. **You are responsible for your own behavior.**

2. **You must be willing to help anyone in your group who asks.**

3. **You may not ask the teacher for help unless everyone in your group has the same question.**

Thom regularly invoked these rules during lessons when students worked in small groups during language arts, social studies, and science, and beginning on September 20, I invoked them during mathematics lessons. These rules served several managerial functions, but they also made explicit the idea that students were to reason about their work whether or not the teacher was present, and that reasoning was the ultimate way to judge whether they were doing the "right" thing.

I acknowledged to the class that we had been doing small-group work for a few days already without following these rules, but I went on to say that we would follow them "from now on."

> Lampert: I didn't expect you to follow these rules up until now because I didn't tell you that these rules apply to math time. But from now on, when we're having individual work, when you have a problem like if you don't understand what you're supposed to be doing or you wanted to discuss a conjecture with somebody, you should ask the people in your group. What that means is you don't sit there and do nothing, waiting for the teacher to come along and answer your question. You ask the people in your group and that's very important.

I went on to tell the students that asking for help was "part of working in a human group" even while recognizing that in school, if not in the larger society, asking for help was an admission of inadequacy. Instead of hiding the fact that there were disparate levels of ability in the class, I again made it explicit and suggested that students use other students as resources for learning.

Lampert: Now sometimes people are a little bit shy about asking
            other classmates for help. 'Cause you think, oh, you know
            if I ask that person for help they'll think I'm dumb or
            something like that, but that's part of working in a
            human group. The people need to get used to asking
            each other for help when they need it. They need to get
            used to asking questions. School time is very, very
            precious and teachers can't get around to helping every-
            body and there are a lot of people in this class who can
            help besides the teacher and so I want you to get used to
            the idea of asking for help and giving help to the people
            in your group.

As I had done in introducing the rules for how we would use pens and notebooks, I added something about the reasons for the small-group rules we
would be observing.

Limiting Interaction

During small-group time, students would not have access to all of the
other students in the class, but only to those who were seated in their group.
I explained this as a condition that would help them—and me—to concentrate on our work. I made my role during small-group time explicit, and
explained that they needed to act in ways that would help me to do it.

Lampert: Now, just to talk about the reasonableness of rules for a
            minute, there may be somebody else in the room who you
            would rather ask than the people in your group. But the
            reason that we made the rule that you should ask people
            in group is because it means that people won't be walking
            around a lot during the lesson and that makes it easier
            for everyone to concentrate, including me, that there's not
            a lot of walking around and then I just can look around
            and see where people are and who's doing, who's doing
            their work and so on.

I finished my lecture by asking for questions, and when no one raised a hand,
I said we would "work on practicing those rules a little bit more for sure." I
did not expect that simply stating the rules and listing them on the wall was
going to make this kind of activity happen, because it is not typical behavior
for ten-year-olds.

Lampert:	Does anybody have any questions about small-group rules?
	Okay, we'll work on practicing those rules a little bit more for sure.

A week after students began to work regularly according to the small-group rules during math class, I wrote in my journal about a situation in which I was able to model the behavior I had been talking about. Two students (Giyoo and Donna Ruth) had not worked on interpreting what the problem indicated they were to do, and said to me, instead, "I don't get it." I reminded them that they were to seek help from their group members before asking me for help, taking a chance that something productive would result, since I did not yet know who I could rely on to help those students who needed some help. In my journal I wrote that I was able to teach Richard that he could help, and to teach Donna Ruth and Giyoo that they could rely on a classmate when they were stuck.

Tuesday, September 26

Richard, Giyoo + Donna Ruth got going together after both Giyoo and Donna Ruth asked me → "I don't get it, what are we supposed to do." I took a chance on whether Richard could clear things up for them—and when I checked back they were all three "on task." It was a nice opportunity for them to learn that they don't need to depend on me to figure things out + for Richard to take a leadership role.

I knew that it would take persistence and continuous attention to support students' independent communications about mathematics.[12] Patterns in numbers or alternative strategies for representing the conditions given in a problem were not something that ten-year-olds were typically inclined to talk about with their peers. Neither were they in the habit of making their own decisions about whether they were on the right track in their work.

Establishing Norms for Written Communication

In the first lesson of the year, I had directed my students to write the date in the upper right-hand corner of their notebook page and copy the Problem of the Day that I had written on the chalkboard before they came into the room. After a few minutes, Awad's page looked like this:

Charlotte's looked like this:

And Eddie's looked like this:

I explained that the reasons for these formalities were:

- to keep your own running record of your daily work; and

- to enable me to look at your work when I collect the notebooks and know what problem you were working on.

Like the use of felt-tip markers, these routines had a functional component, but they also helped connect students, mathematics, and teacher. The notebooks all looked pretty standard until students started to work, and then I could see how they were interpreting the problem and what activities they thought were appropriate to do to work toward a solution. For example, Jumanah:

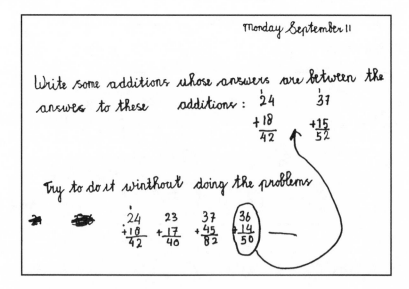

Messima:

and Shahroukh:

```
Math Problems                          9 - 11
 of the day
Write some additions whose answers are between
the answers to these additions:
      24   37
     +18  +15   try to do it without doing the
  32   18   23   22   21   25   24   25        problem
 +18  +28  +23  +23  +23  +25  +25  +26
```

Some students gave me a lot of evidence to go on in assessing how they were thinking, and others gave me very little.

Looking as a Way to Study

In the last week of September, I wanted to introduce a topic that would be new to many of the fifth graders: multiplying by numbers larger than ten. In anticipation of this transition in the mathematical focus of our work, I speculated in my journal about how I might further structure students' use of their notebooks in the service of mathematical investigation. I had two purposes. One was for students to communicate with others, and the other was for them to keep track of their own thinking. Watching their small-group work, I saw that the notebooks could function as a mode of silent communication for students to compare what they were doing with the work of others in their group. I wanted to structure this comparing so that it could foster reflection and communication as activities for studying. It would not help students to learn if all they did was copy one another's work. Writing in my journal, I decided to talk with the class about using a page layout to organize the work they were to do for each Problem of the Day. In addition to writing the date and copying the problem, I added a section called "experiments" and another called "reasoning" where students were to try to write what they were thinking to support the approach they took to working on the problem. I thought of the "experiments" section as something the students would do for themselves to investigate the mathematics in the problem, and the "reasoning" as something they would be using to communicate their thinking to me and their classmates.

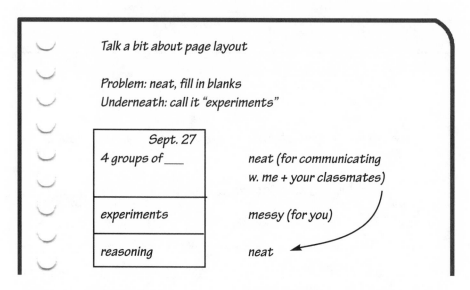

When I went to class the next day, I explained the proposed new layout to the class, conveying my expectation that *everyone* in the class would be doing all of these activities every day. I represented what I was saying on the chalkboard. I referred back to discussions we had had in earlier lessons to explain what I meant by "reasoning." I incorporated the activity of "revising" in my explanation of the parts.

Lampert: I'd like you to think about your notebooks for now, in three parts, actually there are four parts, but one of them is a little bit less important, although it's important. The first part of every day is going to be the date. That's the first part.

The second part is the Problem of the Day. And the Problem of the Day is what I'm going to write up on the blackboard before you come into the room. It will usually have a question mark at the end, or some kind of blanks or boxes to be filled in. By the end of the lesson, you should have an answer to the question which could be revised lots of times, or something to put in the boxes, which could be revised lots of times.

Underneath when you write the Problem of the Day, there's a third part of the page for every day. And that's the part I've been calling "experiments." Now, this part, the experiments part, is usually messy. Because that's where you're trying things out that might not work, and you're not real sure what you want to try out, you're really thinking about the problem. So, this part is for you. The experiments part is things you want to try out.

Then, the fourth part of the page is what I'm going to call reasonings, and that's where you write sentences about why you think what you think. So, in the Problem of the Day, you're going to write, I think there are twenty-five possibilities or something like that, based on your experiments which are in this part, and down here, you're going to answer the question why? Remember, like we did all these additions or subtractions and people said, Oh, I think there are thirteen possibilities. And I asked you to write your reasoning.

Now, we have the date, we have the Problem of the Day, we have experiments—and I expect this part to be messy, but I want to see what your experiments are, so I can see how you think about the problems so I can help you think about them better.

I went on to tell the class about what I would be doing while students did this notebook work, and what kinds of interactions they could expect with me about their written "experiments" and "reasoning." I said that when I was walking around the room, my purpose was to look at their "experiments." The message I was sending here is somewhat ambiguous, reflecting an ambiguity in my own thinking. I had said to the students that the experiments were "where you're trying things out that might not work, and you're not real sure what you want to try out, you're really thinking about the problem. So, this part is for you." But I also act as if the experiments are for me, in that I will look at them to figure out what they are thinking.

Lampert: That's why I walk around the room, and look at your notebooks, and try to talk to people. And then, there's the part where you write your reasoning. Now, every day, you should have these ideas, these kinds of four parts to what goes in your notebook in your mind. Some days, you won't get around to writing your reasoning, there won't be time. Some days, you won't need to do any experiments. You'll just sort of have an idea, and you'll write down your reasoning, and you won't need any experiments. Some people will need lots of experiments, and some people will only need a few experiments.

I am working here at managing the tension between giving students the freedom to figure things out for themselves so that they can learn about that process and finding out what I need to know to support their endeavors.

Clarifying Expectations

During this lecture on what was expected in the notebooks and my role during small-group time, some students raised their hands to indicate that they had questions or comments. As we talked, I modified the routines I had planned to accommodate what I could learn from students' interpretations of their purpose.

Lampert:	Now, people had some questions.
	Yes, Varouna?
Varouna:	Um, Miss, Dr. Lampert if, if, you, if you don't, if you don't want to do experiments can you write the reasoning?
Lampert:	Yes.
	Eddie?

After Varouna asked her question of clarification, Eddie raised his hand, and commented on the sort of work "we do" suggesting that it would always include experiments. Making room for variations and especially for Varouna, I commented that "lots of times, though, people do their experiments mentally and they don't necessarily write them down," but that I liked it better when they were written down so I could see them. I was expressing a matter of my preference, not a hard-and-fast rule.

Eddie:	Actually, the stuff that we do, we always have to experiment and stuff. Most of it.
Lampert:	Okay.
	And lots of times, though, people do their experiments mentally and they don't necessarily write them down. I kind of like it when you write them down, because it helps for us to communicate with each other.

Anthony wanted to clarify more precisely what it was that needed to be explained. I thought I could best respond to this on a case-by-case basis, and I also wanted to leave some of the judgment about what was important to explain to the students, so I could learn more about what they needed to learn.

Lampert:	Anthony, you had a question.
Anthony:	When you, when you explain yourself in the reasoning part, do you have to like, explain why you, why you did this experiment, did this experiment, do you have to explain your experiments? Or do you just have to explain the math Problem of the Day?
Lampert:	Well, you should explain whatever you think is important. And sometimes then, as I'm walking around, I'll say, "I'd like you to explain this, or explain that." And so, sometimes I'll tell you something specific to explain.

The place where this exchange about the notebooks ends points to the complicated ways in which both organizational routines and the mathematical content whose study they are designed to support are mutually constructed. What does it mean to explain your thinking? Philosophers, psychologists, and educators argue about what could count as an "explanation." What I was saying to Anthony here was that we would keep at this work we were calling explanation, and pursue its meaning in the specifics of the mathematics we had before us to explain. By putting the process of having students write "explanations" as part of their daily work, what I wanted to effect was a recurring action pattern that would move all of us toward understanding what it would mean to do that. In chapter 6, I will illustrate the variety of ways in which students used the notebook structure in the lesson on September 28, and how I used their work to structure the large-group discussion on that day.

By having students use bound notebooks and allowing no erasures, a regular record of some of their work would be produced, and they and we could use this documentation as a shared referent for our talk about mathematics. I would be able to see the range of where they might go in relation to mathematical topics I wanted them to study and use what I saw to adapt the subsequent work we would do together to multiple levels of skill and understanding. I could choose from these records the points of interest in individual excursions that I thought could fruitfully be revisited by the whole group. The notebooks would provide students with a nonverbal means of communicating with me and with some of their peers and a scrapbook of experiences to refer back to. I gave some thought to exactly what sort of notebooks would best serve our organizational and mathematical purposes. Having notebooks with grid paper facilitated making graphs, charts, and diagrams in the context of what I had labeled "experiments"—those parts of the mathematical work that involved forays into parts of the territory that students identified as relevant to the problem we were working on.

In addition to walking around and looking in students' notebooks during small-group time, I also wanted the opportunity to get something of a retrospective on their work on a regular basis, and to give students some written feedback. On September 14, I explain my plan to the class. Each week, at the end of the week, I would collect the notebooks and take them home, read them, and write comments. I tell the class again on September 22 that I will "collect your math notebooks and look at what you've been doing all week." On September 29, I decide to collect the notebooks in a way that would enable me to look at them together in groups as the students are seated, linking two of the modes of communication I had established. I want the routine to support my analysis of both written work and what students see and use of one another's work in the notebooks. I tell the class before collecting them that "When I look at your notebooks at home I would like to have them grouped together according to groups." When I collect the notebooks on October 25, I reiterate that what I am going to look at is evidence of "thinking." I tell students, "at the end of the week, I'm going to collect your notebook and I'm going to read about what you did with the problem, and read about your thinking." And on November 6, I add still another mode of communication to writing in notebooks, linking what I have written to students as comments in notebooks with what I will write in parent reports. I tell the class that for parents, "Part of seeing what you've been doing in school is getting a report from me on how you've been doing in mathematics. And I'm basing my reports that your parents will get on what you've been doing in class, and what you've been doing in your notebook. So that's why I need to collect some notebooks every day around this time so I can work on the reports, because I want to have your work in front of me when I'm writing the report. There are some notebooks still to be passed out, but in addition to the, the writing of reports for your parents, I also wrote notes to you in your notebook over the weekend." Here I am using the familiar routine of parent reports to communicate something about the importance of what students write in their notebooks and what I write in response.

What Kind of Work Is This?

Students come into the classroom with multiple purposes: making friends, protecting themselves, arranging dates, earning spending money, and so on. Within this frame, we might construe the work of teaching as adding the studying of school subjects to these purposes and keeping it prominent, at least during school hours. In order to do that, the following conditions need to be in place:

- something that is appropriate to study needs to be made available to everyone;

- teacher and students need to come to an agreement about what activities will constitute "studying"; and

- the tools for doing those activities need to be provided.

In this chapter we have examined how teaching can work to establish these three conditions in a way that is congruent with students doing mathematics problems in school. The resources available to the teacher to do this work are social and physical. She has herself and the students and relationships among them, and she has some desks, chairs, books, paper, chalkboards, and in some classrooms, other materials and technologies as well. All of these can be made into resources for exhibiting that which is to be studied, and for defining and supporting the work of studying in such a way that it is likely to result in learning.[13] Any resources can be used in ways that are constant and regular, or they can be called upon when needed on an occasional basis. The work I called "routine setting" in my teaching journal of September 10 focuses on establishing the constant and regular ways in which the people in my class and the physical environment would interact. My aim was to establish a set of norms that would contribute to a "classroom culture" within which studying could be defined and supported in such as way as to result in learning mathematics. In this chapter we examined what kind of teaching problems are implied in setting such routines.

The work of "routine setting" is more than telling students what the rules are going to be and then enforcing them. It is largely a matter of guiding student talk and action in such a way as to establish shared understandings among everyone present about what it means to teach and to study and how it is to be done, *here*, with this class and this teacher.[14] The definitions of "teaching" and "studying" depend on how they are performed in the particular community in which they are performed. As a reader of this book, for example, you could be said to be studying. In order to study, you do a set of activities that are defined to constitute that work by a more or less formally structured group of which you are a member.[15] If you are enrolled in a course where you have a writing assignment to answer questions based on reading this book, the organization of your "study group" would be a formal one and highly structured. Your study group could also be very informal and unstructured. You may simply be on the mailing list for a publisher's catalogue, reading this book because you have identified it as interesting by virtue of some loose affiliation with a group of people who care about understanding teaching practice for one reason or another. Whether the group of readers to which you belong is formally or informally structured, you would know that you could do other activities in addition to reading this book by yourself as a way to study the practice of teaching. For example, you might investigate the practice of teaching with others using the models and records of practice found in this book, or you might read other materials, create your own alternative models, and look at other records of practice. These are the routines of studying, routines established as legitimate by your membership in some kind of group. Different kinds of groups in which studying occurs will have different goals and purposes and shared understandings of the routines that serve to accomplish them. The complexity of the group's organization will determine the role of routines in accomplishing its purposes.[16]

The goal of the group of ten-year-olds that is my school class, defined by the institution in which we work together, is for students to be prepared for middle school. They will go there after fifth grade, and it is expected that they will have been taught a set of standard elementary mathematical ideas and procedures. But assuming this goal does not define the means to achieve it. As a teacher, I have considerable latitude about how to accomplish this goal. To learn, students need to study, but there are many ways "to study." It can mean:

1. To apply one's mind purposefully to the acquisition of knowledge or understanding of (a subject).

2. To read carefully.

3. To memorize.

4. To take (a course) at a school.

5. To inquire into; investigate.

6. To examine closely; scrutinize.

7. To give careful thought to; contemplate.[17]

For students to be studying mathematics they need to be doing activities that will result in their learning mathematics. For the ten-year-olds in my class, the available time, space, materials, and social interaction patterns need to be arranged to support students' engagement in these kinds of activities and minimize the distractions from such engagement so that they can learn mathematics.

Furniture and People as Tools of Practice

The circumstances in which my students and I find ourselves as we identify the resources available to do our work are typical of a fifth-grade class. The students I teach are usually ten years old. There are always between twenty-five and thirty of them in the room with me at the same time. We are together for about an hour. I am able to arrive in the room where I teach them a few minutes before they do, and I must leave a few minutes after they do. The room contains movable desks and chairs, with barely enough room for thirty of them to be arranged so that children and adults can pass among them. It has a chalkboard on one wall, windows on the opposite wall, doors to the hallway and to the outside, a bookshelf, some cupboards, a couch, and a teacher's desk. In the cupboards are textbooks for various subjects, reference books, and audiovisual materials.

Students bring interpretations of how to use what they find in the classroom and norms of social interaction from diverse family backgrounds and different school experiences. My problem is to choose among the routines for studying that my students already know and add new routines that are likely to engage my students with the mathematics I want them to learn. Whether familiar or innovative, those routines need to be tailored to the tools available in a particular classroom at a particular time. In the classroom, teachers do teaching tasks and use teaching tools, and students have tools and tasks for studying. The distinction between the people in the classroom and the physical tools they use, like furniture and books, is not a clear one. The teacher uses herself and her students to get tasks of teaching accomplished, and students use one another and the teacher to study. Depending on how a class is structured, students may also play the role of teacher and use the tools and tasks of teaching.

The routines that a teacher puts in place function both to display that which is to be studied and to engage members of the class in activities that will connect them with what is displayed in such a way as to result in learning. To get routines to be used, they need to be introduced and students need to have incentives to use them. In order to do this, the teacher can model and demonstrate and label appropriate action, reward appropriate action, or punish inappropriate action. In the classroom, the rewards and punishments that are available are limited, and how the teacher uses them also serves as a demonstration of appropriate action. In a classroom where students are to learn that reasoning about one's actions is the appropriate method of deciding on a procedure in doing mathematics, the ways in which routines are established can be used to display something that is to be studied and learned, namely, that procedures (more commonly called "rules") are based on reasoning about how to get from what is given to what is desired.

Schedule and Task Structure as Tools of Practice

Following the standard definitions of studying, students would need to be able to apply their minds purposefully, read, memorize, inquire, investigate, examine closely, and give careful thought to mathematical ideas and procedures. To do this, the task structure and the arrangement of the room would need to make it possible for appropriate ideas to be displayed for study and for communication to flow in many directions. Students would need to have different social settings for investigating and scrutinizing their ideas and those of others. And I would need to have a reasonable chance of monitoring and responding to what they are doing and talking about.

Not any task structure or arrangement would have been possible, given the constraints of the room and the schedule and the character of the participants. But I came up with one that made several modes of study available to my students while keeping unproductive interferences to a minimum. As we saw, each lesson begins with students working alone, copying the problem from the chalkboard and thinking and writing about it. Then students were to work together with the other students in the group in which their desks were arranged, and I would watch and listen. Even if no talking occurred, the use of notebooks and the expectations I set for what would be written in them gave me and the students something to look at that would tell us something about the work of others. In the second half of the class, I would lead the whole class in a discussion and use the chalkboard to record the salient aspects of our work.

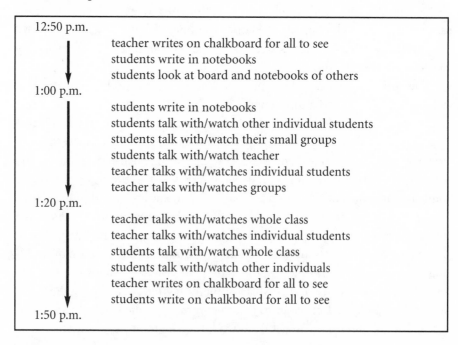

12:50 p.m.

teacher writes on chalkboard for all to see
students write in notebooks
students look at board and notebooks of others

1:00 p.m.

students write in notebooks
students talk with/watch other individual students
students talk with/watch their small groups
students talk with/watch teacher
teacher talks with/watches individual students
teacher talks with/watches groups

1:20 p.m.

teacher talks with/watches whole class
teacher talks with/watches individual students
students talk with/watch whole class
students talk with/watch other individuals
teacher writes on chalkboard for all to see
students write on chalkboard for all to see

1:50 p.m.

The evolution of the regularities in this structure over the first few lessons is documented in my journal and in the instances of interaction described above, illustrating the variety of considerations that come into play and the dilemmas that cannot be solved by any particular arrangement.

Problems in Teaching in the Domain of Establishing Classroom Culture

Putting routines in place to support students' productive engagement with mathematics involves three different kinds of work: identifying what and who I have to work with, devising and choosing routines, and establishing and maintaining routines. These tasks involve thinking and doing; planning, implementing, and observing; inventing and revising. Much of the work occurs toward the beginning of the year, but neither routines nor the conditions they are designed to accommodate are static.

Identifying Affordances and Constraints

Establishing routines to support teaching and studying with problems begins with the identification of the elements of the environment that can be manipulated to engage students in productive work. Before the students arrive on the first day of school, teaching involves finding out what physical conditions one has to work with and what the parameters are for adjusting them. Each situation comes with a set of "givens": What is the size of the room? Where does light come from and how is it controlled? What surfaces are available for writing on or for putting up other kinds of exhibits? Where are the quiet places, and the noisy ones? Where is the door, and what is outside it? What blocks of time are available and what happens before and after them? Other conditions are somewhat more flexible, and can be added to or subtracted from by the teacher: What kind of furniture is in the room, how movable is it, and what can be added and subtracted from it? What books and other materials are available? What informational technology is available? What can be borrowed from elsewhere, and for how long? What can be purchased? Each of these domains provides the teacher with physical "affordances" that can be manipulated toward the purpose of making available opportunities to study and engaging students to take advantage of those opportunities to learn. Each also places constraints on what the teacher can do toward those ends.[18] Some of these affordances will work toward the purpose of supporting study without any intervention from the teacher, and others need to be deliberately introduced and maintained in order to work that way.

Once the conditions of work are identified and characterized, the teacher can work on figuring out: which to use and how to use them, what needs to be added and how to acquire it, what will be the constants in the environment, and what will be changeable and how often it will change. Within the domains of time, space, materials, and social arrangements, productive resources are defined by what can be heard, seen, or manipulated that would offer students an opportunity to study and dispose them in that direction. Routines can define how these resources are to be used to make them productive of learning. What can be heard, seen, and manipulated—and how—depends on where in the room teacher and students are located, what they can get their hands on, who is talking when and what the content expectations are for that talk, as well as who is to be listening to whom, and when. Optimal arrangements will rarely be possible, and so the teacher's work entails making judgments about how best to accomplish appropriate purposes within the given limitations. Groupings of students must be arranged in relation to furniture, doors, windows, and needed display spaces. Materials are acquired, stored, and distributed in ways that are limited by time and by the regularity with which they will need to be used. Expectations about who will talk when and to whom are related to where people are located and are constrained by both the size of the room and its acoustics.

Devising and Choosing Structures for Studying

The tasks of teaching that I am doing as I prepare the structures I have described and put them into place include both the practical setup of time and space and materials and the connection of these routines to linguistic and written communication in the class. To do this work, I am:

- devising/choosing a method for ending the previous class and starting the new class;

- devising/choosing a method for students to record their work;

- devising/choosing a seating arrangement;

- devising/choosing strategies to teach students how the class will operate on a daily basis;

- anticipating what students will do in response to these methods and strategies; and

- devising/choosing methods of handling their responses.

I use both the word "devising" and the word "choosing" here to describe what I am doing as a way to highlight the combination of invention and experience that goes into this work. Over my twenty-five years of teaching, watching others teach, and reading about teaching, I have acquired a large repertoire of possible structures from which I can choose where to start with any particular class. I also know where I can go to get new ideas when I want them. At the same time, I am also devising what I do; it is my own invention, crafted to fit the particular circumstances of my teaching. Words like "devise," "invent," and "contrive" are useful in describing practices of teaching because they mix the thinking with the doing, the planning with the making, the general knowledge of possibilities with the need for creating particular solutions to idiosyncratic problems. I must both decide on how to arrange the seating of my students and be able to bring about that arrangement using the furniture and space in my classroom. As I think through the use of notebooks, I must also engage my know-how to get the notebooks, place them on students' desks, and get students to use them appropriately. Making a schedule entails thinking through the balance of each kind of activity as well as transitioning twenty-nine ten-year-olds from one social structure to another with minimal distraction from the business at hand.

Both designing structures for studying and putting them in place involves confronting existing assumptions about how time, space, materials, and social arrangements are to be used. This teaching involves not only the design and introduction of new structures but also the replacement of unproductive ones. Like any designer, the teacher must work with the given conditions in concert, arranging and rearranging the familiar sights and sounds and manipulatives found in classrooms. Time, space, materials, and social arrangements can become resources if they can be arranged in concert to contribute positively to students' engagement with content. They can be distractions if they are arranged to contribute negatively to such engagement.

Establishing and Maintaining Classroom Culture in a Group

Designing and initiating appropriate routines is teaching work, but routines are established and maintained in a complex set of relationships with a particular group of students. In retrospect, the routines that I designed to fit what I could know about the conditions of my work with students look very rational. If I had simply stated these rational "rules" in my class for using notebooks and doing small-group work, it would seem as if these could be used generically in any teaching situation to accomplish what they accomplished in my classroom. But I have included transcript excerpts in this chapter to provide evidence for the ways in which these rules were only a part of the working routines that were negotiated in the class. Regularities in how my students and I worked together resulted partly from the rules I set and partly from how those rules played out with this particular group of ten-year-olds. With a different group of students, the routines that were in place by the end of September might have looked quite different. What was fundamental was that we had a way of working in which everyone would and could participate productively while treating one another with personal and intellectual respect. That these routines were in place did not mean that everyone always followed them in every lesson. But it was understood broadly in the class that everyone was supposed to do these things, and exceptions were noteworthy.[19] As we will see, students reminded one another of these norms throughout the year as they worked with and without the teacher's supervision. This does not imply that students must have notebooks, or small-group time, or whole-class discussions, but that they have some kind of framework that supports efficacy and engagement.

A consistent social structure that supports studious engagement without constant attention from the teacher has the potential to free up time and energy for the diverse kinds of improvised teacher-student interactions implied by different pathways through the subject matter territory. The scope of the teaching tasks undertaken on this scale is large in contrast to lesson-level teaching tasks like planning a lesson or figuring out what a piece of student work means or getting a small group of students to work cooperatively after a fight on the playground. They are focused on the establishment and maintenance of a classroom culture in which a teacher can teach and students can study. The routines that support a culture seem to be automatic once they are taught and learned. But the establishment of routines to be performed by teachers and students together is a deliberate act on the part of the teacher, and the continuing maintenance of routines requires regular attention. Often the teacher intervenes to revise routines that are not accomplishing what they are intended to accomplish. In the following chapters, we will examine how notebooks, seating arrangements, the variations in interaction groups, and the structure of talk and writing around conjecturing and revising are maintained and woven together with other elements of teaching practice. We will look at the work of teaching through a somewhat finer lens, focusing on how these tools for teaching and studying are used during a lesson later in September and in other lessons throughout the year to support students' opportunities to study the intended content.

Teaching While
Preparing for a Lesson

The task structure that was established in the first week of school in my class meant that every lesson had a similar agenda. To do the kind of teaching I was trying to do, each day I would choose a problem, students would copy it from the board and work on it alone and in groups, and then we would discuss it as a class. So doing a lesson always involved working on three kinds of teaching problems. First I had to prepare[1] the lesson, then I had to structure and monitor students' independent work, and finally, I had to lead the whole-class discussion. These are three forms of work that teachers engage in, no matter what their subject or grade level, whether or not they teach with problems. This chapter focuses on problems of lesson preparation, which involves figuring out how to connect particular students with particular mathematics. I needed to design classwork for my students, choosing a mathematical problem for them from something I had read or heard about, or making one up myself.

Where to Begin, Mathematically?

Toward the end of September, I began to work with my class on the relationship between multiplication and division. On September 28, I would make a deliberate change of course, moving away from studying the mechanics of two-digit multiplication and toward an investigation of how and when to use multiplication and division in problems. I needed to find a problem that would serve to locate me and my students in the appropriate mathematical territory. I wanted to continue to give students practice with computation, but also make it possible for them to focus on the idea of counting by grouping. I used my teaching journal to work on the mathematics of multiplication and division in order to understand what the students in my class might need to study in the mathematics of operations on numbers.[2] At this point, my work involved moving back and forth between mathematics and the structure of the task I could assign. That task would have to relate the particular students I was teaching with the particular mathematics I wanted them to study and learn.

I wondered about what symbols to use and how diagrams and wording might be employed to get everyone in the class going on the problem. I considered which numbers would be likely to raise interesting issues without introducing computational distractions. I reviewed the strategies students had been using to talk about and represent multiplications in earlier lessons, and how they might be used to study these new ideas. I had seen problems in books given in the form "3 groups of 4 = _____ groups of 2." Here, 12 is represented as 3 groups of 4 and also as 6 groups of 2. I thought such a problem form would be useful because it would involve students in doing both multiplication and division. It would make it possible for us to work for a few days on a connected set of ideas and skills because I could vary the given numbers and I could also vary the location of the missing number. These variations would get students to think about different ways of grouping the same quantity and to practice different computations.

As a way to investigate what students might study about how to use multiplication and division in this form of problem, I used my journal to make notes on the various strategies that fifth graders might use to find the missing number.

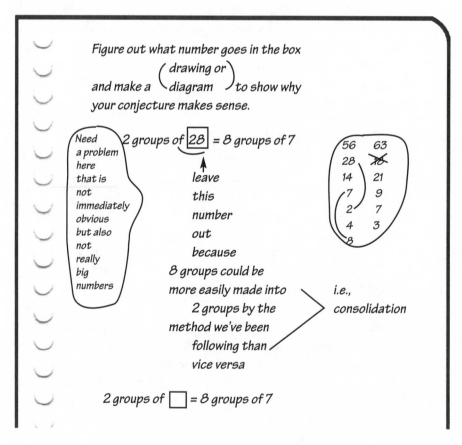

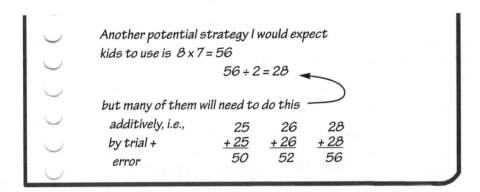

Another potential strategy I would expect
kids to use is $8 \times 7 = 56$

$$56 \div 2 = 28$$

but many of them will need to do this

additively, i.e., by trial + error

25	26	28
+ 25	+ 26	+ 28
50	52	56

With this work, I was anticipating where my students might get stuck or distracted as well as what might provoke productive work. I needed to think of all the things they would or could do when presented with the problem. This kind of preparation showed me what words might be useful in talking about their solutions, as well as what drawings they or I might use to support their studies. To respond to their work in a thoughtful way, I needed to be able to anticipate what they might be able to do independently and where they would need information from me to proceed productively. I figured out that students would need to do some interpretation to recognize that filling in the boxes with numbers is what the problem calls for. They would have to do another kind of interpretation to see that what goes in the box is supposed to "balance" the equation. By using word "groups" in the assignment, I could provide all students a structure within which to work; even if they were not proficient with multiplication, they could add the groups to find the total. They could make groups of groups either by repetitive adding and subtracting or by multiplying and dividing. I knew I would eventually need to give all of my students practice with symbolic calculations and get everyone doing multiplication, but this would give us some kind of a foundation on which to build an understanding of that operation. In speculating about using the structure of equations, I anticipated that my students would be prepared to read the problems in such a way as to arrive at the conventional meaning of the words and symbols I had used. I would have to check to see if my assumption was correct and do something to teach the conventional interpretation if it was not. If a student did not do a more or less conventional reading of the problems, it was unlikely he or she would engage with the mathematics that I intended to teach.

Settling on an Agenda for Classwork

This aspect of my preparatory work is what is conventionally called "lesson planning." The problem I am working on is laying out an agenda for the particular moves I will make and when I will make them. I wrote down a statement of the Problem of the Day and made notes about some ways to use it to support the study of multiplication. I thought I might use paper clips on the overhead projector to project groupings and regroupings of 60 on the wall.

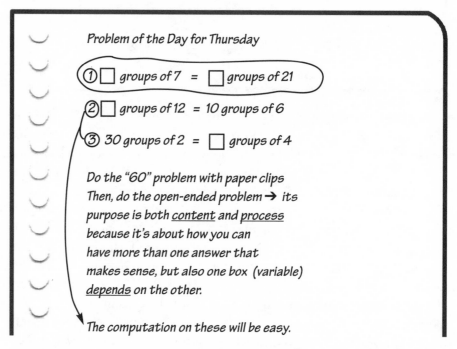

Problem of the Day for Thursday

① ☐ groups of 7 = ☐ groups of 21

② ☐ groups of 12 = 10 groups of 6

③ 30 groups of 2 = ☐ groups of 4

Do the "60" problem with paper clips
Then, do the open-ended problem → its
purpose is both <u>content</u> and <u>process</u>
because it's about how you can
have more than one answer that
makes sense, but also one box (variable)
<u>depends</u> on the other.

The computation on these will be easy.

The part of the Problem of the Day labeled "①" in my journal is more complex because it has two empty boxes. When I put the Problem of the Day on the board, I decided to put that part last, after the two equations with only one empty box. The math lesson on September 28 would begin with this set of problems:

Thursday, September 28

a. ☐ groups of 12 = 10 groups of 6

b. 30 groups of 2 = ☐ groups of 4

c. ☐ groups of 7 = ☐ groups of 21

Once I decided on the numbers, words, and symbols I would use to write on the chalkboard to structure students' mathematical work on that day, I made further notes to myself, anticipating, in mathematical terms, what students would do and where they might run into trouble. (If I had chosen problems from a book instead of designing them myself, as I did for many lessons across the year, I would still need to do this step in preparing for the lesson. It prepared me to be able to understand what my students did during class, and to guide their studies.)

Anticipating What Mathematics Students Might Do

One way to work on the form of problem that I had planned would be to figure out what the expression on the side of the equals sign with the empty "box" is worth by merging the groups into a single quantity. In "part A," for example, you would need to figure out how many units are in "10 groups of 6." Although a fifth grader might know that it was 60, because 10 is a familiar multiple to work with, there are several ways to figure it out, and different computational approaches would engage students with different mathematics. You could think of the problem of merging the groups more tangibly, and add: 6 + 6 + 6 + 6 + 6 + 6 + 6 + 6 + 6 + 6. This adding could be done in stages, first adding pairs of sixes (two of the groups) to get 12 and then adding these bigger groups: 12 + 12 + 12 + 12 + 12, then adding pairs of twelves to get 24 + 24 and adding the other 12 to get 60.

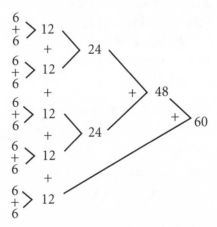

Or you could add sixes on to the total one at a time: 6 plus 6 is 12 plus 6 more is 18, and so on. Students who were just beginning to investigate the relationship between addition and multiplication might approach the problem by first drawing 10 groups of 6 objects.

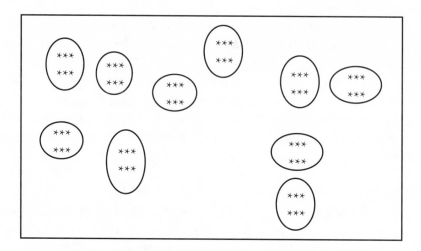

They could then simply count one by one to get the total. These are all options for finding out what the right side of the equation is worth.

Once you know the right side ("10 groups of 6") is worth 60, and assuming you read the "=" to mean that the left side and the right side should be equal, focusing on the left side (where the missing number is) the question becomes, "how many groups of 12 will make 60?" Again, there are several ways to figure it out. Students might argue with their classmates about the benefits of different approaches, and thus engage in studying and evaluating alternative strategies. Here they would be engaging with the mathematical work of creating efficient algorithms for accomplishing quantitative tasks.

I constructed the second part of the task (30 groups of 2 is equal to how many groups of 4?) to capitalize on what I think students might do with the first part, and to push them into less familiar territory. Multiplying by a number as large as 30, even though it is a multiple of 10, is not a familiar activity to most ten-year-olds. Similarly varied strategies could be used to do this part of the problem, with the additional possibility of applying the work from the first part to finding the solution. This variation on the problem form would enable me to find out if using prior work was something students were inclined to do, or if I would have to deliberately call it to their attention as a way to study mathematics. In both parts of the task, each side is also supposed to total 60, a situation that might make it possible for students to play around with related number patterns and study what they contribute to producing the solution.

The third part of the assignment challenges students to figure out a different kind of problem because there are empty boxes on both sides of the equation. Some number of groups of 7 is supposed to equal some number of groups of 21. Because the choice of numbers to fill the boxes is more open-ended in the third part of the task, students would not be "protected" from the possibility of getting into fractions. If they filled in the box on the left with "1," for example, the appropriate number to go in the box on the right would be "⅓" because one group of 7 is a third of a group of 21. Trying to avoid fractions, students would study a different and equally important mathematical idea. The only numbers that "work" as multiples of 7 if you want to avoid fractions have a special characteristic: they are all multiples of 3! Choosing only multiples of 3 to fill in the box on the left assures that the box on the right can always be filled in with a whole counting number.

Putting a number like "5" in the left-hand box in the third part of the problem would make the work of figuring out what to put in the right-hand box quite complex. I thought that the possibility for such a speculation might engage the students who would quickly finish the first two parts of the assignment.

Connecting Student Work with Curriculum Content

I anticipated that as they worked in this way, my students might study:

- number patterns and relationships;

- the connection between addition and multiplication;

- the connection between multiplication and division;

- the six "times table," and the twos, fours, and twelves.

If they did part of the problem by drawing and part by figuring, they also could study the relationship between the two representations of quantities and actions on quantities.

I included the third part, with its new and somewhat more challenging content, because the backgrounds and talents of the students in my class were quite varied. Almost a third of them had come from a different school, and I had not been able to get much information about what experiences and capacities they brought to my class. I wanted to provide everyone with something to study that could be productive of worthwhile learning. I anticipated that some students could use this part of the assignment to investigate multiplication and others would use it to move into the domains of fractions or functions. Because the number of units in the groups is an odd number (groups of 7 and groups of 21 instead of groups of 2 or 4 or 6 or 12), more and somewhat different mathematics gets on the table. Although there are boxes on both sides of the equation, the numbers that go in those boxes have a relationship to one another. One is a "function" of the other. A student working on this problem might begin to study ordered pairs of solutions as a special case of patterns and relationships.

Learning About My Students and Their Capacity to Study This Mathematics

To prepare students to make a productive relationship with the content, given my investigation of the ideas it would entail and the task I was planning to give the class, it would help to know whether any of my students could already multiply large numbers using the conventional procedure. It would help to know if anyone understood that multiplication is about groups of groups, no matter how big the numbers. It would help to know if anyone would be disposed to work independently in ways that were reasonable and if anyone would be likely to focus more on simply producing answers. It would help to know if anyone would have the language facility to describe and reflect on the procedures that they would use. Given a class of twenty-six students, at this point in the year my knowledge of each individual and of how various combinations of students would interact was limited. Some of the students in my class had been in our school in fourth grade, and I know they worked on such things in other classes, but the students who came from other schools may have followed a somewhat different curriculum. And in any case, what anyone had worked on last year and what they were now likely to do might not be the same. I used various means to find out what they would be likely to do now, and how they might think about what they were doing. This is a place where teaching on September 28 also involves actions taken in other lessons, from September 7 (the first day of school) through September 27 (the day before).

Zooming in on Enoyat and Tyrone

To analyze the problem of getting to know students as learners of what I am preparing to teach, I will focus here on my work with two boys in my class in September. Although I did similar work in relation to all of the students throughout the year, I will use my work with these two boys as an example to analyze the elements of this work. Enoyat and Tyrone had been sitting next to one another in an early lesson involving multiplication, and I stopped to look at their work. They were trying to find the missing number in the expression "4 groups of ☐ = 60." I was using this expression to pose a problem to the class because it is deliberately ambiguous as to the appropriate arithmetic procedure for finding the missing number. As stated, the problem does not indicate whether to add, subtract, multiply, or divide to figure out what goes in the box. I noted that Tyrone and Enoyat were working together investigating the relation between addition and multiplication. I took note of their language as I talked with them about what they had written in their notebooks as they worked on figuring out what should "go in the box." Tyrone had picked up the connection between addition and multiplication from Enoyat, but he had not interpreted it in a way that took account of the constraints of the numbers in the problem.

One issue this week is finding out how little sense some of the students have for multiplication. For example, Tyrone had on his paper, under experiments,

$$\begin{array}{r} 15 \\ \times\,4 \\ \hline 60 \end{array}$$ *and*

I asked him to explain he said he knew 15 should be in the box because he "added it up." I noticed in Enoyat's notebook:

$$\begin{array}{r} 12 \\ 12 \\ 12 \\ 12 \\ +\,12 \\ \hline 60 \end{array}$$

and I said no → *"he added it up, you multiplied." Then I asked Tyrone to show me what "adding it up" would look like for*

$$\begin{array}{r} 15 \\ \times\,4 \\ \hline 60 \end{array}$$ *It was hard to formulate a question,*

and I can't exactly remember what I said, but I think he had some sense of what I was getting at because ~~he said~~ *what he did, looking at Enoyat's notebook was:*

$$\begin{array}{r} 13 \\ 13 \\ 13 \\ +\,13 \\ \hline 52 \end{array} \quad \text{then} \quad \begin{array}{r} 13 \\ 13 \\ 13 \\ 13 \\ +\,13 \\ \hline 65 \end{array}$$

I asked why he was adding up 13s and he said "I'm just trying something." It seemed like he should have very readily

---

> seen that if $\quad$ 15
> $\qquad\qquad\quad$ x 4 $\quad$ then the
> $\qquad\qquad\quad$ 60
>
> "adding it up" he needed to do would be $\qquad$ 15
> We did get to that eventually. $\qquad\qquad\qquad$ 15
> but it was not easy. <u>On the</u> $\qquad\qquad\qquad$ 15
> <u>other hand</u>, Tyrone $\qquad\qquad\qquad\qquad\quad$ + 15
> $\qquad\qquad\qquad\qquad\qquad\qquad\qquad\qquad$ 60
> readily translated "10 groups of 6"
> into 10 x 6 : 10 times 6, which did not
> come so readily to some other students.

This observation of Tyrone and Enoyat helps me to understand them, but it also contributes more generally to my understanding of the mathematical territory around multiplication and what students might notice as they investigate it. I can begin to see some ways in which I might support more productive collaborations between these two boys by giving them practice with talking about the procedures they are using and some things I might do with the class as a whole.

Students' Dispositions to Reason and Collaborate

In order to know more about how Tyrone and Enoyat would work, individually and collaboratively, on the kind of problem I was going to give on September 28, I reviewed what I had learned about each boy since school started.[3] Tyrone was not present on September 7, the first day of school, when Enoyat and the others introduced themselves. On that day, Enoyat had introduced himself in fluent English, telling the class that he was born in Sudan and had been at our school for two years. I asked him if there was anything in particular he was hoping to study that year. He said a simple "no" and I moved on to another student. After introductions, we had had an informal whole-class discussion of some mathematical ideas related to things students mentioned. In my reflections on that discussion, I noted that Enoyat was not among the more active participants, but he was not totally quiet either.

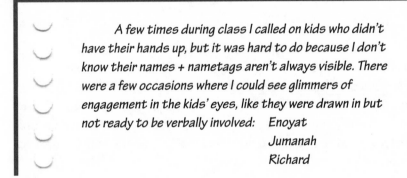

> *I was pleased at the number of students*
> *who participated, given that it was*
> *the first day of school + there were*
> *two video cameras, two teachers, and*
> *three observers!* → *verbal:*
>
> | *Very active* | | *Active* | *Somewhat active* |
> |---|---|---|---|
> | *Charlotte* | | *Awad* | *Leticia* |
> | *Shahroukh* | ← | *Richard* | *Enoyat* |
> | *Eddie* | *Karim* | *Ivan* | |
> | *Varouna* | | *Candice* | *Saundra* |
> | | | *Catherine* | |
> | | | *Ellie* | |

I again noted a "glimmer" of engagement from Enoyat in a whole-class discussion on September 11:

> *A few times during class I called on kids who didn't*
> *have their hands up, but it was hard to do because I don't*
> *know their names + nametags aren't always visible. There*
> *were a few occasions where I could see glimmers of*
> *engagement in the kids' eyes, like they were drawn in but*
> *not ready to be verbally involved:*   *Enoyat*
> *Jumanah*
> *Richard*

On September 12, I had observed Enoyat working productively during the first part of class the first time I assigned a problem for students to work on in small groups.

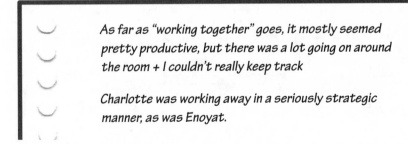

> *As far as "working together" goes, it mostly seemed*
> *pretty productive, but there was a lot going on around*
> *the room + I couldn't really keep track*
>
> *Charlotte was working away in a seriously strategic*
> *manner, as was Enoyat.*

What I probably meant by "seriously strategic" here is that Charlotte and Enoyat were using patterns and relationships to figure out solutions to the problem. This suggested to me that they had some disposition to think that mathematics was supposed to make sense and that they were competent to figure things out that they had not been told how to do.

On September 17, I wrote in my journal about the kinds of mathematical thinking that were being used by different students in response to a problem that I had given them.

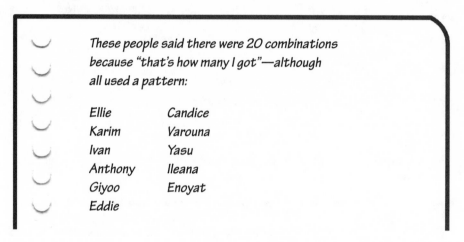

These people said there were 20 combinations because "that's how many I got"—although all used a pattern:

Ellie	Candice
Karim	Varouna
Ivan	Yasu
Anthony	Ileana
Giyoo	Enoyat
Eddie	

I listed Enoyat as someone who was not making abstract deductions from the evidence, but who had arranged the information to show a pattern.

Tyrone joined the class on September 18, a day on which I was not teaching. Thom told me that he had just moved to the area from South Carolina with his stepfather, and that his mother was planning to join them at some future date. When I first met him on September 19, he was seated at the back of the room:

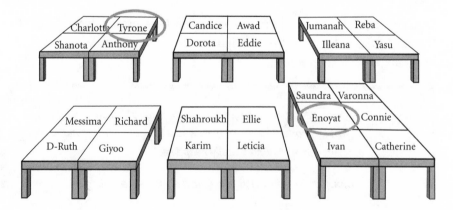

When I came in the next day, I noticed that Thom had rearranged some seat assignments, and now Tyrone was up front, next to Enoyat:

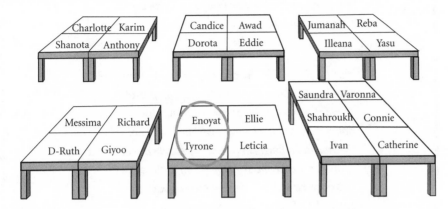

Based on my experience working with Thom, I could use this information to learn about Tyrone. I assumed that this change occurred because he thought that Tyrone needed to be closer to the front of the room, either because of a problem with his eyesight that made it hard for him to see the board, or because he needed to be closer to where the teacher was usually located so that it would be easier to have one-on-one work with him. It might also be the case that Thom had decided that Enoyat would be a good mentor to this boy who was new to the school and the community, and so he seated the two boys together. On September 21, I observed:

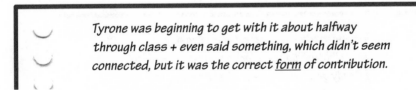

Tyrone was beginning to get with it about halfway through class + even said something, which didn't seem connected, but it was the correct <u>form</u> of contribution.

The next day, September 22, the two boys worked together in a mathematically productive way on figuring out the Problem of the Day: how many ways a subtraction could result in "89." We were working on these kinds of problems to study the process of mathematical "conjecturing." I challenged students to make reasoned speculations about how many combinations there would be, and then to try to "prove" these conjectures to others in the class. I noted that Tyrone needed some help with "routines" in order to participate fully in the work of the class.

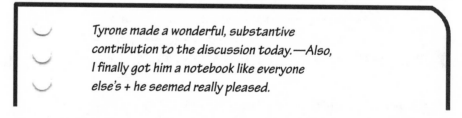

Today there was a bit of nice idea generation
+ engagement between Enoyat + Tyrone -

Enoyat had done

89	88		98
-00	- 01	...	- 09
89			89

and told me "I know there's only one more" →
this is a low level of conjecturing compared
to what some of the other kids have been
doing, but it was nice to have him doing <u>some</u>.
Tyrone had a hard time getting started—I haven't
been very good about helping him with routines—
but once he did, he seemed to productively
copy what Enoyat was doing + he said
"this is neat. This is fun" → noticing the
pattern.

I had given everyone a bound notebook on the first day of school, but because I had not anticipated another student joining the class at that point, I did not have an extra one with me to give to Tyrone on his first day. I did get one for him by September 27, and on that day, I connected a substantive contribution he made to the discussion with his acquisition of a notebook, perhaps symbolic of his mathematical as well as his social inclusion:

Tyrone made a wonderful, substantive
contribution to the discussion today.—Also,
I finally got him a notebook like everyone
else's + he seemed really pleased.

We will come back in a later chapter to examine the role of "the notebook" as a vehicle for supporting students' mathematical investigations.

Students' Computational Skill as Evidence for Understanding

In the first week of school, I used other means of assessment besides observation to learn about what skills and knowledge my students were bringing with them to fifth grade. I looked back at the results of a standardized paper and pencil pretest that was designed to produce evidence of their level of performance on both conventional arithmetic tasks and more open-ended reasoning tasks. On that pretest, I found that there was a wide variation of competencies in the class on all of the content, typical of a heterogeneous group of fifth graders. Narrowing my focus to the domain of multiplication, I still saw a range of variations, but there was a pattern to them. In students' performance on the multiplication calculations in the test, there was a consistent "break" between multiplying by one-digit numbers and multiplying by two-digit numbers.

Enoyat's work on multiplication on the pretest, for example, shows that, like many others in the class, he had not yet made the transition from being able to multiply by a one-digit number to being able to multiply by a two-digit number.

MULTIPLICATION

$$
\begin{array}{r} 213 \\ \times 3 \\ \hline 639 \end{array}
\qquad
\begin{array}{r} 34 \\ \times 4 \\ \hline 166 \end{array}
\qquad
\begin{array}{r} 46 \\ \times 23 \\ \hline \mathit{poo} \end{array}
\qquad
\begin{array}{r} 253 \\ \times 30 \\ \hline 394 \end{array}
$$

Tyrone was not present when the pretest was administered.

To know how to teach Enoyat, I needed to look not only at his work, but also at how it compared with what other students could do. Some did the multiplications by two-digit numbers differently than Enoyat but, like him, did not take account of the meaning of the numbers involved. Karim, for example, handled the tens and the ones in the second two multiplications as if they were independent single-digit multipliers. "23 × 46" was treated as if it was 3 groups of 46 added to 2 (rather than 20) groups of 46, and "30 × 253" was treated like 3 (rather than 30) groups of 253.

MULTIPLICATION

$$
\begin{array}{r} 213 \\ \times 3 \\ \hline 639 \end{array}
\qquad
\begin{array}{r} 34 \\ \times 4 \\ \hline 136 \end{array}
\qquad
\begin{array}{r} 46 \\ \times 23 \\ \hline 138 \\ + 92 \\ \hline 230 \end{array}
\qquad
\begin{array}{r} 253 \\ \times 30 \\ \hline 000 \\ + 759 \\ \hline 759 \end{array}
$$

Like Karim, Varouna carried out the one-digit multiplications appropriately, but when multiplying by more than one digit, she did some combination of multiplying and adding, and it is hard to see any logic in this work:

```
MULTIPLICATION

   213          ¹3 4          ⁴4 6          ¹2 5 3
   x 3          x 4          x 2 3          x 3 0
   ────         ────         ─────          ──────
   639          136           9 8           1 5 0
```

or in Shanota's:

```
MULTIPLICATION

   213          3 4          4 6           2 5 3
   x 3          x 4          x 2 3         x 3 0
   ────         ────         ─────         ──────
   639          136          1 3 8          2 5 3
                            + 1 2          + 6 9
                            ──────        ──────
                             2 5 8         9 4 3
```

The mixture of addition and multiplication in the work of these students suggests that the idea of multiplication as "groups of groups" is not guiding their work.

A few students produced correct answers to all the multiplications by using the conventional procedures, but it was hard to tell from these calculations what they understood about the meaning of the numbers or the procedure.

```
MULTIPLICATION

   213          ¹3 4          ¹4 6          ¹2 5 3
   x 3          x 4          x 2 3          x 3 0
   ────         ────         ─────          ──────
   639          136          1 3 8           0 0 0
                              9 2            7 5 9
                             ──────         ───────
                             1 0 5 8         7 5 9 0
```

Although it is more efficient to leave out the zero in the second "partial product" ("92" and "759" in the work above), it leaves the teacher wondering if the student knows that these numbers are not what they appear to be. Others performed correct procedures that were more revealing of their understanding. Connie, for example, demonstrated the skill of using the procedure correctly for multiplying by two-digit numbers in the case of the third multiplication calculation, and she also demonstrated a knowledge of place value by indicating that 20×46 results in 920 and 30×253 results in 7,590.

```
MULTIPLICATION

    213           ³3 4          ¹4 6          ¹2 5 3
    x 3            x 4          x 2 3          x 3 0
   ─────          ─────         ─────         ─────
   6 3 9          1 3 6         1 3 8          0 0 0
                                9 2 0          7 5 9 0
                               ───────        ─────────
                               1,0 5 8        7,5 9 0
```

Some of my students did not attempt to do any of the calculations involving multiplication, and left all of these questions on the test blank:

```
MULTIPLICATION

    213            3 4           4 6           2 5 3
    x 3            x 4          x 2 3          x 3 0
   ─────          ─────         ─────         ─────
```

Problems in Teaching in the Domain of Preparing a Lesson

To prepare a lesson, I use information like what I have described in the cases of Enoyat and Tyrone for all of my students. I put this information together with what I am able to learn about my students' learning by investigating the mathematics in what I wanted to teach them. I also think about what I know about the role of reasoning in mathematical practice in relation to the material I intend to teach, and what I know about fifth graders. Using all this information, I tentatively judge whether the tasks I am planning are likely to be engaging and appropriate for everyone in a particular class. Both my analysis of the mathematics and my review of the students' performance on the paper-and-pencil pretest suggest that the difference in the mathematical ideas that need to be activated to correctly perform the procedure for a multiplication like "4×34," and the ideas that would support performing the procedure for a multiplication like "23×46" (both of which appeared on the test) is significant for this class. Using this information, I am able to speculate about where in the terrain of multiplication I might begin a lesson about multiplication and division as "grouping."

The problem I am working on is how to engage *this* class, with *its* particular variation of skills and understanding, in the study of the ideas surrounding *this* piece of mathematics. To address this problem, I need to get the students simultaneously involved with the process of aggregating equal groups and the process of making sense of large numbers by taking them apart into their components. I need to create a work environment where they can recognize what multiplication would mean in the problems they are trying to solve, and examine various approaches to carrying out this operation on large numbers. I need to provide them with an opportunity to take numbers apart into their components and then recombine them in ways that are mathematically legitimate *and* make sense to them so that they can study the constraints of the system. At the same time, I need to challenge students like Connie who are already able to operate competently in this domain.

It would be unusual for a teacher always to invent activities for students "from scratch" as I did on September 28. More typically, I and other teachers would use a book of some sort to narrow down the possibilities and get advice about good places to begin. But even with the availability of such resources, one must prepare to use a particular activity with a particular class by investigating the intellectual content of the work entailed in such a way as to be able to support the relationship between that content and a specific group of students.[4] Teaching a lesson begins with figuring out where to set the particular students one is teaching down in the terrain of the subject to be taught and studied. Teachers must figure out where to start a lesson whether they are making up assignments for their students or directing them to complete exercises in traditional textbooks. Solving this problem can be as simple as "picking up where we left off yesterday" or choosing the appropriate page in a textbook, or it can entail designing a unique, context-specific problem that may take weeks to complete. Once a starting point for a lesson is chosen, it may be rejected as inappropriate after the lesson is under way, but that judgment cannot be made without starting somewhere.

Because each student comes with different experiences and capacities, addressing the problem of where to begin a lesson involves working on two constituent problems with interdependent solutions. I need to:

- characterize the subject matter to be taught, and

- characterize the students to be taught.

I use the word "characterize" here rather than the word "know" to imply an active, constructive kind of cognition, and to indicate the practitioner's responsibility for the unique content of the characterization. Such characterizing is a matter of creating context-specific knowledge; it is enhanced by knowledge brought from coursework or reading, but it can not be replaced by it. The picture of students and subject matter that I create for myself going into a lesson is not an exact representation of the students or the subject. Some characterization needs to be done to embark on the lesson, but it is always tentative, open to revision with each new interaction and reflection.

The work described in this chapter prepares me not only to *teach* the lesson, but also to *learn from* whatever happens in the lesson so that I can more productively teach other lessons in the future.

In making judgments about what students should be expected to do during a lesson I also need to:

- figure out what kinds of activities a particular problem will elicit from the students in my class, and

- specify how the activities implied by the problem can support the teaching and studying of the intended subject matter for these students.

These teaching problems involve work in relationships with students and with content simultaneously. To be appropriate, the activities implied need to make it intellectually and socially possible for all of the students to work on the tasks in a way that supports *studying the intended content*. What students are to do also needs to make it intellectually and socially possible for me to *teach the intended content using students' work*. Preparation produces resources for use in completing other practical work. The understanding of content and students acquired in preparation for a lesson is generated both during prior lessons, in interaction with students, and in private or professionally collaborative reflective analysis. Still, how much the teacher comes to know beforehand about the students in the class and about the nature of the content will vary with the teacher's interest and the time available, as well as with the teacher's ability to investigate such matters and the institutional supports for doing so.

Although the analysis here is situated in a particular kind of teaching, and I am teaching fifth-grade mathematics, the work of preparing is not particular either to teaching with problems or to the kind of students I teach. It is the sort of work that a teacher does to get ready for a lesson. More or less of such preparation can be done, it can be done well or it can be done poorly, and it can be done in closer or not so close proximity to any particular lesson or group of students. Depending on how the preparation is done, the teacher will have more or fewer resources to call on while teaching. In subsequent chapters, I will show how the work done in preparing is continually re-engaged as a resource during a lesson, and in the lessons that follow it.

6

Teaching While Students Work Independently

One of the intractable problems of teaching when it occurs in school class-rooms is managing the tension between working with individuals and work-ing with the whole class. Another is managing the conflict between leaving students alone to see what they can do on their own and guiding their activ-ity to make it productive. In this chapter, work on these two problems is cen-tral. I zoom in on teaching as it occurs during small-group time when students are working alone or with their peers on the Problem of the Day.

Teaching the first part of the lesson on September 28 involves several dif-ferent kinds of work. I need to watch and listen to see what my students actu-ally do with the problem I prepared. I need to enable relationships among the students, and between the students and the subject matter, so they can study the intended subject matter. But I also need to learn more about how they interact with one another, how disposed they are to talking about math-ematics, and what their communications skills are like when I am not around to help or guide them. I need to acquire information I can use later in the les-son and in future lessons. I need to watch and see who gets along with whom, who would prefer to work alone, and where the social trouble spots might be. With these purposes in mind, choosing an appropriate level of interac-tion for guiding student work during this part of the lesson is tricky. If I intervene too much, I will not be able to learn what I need to know about my students to teach them.

Because this part of the lesson is structured to have students working alone or with one another, my need to pay attention to everyone and every-thing is somewhat diminished. Some students talk among themselves, and I can listen as they try to figure out how to work on the problem. Some stu-dents work alone, and I can watch as they experiment with different strate-gies in their notebooks. I have some opportunities to interact with one or two students at a time while other students are less likely to be watching or listening.

The analysis of practice in this chapter begins with a look at the most explicitly interactive element of the work of teaching while students work independently: the problem of guiding and inquiring into individuals' think-ing. I then examine the problem of creating and maintaining a task structure that will enable students to interact with one another to study and teach *each other* mathematics. Finally, I consider what it takes to make sense of the range of student work that is produced. In all of these elements of practice, the analysis of students' individual performances is integrated with a continued investigation of the mathematics that was identified in preparation for the lesson.

Teaching Problems in One-on-One Interactions with Students

While students work on the assigned tasks in their small groups, I have the luxury of choosing a few individuals for one-on-one interaction. Some of that interaction takes the form of direct intervention, as when I see a student heading down an unproductive path and needing some support— mathematical, social, or personal—to focus on the work at hand. These direct interventions can be "big," as when I spend five minutes or so with my attention directed to one idea with one student. They can be "small," as when I simply place my body a certain way or point to a particular spot on a notebook page in a way that catches a student's attention. Some interactions are active, and others are more passive on my part. I watch and listen, sometimes asking questions about what I see or hear. Even when I am "just watching," I am also teaching a lesson about the study of mathematics. I deliberately talk and stand and look in ways that intend to communicate that it matters to me what they say and do, even if I do not comment on it.

What I am able to do with individuals depends on my doing another piece of work simultaneously: assessing how things are going in the surrounding area. I assess the tenor of the whole class from moment to moment, and I also consider the disposition and activity level of the students sitting adjacent to the one I want to work with. This simultaneous assessment of individuals and the environment is necessary because I am teaching efficacy, civility, and task structure as well as mathematics. Considering these multiple goals, I need to direct individual students' work in a way that maintains their sense of mathematical competence and their standing among their peers while obtaining as much information as I can about the strengths and limits of their understanding. This depends on being actively sensitive to what others, sitting nearby, will make of what I am doing.

In the small-group portion of the lesson on September 28 (between 1:00 and 1:32), I made two passes through the class, each lasting about seven minutes. Then I spent the next six minutes with one group of four, working both with individuals and with the whole small group. In all, I spoke to students twenty-one times in twenty minutes, addressing fifteen different students, some individually, some in pairs, and some as a group. Four times, I stopped and addressed the whole class briefly about matters of procedure. I spent about twenty minutes out of the thirty-minute small-group part of the lesson just watching and listening, and the rest of the time interacting. As I walked around watching students work, the teaching I did was constructed in response to whatever I saw or heard on the spot. Here I give examples of two instances of the one-on-one teaching that occurred—one a more directive and the other a less directive interaction—and I explicate the work entailed.

Zooming in on an Interaction with Varouna

As I walked around and watched on September 28, I saw that Varouna had begun to work on part C of the problem by writing the equation as I had it on the chalkboard and putting the number "1" in the box on the left-hand side of the equation:

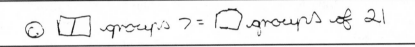

Having done that, she was sitting and staring at the page. She had tried an experiment and was now thinking about how to cope with its consequences. I knew the equation Varouna had constructed could be made to be true by putting the number "⅓" in the second box. But based on my previous interactions with her, I also suspected that she was not likely to use fractions in this way on her own. This was a lesson about the meaning of multiplication, and I knew Varouna needed to learn about that, so I did not intend to teach her about fractions unless she took me down that path.

I anticipated that Varouna would be self-conscious if I spoke to her because of how she had acted in previous encounters, so I stooped down so that we would be face to face and my presence next to her was less obtrusive. I did not want to entirely ignore her initial effort to work on the problem, so I suggested drawing a picture as a way to examine the meaning of *one* group of seven in relation to some number of groups of 21. I connected the idea of such a drawn representation of grouping with something I had shown the whole class in the lesson the day before:

Lampert: [to Varouna] Remember yesterday when we put those, the um, paper clips up on the board?

So one way to think about [this] is to make a drawing and you could make a drawing that would have one group of seven [pointing to the left side of the equation which she had filled in to read "1 groups of 7"].

Can I make groups of twenty-one out of this? Try—

For the one in this spot [pointing to the box on the left side of the equation with the one in it], is there anything that could fit in this spot [pointing to the empty box on the right] that would be true?

In response to my question, Varouna put a "3" in the second box so that her equation now read "1 groups 7 equals 3 groups of 21." My work here was to interpret and respond in a way that taught her something about the mathematics of multiplication and also respected her efforts to make sense. I interpreted what she did as an indication that she was trying to apply her knowledge that 3 sevens are 21, but she was having trouble representing that knowledge in this problem form. Since I wanted her to learn to evaluate her own thinking, I needed to put some language and pictures in the environment that she might be able to make use of to take another step.

To teach Varouna, I stated the implications of what she had written in the form of a question. When she didn't answer, I made a drawing in her notebook. I created a representation of what she had done that involved words, numbers, and graphics so that she could use it to continue to work on the problem without my help.

Lampert: [to Varouna] Is one group of seven equal to three groups of twenty-one?

Here let me show you, in this notebook [drawing in her notebook].

I'll make a group of seven boxes.

So that is one group of seven.

> Now I'm going to make groups of seven and I'm also
> going to make a groups of twenty-one, and I want them
> to be equal.

As I talked through the relationships in the mathematics of multiplication, I drew some more in her notebook to give her a visual representation of the two different quantities showing that a "group" of 21 would look like 3 groups of 7.

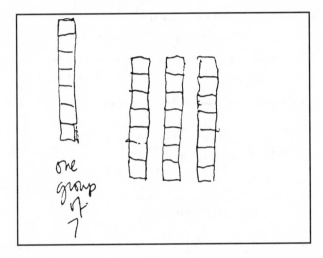

And then I asked, leaving room for her to answer that it would be a fraction of a group, if that is what she perceived.

> Lampert: [to Varouna] If I have got one group of seven could that be
>   equal to any groups of twenty-one?

My intention was both to probe Varouna's thinking and to teach her how to work on this kind of problem independently. I wanted to direct her work but in a way that was not a simple "telling" of the answer.[1] There was a particular mathematics content in our exchange, about multiplication as grouping and regrouping. But I was also teaching Varouna that making a certain kind of picture is a strategy for finding the solution to this kind of problem. I was teaching her that making pictures is a way to solve math problems more generally, and that it is a legitimate thing to do in school, in this class, to *study* mathematics. I was also teaching her what her notebook is for and how to organize it. At the same time, I was teaching her that what we did the day before might be relevant to what she needs to do for this.

Zooming in on an Interaction with Richard

I had other exchanges with students about the content during their independent work time that were more like interviews. In the effort to answer my questions, a student has the opportunity to study some piece of mathematics and clear up a misunderstanding. But that did not always happen, and I did not always push the interaction to that point. It was also important to me to know when that would *not* happen if students were working independently.

As I walked around the room, I saw that Richard had written something in his notebook that merited inquiry. I pointed to what troubled me:

$$30 \ groups \ of \ 2 = \boxed{12} \ groups \ of \ 4$$

and asked him a series of questions:

Lampert: [to Richard] What's happening here?

[several seconds of silence]

How did you figure this out?

[several seconds of silence]

What is twelve groups of four?

[several seconds of silence]

Is that the same as thirty groups of two?

[several seconds of silence]

Richard continued to look at his work as I talked and did not answer, until after the last of these questions, when he shook his head "no." Although he was silent, he seemed to be thinking rather than resisting the interaction, so I continued my questioning:

Lampert: Can you think of a number that would go in here [pointing to the box where he had written "12"] that would make it stay within thirty groups of two?

[several seconds of silence]

Is twelve too big?

Or too little?

He shook his head "yes" when I said "too little," and I ask him to explain:

Lampert: [to Richard] How do you know? How do you know it's too little?

I did not wait for a response but left Richard to think by himself about what he had said. I worked on interpreting his responses, both in the interaction and as I thought later about how to teach him to be more mathematically assertive. His cautious agreement with "too little" suggested to me that he had some appreciation of the task and the way multiplication entered it. Richard was not particularly verbal in other situations I had observed, and one thing I was doing here was putting words to what he had written down on the page, words that connected symbols with their mathematical meaning. This exchange focused on the mathematics of regrouping, but it was also a lesson in how we would do mathematics in this class, going beyond the "answer" to probe the reasoning behind any assertion.

Teaching Students to Study Collaboratively

Thom and I chose the seats to which students were assigned deliberately to foster productive interaction during their independent work time. It was our intention that they could use this time to teach one another. If I was going to use student relationships to teach, I needed to observe actively if those relationships were working for that purpose, or not. This would prepare me to do something about it if they were not working.

Observers' notes on the September 28 lesson offer some evidence about how students might have influenced one another's direction in the mathematics:

Donna Ruth explained the process to Giyoo.

Tyrone and Enoyat conferred.

There was an interesting conversation between Eddie and Awad, during which Eddie inquired, "What did I do wrong?" and Candice and Dorota entered the conversation. Candice directed Dorota to look for a reason why she thought she had a solution, mimicking language used by Lampert earlier.

Although these notes are more sparse than one would like, they do indicate some efforts on the part of some students to "teach" others mathematics. The students that the observers chose to comment on were sitting near one another in their groups.

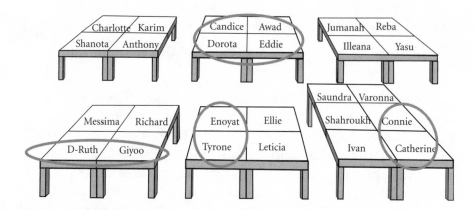

Consulting the students' notebooks as another source of data on students' teaching of other students, I can see several sets of students whose work seems similar:

Catherine & Connie

Shahroukh & Yasu

Donna Ruth, Richard, & Jumanah

Dorota, Giyoo, & Saundra

Candice, Ellie, Reba, & Leticia

Anthony & Ivan

The similarity in their approaches to solving the problem suggests that these students may have at least looked at one another's notebooks. But if we look at where these students were sitting, only three of these pairs, Donna Ruth and Richard, Connie and Catherine, and Ellie and Leticia, were near one another.

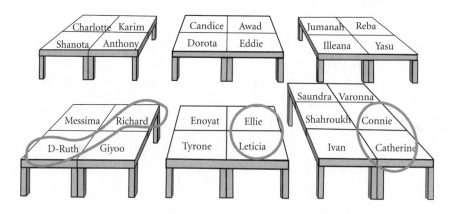

In these cases, we might imagine that one student's work might have been influenced by another student as well as by the teacher.

Zooming in to Examine a Collaboration Between Ellie and Leticia

Looking at the notebooks of Ellie and Leticia, there seems to be some mathematical communication between the two girls about how to use grouping strategies to find the solution. As we saw in chapter 5, the problem does not require that students use multiplication to solve it. Ellie clumps together 3 groups of 4 as a strategy for adding 15 fours. She makes both numerical and graphic representations of the groups, seemingly to examine her strategies and see if they produce the same total:

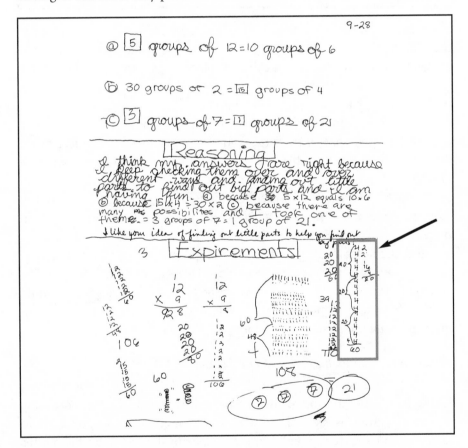

Ellie calls her strategy "finding out little parts to find out big parts."[2] The language she uses here is not similar to anything I had said to the class.

Leticia uses a similar strategy, doubling and then doubling again, to multiply, but she uses it with different combinations of numbers (4 + 4 = 8, 8 + 8 = 16).

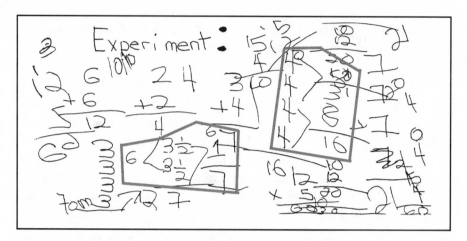

She uses the same strategy to add 3½ and 3½, first adding the two 3s to get 6, then adding the two halves to get 1, and then adding 6 and 1 to get 7. It could be that because Ellie did what she did in a place where Letitia could see it, she is teaching her something about the strategy of decomposition and recomposition and when it is appropriate to use it.

Moving away from Ellie and Leticia to look at Donna Ruth and Richard, the collaboration appears from the evidence to be less mathematically productive. In both Donna Ruth's and Richard's notebooks, the empty boxes are filled in with numbers that bear no relation to the mathematical task as set by the teacher. Perhaps one of them has "taught" the other that it is better to have the boxes filled in with *something* than to leave them empty, even if there is no clear reason for the numbers chosen, or perhaps they did not interpret the task as having to do with multiplication. Can we say that these students were studying any mathematics? There is little evidence that the design of the problem was productive of the kinds of constraints that would get them into worthwhile territory. I would need to pay special attention to them in future interactions to get more information.

Zooming in on Richard, Enoyat, and Leticia

During the interaction with Richard I described earlier in this chapter, Enoyat had turned around to attend to what I was saying. He was not sitting in the same group as Richard. His actions presented me with an occasion to teach the task structure of collaboration explicitly. I asked Enoyat about his mathematical ideas, but I then deliberately refocused him socially back toward his own group. I needed to manage a conflict between gaining his enthusiasm for the work and maintaining an order that would support everyone's work. I attempted to communicate, albeit indirectly, that the relevant work team for Enoyat was the people sitting in his group. I waved my arm in a way that encompassed him and the group he was sitting with while saying "you" needed to come to an agreement.

Next I spoke with Leticia, who was sitting in the same group as Enoyat but working on a different problem, using a different strategy. I verbally interacted with Leticia and referred to her notebook page in a way that would make it possible for Enoyat to redirect his attention toward his own group, using my interaction with her to teach him something about how to use diagrams to study multiplication as grouping. I referred specifically to what she was doing in her notebook under "experiments."

Besides trying to strengthen the relationships between particular students and particular mathematical ideas so that their independent studies of these ideas would be productive, I also did work that was directed toward structuring the environment with routines that would enable all students to make productive use of one another. Although I sometimes did this kind of thing explicitly, I also communicated about collaboration implicitly in the way I arranged the seating in the classroom and by the kinds of resources, like notebooks, that I made available to students. My students were seated in such a way as to make it possible for them to see the work of a few other students easily. Talking with one's immediate group-mates was encouraged. Under these conditions, students could find out that not everyone did the same mathematics to work on the problem. Besides looking at the nearby notebooks, they could hear students in other groups nearby talking with one another, and notice, for example, that others might be talking "division" whereas what *they* were doing was addition. They may or may not confront these differences, but they had the opportunity to be aware of them.

Observing and Making Sense of the Range of Student Performance

As a final look at elements of the practice of teaching as it plays out during students' independent work in small groups, I will zoom in to look at the notebooks of a few students during the lesson of September 28. What we will see from this vantage point is the variety of mathematics that I, as the teacher, had to work with in constructing my interactions with individuals, groups, and the class as a whole. The mathematics each student studied in working on the problem I assigned depended on how he or she chose to work on the assignment. My ability to look at this student work and make teaching out of it on the spot depends on the work that I did to prepare for the lesson and so is continuous with the work described in the previous chapter.

We will look in some depth at the notebooks of a random sample of students[3] in order to examine a range of possible approaches. I describe the particular mathematics I was able to see in each of these in annotations on the students' work. (These written annotations were not part of my teaching at the time, but they are included here for the reader.) All of the students whose work we see here were responding to the same stimulus: the problems I had put on the board at the beginning of class. They had been directed on each day since the first week of school to copy what I had written on the board, write the date, do some experiments to help them think about how to solve the problems, make a conjecture about the solution, and write their reasoning.

Students' notebook work for the lesson of September 28 is presented here to illuminate two aspects of my work as their teacher. One is the work of designing a structure that can make it possible for such work to happen. The other is the work of "reading" students' mathematics off the pages they produce. The results of such work are represented here by the annotations on the student notebook pages.

Zooming in on Karim's Work

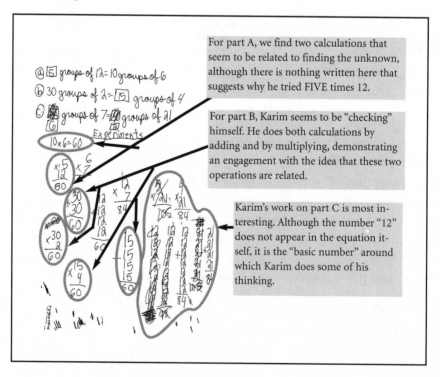

For part A, we find two calculations that seem to be related to finding the unknown, although there is nothing written here that suggests why he tried FIVE times 12.

For part B, Karim seems to be "checking" himself. He does both calculations by adding and by multiplying, demonstrating an engagement with the idea that these two operations are related.

Karim's work on part C is most interesting. Although the number "12" does not appear in the equation itself, it is the "basic number" around which Karim does some of his thinking.

Karim tries to add eight 12s twice, but crosses out his effort. Then he adds seven 12s to get the answer, 84, and seems to then try to find out how many groups of 21 he would need to equal seven 12s. He tries 5, too big, then tries 4, and gets 84. (He also records these as multiplications.) But for some reason, he does not use the results of this figuring in filling in the boxes in part C—he does, then crosses out what he did. It is hard to read what was under his crossing out, but the mistaken representation—7 groups of 12 instead of 12 groups of 7—may be what got him hung up here. He finishes up with 6 groups of 7 equals 2 groups of 21, with no experimental indications of how he arrived at that solution, except an unfinished computation of 6 times 7.

Zooming in on Charlotte's Work

Charlotte was sitting across from Karim, but when I watched them, they did not appear to be sharing ideas. Their notebooks show evidence of very different levels of mathematical competency.

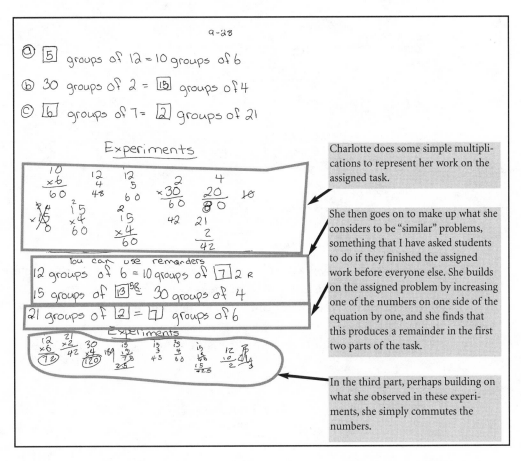

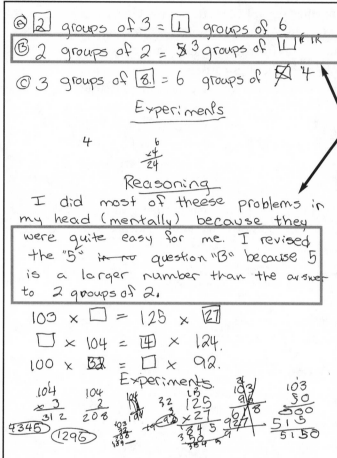

(A) 2 groups of 3 = 1 groups of 6

(B) 2 groups of 2 = ~~5~~ 3 groups of 1 " IR

(C) 3 groups of 8 = 6 groups of ~~4~~

Experiments

4
×4
24
6

Reasoning

I did most of theese problems in my head (mentally) because they were quite easy for me. I revised the "5" ~~to~~ question "B" because 5 is a larger number than the answer to 2 groups of 2.

103 × □ = 125 × 27

□ × 104 = 4 × 124.

100 × 32 = □ × 92.

Experiments.

104   104   32   125   103   103
× 3   × 2   × 27   50
312   208   500
4345 1296   515   5150

Charlotte went on to try more experiments with this problem structure, using what look like fairly simple numbers. But even with this constraint, she gets herself into some interesting mathematical territory. As she explains below in her "reasoning" section, she found that there was no number that would work in the equation "2 groups of 2 = 5 groups of ___." In formal mathematical terms, she is recognizing here that the domain of the independent variable constrains the range of the dependent. Although Charlotte was able to cope with the earlier problems requiring remainders, she did not push on here into the domain of numbers smaller than 1.

Finally, Charlotte moves on to larger numbers and is engaged in multidigit multiplication. It is interesting that she does "guess and check" multiplication rather than division to find the missing terms.

Zooming in on Eddie's Work

Eddie's work on the September 28 problem is embedded next to some work from the day before. This tells me he is attentive to the task structure at some level. He might benefit from some more explicit directions on how to organize what he is writing down so that his work can be maximally productive as an opportunity to study the mathematics the problem engages.

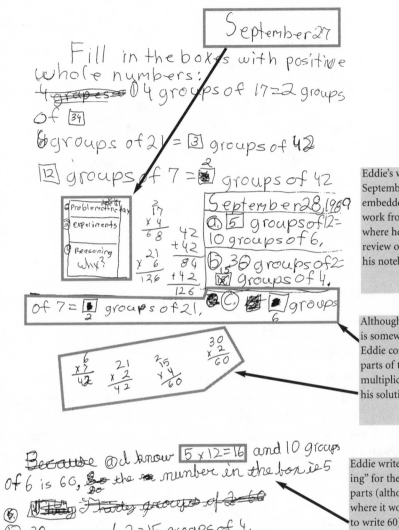

September 27

Fill in the boxes with positive whole numbers:
~~4 groups~~ 0 4 groups of 17 = 2 groups of 34

6 groups of 21 = 3 groups of 42

12 groups of 7 = 2 groups of 42

Problem of the day	$\begin{matrix} 17 \\ \times 4 \\ \hline 68 \end{matrix}$	42	September 28, 1989
experiments		+42	A. 5 groups of 12 = 10 groups of 6,
Reasoning why?	$\begin{matrix} 21 \\ \times 6 \\ \hline 126 \end{matrix}$	$\begin{matrix} 84 \\ +42 \\ \hline 126 \end{matrix}$	B. 30 groups of 2 = 15 groups of 4,

of 7 = 2 groups of 21, C. 6 groups 6

$\begin{matrix} 6 \\ \times 7 \\ \hline 42 \end{matrix}$ $\begin{matrix} 21 \\ \times 2 \\ \hline 42 \end{matrix}$ $\begin{matrix} 15 \\ \times 4 \\ \hline 60 \end{matrix}$ $\begin{matrix} 30 \\ \times 2 \\ \hline 60 \end{matrix}$

~~Because~~ @d know $5 \times 12 = 16$ and 10 groups of 6 is 60, ~~so~~ the ~~no~~ number in the box is 5

B. ~~Thirty groups of 2 = 60~~

B) 30 groups of 2 = 15 groups of 4,

C) Six groups of 7 = 2 groups of 21.

Eddie's work on the September 28 problem is embedded next to some work from the day before, where he took notes on a review of how to set up his notebook page.

Although the arrangement is somewhat hard to read, Eddie completes all of the parts of the task with a few multiplications to check his solutions.

Eddie writes some "reasoning" for the first of the three parts (although he writes 16 where it would make sense to write 60), but for the rest, he simply repeats the equations, changing only that the numeral "6" is replaced by the word "six." He is experimenting with what it might mean to "reason" about something like this.

Zooming in on Giyoo's Work

What appears on this page gives a teacher little information about what Giyoo was working on mathematically.

Zooming in on Saundra's Work

Saundra's work also gives little information about her connection with mathematics. The first equation, where she inserts "1" into the box, is puzzling, and there is no other work on the page to help interpret it. What we can see is that she made up an equation herself, unrelated to the assigned work, possibly signifying some sense of mathematical efficacy.

Saundra does make up an additional task for herself.

Zooming in on Varouna's Work

This is the work of Varouna, the student I described previously in terms of the direct support I had given her during the small-group part of the lesson to get her going in a productive direction.

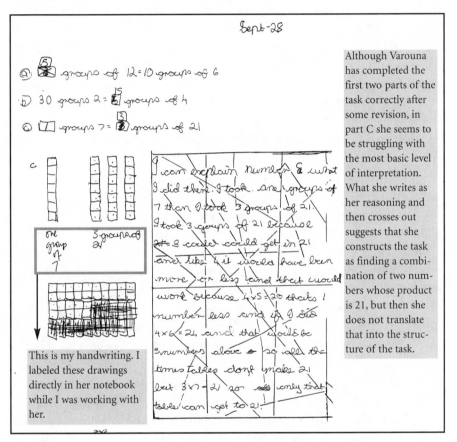

Sept-28

ⓐ 5 groups of 12 = 10 groups of 6

ⓑ 30 groups 2 = 15 groups of 4

ⓒ ☐ groups 7 = 3 groups of 21

c   one group 7   3 groups of 21

This is my handwriting. I labeled these drawings directly in her notebook while I was working with her.

I can explain number & what I did them. I took one groups of 7 than I took 3 groups of 21. I took 3 groups of 21 because 3 could could get in 21 and like 4 it would have been more or less and that would work because 4×5=20 that's 1 number less and if I did 4×6=24 and that would be 3 numbers above or so all the times tables don't make 21 but 3×7=21 so only that table can get to 21.

Although Varouna has completed the first two parts of the task correctly after some revision, in part C she seems to be struggling with the most basic level of interpretation. What she writes as her reasoning and then crosses out suggests that she constructs the task as finding a combination of two numbers whose product is 21, but then she does not translate that into the structure of the task.

Although the work they did in their notebooks represents only a partial trace of what any of these students studied during the lesson, it does illustrate the range of performances that I, as their teacher, needed to interpret. To teach these students, I needed to locate each of them in the mathematics I had anticipated that the lesson would be about. I also needed to expand my own mathematical understanding to interpret what each student did with the problem. The study Karim records in his notebook is relating multiplication and addition to "check" his computation. He investigates the meaning of multiplication in the columns of numbers he writes down and adds, even though his computation is not always accurate. I might say he is "practicing" that meaning. I wonder whether he is representing the meaning accurately, because he transposes 15 groups of 4 into four 15s. What he may be doing here, however, is the mathematically legitimate move of finding a shorter way to figure out what he wants to figure out. Adding up four 15s is less trouble than adding up fifteen 4s, and he could be using his knowledge that they are equivalent to make his work more efficient. When I turned to Charlotte's work, I could see that she completed the assigned task quickly. She takes the initiative to study what happens when the numbers "don't come out even." She studies the characteristics of different kinds of numbers—the mathematical domain of number theory—as she investigates the effects of additive changes on the multiplicative structure of the problem. She also is working on examining the boundaries of the solution set. Eddie is working in another domain—mathematical communication—trying to figure out what he might do that would be called "reasoning" in relation to the assigned task as he experiments with exchanges between numerals and words. I think he is trying out various possibilities because the form of his "reasoning" for the first part is repeated and then crossed out as he tries to write about the second part. He seems to be engaged in the sort of first-draft work that writers do, getting something down on paper and then revising it. Varouna is also studying mathematical communication, but in contrast to Eddie's work on writing, she is working on reading and translating words and numbers into graphic representations. She has mislabeled 3 groups of 7 as 3 groups of 21, but by having the drawing in front of her and counting the figures she has drawn, she can work on resolving the conflict between the two representations.

We do not get much information from their notebooks about what Giyoo and Saundra are working on, except that Saundra did some thinking about the structure of these equations and came up with a parallel expression using different numbers. Looking at their work in retrospect, it may be that they thought or talked with peers about mathematics that did not get written in their notebooks, or it may be that they were distracted and could have used some help to get going on the mathematics.

Zooming out to the Class as a Whole

A survey of all of the notebooks from September 28 shows that the types of work students did on this day varied greatly, including:

- drawing and using the multiplication algorithm
- drawing and using repeated addition
- labeling drawings with numbers
- drawing things in containers

- drawing things in rows

- referring to the relationship between multiplication and division (stated in a way that is related to them as operations or stated in a way that indicates a mechanical process)

- identifying which operations are needed to solve the problem, e.g., "I multiplied" or "I divided"

- stating processes of thinking about the problem

- using patterns

- ordering possibilities

- column repeated adding

- iterative repeated adding

- doubling to add

- filling in boxes with no explanation and no obvious relation to the problem

- drawing with no obvious relation to the problem

- indicating confusion in writing

- decomposing/recomposing to multiply

- making up more problems (with different numbers).

These eighteen kinds of activities were found among the twenty-six students in the class who were present for this lesson. As communication from students to teacher about content, this work reveals characteristics of the students as mathematics learners as well as aspects of the mathematics under study. Their notebook pages display the intersections between students and content where teaching and studying were possible.

Teaching Problems in the Domain of Supporting Students' Independent Work

While my students worked independently on the problem I had prepared for them, I used and expanded my relationship with the mathematics of multiplication to figure out what they were doing and what they needed to learn.

And I did several things to connect my students with that mathematics, including:

- watching and listening;

- interpreting written products and actions insofar as I could see or hear them;

- clarifying, inquiring, probing;

- redirecting, representing, revoicing;

- simultaneously assessing individuals and their environment;

- maintaining the task structure;

- locating students' observed performances in an anticipated mathematical domain;

- analyzing students' individual performances in concert with a continued investigation of the mathematics I had prepared to teach;

- revising my knowledge of the domain to accommodate student performance;

- providing and maintaining appropriate use of notebooks and seating assignments; and

- fostering productive communication and limiting unproductive communication among students.

My decisions about when to intervene and when to let students alone have partly to do with how I solve another teaching problem that I was working on at the same time. Besides teaching and observing, I was also figuring out what to do in the second part of the lesson, when I would bring the whole class together and coordinate collaborative work and discussion. Even if I had planned to do something as formal as a lecture during that time, I would need to use my interpretations of student independent work to modify my plans to accommodate what I was learning about my intended "audience." If I watch and listen during small-group independent work, I am then able to use my observations retrospectively to decide what and who to make focal in the second part of the class as I guide the class's reflections on particular mathematical aspects of the problem and further investigations. When I choose to intervene, it is often to get a better sense of what a student is doing or thinking.

Teaching Problems in Other Domains Caused by Students' Independent Work on Mathematics Problems

The kinds of teaching problems described in this chapter are part of my practice in the first part of every lesson because I have chosen to make it possible for my students to work on mathematics problems alone and collaboratively, in small groups with their classmates. Independent mathematical work by individuals and small groups can be a fruitful structure in which to study and a rich opportunity for the teacher to learn about students. But some of the records of student work I have displayed here suggest additional teaching problems that would need to be addressed as a result of the way I chose to structure students' independent work.

One kind of problem that I need to face because I choose to begin every lesson with small-group work is the perception by students that I am not being fair. In the kind of classroom structure I established, I could not get around to everyone during the first half of every class. There was a structure in place whereby students could make use of other students to support their studies. There were also some opportunities for me to "catch up with" the students who needed direction built into the task structure. But I needed to figure out when and how to make use of these opportunities. If too many students needed support to make their work productive during this period, there would be many distractions from the study of mathematics.

A second problem that I face as a result of having students work independently is building coherent instruction in the face of the diversity of student activity and knowledge that this way of working makes possible. I deliberately chose the form of the problem we worked on during the September 28 lesson to make it possible for mathematical diversity to surface in a way that might have remained invisible on textbook-type exercises. Once the differences among students' work become apparent, however, it is hard to "put the genie back in the bottle." Diversity can be a rich resource, *if* I can figure out how to make use of it. The mathematics that I had anticipated (described and explicated in chapter 5) clearly came into play. But opening up the potential for students to respond on many levels of competency revealed to me the wide expanse of mathematical territory I needed to cover. Among my fifth graders, a wide range of experience with and understanding of the mathematics under consideration showed itself as they worked. We had been in school for three weeks, and I was learning more about that diversity every day.

Finally, as a result of allowing students to teach one another, I have the problem of coping with the consequences of students taking other students down mathematically unproductive paths. By having students be able to look at one another's approaches to the problem, I generate more teaching resources but I also take a risk. The gamble is that more collaborations will turn out like the one between Ellie and Leticia than the one between Donna Ruth and Richard. I can influence the odds somewhat by intervening as I walk around the room. But over the long haul, since establishing students' sense of mathematical efficacy is an important goal of my teaching, I needed to establish norms in the class that favored sense-making instead of simply getting the task done, *even if I was not there watching.* Where I perceived persistent patterns of counterproductive collaborations, I could try changing students' seat assignments. I would not, at least for now, address this problem by redesigning the task structure of the lesson to eliminate the influence of students on other students, because the potential for them to teach one another remains.

I could work on some of the problems that arose in the small-group and individual work during the next part of the lesson. Some I would be addressing at the level of practices that continued over the whole year. And some would work themselves out as we continued through this curricular unit, studying the mathematics of multidigit multiplication.

7

Teaching While Leading
a Whole-Class Discussion

The most common image of the teacher at work has her in the front of the room, either addressing the whole class or choosing students to answer questions. In this chapter, I examine problems of practice that arise in this kind of work. Considering actions that involve the teacher in communications with the whole class, I zoom in to investigate who is being taught, what they are being taught, and how they are being taught. I examine the work that this teaching entails. As I interact with the whole class at once, I need to maintain overall coherence while drawing different kinds of individuals into a common experience of the content. I do this, in part, by calling on students to say something that will contribute to the common experience of the class and then constructing responses to what they say. Equally important are the actions I need to take to engage those students who are not verbal participants, such as drawing on the board.

In order to examine practice at this level, I bring a microscopic lens to work that I performed in the whole-group portion of the lesson on September 28. I analyze that work action by action to link teaching individuals with teaching the class as a whole. The talk in this part of the lesson was divided by its attention to the three parts of the task the students had been working on, labeled A, B, and C.

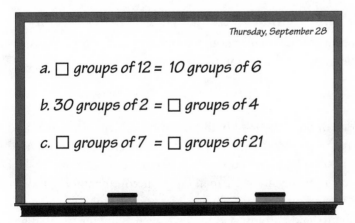

Thursday, September 28

a. ☐ *groups of 12 = 10 groups of 6*

b. *30 groups of 2 =* ☐ *groups of 4*

c. ☐ *groups of 7 =* ☐ *groups of 21*

The discussion divides into one segment whose focus was on the mathematics of multiplication as grouping (during which we discussed problems A and B) and a second segment whose focus was on patterns and relationships

143

in ordered pairs of numbers (during which we discussed problem C). Using video records of interactions in each of these segments, I closely examine a ten-minute portion of the discussion of problem A and a smaller portion of the discussion of problem C. I break each segment into many discrete "teaching and studying events" to illustrate the range of teaching problems that arise at this scale and the work entailed in addressing them. (A transcript of the entire large-group discussion is included in appendix A so that the reader can also investigate these events in relation to the continuous flow of talk during the discussion.)

In the teaching events that I examine here, the mathematical scope is wide, and the relationship in focus is my relationship with the class as a whole. In addition to the problems of teaching the mathematical content, I was trying to teach everyone about mathematical discourse, about how to participate in a conversation with twenty-six other people, and about themselves as capable doers of the task and thinkers about the ideas in it. Through these wide social lenses I analyze teaching in small units of time to see how these broader efforts play out in each moment of interaction. This microscopic analysis is at times tedious and complex. But it reveals that each word and gesture the teacher uses has the potential to support the study of mathematics for all students, or not. The labels I have placed on each event identify the actions a teacher takes to support studying by the class as a whole while interacting with individuals. These actions are intended to create opportunities for everyone in the class to study something. Particular students may or may not take advantage of these opportunities, but my work is to make them broadly available.

Teaching in the Moment so the Whole Class Can Study

I guided a discussion for about ten minutes that began with one student's speculation about the solution to problem A:

$$\square \text{ groups of } 12 = 10 \text{ groups of } 6$$

The studies of the class that I built from this problem were organized around an exchange with the first student who volunteered an assertion, Richard. I asked him to explain his solution and I recorded parts of his explanation on the board, inserting my own mathematical commentary. I involved other students in supporting and furthering Richard's thinking. As I responded to what students said and inserted my own agenda, he reevaluated his original assertion. The nature of the discourse shifted around including both rehearsals of multiplication tables and reasoning about grouping. I used this talk to assemble an argument for why Richard's assertion was wrong. After he reevaluated what he said, I made another incorrect assertion about what might go in the box and invited students to evaluate it. Then we moved on slowly, almost painstakingly, to construct a correct assertion about what number would go in the box and why. I guided this construction in a way that kept the talk strongly linked to the representation of multiplication in terms of grouping and regrouping and the idea of multiplication as repeated addition. Several students made use of the diagrams I made on the board during the interaction with Richard to support their assertions.[1]

Although the focus in the following analysis is on what I did to teach, the actions that I took were constructed in concert with my observations of what students did to study and what they were studying as individuals, dynamically constituted groups, and as a whole. The topics of our work together included talk about conventional mathematical content as well as aspects of mathematical practice and of the practice of "studenting"—or learning how to learn—in this classroom setting. In what follows, I focus on the details in my speech acts because particular words and intonations are some of the most important tools I can use in this setting to maintain continuity and coherence for the class while responding to individual students.

Teaching and Studying Event #1:
Teacher Formulating and Asking a Question to Begin the Discussion

Lampert: [referring to the first problem] Okay, who has something to say about A?

By asking this opening question in the way I do, I make use of an opportunity to teach students that mathematical talk can have a broad range, and not just be about right and wrong answers to teachers' questions. With this particular choice of words, I open the floor to students for reflection. They can answer my question whether or not they think they have solved the problem. "Something to say" here *can* include the "answer." That is what students are likely to expect the teacher to ask for. But students might also legitimately respond by saying "I finished it," by making assertions pointing toward the mathematics like "that was the easiest one," or with other kinds of commentaries on the work. As students contemplate whether and how to respond to my question, they must interpret what is meant, in the context of this discussion by "something to say."

Teaching and Studying Event #2:
Teacher Calling on a Particular Student to Answer

Lampert: Richard?

Several students had raised their hands. Ellie, Connie, Shahroukh, Candice, Enoyat, and Leticia all seemed eager to answer. Because I knew what many students had been doing in the first part of class as they worked independently with their peers, I could exercise the option to call on someone in the class to get a particular piece of mathematics on the table. I decided to call on Richard, even though he had not volunteered to speak. I used my choice of whom to call on to get a particular piece of mathematics up for consideration. I could then direct other members of the class to examine the initial speaker's mathematical work, which would make it possible for them to both study the topic and engage in the practice of mathematical communication.

So why did I call on Richard? How and what and who could I teach by calling on *him*? What would I make available for students to study? And how? In my journal, after the lesson, I wrote about my worries about Richard and another student, Jumanah, doing computations randomly without thinking about the appropriateness of what they were doing to the problem context.

> *I don't understand at all how Jumanah*
> *is thinking* → *she puts numbers in the spaces*
> *in* ~~here~~ *her notebook that have no*
> *conventional relationship to the problem*
> *being posed, and she is not at all verbally*
> *expressive. In her case, from what little*
> *evidence I can gather, as well as in the*
> *case of Richard, there seems to be a*
> *"put these numbers together in <u>some</u> way,"*
> *vs. any attempt to see meaning in what is*
> *happening.*

I called on Richard because I wanted to teach him and others in the class that everyone would indeed be asked to explain their thinking publicly. I also wanted to teach everyone that what they said would be expected to be an effort to make mathematical sense. (As we see in the following parts of the lesson, at this point in the year their efforts to make a sensible explanation would be scaffolded, sometimes heavily; students would not be expected to do this entirely independently, or even to know what is meant by an "explanation.")

One thing students in the class can study as I make my choice to call on Richard is that I take this action in the face of several students' raised hands.

Many would no doubt make their own conjectures about why I called on Richard and why I did not call on someone else. They would continue to conduct experiments to learn more about how to get called on or not, depending on their purposes.

Teaching and Studying Event #3:
Student Asserting and Teacher Repeating His Assertion

When Richard responds, he has the opportunity to study how his teacher and his peers will respond to his assertion.

Richard: I think that if, A, is twenty-two. Groups.

Lampert: [addressing the whole class while writing "22" in the empty box on the board and pausing while stressing the word "of"] Okay, so twenty-two groups OF twelve equals ten groups OF six [pointing to what is on the chalkboard].

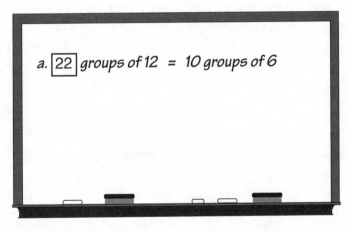

In this exchange Richard volunteers an answer. He uses the words "I think" to preface his assertion. I fill the empty box on the chalkboard with his assertion, revoicing it in terms of the problem structure. I repeat his answer in the form I had designed for the problem and write it on the board. By recording Richard's conjecture on the board, I intend to teach my students that any assertions they make would be taken as a serious indication of what they thought was a reasonable solution to the problem as posed (whether or not that is how they intended them to be taken).

Teaching and Studying Event #4:
Teacher Asking a Student to "Explain His Reasoning"

Lampert: Can you explain your reasoning about that, Richard?

As my preparation for this lesson indicated, I wanted to get students working on tasks that would engage them in thinking about when it would make sense to use multiplication to solve problems. By asking Richard to explain his reasoning, I initiate a discussion of why he might have done what he did. I was preparing the social framework in which I would ask other students to agree or disagree with him. I did what I did knowing that several students in the class would have already decided that Richard's answer was wrong because I had seen what they did in their notebooks prior to the discussion. I conduct the discussion as if there was a shared assumption that there would be *reasoning* behind any assertion that would explain why it would make sense. Even though Richard's assertion did not seem to make sense, I respond respectfully, hoping to "dignify with pertinent curiosity" his contribution to the discussion.[2]

Throughout this segment, Candice has her hand up, as does Shahroukh. Although we cannot know for sure, patterns of classroom discourse lead me to suspect that the two students who were indicating they wanted to speak wanted me, and others in the room, to know that they would disagree with Richard. I stick with him at this point instead of entertaining their contributions. This choice produces additional work, as I am also responsible for keeping Candice and Sharoukh engaged, even as I suspect that they are not on the same mathematical path as Richard.

Teaching and Studying Event #5: Student Interpreting "Explaining" and Responding

Richard: Because, I timesed twelve and ten. Twelve times ten equals twenty-two.

In his response, Richard seems to confuse addition and multiplication. Although he *says* "Twelve times ten equals twenty two," he seems to have added instead of multiplying. He has correctly added a group of 10 and a group of 12, to arrive at 22, and there is a "10" and a "12" in the expression. That particular computation is not relevant to finding the unknown, however, given that the problem questions how many *groups* of 12 you need to equal 10 *groups* of 6. He has also transposed the 10 and the 12 in a way that does not fit the problem context.

Richard has presented me here with both a problem and an opportunity. The idea that multiplication is about a particular kind of *grouping* was the central focus of my planning for this lesson, and so here I have an opportunity to demonstrate the meaning of the operation by contrast with Richard's interpretation. The placement of the empty box asks, "How many groups of

12?" or "What number times 12?" would be equal to 60. Richard's assertion was "Twelve times ten equals twenty-two." So there are several bits of mathematics to be sorted out here, some of which have to do with the meaning of multiplication and others of which have to do with the different representations of multiplication in words and symbols. The problem is that I must somehow both teach Richard and engage the whole class in worthwhile mathematical activity at the same time.

To respond to Richard's assertion, I initiate activities that will make it possible for all of the students to study the connection between the action of grouping and the arithmetic operation of multiplication. Based on my observations of their notebook work in the first part of class, I choose representations for communicating both what I am trying to say and what I think students are trying to say. These activities are structured both for participation by Richard and for participation by others in the class in studying multiplication. The others in the class I teach in this way may need to study precisely what Richard needs to study—that multiplication means grouping and that "☐ groups of 12" is translated as "what number times 12"—or they may need to study related topics.

After listening to Richard answer that he "timesed twelve and ten," I move the work of the class into the domain of representation, making available several alternatives for study. By choosing not to call on either Shahroukh or Candice, I intended to hold off on any talk about answers other than the one Richard had given. I also tried to push Richard further toward making sense of the problem, demonstrating both to him and to everyone else that this was a possible teacher move in this circumstance.

Teaching and Studying Event #6:
Teacher Making Representations of Student Talk

My next teaching move is to address the "translation" problem. Here I give Richard and his classmates familiar representations to ponder in relation to the words that Richard used and the problem structure as I presented it.

Lampert:	Ten times twelve.
	Or—, I'm sorry, twelve times ten is like this.
	[I write first the 12, then the times sign (×), then the 10, and then put a line under the 12.]

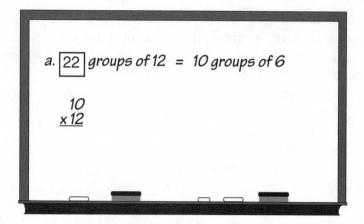

[to Richard] Is that how you did it?

[to the whole class] Okay, now I want to remind you that this [pointing to the multiplication] means twelve groups of ten [writing on the board, 12 first, then ×, then 10, and a line under the 10]:

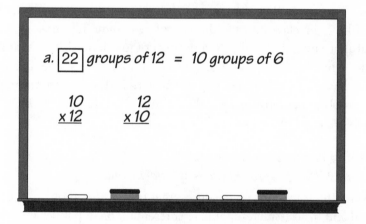

This [pointing to the second multiplication] means ten groups of twelve.

The content of what I am doing here is multidimensional. In one dimension, it has to do with teaching topics, terms, and symbols. I am teaching Richard and the class how to write down a multiplication so that the way they write it down matches what is commonly seen, and how to read it, conventionally. In another dimension, it has to do with teaching the practice of studying mathematics in school. In order to study together, students need to be able to have a shared set of terms and symbols to which their talk refers.

Teaching and Studying Event #7:
Teacher Interpreting Symbols in Terms of an Alternative Representation

As I continued to teach, I continued to mix mathematical content with learning-to-learn content, next showing a more graphic representation of multiplication. I begin the representation only to hint at its usefulness. I refer to the drawings I had guided some students to make in their notebooks during their independent work time to draw in those like Varouna who I knew needed to know more about the meaning of multiplication.

Lampert: One of the things that I came around and did with some
              people is to draw a picture that would help you to reason
              about these problems. Twenty-two groups of twelve, you
              could draw as a twelve, a twelve, a twelve, and so on until
              you got twenty-two of them [drawing circles around
              12s as I talk].

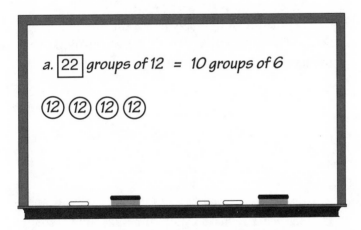

Or you could even put little Xs in the circles like I did
yesterday with the paper clips. Twenty-two groups of
twelve seems to me like it would be quite a lot of stuff, if
I did twenty-two of these [pointing to the four 12s
circled on the board].

By choosing to teach Richard in this way, I show him and the other students what "we" do to learn math. Throughout this demonstration, I intend to teach everyone, including Richard, that this is not going to be a class in which the teacher says whether an answer is right or wrong as the first response to any assertion. Rather, I will provide students with tools for reasoning themselves about the appropriateness of their answers.

Here I do mathematics by ranging around various ways to interpret "ten times twelve," making my activity available for observation. I demonstrate another representation for "ten times twelve" to put alongside these words, spoken by Richard. The mathematical work I expect of students (including Richard) is that they study these representations by using them to reason about Richard's assertion. What I did was designed to teach the class that the number they put in the "box" should make sense according to the meaning of the words and symbols we are all using. It was also designed to teach the class that drawing a picture is a way to give words and symbols a publicly available meaning that could then be assessed for its reasonability. I did not tell them the meaning, I created a representation of it for them to look at and interpret. I wanted to teach everyone that "drawing pictures" is not just for those students who could not do computation (i.e., the ones I worked with earlier in the lesson). I also wanted to demonstrate that teaching could happen in both small-group and large-group settings, and that what is taught and studied in these settings is related.

Working at the juncture of words, symbols, and pictures, I began to create a "hybrid" kind of representation. It was a mathematical shortcut, more abstract than making twenty-two of these:

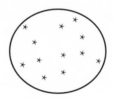

but more concrete than writing "22 x 12" or saying "twenty-two times twelve." By making what Richard called "timesing" into "grouping" I have used language to place my students (including Richard) in a mathematical environment where they can study and evaluate Richard's assertion that "twelve times ten equals twenty-two." I conclude this segment of teaching with an assertion, which I had been laying the groundwork for with my representation: "twenty-two groups of twelve seems like it would be quite a lot of stuff." I leave that assertion hanging in the air. I connect it with *my* reasoning but I do not connect it back to Richard's assertion, seeking to teach Richard and the class that it is up to them to decide what the implications are for judging Richard's assertion. By doing this drawing, I show Richard and the class how drawing a picture could be used to check your assertions, and that there is a particular kind of drawing that would work to check in relation to these kinds of problems. However many groups of 12 we had was supposed to be equal to 10 groups of 6.

Teaching and Studying Event #8:
Teacher Highlighting Patterns to Give Meaning to Multiplication

I leave my representation of "22 groups of 12" unfinished and leave Richard and the others to contemplate what 22 groups of 12 might look like. Moving over to the other side of the equation to represent the groups of 6, I cover up the groups of 12 I had drawn by positioning myself in front of them.

Lampert:	But let's look at ten groups of six for a minute [drawing on the board, next to what I had already done]:

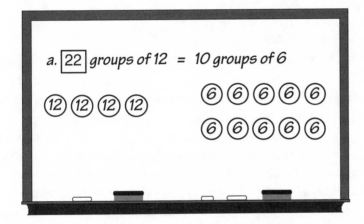

Six, six, six, six, six [pointing to the 6s in the circles].

The lesson in the discussion so far could be said to be about how to represent an assertion made in words and symbols in a drawing so as to judge whether it makes sense. With this new representation of groups of 6, I shift to a more fundamental level of teaching about multiplication and shift the focus away from Richard somewhat.

Teaching and Studying Event #9:
Student Interpreting the Public Representation

What I do next is designed to accomplish two aims, to teach students to notice and use patterns in the drawings they produce and to teach them that mathematics is characterized by finding such shortcuts.

Lampert:	How do I know that I have ten groups of six there without counting them? Ellie?
Ellie:	Because you made um, on the top you made five of them, but, you made five rows on the top and you just made a line exactly like that on the bottom.

Lampert: Okay, that's the story of a mathematical shortcut. I only had to count the first row and then I gave each one of them a partner and that gave me ten groups of six.

Now I give the class a new task: figuring out *my* reasoning. I am using patterns to design and justify a strategy for calculating a total instead of counting "by ones." I am demonstrating what my strategy gets me in this problem context. I challenge the class to imagine and describe what I did. Several students volunteer and I call on Ellie. Together, this student and I assert that counting "by ones" is not the only way to find the total when presented with an array of objects.

Teaching and Studying Event #10:
Teacher Relating the Idea of Groups to Practicing the "Times Tables"

I have made a shift away from the representation of 12 times 22 toward the use of patterns to accomplish calculation. We are still within the domain of giving meaning to multiplication because the particular pattern that this bit of teaching focuses on is doubling the number associated with one group when you can see that two groups have the same number of objects. I will switch again, in the same utterance, to teaching students that counting by sixes is a rehearsal of the six times table. I will then switch yet again, back to the language of grouping, to teach the class that the times tables are about counting *groups* of objects. The patterns in the numbers and in the way we talk about operations on numbers are verbalized and available for study. Also available is a different participation structure: chorusing a simple answer to a simple question. This mode of participating makes it possible for students to try out their thinking in another kind of medium than the single-student answer.

Lampert: Now, let's count by sixes here.

[pointing to the circled 6s] Six, twelve, eighteen, twenty-four, thirty, thirty-six, forty-two, forty-eight, fifty-four, sixty [students counting with Lampert].

That's our six times table. One group of six.

Eddie and Awad you should be looking up here [circling my finger around one 6].

One group of six is six.

Two groups of six is—[circling my finger around two 6s]

Students:	Twelve.
Lampert:	Three groups of six is—[circling my finger around three 6s]
Students:	Eighteen.
Lampert:	Four groups of six is—[circling my finger around four 6s]
Students:	Twenty-four.
Lampert:	Five groups of six is—[circling my finger around five 6s —the whole "top" row]
Students:	Thirty.
Lampert:	Thirty, and now I can do the same thing. If this much is thirty [again circling my finger around five 6s], how much is the whole amount [circling my finger around both rows of five 6s] going to be? Leticia?
	Sixty.
	So I have ten groups of six here.

I use the blackboard representation and point with my finger to show a connection between what we say and the pictures of groups of objects. And within this switch, there is another topic to study: the six times table itself, and the importance of developing familiarity with that particular set of "ordered triples" [i.e., (1, 6, 6), (2, 6, 12), (3, 6, 18), (4, 6, 24), and so on.] There is also a social switch away from Richard, and a cognitive switch, away from reasoning to remembering. What I do next with students is to practice associating the numbers in those triples and fix them in everyone's auditory memory by chorusing. I assume that students vary in their facility to recite the six times table and that such chorusing would help to move everyone up a notch on the memory scale.

Teaching and Studying Event #11:
Teacher Again Asking for an Explanation

All of this time, as I had been teaching the whole class various aspects of multiplication, I also had been trying to give Richard a way to make sense of his assertion, which was still up on the board: "22 groups of 12 = 10 groups of 6." I focus again on questioning this particular student, while attending to the class in the background.

Lampert: Now, Richard, what do you think about this twenty-two groups of twelve thing? [several seconds of silence]

                  What if I had just ten groups of twelve? How many would that be?

Richard: I don't know.

At the time, it is unclear whether Richard has learned something from the discussion. He had earlier said, "I timesed twelve and ten. Twelve times ten equals twenty two." Now he says "I don't know." This could be progress. I had been engaging the class in different activities that would illustrate the connection between "timesing," "multiplying," and "grouping," and wanted to find out now if Richard would see that adding 10 and 12 was not an appropriate action to take to find out the answer to my question. He did not repeat his earlier assertion that "Twelve times ten equals twenty-two." Richard's response suggests that he had learned that as a number to go in the box, "22" did not make sense, but he also learned that he did not know what did make sense.

Teaching and Studying Event #12:
Teacher Linking the Explanation to the Public Representation

To make a connection between Richard and the rest of the class that both Richard and I might be able to use, I return to the representation I had been generating earlier and had asked students to complete in their imaginations. I add more circled twelves to the earlier "groups of 12" until what is on the left side of the board is symmetrical with the representation of 10 groups of 6 on the right side.

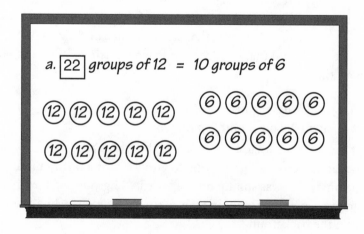

In addition to teaching Richard how to figure out the answer to my question, what I am doing is designed to teach him that he is capable of figuring it out. I am also teaching the rest of the class that Richard is capable of figuring it out and of talking about his thinking.

Teaching and Studying Event #13:
Teacher Representing, Student Asserting

Next I did some of the calculation, scaffolding Richard's participation and focusing him on the "doubling" strategy I had earlier discussed with Ellie.

Lampert:	Okay, let's do the top row [pointing to circles].
	Twelve plus twelve is twenty-four, plus twelve is thirty-six, forty-eight, sixty.
	[pointing to a row of five circled 12s] Now if the top row is sixty, how many am I going to have altogether? Richard?
Richard:	One-twenty.
Lampert:	One-hundred and twenty. Now this is ten groups of twelve. Richard, what do you think about your idea of twenty-two groups of twelve?
Richard:	It's wrong.

Here I am teaching Richard and the rest of the class that it is their job to evaluate their own thinking and that a drawing is a useful tool for doing so.

Teaching and Studying Event #14:
Student Evaluating Earlier Assertion

I now ask Richard to position his earlier assertion in relation to his current thinking.

Lampert:	Is it too big or too small?
Richard:	Too big.

As I have been teaching the whole class various aspects of multiplication, I have been trying to give Richard a way to make sense of his assertion, still up on the board. I move back from interacting with other members of the class to questioning him. This part of the journey comes to an end when Richard publicly recants, saying that his idea of 22 groups of 12 is "too big" and that 10 groups of 12 is not right either. By asking Richard to evaluate his answer in terms of too big or too small, I am teaching everyone that getting "in the ballpark" is an appropriate first step toward getting a precise answer.

Teaching and Studying Event #15:
Teacher and Student Reason Collaboratively

In terms of ordinary classroom norms, Richard is being asked to be extraordinarily courageous here. I am demonstrating something to the class using my interaction with him. Because I am teaching him in such a public way, I need to manage the problem of helping him save face with the rest of the class even though he has publicly admitted that he was "wrong." Gingerly, I stick with him, believing perhaps that if I can elicit some publicly respectable reasoning from Richard, I will be able to rescue something of his image as a mathematical problem solver. I reason for and with Richard that if 22 is too big, then what goes in the box needs to be "lower" than 22, giving him some language to continue his nascent reasoning process.

> Lampert: Okay, so we have to make this [pointing to the number in the box] lower. Can it be ten [replacing the 22 in the box with a 10]?

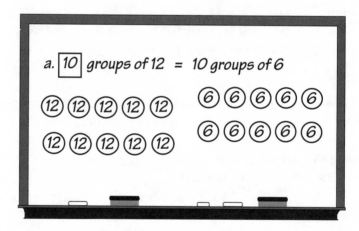

To model the "guess and check" strategy, I deliberately choose a lower number that does not fulfill the conditions to solve the equation and address a question about whether "it can be ten" to the whole class. Minimal reasoning is required to conclude that 10 groups of 12 cannot equal 10 groups of 6, but reasoning is required. When I put the "10" in the box, Richard said "no," and others chimed in as well, possibly indicating some camaraderie.

Zooming out from Particular Exchanges to the Class as a Whole: Linking Students with Content Across Events

At most, six minutes of class have gone by since I first asked for a student to speculate about problem A and Richard raised his hand. I have segmented those minutes into fifteen "events," each of which can be distinguished by the content made available for the class to study. Most of that time my mathematical focus was on issues raised by Richard, although I made some small moves to draw others in to my work with him. But zooming out to my work with the class as a whole, I have also been teaching everyone to participate in a classroom culture in which students:

- are publicly willing to reason their way from confusion to making mathematical sense;

- are publicly willing to talk about what they are thinking; and

- respect what others say even if it does not seem to make sense.

Through all of the events I have described, my job is to teach Richard (and everyone else) that he (and anyone else) who speaks publicly in class is responsible for reasoning through a piece of mathematics. This element of my practice is so fundamental to teaching students to engage in mathematical work that it leads me into dangerous social territory, where Richard's self-image and his standing with his peers is at stake. Whatever the outcome of this exchange, it will have consequences for his future and the future of the class, socially and mathematically. Although it might have been temporarily more comfortable for him to be "let off the hook," the consequences of doing that would interfere with his capacity to study mathematics through engaging with problems. The alternatives I might have taken were to simply move on to someone else, who might have given and even explained the "correct" answer, or to correct Richard myself. But students' engagement in mathematical sense-making is the foundation on which studying mathematics by working on problems is built. If they learn to expect me or their classmates to step in when they do not make sense, rather than learning to get themselves out of a difficult spot, they will not be likely to do mathematics when completing the assigned problems.

It is important to note that this is not a "sink or swim" situation. The work I am doing here is not started or finished in this six-minute exchange. Recognizing the dangers in the situation, I gave Richard several tools with which to build his sense-making skills and his image as a competent mathematical reasoner. In addition to scaffolding Richard's participation in this discussion, I would also be monitoring his continuing participation on a daily basis and inventing interventions to cope with any problems that might arise as a result of what I chose to do here. These tools included various symbolic representations of the multiplication of two two-digit numbers; language for talking about the meaning of multiplication; and a culture in which the norm was changing one's mind in public. While he was using those tools, I maintained a nonjudgmental stance in the conversation. The tools I provided were proximally available to Richard in his conversation with me, but they were presented in a way that would make them public property as well. My assumption that the "public" might be able to use such tools was founded on my earlier interactions with members of the class. Although I was adding to my cognitive load yet another concern to worry about in the future, the risk seemed worthwhile. Internally, I was cheering Richard on, but I needed to work at not making a big deal of it when he finally judged his original assertion to be "too big" in order to convey to him and the class that this exchange we were having was ordinary mathematical practice. I did not celebrate his answer because my purpose was to get the class to reason about the meaning of the problem, not just to get the right answer.

I didn't press Richard to make any further speculations, but instead I turned to several other students in quick succession to reiterate the ideas that I had gotten out on the table for him to study. At this point, having spent a long time with one student, I had to work on ascertaining who was still "with me" in the mathematical territory of multiplication. I did this by questioning students in a way that challenged them to interpret what was on the chalkboard in relation to the problem we were discussing. By using this public representation in this way, I was attempting to convey that I intended the lesson I had so far been teaching to be for everyone, not just for Richard. The representation on the board served as a kind of cement among the parts of this discussion, making it possible for students to move in and out of active engagement with the ideas. If they had been bored or irritated by my focus on Richard and "tuned out," they could find some clues about how to "tune back in" by looking at what was in front of them.

I shifted the purpose of the discourse further away from figuring out the answer and closer toward a discourse of explaining why it made sense as I challenged students with a question about why "10" does not make sense as the missing value. I continued to pursue the *analysis* of the problem rather than the *answer*, teaching the class that this is a legitimate way to study mathematics in school.

We now had "10 groups of 12 = 10 groups of 6" on the chalkboard. We needed to revise it.

| Lampert: | Why not? Who can explain why not? Karim? |

| Karim: | Because it won't be like, if you times ten and twelve then you times ten and six, they won't be both the same answer. |

Karim gave part of the explanation and I reiterated it, fitting it into the larger picture. It cannot be 10 groups of 12 because the symbols and words mean that what is on either side of the equation has to be worth "the same"—I deliberately did not use Karim's word "answer" to refer to the values of the two sides of the equation.

Lampert:	[pointing to the expressions on either side of the equals sign] Okay, so whatever I have on this side has to be the same as what I have on this side.
	So it seems like it said ten times twelve is going to be a little bit, or maybe even a lot, too big.
	What do you think?

I kept the discourse in the realm of explanation rather than returning to figuring out what goes in the box. By asking "What do you think?" and not "What do you think goes in the box?" I continued with teaching that the "answer" is not the only thing we are after here. I next called on Charlotte, who taught the class more about multiplication by using the representation I had earlier created on the chalkboard.

| Lampert: | Charlotte? |

| Charlotte: | You could find out that if you tried ten times twelve, that it would have to be five times twelve, because what we did was we counted by twelve in the top row and then we added sixty, and sixty, and it came out to sixty. Then you know that only the half the ten would be sixty. Half of the ten groups of twelve. |

In addition to the multiplication content, Charlotte and I together taught the class that we can use what we did "before" to reason about what we are working on "now." I followed her lead and asked some other students whose hands were raised to comment further on the connection with the representation. I used the words "think" and "explain" in my talk to identify what it is we were doing here. And I used the chalkboard representation to record the representation of students' contributions and connect them with my mathematical agenda. The following piece of the discussion provides closure for this segment and a link with the teaching I will analyze in our consideration of problem C, later on in the lesson.

Lampert:	So you're basing what you're saying there on what we just did. When we counted all these, we got up to, Donna Ruth, what did we get up to on the top there?
Donna Ruth:	We got up to sixty.
Lampert:	Okay, and that is really exactly what we want because we have ten groups of six over here and that's sixty. So what number should go here? What do you think? Yasu?
Yasu:	Five.
Lampert:	Five groups of twelve.
	Can somebody please explain why it should be five groups of twelve? Leticia?
Leticia:	Because ten times six is sixty. Five times twelve equals sixty.
Lampert:	So ten groups of six, the arithmetic we can do for that is ten times six, and the arithmetic we can do for twelve, is five times twelve. But if you don't happen to know what five times twelve is, you can do it another way.
	Tyrone, can you explain another way if you don't happen to know five times twelve? What else could I do?
Tyrone:	Add twelve, five times.
Lampert:	Add twelve, five times. [I write five 12s on the board.]
	Okay. One, two, three, four, five times twelve.
	[adding the twos] Two, four, six, eight, ten, twel—
	Two, four, six, eight, ten carry the one [adding the tens]. One, two, three, four, five, six. Five times twelve is sixty. Okay?
	Shahroukh?
Shahroukh:	I think—
	The reason I think it's correct is because twelve groups of five is sixty.

	And ten groups of six is sixty, too, so they're both equivalent.
Lampert:	Okay, that's good.
	That's what we're trying to do here. Equivalent and equals mean the same thing. Another way you could think about this problem and use a drawing to help you think about it is to look at your ten groups of six. How could I make a group of six into a group of twelve? What sort of regrouping could I do here that would help me to think about groups of twelve? Donna Ruth do you have some ideas about that? How could I make these into groups of twelve?
Donna Ruth:	You could get two sixes and um—
Lampert:	[circling the two circled 6s with brown chalk] Okay, two sixes.
Lampert:	Now what do I have inside the brown circle there?

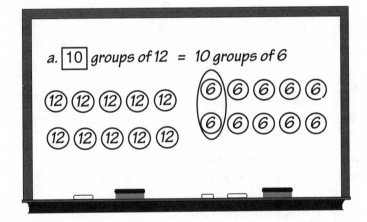

Donna Ruth:	I don't know.
Lampert:	Ileana, what do I have inside the brown circle?
Ileana:	Twelve.
Lampert:	Twelve. Six and six. How many times can I do that here? Altogether? Connie?
Connie:	Five.
Lampert:	Five times [making five sets of two circled 6s]. So I make groups of twelve out of my groups of six [replacing the 10 in the box with a 5].

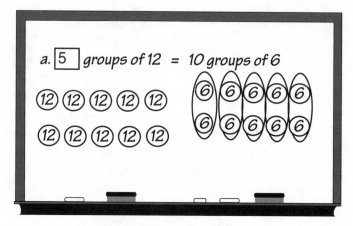

Drawing a picture, it's not really a picture, it's sort of a diagram and I heard you talking about diagrams in science yesterday, helps you to think through the problem. So when I see you being stuck and not being able to make any progress, or if I see your thinking being confused, I'm going to ask you to draw a picture because that is something that is very important to do in mathematics.

Lampert: Tyrone turn your chair around and sit on it properly please.

Okay. So that was problem A.

How about problem B?

We had a short discussion of problem B, involving three students who had not yet had anything to say, and then I moved us to problem C.

Using Students to Take the Class into New Mathematical Territory

I began the last part of the discussion—in which we would talk about problem C—knowing, and announcing to the class that I knew, that not everyone in the class had worked on this piece of the Problem of the Day during their independent work time. I am teaching the students that *we will*, and that *they can* discuss a problem, even if they do not "finish" it during small-group time. Even if all students do not participate in this part of the discussion, it indicates to all where our mathematical work will be going later in the year. Like toddlers first learning to speak, or travelers in a foreign land, they can learn from listening, even if they do not quite understand everything that they hear. My assessment of the overall success of a lesson segment like this would occur in the future, in the next few lessons, and later in the year when we came to studying functions more deliberately.

Bringing a microscopic lens to the lesson again, we now consider the similar and different teaching moves that occurred, event by event, as the content and the participants changed.

Teaching and Studying Event #1:
Teacher Asking a Question to Begin the Discussion

I begin this part of the discussion by inviting some commentary on how working on problem C is different from working on problems A and B. (See page 143.)

> Lampert: What do you think?

Again, I begin work on the problem by asking the question in a way that is intended to teach students that there is more to think about in doing mathematical work than finding the answer. After eliciting some comments on how problem C is different from A and B, I construct a question that keeps us on a more reflective plane. By addressing the whole class with the question "What do you think?" I leave open the possibility that someone could either make a general statement or talk about the missing values. Several students raise their hands, and I call on Anthony.

Teaching and Studying Event #2:
Teacher Calling on a Particular Student to Answer

> Lampert: Anthony?

As with my choice of Richard to begin talk about problem A, the choice of Anthony here is a deliberate teaching act, meant to get at a particular piece of mathematics and a particular aspect of my relations with students. Anthony had been silent so far in the discussion, and I knew from watching him earlier that he had spent most of small-group time working independently on problem C. If there was a segment of the class that did not get to problem C, there was also a segment who, like Anthony, got through problems A and B quickly, who were more proficient in multiplication, and for whom problem C was designed. I wanted to teach them that they needed to attend to a part of the discussion that might have been less interesting to them, but also that we would get to more challenging investigations in this public forum. I wanted to teach those students who had not done the sort of work that Anthony had done on problem C that there were others in their class who were working on mathematics at a different level, broadening their notions of what mathematics could be about. Even if they could not do it, I could conduct the discussion in such a way as to make it possible for them to watch it being done.

Teaching and Studying Event #3:
Student Asserting and Teacher Responding with a Representation

What was up on the chalkboard now was ☐ groups of 7 = ☐ groups of 21. Anthony told us what he was thinking.

> Anthony: There are many possibilities, like it could be three groups of seven and one group of twenty-one, or it could be six groups of seven and two groups of twenty-one. You can just double it all the time.

First Anthony mentions some of the possible values that would make the equation true, and then he makes a conjecture about how to find more values. Using the word "all" suggests a mathematical generalization. This is a different kind of mathematical work than finding particular pairs of numbers that would make the equation true. I respond to this change in the level of the conversation by putting both pairs of numbers [(3, 1) and (6, 2)] on the board under the equation:

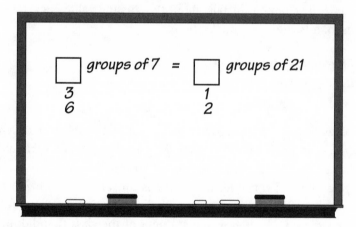

Teaching and Studying Event #4:
Teacher Invites Reflection and Student Constructs a Hypothesis

> Lampert: What does anybody else think about that?
>
> What do you think Shahroukh?
>
> Shahroukh: I think he's right and that pattern would keep on going.

At this point, I am making a change from the routine I followed in responding to Richard's answer. I did not, at this point, ask Anthony to "explain his thinking." Instead, I invited another student to comment on Anthony's assertion, making a major shift in the direction of our mathematical journey.[3] We are not exactly leaving the territory of multiplication, but we are enlarging the scope of what we look at in that area to the broader domain of multiplicative structures, encompassing multiplication but also verging on functions. Shahroukh keeps the conversation on this abstract plane. I next ask the class to explain the pattern in the pairs.

Teaching and Studying Event #5: Teacher Elicits Further Reflection on Assertion and Representation

Lampert:	Why does that work [pointing to the pairs on the board]?
	Three groups of seven equal one group of twenty-one? Six groups of seven equals two groups of twenty-one?
	What do you think? Candice?
Candice:	Because three times seven equals twenty-one, and twenty-one ones equals twenty-one, and that means six times seven equals forty-two, and twenty-one two times equals forty-two.
	You can go on.
Lampert:	If I do three times seven I get twenty-one, and that's one group of twenty-one. Shahroukh?

In my response to Shahroukh, I had chosen to straddle the fence between the specifics of the multiplication at hand, and the more general idea of functions. I refer back to the chart I made based on Anthony's response to see whether this kind of mathematical generalization would continue. Candice carries on in the same vein as Shahroukh's earlier contribution. The first part of Candice's response refers to the two specific pairs of numbers. She is explaining why you double the product of 3 and 7 to get the product of 6 and 7, using the language of groups; she describes 21 as "twenty-one ones" and 42 as "twenty-one two times." But the second part of her response ("You can go on.") is like Anthony's and Shahroukh's assertions in that she is recognizing that the relationship between the two empty boxes in the equation means that the list of pairs "goes on" following the same pattern. I begin to revoice her more concrete assertion, perhaps to rephrase it as "one group of twenty-one" and "two groups of twenty-one" to make a more direct link to the earlier part of the discussion.

But I let Shahroukh interrupt me. I had chosen not to engage either Shahroukh or Candice when they were bidding for attention early on in the lesson when I was interacting with Richard. Here they were competing with one another.

Teaching and Studying Event #6:
Teacher Responds to Student-Initiated Direction

Shahroukh: You can keep on adding three on this [side of the] board. Like it could be nine times seven equals sixty-three and three groups of twenty-one, and you can keep on adding three on this board and keep on adding one on that [side of the] board. So, you can go on forever.

Here I was teaching students that it is possible to interrupt the teacher and change the direction of the conversation. When I called on Shahroukh, he made a general assertion as well, expanding on what Candice and Anthony had said.

Teaching and Studying Event #7:
Teacher Interprets Student Assertion to Increase Accessibility

My next move takes the generalizations made by Shahroukh, Candice, and Anthony to the rest of the class for consideration. Recognizing that a bridge was necessary between the concrete task of "filling in the boxes" and the work of looking for and making predictions from patterns, I again use the chalkboard to unpack the ideas under discussion.

Lampert: So, let's just test that out though. I'm going to write the answers to these multiplications then and this colored chalk here, although this one's a little bit bigger. Let's see. Three times seven is twenty-one, I am just putting this in here and one times twenty-one is twenty-one. On this side. Then next I have six times seven, which is—

Students: Forty-two.

Lampert: Forty-two, and on this side I need two groups of twenty-one is forty-two. [now on the board:]

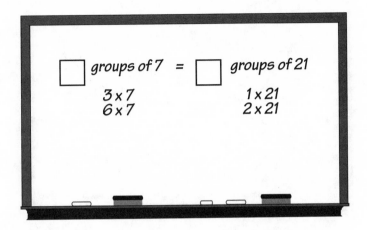

Teaching and Studying Event #8:
Teacher and Students Collaboratively Continue the Pattern

Again, I shift the mode of discourse, moving away for reiterations of the generalization toward getting more examples of ordered pairs in the public eye for everyone's consideration. I call on several different students to contribute, both verbally rehearsing the relevant multiplication "facts" and illustrating where such facts could fit in some larger scheme of reasoning.

Lampert:	Now, what would the next one be? Connie?
Connie:	Seven times nine?
Lampert:	Okay, but since I'm writing it this way and I want to follow a pattern, I'm going to write nine times seven. And what's nine times seven?
Connie:	Sixty-three.
Lampert:	Okay, nine times seven is sixty-three. Now on this side we're going to have what?

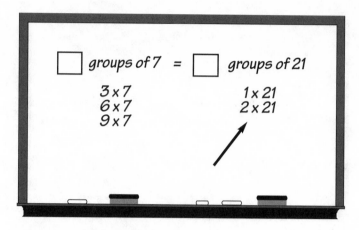

Lampert: What should that be? Donna Ruth?

Donna Ruth: Three times twenty-one?

Lampert: And what is three times twenty-one?

Donna Ruth: Sixty-three.

I wrote in my journal after class about what I had done here, commenting on how the discussion had gone along somewhat differently than I had anticipated.

> *Yesterday, Working on problem ⓒ*
>
> ☐ *groups of 7 = ☐ groups of 21*
>
> ~~*Several*~~ *Well, about 1/4 of the class seemed
> to come up with the idea that this was
> a case of multiple solutions. It did* _not_
> *occur, as I thought it might, that one*
> *solution*
> *student gave one alternative ^ + another
> gave another. Rather three or more students
> volunteered right off the bat the idea that
> there were "endless" solutions.*
>
>   *What I put up on the board was this:*
>
>   ☐ *groups of 7 = ☐ groups of 21*
>
> | 3 | 1 |
> |-----|-----|
> | 6 | 2 |
> | 9 | 3 |

*and then partway through the discussion,
I added:*

☐ *groups of 7* = ☐ *groups of 21*

3 x 7	*1 x 21*
6 x 7	*2 x 21*
9 x 7	*3 x 21*

*We did the multiplication to "check"
the equalities, which* ⓐ *drew more kids into
the discussion and* ⓑ *allowed me to reinforce/
introduce "mental multiplication," i.e., decomposing
and recomposing the numbers—the fact
that the multiples are written horizontally
helps with this, I think, because it is* ~~more~~ *less
likely the that kids will just click into the
algorithmic approach.*

*Teaching and Studying Event #9:
Teacher Leads a "Practice" Session on Multiplication
Procedure to Use with Two-Digit Numbers*

Here I recognized a point in the discussion where it would be appropriate to bring to the table an idea I had prepared the lesson to address: multiplying by two-digit numbers. This was a skill I knew many of my students needed to learn based on what I saw them do on the pretest at the beginning of the year. I would represent this process verbally and on the chalkboard as we filled in the chart of ordered pairs in problem C of this Problem of the Day. The problem I faced here was keeping both the arithmetic procedure and the mathematical generalization in focus at the same time because I was teaching a diverse group of students. I called on several collaborators to do a quick series of multiplications by decomposing and recomposing to "test" whether the conjecture about the pattern would continue. I named what we were doing "practicing mental multiplication." We needed to obtain the products of these multiplications to test whether the pattern that Anthony and others conjectured "works."

9×7	=?	3×21
12×7	=?	4×21
15×7	=?	5×21

In order to test this generalization and also to practice computation, we would not take the truth of his assertion for granted.

Lampert:	Let's try to practice a little mental multiplication. Three times twenty is twenty plus twenty plus twenty. That's sixty.
	Three times one, that's pretty simple, is three.
	So, three times twenty-one is going to be sixty-three.
	So I get the same thing on both sides.
	What should be the next problem on this side? We had three groups of seven, six groups of seven, nine groups of seven. Yasu?
Yasu:	Twelve groups of seven.
Lampert:	Twelve groups of seven. Twelve groups of seven I can get by doing twelve times seven. Now, again, what's the mental multiplication here?
	Twelve can be broken up into two parts.
	Ten and two.
	What's ten times seven? Varouna?
Varouna:	Seventy.
Lampert:	Seventy.
	What's two times seven? Leticia?
Leticia:	Fourteen.
Lampert:	Fourteen. If I have seventy and fourteen, what's twelve times seven?
	Seventy and fourteen. Donna Ruth?
Donna Ruth:	Eighty-four.
Lampert:	Eighty-four. The tens have to go up by one, and the one becomes fourteen. Gotta start doing these things in your head.
	What's the problem I need on the other side of over there? Reba.
Reba:	Four times twenty-one.

Lampert:	Okay, four times twenty-one.
	Again, what's four times twenty? Reba?
Reba:	What?
Lampert:	What's four times twenty?
Reba:	Four times twenty is um, eighty?
Lampert:	Eighty. And then four times one is—
Reba:	Eighty-four.
Lampert:	So four times twenty is eighty, and four times one is eighty-four.
	So it comes out the same. Okay. Let's see.
	We'll do one more.
	What's the next problem on this side? Connie?
Connie:	Fifteen times seven.
Lampert:	Okay, fifteen times seven. Now we have fifteen, break it up into two parts. Ten times seven is—
	Ivan what is ten times seven?
Ivan:	Seventy.
Lampert:	And five times seven?
Ivan:	Thirty-five.
Lampert:	Thirty-five. Now I need to add in my head seventy plus thirty-five. Well, seventy plus thirty is a hundred. Plus five is a hundred and five.

Candice and I then solved 5×21 using a similar reasoning, and I summarized our findings.

| Lampert: | So it seems like this conjecture that you can keep on going works. |

I was intending to end the lesson here as we were already past our scheduled ending time, but several other students were bidding for the floor. As I called on them one after another, Ivan, Charlotte, Karim, Yasu, Anthony, and Donna Ruth asserted additional patterns they had noticed in the ordered pairs that would generate more ordered pairs, ad infinitum. Charlotte and Karim commented as they made their substantive contributions that this approach made doing the mathematics "easier" because you did not have to multiply large numbers to find the missing factors. These closing activities brought coherence to the lesson, both mathematically and socially. The students who made these assertions at the end of the lesson included both those who were just learning two-digit multiplication and those who were working on understanding functions.

Problems in Teaching in the Domain of Leading a Whole-Class Discussion

The teaching events described here are only a subset of all of the events that occurred during the half-hour-long discussion on September 28, but they are useful for identifying the kinds of work the teacher does when in front of the whole class. If we look for patterns in those events, we see a variety of moves made by the teacher to address the problems of getting mathematics into the conversation and getting that mathematics to be studied. Elements of the work of teaching within this structure include:

- creating visual representations of the ideas under discussion as a common record of the class's journey and referent for discussion;

- deciding who to call on from among those who are and are not bidding for attention;

- simultaneously teaching individual students and engaging the group as a whole in worthwhile mathematical activity;

- keeping the discussion on track while also allowing students to make spontaneous contributions that they considered to be relevant;

- monitoring the pace of the discussion with attention to the scheduled end of the class period; and

- adjusting to the few students who need to leave or enter the room during the period.

These are the problems I faced while in front of the whole class. The actions I take to address these problems are both managerial and intellectual. They serve both to move the discussion along for everyone and to infuse its content with the mathematics students are to study.

In each interaction in a public discussion, a teacher can use a student or a student's connection with some mathematics to teach the student while also teaching the class as a whole. At the same time, she might also teach a particular group of students like "those who finished problem C" or "those who are not yet facile with times tables." A problem at the intersection of my relationship with students and my relationship with mathematics is how to begin each new segment of the discussion. In the example above, I begin segments of the discussion with one or more of these actions:

- choosing the question to begin a segment of discussion;
- choosing who has the floor in response to a question; or
- choosing to give someone who is bidding for the floor an entree into the discussion.

In making such choices, a teacher identifies possible resources that are available in the work environment. Structuring interaction is fundamental to being able to use these resources and use them productively.

When the student who is chosen responds, another kind of problem comes into focus. There are several subsequent moves that can be made to turn that response into a resource productive of teaching and studying:

- when an assertion is made, choosing to stay with the student who made it and requesting an explanation;
- when an assertion is made, choosing to stay with the student who made it and suggesting my interpretation;
- when an assertion is made, moving to other students and requesting a counterspeculation; or
- when an assertion is made, moving to other students and requesting an explanation.

Whichever of these actions is chosen, the teacher can then continue by

- asking additional students to comment on another student's thinking;
- rephrasing a student's explanation in more precise mathematical terms and asking him or her to comment; or
- creating a representation of the students' talk on the chalkboard.

Each of these acts of teaching makes more potential resources available. Students can take advantage of them as opportunities to study, and the teacher, to teach.

To address the problem of infusing mathematics into the discussion in conjunction with attending to social issues, a teacher can:

- alternate between persistent engagement with one student and quick moves around the class, or

- alternate between single student answers and chorus-style participation.

At any point in the discussion the teacher can step out and

- comment on what kind of problem or what kind or work this is, or

- name a process or a kind of number with either a contextually invented term or a term from the public domain of mathematics.

These actions, taken to manage the discussion both interpersonally and intellectually, need to be aligned with both the mathematical and the social context. Each move is designed and enacted in a particular moment to bring a particular piece of mathematics to students and particular students to mathematics. The work of teaching is not only *deciding what to do* at each of these levels, but also *doing it*, and keeping track of the studies it enables for students.

At each juncture, there are many ways in which the conversation in a discussion like this can go, and multiple influences on where it does go. But the teacher consistently works at teaching students both mathematics and how to study mathematics by asking students to reason, to explain, to attend to and to interpret the assertions of others, and by reasoning, explaining, attending, and interpreting the mathematics herself in concert with their responses. During the half-hour discussion we have analyzed here, it is interesting to note that the teacher used variants of the word "think" thirty-two times in ninety turns at talk, and students used variants of the word "think" sixteen times. Eighteen students participated in the discussion verbally, and thirteen of them had more than two turns to talk.

Problems in a Lesson Lead to Larger-Scale Problems

Although several students had made verbal contributions to the discussion, I wrote in my journal after class that I had been concerned about the level of participation. I was still getting to know the students in this class, and some of them continued to puzzle me. I worried that some students were volunteering often, perhaps being frustrated that they did not get to talk more in the large group. And I worried that some students were still unknown to me in this, the third week of school.

Evident in the patterns of talk on September 28 is the diversity of the students' capacities for doing mathematics in a thoughtful, productive way. What I had to work hard at teaching to Richard was different from what I was trying to teach Anthony or Charlotte or Shahroukh, and yet I was teaching all of these students how to participate in a common discourse of mathematical reasoning. As I was getting to know the students, I was becoming aware of the range of their mathematical diversity and the differences in their dispositions to reflect and make sense of what we were working on. I had tried a few strategies to be responsive to the diversity in this lesson, and I would need to monitor future lessons to see what effect these had on students. Would Richard be reluctant to offer another assertion in a whole-class discussion, either for reasons of his own or because other students teased him? Would Shahroukh or Candice or Anthony "tune out" because they were frustrated by the level of some of the discussion? What teaching strategies could I employ to head off these possible results of today's work?

And what of the mathematics we never got to? Reviewing the way in which the large-group segment of this lesson went lays bare some of the mathematics that we might have talked about in the context of these problems but did not. Of particular concern is the mathematics that students were working on during the small-group portion of this lesson that we did not talk about. I now faced the problem of figuring out not only whether we should but when we would.

Standing back from the event-by-event analysis of teaching here, we can identify two big problems that stand out when the events are aggregated. Both have to do with a kind of "coverage." In the discussion, I was not able to interact with all of the students who I would have liked to hear from. Neither was I able to get to all of the mathematics that seemed important. These two teaching problems need to be addressed across time as well as in particular events. We will look at large-scale "teacher moves" that address teaching problems at this scale in the next section of the book, zooming in on more lessons to see how they play out in practice. The work to be considered entails both long-term design work, like considering the scope and sequence of mathematics across the entire year and figuring out how to structure written and spoken participation in discourse. It also includes continuously maintaining, monitoring, and modifying the structures that are in place to accommodate what is learned about students and mathematics along the way.

8

Teaching to Deliberately Connect Content Across Lessons

In this chapter we zoom out to investigate a different dimension of practice: the teaching problems that come up in connecting content across lessons. We all make intellectual and practical connections as we move from one experience to another through time. Such connections can be as superficial as remembering what one was wearing on two subsequent visits to a museum or as substantial as identifying common themes across examples of painting and sculpture from the fifteenth century. In school, students will connect what they learn in one lesson to what they learn in the next lesson in one way or another. The teacher can work to *deliberately structure* the making of connections to enable the study of substantial and productive relationships in the content. If the teacher can make the conceptual connections among lessons obvious, students will have the opportunity to study aspects of the content that are not easily contained in single lessons. They will be able to study the kinds of ideas that make a subject coherent across separate topics.

The sequencing of the problems from one lesson to the next and the use of a common representation of mathematical relationships to tie work together over time are examples of the deliberate structuring of students' experience to teach coherence. Over a series of lessons, I investigate these and other ways in which a teacher can address problems in the domain of making connections. I analyze teaching in a series of lessons that occurred in my classroom during the first part of an "instructional unit" on time-speed-distance relationships that lasted from mid-October through November.[1] In my class, time-speed-distance relationships were a "problem context" for studying ideas about fractions, division, and ratio over time, just as number sentences with empty boxes were a problem form for studying multiplication in the lesson described in chapters 5, 6, and 7. The kinds of resources these forms and contexts afforded for addressing problems of practice are the focus of my analysis. The particular problem forms and problem contexts that I used in lessons and across lessons are interesting, but not unique. I drew on a number of resources to find problem contexts, but the kinds of work I needed to do with those contexts is similar to what any teacher would need to do using a problem-based curriculum, even if it is laid out in a textbook. By investigating the problems entailed in choosing and using problem contexts to tie lessons together, we can see elements of teaching work that cross lesson boundaries.

Paralleling the analysis of preparing a single lesson in chapter 5, here I examine the preparation that goes into extracting a connected set of mathematical ideas from a particular context over a series of lessons. I then examine how I used student work as a resource for building coherence, and the work of creating representational and linguistic threads to link ideas and students over time. I consider how a teacher can make use of such threads to "carry" the mathematics from one lesson to another, and to make it possible for teacher and students to communicate about a complex web of mathematical ideas.

Choosing an appropriate context and identifying the kinds of generative Problems of the Day that can be derived from it is teaching work that extends over several lessons. It is similar to the smaller-scale problem of choosing the particular problems that students will work on in any given lesson, but it is work that is done over longer stretches of time as the problems follow one another to connect the mathematics in a coherent way. As with individual problems, there are many sources from which a teacher can choose a problem context that is appropriate for a particular class to use to study a particular set of topics. Perhaps the most engaging contexts a teacher can choose to work with are those that grow directly out of an actual problem faced by the class. This happened in my class when students and I were planning for an upcoming parents' night. Each member of the class was to introduce him- or herself and attending family members and tell the group something about each person. The amount of time we had to do this was limited to forty-five minutes. As a class we worked on how to allocate that time fairly, given that different students would have different numbers of family members to introduce. Problems like this are valuable teaching tools because they help students to recognize that mathematics can be directly relevant to their ten-year-old lives. But it is not easy to find enough of them to build a whole year's curriculum.

Anticipating the Connections That Can Be Made in a Problem Context

In October, my class was beginning an integrated unit in science, language arts, and social studies. Their work in all of these subject areas would center around a dramatic tale called "The Voyage of the *Mimi*."[2] "*Mimi*" is the story of a group of people (three researchers, their high school assistants, a ten-year-old boy, and his grandfather) who spend the summer on a sailing ship (named *Mimi*) studying whales off the coast of New England. Using a story written to engage students' interest, a series of thirteen fifteen-minute video episodes illustrates several ways in which mathematics, science, and technology are used in the world outside of school. From my point of view as a teacher, having my students investigate how mathematics plays into the story of a summer on the *Mimi* was the next best thing to being able to put them into a situation where solving mathematics problems mattered directly to their lives. And given that I was teaching them for only one hour a day, the story provided a useful framework for integrating what I was doing in mathematics with what they were doing in the rest of the school day.

Identifying the Curriculum in a Problem Context

Navigation is a prominent problem-solving context in the story of the *Mimi*. The characters are challenged with finding their way on the sea, where there are no highways or road signs to help locate either where they are or how far they have gone. These problems are solved using calculations and geometry. The mathematical elements of the problems are revealed as the captain of the ship tries to keep the journey on course and the crew safe. The whales that the crew wants to observe are found on "George's Bank," but sailing in this area is risky because of sudden shallow spots in the water and submerged shipwrecks. It is important to know exactly where the *Mimi* is and where it is going. This requires "reading" a nautical chart and figuring out mathematical relationships among time, speed, and distance. Captain Granville, the owner and captain of the ship, explains how he solves navigation problems to the crew of researchers and to his ten-year-old grandson. To the extent that the drama is successful in getting viewers to identify with the characters in the story, these problems become real and important to students.

Within the broad frame of navigational challenges, I chose to work with my class on time-speed-distance relationships. (In other years, I had also used this navigational context to teach about angles and vectors.) On a ship, knowing how time, speed, and distance are related is crucial to arriving at one's intended destination and avoiding danger. I knew that this relationship could be modeled in ways that could take us into the mathematics of multiplication, division, and fractions at a level appropriate for study in the fifth grade. My aim was not to prepare my students to solve a particular kind of "real world" problem. It is very unlikely that they would ever find themselves in a situation where they would face the same navigational challenges as the *Mimi* crew, but if they did, there would be many contextual tools they would be able to use to supplement their mathematical skill and understanding.[3] Rather, I considered their engagement with time, speed, and distance relationships, like their interest in finding all the two-digit pairs that would add up to 51, as a "way in" to some mathematics worthy of investigation. It seemed particularly useful as a familiar context in which fractions are needed to model reality where we could use those numbers with meaning before setting off on studying the more technical aspects of rational numbers.

Within the "*Mimi*" drama, a group of scientific investigators face problems and solve them using these mathematical ideas and tools. The print materials and software that accompany the video pose similar problems for students to work on with the same context as a referent and the upper elementary curriculum as a guide to topical content. There is a particular problem that arises in the drama and is solved by the captain that I wanted my students to be able to think about in a sensible way. This problem had been a frame for my teaching various topics to fifth graders in several different classes over the prior ten years. I had a good sense of what it would take in the way of teaching and studying to get a group of fifth graders to understand something of the mathematics entailed in the captain's problem-solving strategy.[4] He drops a piece of bread off the bow of the ship (which he knows is 58 feet long) and one of the crew members uses a stopwatch to time how many seconds it takes for the ship to pass the bread. The strategy is one of those bits of mathematics that can seem like "magic" unless you think about it through the lens of speed as a constant relationship between distance and time.

It took several weeks of working with time, speed, and distance relationships before I would actually try to analyze the "bread on the water" problem with my class. After watching a video of episode 2 of "The Voyage of the *Mimi*" on October 23, we discussed a much simpler problem that arose and was solved by the captain early in the voyage. In charting the course for the next day, he needed to let the crew know what time they would get to the place where they anticipated some whales might be spotted. Given the speed and direction of the wind, they could anticipate sailing at a constant speed of 5 knots. They needed to travel 50 nautical miles. How long would it take to get there? What time would they need to set sail in the morning in order to be there at the time of day they could expect to encounter the feeding behavior of whales that they wanted to observe?

We spent a week doing problems similar to this one, with different speeds and distances to pose different mathematical challenges. During this week, the class and I used a representation to organize our talk and our work that we came to call "the journey line." It was used in each different problem to link distances with times for the given speeds.[5] In the strategies students used to solve the problems, they studied multiplication by relating it to repeated addition and they figured out divisions by estimating and doing multiplications (as we saw in chapter 2). Calculators were brought in as a tool for working with large or otherwise unwieldy numbers, so when divisions did not come out even, we were confronted with interpreting decimal representations that were unfamiliar. On October 31, we digressed into working on translating fractions of an hour into minutes and vice versa. Students grappled with how to label fractional parts of the clock face that was used as a representation of one hour. They struggled a bit over how to translate the term "quarter hour" into minutes because of the association of a quarter coin with twenty-five cents and the decimal representation of one-fourth as ".25."

On November 2, we shifted from the nautical context to problems about car travel, beginning with a situation that had conditions I assumed would be familiar to children who travel on the highway. "A car is going 50 miles per hour; how far will it go in 10 minutes?" Although this is a familiar situation, the mathematics of this problem is difficult.[6] At first, almost everyone in the class was sure that the car would go 5 miles. Using the model of the journey line from earlier in the unit, some students asserted that the car could not be going 5 miles in 10 minutes and *also* be going 50 miles in an hour. I left this problem "hanging" for a few days. During this time, I made up similar problems with different times and speeds that I thought might jog my students out of simply doing the easiest calculation with whatever numbers appeared in the problem.

While we worked on time-speed-distance problems, we consistently used the journey line to represent hours and minutes, miles, and fractional parts of a mile and to make connections between the problem context and the calculations. We returned to the "50 miles per hour for 10 minutes" problem several times, generating and evaluating many alternative assertions for the distance the car would travel. The tools and representations that we used raised questions about the connection between common fractions and decimals and provoked arguments about accuracy and how much of it was required. Disagreements about the solution to this problem were more or less resolved by November 14. On November 16, I gave the students a quiz. After the quiz, we did two more days of "car" problems, raising some new issues around fractions and division, but mostly refining the ways in which the journey line could be used to represent equivalent ratios generated by the same rate. The lesson described in chapter 2 occurred during this period.

While we were working on these "car" problems, the class was proceeding through episodes of the *Mimi* drama in other lessons. When they came to the episode in which the captain uses a piece of bread and a stopwatch to determine the speed of the ship, we moved back to working in the nautical context. Now we were using fractions as well as multiples of an hour as the given time and using knots for the given speed. In the rest of this chapter and the next, I focus the analytic lens on teaching in different parts of this long unit to look at what math was being taught and studied. I examine what mechanisms brought that mathematics into play and identify teaching problems that I confronted when making connections among ideas across lessons.

In any concrete problem-solving context, there are many ways in which mathematics can be applied and thus many kinds of mathematics that could be studied. My teaching problem in the time-speed-distance unit was to use *this context* to teach the relationships among mathematical ideas and skills that *my class* needed to learn. A connected curriculum was not going to emerge from the context unless I designed problems that would focus my students' activities. Students might make their own connections, but they might not see important relationships among mathematical concepts unless I made a deliberate attempt to teach them.

Although I was drawing on a published set of activities that came with the "*Mimi*" videos, I made use of my own knowledge of the mathematics of navigation to understand my observations of student work and to produce a tentative map of the mathematical terrain we might expect to cover.

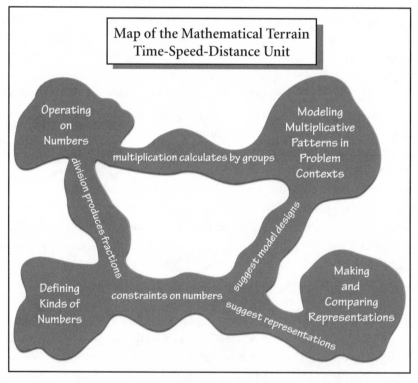

**Map of the Mathematical Terrain
Time-Speed-Distance Unit**

Operating on Numbers

Modeling Multiplicative Patterns in Problem Contexts

multiplication calculates by groups

division produces fractions

suggest model designs

Defining Kinds of Numbers

constraints on numbers

suggest representations

Making and Comparing Representations

I am calling this kind of teaching work "anticipation" because it is about developing the foreknowledge that I would need to take advantage of the opportunities that would arise to make mathematical connections as students worked in the time-speed-distance context. It is analogous to the work of lesson preparation described in chapter 4, but it extends over all of the lessons in which a particular context is used to frame students' work.

The work of creating a map of the mathematical terrain that I could anticipate as the focus of time-speed-distance problems extended over several years. From the first time I used the "*Mimi*" materials in 1983 until the year under consideration here, I investigated activities students might do with these materials to learn the mathematical content of the fifth-grade curriculum and how to make connections among ideas and skills. Here I give an overview of the possible connections I had learned to anticipate.

Connecting Rates of Speed with a Mathematical Model

If Mimi's speed is 7 knots (nautical miles per hour) and there are rocky shoals 50 nautical miles away in the direction the ship is traveling, the crew needs to figure out how much time there is to decide on a new direction and change course. The unknown here is a matter of hours and minutes. The mathematical problem is figuring out how to relate the numbers that we know to the ones that we want to know. In order to use mathematical tools to solve problems, the information that you know has to be organized in some way so that patterns and relationships can be found in it. When the patterns and relationships in information match patterns and relationships in numbers, this match can be used to construct what mathematicians call a "model" of the problem situation. In the domain of travel at a constant speed, for example, the phenomena are modeled by defining "speed" as the ratio between any distance and the time it takes to cover it. The model helps you to decide which operation to use to find out what you want to know—the "solution" to the problem. The particular piece of mathematics used most to find unknown information in these kinds of problem contexts is the operation of division.

I anticipated that working with time, speed, and distance would mean getting into a domain where fractions, multiplication and division, and functions all reside along with rate and ratio. Besides working with the internal relationships among mathematical ideas in this domain (for example, the relationship between division and fractions), I also figured that students would need to connect the mathematics to the "real world" constraints on measuring time and distance. They would need to link their familiarity with travel on land to the less familiar domain of travel on the water, where the conventions and constraints of measurement are different. I anticipated that students would be confronting a new kind of quantity in using numbers to talk about speed. Because speed is about the relationship between distance covered and time traveled, it is not quantifiable in the same way as miles or seconds or feet or hours.[7] Quantities of time are measures of seconds or minutes or hours. Quantities of distance are measures of feet or yards or miles. Quantities of speed are a different kind of number altogether because the numbers we associate with speed are not about counting but about *relating* two kinds of quantities, distance and time. This makes "speed numbers" more abstract than "time numbers" or "distance numbers." A quantity like "7 miles per hour" cannot be understood in a problem context apart from a relationship between a particular number of miles and a particular number of hours, and yet, as a rate, it does not imply a journey of a particular time or distance. This dictates both the kinds of problems that can be posed in this context and the mathematics that must be engaged to solve them.

Connecting Addition, Subtraction, Multiplication, and Division

If my students were going to study math with time, speed, and distance problems, I would have to make it possible for them to investigate the relationship between two different perspectives on the problems. They would need to move back and forth between a *mathematical* frame in which numbers are related according to certain constraints and a *navigational* frame in which quantities like time and distance are related according to their own set of constraints. In the navigational frame, we would be trying to figure out an unknown time or an unknown distance, while in the number frame we would be finding the result of a division or multiplication. We would be referring to actual travel, and yet we would be assuming that the ship is always going at a constant speed in the same direction. (This is more "realistic" on a ship than in a car.) We would be trying to figure out what operation (add, subtract, multiply, divide, or some combination) to do with the numbers using a strategy associated with the information given in the problem.

Given the mathematical levels at which fifth graders function, I figured out that I would need to make it possible for them to study division if they were going to work with rates of speed. Dividing is related in fundamental ways to both multiplying and subtracting, and so students would have to study those operations as well, and how they could connect to dividing. I laid out for myself what the relationships among the operations were so I could bring them into my teaching when appropriate. In any operation, two numbers are given and the third is to be determined. One of the given numbers "operates" on the other to produce a new number. Addition and subtraction, and multiplication and division, are pairs of "inverse" operations because of the special relationship they have with one another in these "triples." For example:

$$5 + 4 = 9 \qquad\qquad 4 \times 5 = 20$$
$$9 - 4 = 5 \quad \text{and} \quad 20 \div 5 = 4$$
$$9 - 5 = 4 \qquad\qquad 20 \div 4 = 5$$

Another kind of relationship exists between addition and multiplication, and between subtraction and division. Multiplication can be accomplished by repeated addition of equal quantities (as we saw in chapter 4) and division can similarly be accomplished by repeated subtraction of equal quantities. For example:

$24 \div 6 = 4$ or "how many groups of
6 are in 24?"

can also mean, "how many times can I take a group of 6 out of 14"

or:

$$
\begin{array}{rl}
24 & \\
\underline{-6} & \text{One time} \\
18 & \\
\underline{-6} & \text{Two times} \\
12 & \\
\underline{-6} & \text{Three times} \\
6 & \\
\underline{-6} & \text{Four times} \\
0 &
\end{array}
$$

In the problem context of time-speed-distance relationships, studying these inverse relationships would be occurring as students tried to figure out how long a journey would take at a given speed or how far a ship would go at a given speed.

Connecting Division, Remainders, and Fractions

There is another much more messy but essentially important mathematical idea that I anticipated would need to be engaged in our teaching and studying work because the operation of division is key to working out time-speed-distance relationships. It has to do with what kind of number you get as an "answer" when you do division. In addition, subtraction, and multiplication, if the given numbers are whole numbers, the result of the operation will also be a whole number.[8] In division, the new number could be a whole number, but it is not always a whole number. There are two things that can happen when we divide; either the division "comes out even," or it does not. The division comes out even when the number to be divided is a multiple of the divisor. In this case, it is easy to find the answer to a division by multiplying. For example, to "divide" 24 by 6, you can work out what number multiplied by 6 will give you 24. But this approach to doing division is less straightforward when the division does not "come out even." For example, there is no whole number that you can multiply by 6 to get 26. If you try to do the division by repeatedly "taking away" or subtracting groups of 6 from 26, you will be left with "2," and in a practical problem-solving context, this means figuring out "2 what?" Miles? Hours? Minutes? A variation on this challenge, even more messy, arises when you need to divide a smaller number by a larger one. For example, if you wanted to divide 1 by 6, there is no whole number multiplied by 1 that would yield a product of 6. In both of these cases (26 divided by 6, and 1 divided by 6) you need to use fractions to find the number to multiply by 6. Doing division therefore means inventing/learning about this new kind of number, which mathematicians call "rational" because it involves a ratio.

By doing this anticipatory work, I recognized that I could connect the problem context of travel on the sea to the study of several topics in the fifth-grade curriculum. I could see that there was a whole set of connected ideas here, all of which we would be confronting at once. If I could deftly move around in this web of connected ideas, I could have students working at different levels on the same problem. Some would be using addition and subtraction where others would be using multiplication and division. Some would be trying to make sense of the differences in fractions and decimal notations, and figuring out how to represent the "leftover" would challenge others. If I could use the whole-class discussions to keep all of these ideas on the table, students would get some sense of the whole territory, even if they did not learn to operate with facility in all parts of it.

Teaching This Mathematics to This Class

On October 23, I watched episode 2 of "The Voyage of the *Mimi*" on video with my class. In this episode, the captain is charting the course for the day, and he explains something of what he is doing to his ten-year-old grandson. In the time left after the class viewed the video, I posed a question for informal discussion using the same form as the captain had used in the video. My problem used different numbers: "If *Mimi*'s speed is ten nautical miles per hour, how long will it take for the ship to go *two* nautical miles?" (In the video, the question had been how long to go five nautical miles.) I did not demonstrate any procedure for figuring it out, and I tried to effect a very low-key interactive atmosphere so that students would feel safe saying whatever they thought about the problem. I did reiterate an explanation from the video: that "nautical miles" were a measure of distance used on the sea, and that they were roughly equivalent to miles on land, but not exactly the same distance. "Knots" is also a term used in the video, and I reviewed the captain's explanation of how it was used to mean "nautical miles per hour."

Learning What Students Know and Can Do

In my journal after the October 23 lesson, I reflected on the mathematics that was elicited in some of the students' responses in this initial exploration of their thinking:

Monday, October 23

*After watching part of episode 2, I posed
the problem:
If ~~speed is~~ Mimi's speed is
10 nautical miles per hour (knots)
   will it take
how long ^ to go 2 nautical miles?*

*Dorota—50 minutes—explains something
   about 100 ÷ 2
others—5 miles = ½ hr
   2½ miles = 15 min.*

*Ivan used something like this
to estimate: 10 minutes
then Catherine did a messy
   bit of reasoning which
   included 5 is half of 10
   so for the "extra" five minutes
   in 15 minutes (10 + 5)
   she added on another mile →
      3 miles in 15 minutes*

*Shahroukh did the calculation: 10 ÷ 2 is 5,
   one-fifth of 60 minutes is 12 or something
   like that.*

I also reflected about students' social engagement as it related to their capacity to explore mathematics in the context of the problem I had posed.

> *I think what Ivan said was a response/challenge*
> *to Dorota's 50 minutes: he said it had to be*
> *less than that because in ½ hr it could go*
> *5 miles and we only were looking for 2 miles.*
>
> *Ivan's contribution here is interesting*
> *because he thinks it is legitimate ⓐ to challenge*
> * *Dorota's answer (i.e., he doesn't only think*
> * *of that as the teacher's job) and ⓑ to*
> * *reason about why her answer must be*
> *wrong in an approximating sort of way*
> *(rather than seeing the work of*
> *doing math in school as only coming up with*
> *right answers).*
>
> *I wonder through it all about Shahroukh,*
> *how confirmed was he in the idea that his*
> *answer + his way of thinking about this was*
> *right. I wondered if he was thinking: "Why is*
> *this teacher entertaining all these other ideas*
> *when I have clearly answered the question?"*
> *or "why doesn't she tell them that they are*
> *wrong and/or show them how to do it my way?"*

I was focusing here both on the students' relationship with the mathematics and the kinds of relationships with one another that this problem-solving context would be able to support. I commented on how Ivan used the context to challenge an assertion made by Dorota. I wondered about Shahroukh's attitude toward my working with other students once he was satisfied that he had the correct answer, wondering how I could use this context to open him up to multiple ways of thinking. Both the mathematical responses and the social responses in this first class gave me some initial background for thinking about how I was going to use the time-speed-distance context to teach and what my students needed to study in this unit. I listened to their informal speculations to gain information that would help me to formulate problems that would stretch their thinking in new ways.

The problems I assigned in the next lesson would be the basis for beginning to study the mathematical relationships entailed in finding out how long a journey will take when you know the speed and the distance to be traveled. The first problem I posed followed the form of the problem that the captain solved in the video. But I also posed a problem that would involve students in thinking about rates and ratios as well as computing a particular time, given speed and distance.

> Monday, October 23
>
> 1. If the Mimi travels 60 nautical miles at a speed of 5 knots, how long will the journey take?
>
> 2. If Mimi travels at a speed of 8 knots, will the journey take more or less time?

In choosing this form for the Problem of the Day, I wanted to build on the context and also get students thinking about relationships among mathematical ideas. I did not ask them to find out exactly how long it would take if the speed was 8 knots (part 2) because I wanted to get a sense of their comprehension of rate, without challenging their computational skills. Sixty miles does not evenly divide into eight segments. I was hoping they would not get distracted by trying to do the computation if the task could be completed without it, but I was also interested to see if anyone would tackle it and how they would go about it. The two problems together would give me additional information about my students that I could use to start working with this class on the web of ideas I had prepared to teach them.

Finding a Usable, Durable Representation to Carry Ideas Across Lessons

In chapter 4, we saw some of the problems entailed in establishing a culture in which students would engage in sense-making as an element of their mathematical studies. The teaching described in that chapter needed to be done across every problem context, across every interaction, throughout the whole year. Within particular problem contexts, I needed to add context-specific tools to the learning environment that students could use to support particular kinds of "sense-making." After the lesson in which we worked on the two problems above, I wrote in my journal about a decision I made about how to do this as I watched students and listened to them talk, and considered something their other teacher had told me about them:

> *I decided in the midst of the class to make the <u>diagram</u>,*
> *partly based on what Thom said yesterday about how*
> *their knowledge of division was "fragile." Only Shahroukh*
> *solved the problem, eventually, by dividing 60 by 5 to get 12.*
> *There were several other strategies making very*
> *good use of the diagram. Now I wonder whether they will*
> *draw diagrams on their own.*

The "diagram" I referred to in this journal excerpt looked like this:

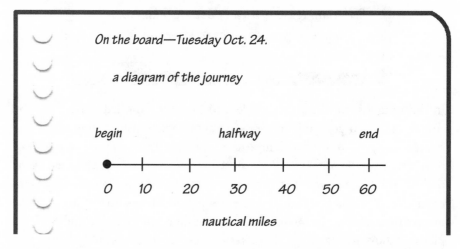

> *On the board—Tuesday Oct. 24.*
>
> *a diagram of the journey*
>
> begin   halfway   end
>
> 0   10   20   30   40   50   60
>
> *nautical miles*

I intended this diagram to be a tool for relating what we were doing with the numbers (multiplying or dividing, adding or subtracting) with the conditions given in the problem context (the speed of the ship, how far it needed to go, how long it would take). As the lessons on time-speed-distance unfolded, the diagram had another use besides mathematical sense-making at an individual level. It became a means of communicating about what someone was assuming, a representation of our shared understanding of the complicated web of ideas under consideration. Different students could use this tool to "tap in" to mathematical relationships at different levels. It could be displayed in students' notebooks and on the chalkboard as a way of keeping track of all of the mathematical elements in the solution of a problem. It served as a bridge[9] between the words, symbols, and ideas associated with rate and ratio, and the vivid image that we had seen on the video of the sailing ship making its way through the waves.

Teaching this representation was not something that I had planned on in advance. It was not derived from the video or the print materials that came with the curriculum guide, but it seemed like something that this class needed in order to proceed with productive activities in the context of these problems.[10] In making a diagram, which I called a "journey line," as a spur-of-the-moment aid to progress, I partially "mathematized" the real situation of the ship on the water as I thought the problem through together with my students.[11] I had not ever used this tool before, and so I was not sure what would happen when students encountered it. I did not direct students in how to make a journey line or require that it must be used in these problems at this point. I wanted to see what students would do with the journey line independent of my suggestions: how they would use it, modify it, and relate it to different kinds of conditions and calculations.

As we discussed the problem of the *Mimi* sailing 5 nautical miles per hour for 12 hours, I elaborated the diagram, linking miles and hours at several points along the way. I recorded the results of that elaboration in my journal:

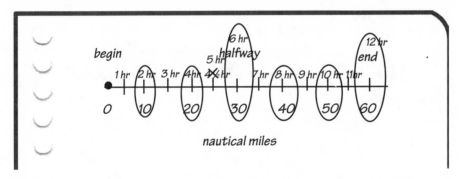

In the "journey line" for this problem, I was trying to demonstrate the meaning of rate, showing graphically how the distance changes *in relation to* the time. I wanted to show how multiplication and division, addition and subtraction were all connected in the time-speed-distance problem context. I was deliberately consistent in labeling hours above the line and miles below but I had not taken account of an important convention in the way we express speed. Speed is conventionally expressed as *miles per hour* (miles over hours), but the fractions suggested by my diagram where the hours were on top (i.e., $\frac{2}{10}$ $\frac{4}{20}$ $\frac{6}{30}$ $\frac{8}{40}$ $\frac{10}{50}$ $\frac{12}{60}$) expressed the rate of speed as *hours per miles*.

On the first day I presented it, several students made their own version of the journey line in their notebooks. We might say they "customized" the vehicle that I had presented them with. Some put hours on top of the line and miles under it, as I had. For example, Dorota:

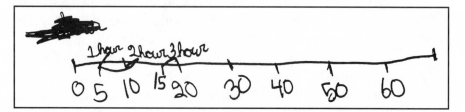

and Ellie:

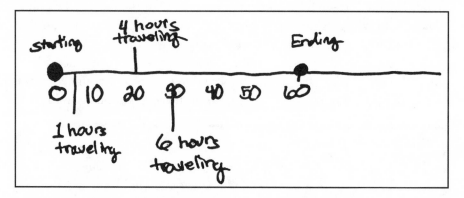

Some, like Candice:

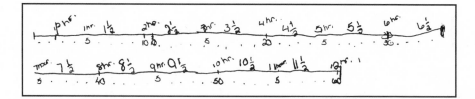

and Jumanah:

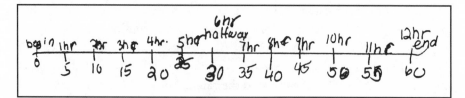

had more detail in their diagrams.

And others, like Eddie, had less:

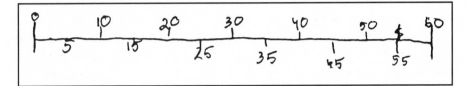

Charlotte put both miles and hours below the line:

and Richard only labeled intervals of 5 between 0 and 60.

These variations of what I wrote on the board suggest that in making their representations, students were negotiating between my effort at mathematizing the situation and their own thinking about it. Most were not yet using the diagram to figure out the relationships in the problem.

The journey line served over several lessons as a useful tool for communication, but it also illustrates a task of teaching that occurs across lessons when such shared use becomes common. Asking students to put their own representation of the journey line in their notebooks gave me some information about their capacities for using and interpreting the mathematics of rate. But it also presented me with several new teaching problems to solve. How would we use this diagram as a communications tool if the ways in which students represented time and distance on the journey line were not consistent? How could I organize our work so that expertise in using this kind of tool could be shared among class members, rather than having them rely entirely on me as the single most experienced model-maker? If I focused on consistency, it would be harder to make use of the good ideas that students brought to the work. If I allowed all the possible variations students could come up with, it would be hard to assess their understanding and it would make sense-making communications among students more difficult. This became a problem further into the unit when the vehicle in question in the Problem of the Day was traveling for less than one whole hour at a time. In these kinds of problems, a representation in which miles are "on top" and hours are "on the bottom" is much simpler to manipulate than the other way around. I would need to make some decisions along the way about how to manage these dilemmas. I would need to structure our work so that I could find out whether students were actually modeling the situations in the problem or joining in to a community practice without making that connection. This was a teaching problem that would extend over several lessons.

Choosing Problems to Move Us into New Mathematics

Once I had tentatively settled on a form for the problems we would work on, I needed to figure out just which numbers to put in the problems to challenge students but still make the work accessible to everyone. All of our work on October 23 had been around the first part of the problem. Because I spent so much time during the lesson developing the journey line to represent the information in the first part of this problem, there had been no time to publicly reflect on the second part. Given my observations of how variously students used the journey line as they worked independently on the first part of the problem, I wondered after class if I should go back there the next day, work on part 2, or start with entirely new numbers.

When I looked at their notebooks, I saw that only two students, Anthony and Shahroukh, had written straightforward assertions that the journey would be shorter at a speed of 8 knots because the ship was going faster. Charlotte was the only student who actually tried to figure out precisely how long it would take the *Mimi* to go 60 nautical miles at 8 knots. Because she attempted work that was beyond what I had anticipated, I was able to use her thinking to figure out what would happen if others tried to do these kinds of problems. At first glance, I saw that she had used the journey line for the first part of the problem, but she only did calculations for part 2. Because Charlotte ventured into mathematical territory that was new for her (and would be new for everyone else in the class as well) she gave me a resource for preparing to cope with the difficulties students would have in future lessons.

oct 24

1. If the ~~mmm~~ mimi travels 60
~~nautical miles~~ ~~kilometers~~ at a speed of 5
nautical miles ~~knots~~ ~~knots~~ per hour, how long
will the journey take?
2. If its speed increases to 8 nau-tical ~~knots~~ mile per hour.
will the time be longer or shorter?
EXPLAIN

Defination
A krot is one
nautical mile per
hour. Equal to ap-
proximately
6076 ft. A land
mile is 5280 ft

EXPERIMENTS

60 ÷ 5 = 12 hours

$\frac{60}{15}$

45
9

30
10

12
5
60

7 R4.
8)60

592
6076
5280
$\overline{796}$

6000
5000
1000

ROUND TO NEAREST
100 is 800

8
9/12

60
12

8
8
64

60 N.M. ÷ 5 NM per hour = 12 hours for the journey.
7 40 min journey.

56   8)60

REASONING

① If the mimi ~~travels~~ 60 nautical
miles at a speed of 5 nautical
miles per hour, The journey will take
12 hours because 60 ÷ 5 = 12 hours.

0 | 10 | 20 | 30 | 40 | 50 | 60 end-ing
Beg Beginning
traveled traveled 5 hours 7 hours 9 hours 11 hours 12 hours
1 hour. 2 hours

      Using the diagram I made I
can show you that it is 12 hours to
completed the journey. Every 5 miles
it is 1 hour completed. To get to
60 miles, you have to take 12
hours if you are traveling at a
pace of 5 nautical ~~you~~ miles.

② If the mimi travels 8 nautical miles per hour, and you
are going 60 miles. The answer
then is 7 hours and 40 minutes
to completed the journey. I
think this because 60 ÷ 8 = 7 R4.
Each remainder is 10 minutes.
This gives you the answer.

Using student work like this to figure out what kinds of problems to pose in future lessons was something I did often across the year. Analyzing what one student did gives me a concrete ten-year-old's perspective on what needs to be studied and how we might study it. Charlotte's interpretation of the remainder in part 2 of the problem signaled a trouble spot that I knew other students would run into if they tried to do this division. Looking at what Charlotte did to figure out how long it would take for the *Mimi* to go 60 nautical miles at 8 knots gave me a view of the mathematical horizon,[12] and some signposts directing me toward the mathematics I wanted to teach.

The work that I did using Charlotte's solution as an inspiration involved me in my own studies of the mathematics of time, speed, and distance relationships and how they are expressed in terms of division and fractions. In what follows here, I recount the kind of thinking that I did to prepare myself to teach not one lesson, but a whole series of related lessons on a set of related topics. By unpacking the problems that Charlotte faced when she tried to figure out the meaning of the remainder, I would be able to make up several days' work for my students. I would not make up the daily problems all at once, but I would take the material a little at a time and see how far we could get with it. The work I am about to describe not only prepared me for a series of lessons in this problem context, but it also prepared me to work in the other problem contexts that I would use to teach fractions, division, rate, and ratio.

Figuring out Where Students Will Have Difficulty, and Why

Charlotte had simply divided 60 by 5 to figure out part 1 of the problem to find out how long it would take the *Mimi* to go 60 nautical miles at 5 knots. After she did this computation, she explained the connection between what she did with the numbers and the problem by using the journey line. Instead of using the journey line to guide her computation, she used it as a kind of "proof" or "explanation" of the connection between the computation she had done and the conditions of the problem:

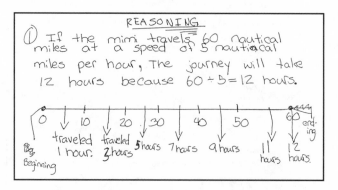

Although her diagram is quite similar to the one I put on the board, she claims it as her own tool when she writes her "reasoning." She says, "Using the diagram I made, I can show you that it is 12 hours to completed [sic] the journey."

> Using the diagram I made I can show you that it is 12 hours to completed the journey. Every 5 miles it is 1 hour completed. To get to 60 miles, you have to take 12 hours if you are traveling at a pace of 5 nautical ~~you~~ miles.

Charlotte's solution helped me to think about how to guide the other students in the class in their use of the journey line. What made sense to her was to do the computation and then think about what it meant by using the diagram. In my future interactions with the class, I could follow her lead and speak about the journey line as an explanation and as a way of judging whether a particular computation makes sense as a strategy for solving the problem.

Having successfully expressed her arithmetic-based solution in terms of her diagram, Charlotte followed the same computational strategy to tackle part 2 of the problem.

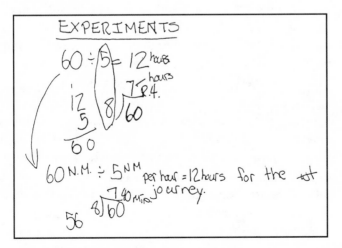

But although she used the journey line to justify her solution to the first part of the problem, she only did calculations for part 2. Perhaps this was because she ran out of time or because the work she did on part 1 confirmed her thinking that this was a legitimate approach. It seemed that she had "studied" how this sort of problem worked mathematically in part 1, and applied what she had learned to the second part. Because of the numbers involved, she ran into an additional challenge—the remainder—and she did not use the diagram to confront it in a sensible manner.

In writing her "reasoning" for part 2, Charlotte simply asserts, "Each remainder is 10 minutes."

Figuring out what she might have done to arrive at that conclusion helped me to understand what and how I would need to teach if students were going to learn to interpret remainders appropriately.

Using the problem context to give meaning to the remainder is something I would want everyone in the class to be disposed and able to do. In order to do this, they would need to study the relationship between division and fractions. Charlotte does not give any indication of why she thinks "each remainder is 10 minutes." I wondered if her idea about this may have been derived from the diagram she made for part 1 of the problem, and how that diagram might be employed to challenge her mistaken conclusion. To make sense here, she (and everyone else) would need to investigate both fractions of a mile and fractions of an hour and how they are connected to rate expressed as "miles per hour." I investigated how I could use the journey line to teach this material in the context of time-speed-distance relationships.

Charlotte's work made a particular mathematical question prominent: What does the "remainder 4" mean when you are dividing 60 *miles* by 8 *nautical miles per hour*? I had not expected students to do this calculation on October 28, but I wanted them to be able to do it in the future and to interpret the remainder in a sensible way. So I unpacked the mathematics in Charlotte's work and used it to prepare future lessons.

I made notes for myself to show that in the situation that is posed in part 2 of the problem (p. 191), I could use multiplication or repeated addition to figure out that at a speed of 8 knots, the ship would travel 8 miles in an hour. It would go 8 + 8 or 16 miles in 2 hours, 8 + 8 + 8 or 24 miles in 3 hours, and so on, up to 56 miles in 7 hours. In another hour, at the same speed, the ship would go 8 times 8 or <u>64</u> miles. But the problem says it only goes <u>60</u> miles. So before getting into remainders, I would stop at 7 hours. At that point, written as a formal ratio, the relationship between the speed as given (8 knots) and the bulk of the journey (56 miles) would look like this:

$$\frac{8 \text{ nautical miles}}{1 \text{ hour}} = \frac{56 \text{ nautical miles}}{7 \text{ hours}}$$

The statement of the ratio suggests the division of 56 by 7. Although the form is familiar it suggests some of the potential difficulties that would be involved in linking the information given in the problem (a journey of 60 miles) to the numerical relationship stated in the equivalence between $\frac{8}{1}$ and $\frac{56}{7}$. What the familiar form says is that the ratio of 8 to 1 is the same as (or equal to) the ratio of 56 to 7. This equality holds for these ratios, even though the left side of this equation represents a journey of only 1 hour and covers 8 miles, while the right side represents a journey of 7 hours and covers 56 miles. The "constant" here is the ship's speed, which stays the same over the whole journey but is a more abstract number than the numbers that measure time and distance.

Figuring Out How to Teach so Students Can Get out of Difficulty

So how might I go from here to thinking about how to teach students what to do with that "remainder 4"? I remind myself that the condition given in the problem is that the ship travels 60 miles, not 56. It will take longer than 7 hours to make this journey, but how much longer? To complete a journey of 60 miles, the ship needs to go 4 more miles, and we know it travels 8 miles in an hour. Intuitively, we can imagine that the rest of the journey will take half an hour. But Charlotte does not think about the problem in this way. Having used the conventional algorithm to divide in her earlier work, and having shown herself that this would lead to a sensible solution by connecting what she did with the journey line, she uses that strategy again and is confronted with a remainder. Now she has a new problem: How is she to give meaning to "R.4" in this problem situation?[13]

After the hour, the next smallest familiar unit of measure in the domain of time is the minute, so the question becomes, how many minutes more than 7 hours does it take to go the final 4 miles? In order to figure that out, I need to recall that there are 60 minutes in an hour. When Charlotte claimed that "each remainder is ten minutes" she was working with a ratio. Her remainder was "four," and she said every "one" was related to "ten." In terms of a ratio, she was claiming:

$$\frac{1 \text{ remainder}}{10 \text{ minutes}} = \frac{4 \text{ remainders}}{40 \text{ minutes}}$$

Charlotte stopped short of making the connections that would have suggested a full understanding of how division was related to rate and ratio in the domain of time, speed, and distance. Her work allowed her to correctly answer the question that was asked in the problem in the sense that it produced the conclusion that the ship travels a shorter distance if its speed is increased. But when she went into less familiar territory, she moved away from making sense in terms of the "givens" in the problem.

What Charlotte wrote about part 1 of the problem suggested to me that more work with the journey line might help students to grapple with rate, ratio, and division. On such a line, at regular intervals, quantities of time could be represented in relation to quantities of distance, maintaining a series of equivalent ratios to represent the constant speed across the journey. Using the referent of the line, maybe students could talk both about the journey as a concrete situation and about the relationships among the numbers they were manipulating.[14] Translating what Charlotte may have been thinking into graphic terms, we can see where the "remainder" shows up on the journey line:

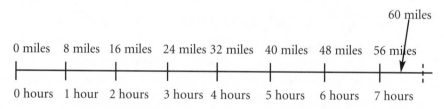

As we focus on the segment of this "journey line" that represents the seventh hour of the journey, we can figure out more precisely how long it will take to go 60 miles by dividing that hour into 10-minute subsections.

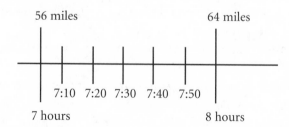

If Charlotte's assertion that "each remainder is worth ten" were correct, then 60 miles would need to be associated with 7 hours and 40 minutes. What *is* the "remainder 4" if not 4 blocks of 10 minutes? What does it *mean* to divide 60 miles by 8 miles per hour? The "answer" is going to be some amount of time—the whole number part of the answer is 7 hours, so it seems reasonable that the leftover part or the "remainder" will be some fraction of an hour. But if we reason that 7 hours uses up 56 of the 60 miles that we have to travel, we see that what we have left is 4 *miles, not 4 units of time.*

I wrote in my journal, reflecting on these matters as a basis for making up future problems. I tried using other possible numbers for distance and speed:

> There are two ways to have a remainder—
> leftover time (for which you need to figure out
> distance) and leftover distance (for which you
> need to figure out time). Dealing with the
> remainder is so clearly a matter of
> proportional reasoning!
>
> > Going 180 naut. miles at 8 knots
> > > means you have leftover <u>distance</u>
> > > 160 naut. miles would be "easy" ➜ 20 hrs.
> > > another 16 ➜ 20 hrs.
> > > but then there are 4 <u>more</u>.
> > > here the term <u>knots</u> gets us in trouble:
> > If the meaning "8 nautical miles per hour"
> > is articulated, it seems much easier to see
> > how you'd need <u>half</u> an hour to go those
> > extra four miles.

Reworking Charlotte's ratio, in which she was attempting to give meaning to the remainder in terms of the problem situation, we can give meaning to the "R.4" by reference to what we know about the speed of the ship:

$$\frac{8 \text{ miles}}{60 \text{ minutes}} = \frac{4 \text{ miles}}{30 \text{ minutes}}$$

Examining the mathematics involved in Charlotte's assertion led me to think that I should pose problems that would engage students with these ideas. Although Charlotte may have been ahead of everyone else in confronting the problem of giving meaning to the remainder, I could use her work to clue me in to the kinds of things other students might do and what they should be able to do. The challenge for me would be to structure the learning environment so that neither Charlotte nor anyone else would be satisfied with an assertion about the remainder like the one Charlotte ventured without returning to the constraints of the problem situation to see if it fits.

My use of Charlotte's mathematics illustrates a piece of teaching work that occurs across the boundaries of lessons. Even though her work was unique in the class, it foreshadowed something I wanted to teach and gave me some clues about how to teach it. I could learn something from this kind of investigation about what and how to teach both Charlotte and the rest of the class about multiplication, division, and fractions within a unit on time, speed, and distance relationships. In order to make a link between the way Charlotte thought about the "remainder" and the mathematics I wanted to teach, I needed to do some unpacking of the problem in relation to what she did with it. I needed to understated why the remainders were not worth 10 minutes in the second part of the problem although they would have been in the first part. This would prepare me to teach both Charlotte and any other student who made similar kinds of assertions.

Moving Ideas Through Time with Problems

The progression of problems that I devised following this reflective analysis began with a problem that had no "leftovers."

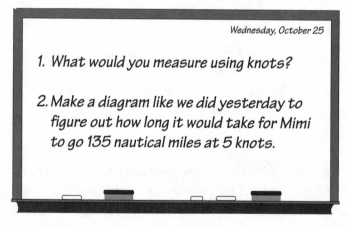

Wednesday, October 25

1. What would you measure using knots?

2. Make a diagram like we did yesterday to figure out how long it would take for Mimi to go 135 nautical miles at 5 knots.

Instead of going directly into fractions of hours and fractions of miles, I gave students problems they could use to study how multiples of time would relate to multiples of miles. I also wanted to get some sort of a read on how they were thinking about the term "knots" before going on to this new material. If they were not translating that term into "nautical miles per hour" I would have to provide some opportunities for them to practice using that terminology before embarking on how to interpret the "leftovers." The next problem engaged them with similar work:

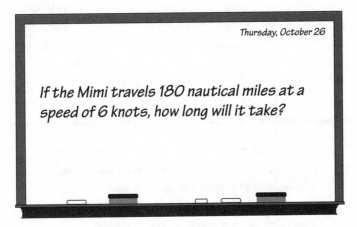

Two days after I reflected on the big ideas in Charlotte's work, I challenged the whole class with a problem that would not "come out even." I changed the speed in the problem from the day before only slightly, to 8 knots. I kept the distance the same to see if any students would use "6 knots" from the previous problem as a benchmark. If they did this, it would constrain their reasoning about the time it would take to go 8 knots, leading to the conclusion that it needed to be less than 30 hours, since the ship was going faster.

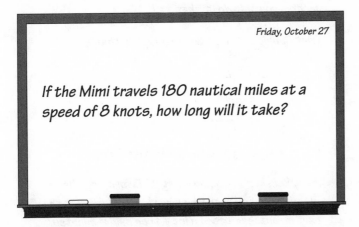

With this change in speed from 6 knots to 8 knots I was hoping that I could place everyone in the class in the same mathematical territory as Charlotte had been exploring in the switch from the first part of the problem to the second part of the problem on October 23 (p. 191). Dividing 180 by 6 did not leave any leftovers to interpret, but dividing 180 by 8 would not "come out even." The remainder would somehow need to be expressed as a period of time.

In my journal, I made some quick notes during class to help me remember what Candice, Shahroukh, Yasu, Ivan, Anthony, Tyrone, Connie, and Enoyat did with this problem. These students represented a wide range of responses and provided me with more mathematical signposts to help me guide the class's journey. I later returned to my notes and analyzed the mathematics in their work:

The "second" problem—the one that didn't come out even—was the first place where their algorithmic knowledge was pressed to see if it was undergirded by understanding: many kids seem to know the division algorithm, but not much of what it means.

Connie explained that she did 6

$$8\overline{)180} \begin{array}{r} 2 \\ \hline 180 \\ -16 \\ \hline 20 \end{array}$$

And I challenged her about how 2 turned into 20.

She couldn't explain & Dorota had had a similar road block—you just do it, that's all.

(But Connie did go on later to explain that

$$8\overline{)180} \begin{array}{r} 22 \\ \hline 180 \\ -16 \\ \hline 20 \\ -16 \\ \hline 4 \end{array}$$

meant ~~possibly~~ you could go another half-mile)

many kids kept on going + get 22.5 following the algorithm—i.e., Yasu who when I asked her what the .5 part meant, hesitated a lot + then said 5 minutes.
Charlotte & Anthony explained that the 16 was really 160, and so the 2 was really 20.

Ivan asserted that the "remainder 4" meant "4 minutes."

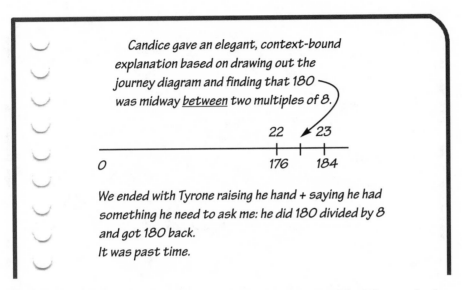

Candice gave an elegant, context-bound explanation based on drawing out the journey diagram and finding that 180 was midway <u>between</u> two multiples of 8.

We ended with Tyrone raising he hand + saying he had something he need to ask me: he did 180 divided by 8 and got 180 back.
It was past time.

After these analyses, I wrote some ideas in my journal for what to do the following week.

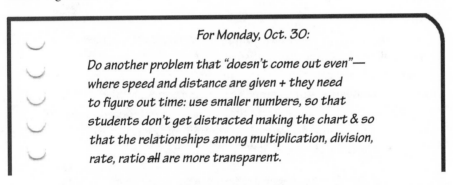

For Monday, Oct. 30:

Do another problem that "doesn't come out even"— where speed and distance are given + they need to figure out time: use smaller numbers, so that students don't get distracted making the chart & so that the relationships among multiplication, division, rate, ratio ~~all~~ are more transparent.

I then played around with some numbers to see how they would relate to the journey-line representation. I wanted to design a problem that would influence students to look to the journey line as a useful tool. I hoped to teach them, in this way, that making diagrams is a central aspect of mathematical practice.

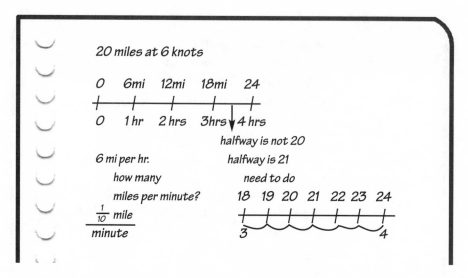

I chose 6 knots for the speed to remain consistent with what we had worked on already, but I made the distance a short one so that counting by sixes would not be a major preoccupation, thereby focusing work on what to do with the "leftover."

As I was investigating what would happen with the numbers in the problem, I realized that at a constant speed of 6 nautical miles per hour, the ship would go 1 nautical mile in 10 minutes, and ⅒ of a nautical mile each minute. This relationship seemed interesting to me, and so I included some reference to it in the way I wrote the problem on the board on Monday, just to see if anyone would go toward the domain of fractions using this problem in the same way I did.

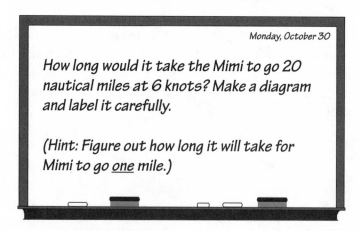

The student work I observed and heard over the course of their studies using these time-speed-distance problems led to a few days of lessons in which we focused only on time. We zoomed in on a particular challenge having to do with time: the change in perspective as one moves from hours to parts of an hour, and what happens to the numbers when parts of an hour are expressed in another unit of measure, namely, minutes.[15] This challenge, common to all kinds of measures, is an instance in which a big mathematical idea comes into play. In measuring length, the relevant units are miles, feet, inches, and so on; in volume, ounces, pints, quarts. The way these different kinds of units are related in each domain causes a counting problem. In the arena of time where we were working, a ship could travel for 5 hours, which is a simple multiple of 1 hour. The distance it covers in 5 hours would be a simple multiple of the distance it covers in 1 hour. If, however, the ship only travels for 15 minutes, we have a much more complicated situation. Fifteen minutes is 15 times *1 minute*. But in relation to *1 hour*, 15 minutes is a fraction: one-fourth of an hour. Instead of multiplying (by 15) we divide (by 4). The Problems of the Day I assigned at this point were intended to give students the opportunity to study this complication, which they would need to appreciate if we were to go any further in our work on time-speed-distance relationships. I began with having students translate whole hours into equivalent numbers of minutes, and then I moved on to simple fractions of an hour.

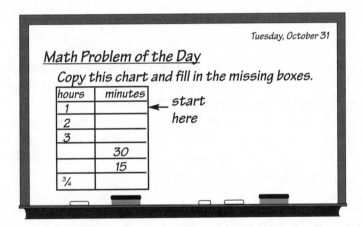

Finally, I added more complex fractions to the mix and invited students to "make up their own" equivalents.

We continued on this kind of work for two more days. We then switched contexts somewhat, investigating time-speed-distance relationships in automobile travel, where speeds are faster, making the numbers that have to be manipulated larger, and offering more occasions for encountering fractions of a mile and fractions of an hour. I described some of this work in chapter 2, and I will describe more of it in chapter 9, where I take up the teaching problem of covering the curriculum across the whole year.

Problems in Teaching in the Domain of Deliberately Connecting Content Across Lessons

In the case of teaching across time that I have investigated here, I address my teaching problems by using a common problem context (time-speed-distance relationships) and a common representation of connections among mathematical ideas (the "journey line"). I analyze where understanding and skill break down in one student's efforts to take on new mathematics and use that analysis to figure out what problems other students might encounter. Work in this domain of practice involves:

- creating graphic representations that enable students to make bridges from context to content;

- making connections between the context and the content that support students' reasoning about the use of arithmetic procedures;

- building a shared language for talking across lessons about ideas and standardizing the representation so it could be used in mathematical argument; and

- investigating student work to construct a foundation on which further teaching can be built.

Moving out from the lesson level makes it possible to see the problem-solving paths that are constructed across several days both in teaching decisions and in the mathematics that students are studying.

As with the elements of teaching working at the lesson level, practice is situated simultaneously in relationships with students and relationships with content. The notes that I made from day to day during the unit illustrate the interplay between assessing students' performances, reflecting on my own mathematical activities, and designing instructional strategies to get at specific mathematical topics. As planned activities played themselves out over time, investigations of mathematical relationships were dropped and picked up again over the course of several lessons. Students realigned themselves into different groups, changing both the mathematical and the social chemistry of their interactions. As I assessed their work and mine over the course of time, I learned more about the range and content of the knowledge and skills they brought to the study of rate and ratio.

Although problems are chosen and tasks assigned on a daily basis, the work in focus in this chapter involves devising and choosing problem contexts or themes for a class that will tie together a series of problems stretching over several days. Using contexts or themes to make connections is an iterative process of trying out activity settings, forms of problems, and tools.[16] Choosing a context or representation that will span over several lessons, like choosing a problem, is only the beginning. More pedagogically challenging is the problem of figuring out how to *use* a context, both to bring students in contact with the connected universe of important mathematical ideas that the problems posed make available and to make the contact that they have with those ideas productive of learning. Even if the problem contexts and Problems of the Day a teacher uses to teach are chosen by someone else—a curriculum designer or teaching team, for example—the teacher must work at figuring out how to use these resources. Unlike the curriculum developer, she is using them over time in a particular classroom, with a particular group of students, making a coherent program of study available by deciding how long to spend in any problem context and what aspects of the mathematics it engages to focus on. This element of teaching practice occurs at the boundaries between lessons, between interactions, and between topics.

Teaching to Cover the Curriculum

The curriculum I was expected to "cover" in my fifth-grade class was set by the school district within boundaries outlined in a state framework.[1] Teachers generally used two textbook series suggested by the district (Comprehensive School Mathematics Program and Scott, Foresman) as standards for determining what should be in the curriculum, even if they were not actually using the recommended textbooks.[2] With several years' experience as a fifth-grade teacher, I had a firmly fixed mental checklist of all the topics in the curriculum, and I was able to structure lessons to bring them into students' work. I was also able to take note of when required curriculum topics came up as a result of students' independent investigations. As I mentioned in chapter 1, I was expected to teach multiplication and division with "big numbers," division with numbers that "don't come out even," fractions beyond a half and a quarter—including comparing, adding, and subtracting them—fractions written as decimals, properties of basic geometric shapes, area and perimeter, and averages. The analysis in this chapter begins by looking at a series of lessons in the time-speed-distance unit to identify what topics were covered over time in students' work. I then go on to investigate what kinds of teaching actions get students connected with these topics. Along the way, I reconsider what it means to "cover" a topic when students study mathematics by working on problems.

Teaching to Cover Topics with Problems

At the beginning of each chapter of the Scott, Foresman text series that was used by other fifth-grade teachers in my school district, there was a "General Objectives Reference Chart." This chart listed each lesson, its associated objective, and the one or two pages in the students' text that a teacher would use for working on that objective.[3] Looking through the reference chart for topics that might identify what mathematics we were covering in the time-speed-distance lessons, I find some of the topics in the lessons at "Level 29," which has three chapters:

1 Meaning of Mixed Numbers

2 Adding and Subtracting of Mixed Numbers

3 Measuring Angles.

Each of these chapters contains several lessons. The topics of the lessons are indicated by their titles. For example in chapter 1, the lessons include:

Meaning of Mixed Numbers
- Mixed Numbers
- Mixed Numbers on the Number Line
- Using Mixed Numbers in Measurement
- Comparing Mixed Numbers: Baseball
- (Time out)
- Mixed Numbers and Improper Fractions
- (Keeping Skillful)
- Dividing to Find Mixed Numbers
- Changing Improper Fractions to Mixed Numbers
- Using the Remainder in Division Problems
- (Keeping Skillful)
- (MixoFracto Game)
- (Check Yourself [test]).

Using an expanded version of such a topics list, I investigated a continuous sequence of six lessons in the middle of the time-speed-distance unit to assess what topics were covered by student work.[4] The lessons occurred on November 2, 6, 8, 9, 13, and 14 and were chosen from the twenty lessons over which this unit occurred.[5] The inquiry focused on a sample of eight students out of the class of twenty-nine. Although I knew that these students were not always working independently, I used the single student as the unit of analysis, since I had to cover the same curriculum for every student. The sample included boys and girls, native and non-native English speakers, students who had been in the school since kindergarten and those who joined the class that year, students across the range of races and ethnicities represented in the class, and students who had a variety of different kinds of mathematical strengths and weaknesses. Working with a list of possible topics drawn from several fifth-grade textbooks, our state's curriculum guidelines, and the *Curriculum and Evaluation Standards for School Mathematics* from the National Council of Teachers of Mathematics, my research assistants categorized student work for the days whose content we were investigating.[6] To find evidence for what students were working on they consulted several kinds of records of what students were doing.[7] They looked at videos and transcripts of individual, small-group, and large-group work for each of the six hour-long lessons; all of the written work of the eight focal students; and observer's notes on these students. The data in tables 9.1 and 9.2 represent the findings of this investigation.

Table 9.1. Curriculum topics covered, ordered by theme.

Mathematical Content	Nov. 2	Nov. 6	Nov. 8	Nov. 9	Nov. 13	Nov. 14
Meaning of terms—miles per hour	•	•••	•			
Meaning of terms—knots				••		••
Symbolic notation—fractions	••			•	•	
Symbolic notation—equivalent notations				•••	•	•••
Symbolic notation—number words						••
Symbolic notation—remainders						
Concept of speed	••	••	•••	•	•	
Concept of rate/ratio	••	•••••	•••	•••	•	••
Concept of irrational #s & repeating dec.						
Concept of fractions			•	•	•	••
Concept of mixed numbers				•••		•
Number sense—distributive law	•••			••	•	
Number sense—community		•		•••	•••	••
Number sense—associativity		•••		•••	•••	
Operations—relationship b/w mult. & div.		•	•	•	•	
Operations—mult. as repeated addition		••		•	•	
Operations—division as partitioning		•••				
Operations—meaning of a remainder						
Operations—practicing comp. w/whole #s						
Operations—practicing comp. w/mixed #s						

Mathematical Process	Nov. 2	Nov. 6	Nov. 8	Nov. 9	Nov. 13	Nov. 14
Reasoning about the appropriate operation	••••	••	•••	•••	••	•••
Making equivalent ratios for the same rate			•••	•••		•••
Making sense of patterns—organizing data	••			••	•••	•••
Associating numbers with quantities				•••	•••	•••
Trial & error/successive approximation	•••	••	•		•	•••
Estimation	•••	••	•••	•••	••	••
Converting (miles, feet, hours, minutes…)			••	•••	•	•••
Making/using diagrams			••	••	••	••
Proving that a conjecture is wrong					••••••	
Interpreting/evaluating soln. to a problem					••	
Reasoning-implications of assumptions			•	••	••	
Convincing other people						
Using semantic structure w/new conditions					••	•

Table 9.2. Curriculum topics covered, ordered by range of student activity.

Mathematical content/process	Nov. 2	Nov. 6	Nov. 8	Nov. 9	Nov. 13	Nov. 14
Associating numbers with quantities	⋮	⦙	⋮	⋮	:	
Concepts of rate/ratio	⋮	⦙	⋮	⋮		
Concept of speed	⋮	⦙	⋮	:·:		
Converting (miles, feet, hours, minutes...)	:		⋮	:	⋮	⋮
Estimation	⦙		·	⋮	⦙	⋮
Making/using diagrams	:	⦙	⋮	⋮	⦙⦙⦙	⋮
Making equivalent ratios for the same rate	⦙		⦙	⦙:	⦙	
Making sense of patterns—organizing data	·			·		
Meaning of terms—knots	·				·	
Operations—relationship b/w mult. & div.	:	·	:	:	:	::
Reasoning about the appropriate operation	:	·	·	·	·	
Symbolic notation—equivalent notations	·		·	:	·	·
Convincing other people					·	
Interpreting/evaluating soln. to a problem		·	·	·	·	
Meaning of terms—miles per hour	:	·	·:	:	·:	·
Operations—meaning of a remainder		·		·		
Operations—mult. as repeated addition	·	⦙	·	:		⦙:
Reasoning—implications of assumptions	·	·		·	·	⋮
Concept of mixed numbers	:			:		
Operations—practicing comp. w/mixed #s				·		·
Concept of fractions		:		·	·	·
Trial & error/successive approximation				·		
Number sense—distributive law				·	·	
Operations—practicing comp. w/whole #s				·		·
Proving that a conjecture is wrong				·	·	
Symbolic notation—fractions				·		
Symbolic notation—number words	·		·	·		·
Symbolic notation—remainders	·		·			
Number sense—associativity		:		·		⋮
Number sense—commutativity	·	⦙	·	·	·	
Using semantic structure w/new conditions		·	·	·		·
Concept of irrational #s & repeating dec.	·	·		··	⋮	⋮

In the first table, the topics of possible study are listed as they might be ordered in a textbook or a curriculum framework. In the second table, the same set of topics is rearranged to display the order in which topics came up in students' work in the course of the time-speed-distance lessons. In both tables, each dot represents a piece of evidence that one of the eight focal students was working on that topic.

These representations of the topics covered in students' work reveal several points that are fundamental to understanding teaching to cover the curriculum using problems:

- given the same Problem of the Day, different students are working on different topics;

- some topics are engaged by several students, while others may be engaged by only one student;

- some students stay with a topic over time, and others jump around among many topics;

- the range of topics under study by members of the class increases over time;

- there is a mixture of engagement with conceptual content and procedures every day.

What this analysis reveals is that the teacher using problems can not simply work with one topic at a time and teach topics one after another. As we saw in chapter 3, connecting students with content is a fundamental element of the work of teaching. In order to monitor student work and promote learning for everyone in the class within a problem context, the teacher must be simultaneously engaged with several topics in each lesson. Both students and teacher are involved at different levels of multiple conceptual hierarchies, moving back and forth between big ideas and the facts and procedures that logically flow from them.

Viewing the Teaching of Topics Through Wide-Angle Lenses

With these findings in mind, I broadened the field of my analysis to include all of the lessons in the whole year. I used the lists of what I wanted to teach that I had made at the beginning of the year retrospectively to see what I had covered and how. Based on evidence in my journal I first made a simple chart to show how many weeks we spent working in each problem context:

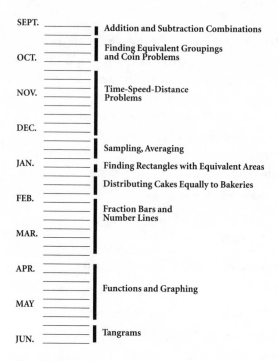

A close look at this chart reveals a basic component of teaching work entailed in covering the curriculum in a classroom: negotiating between the mathematics to be taught and studied and the vagaries of the school calendar. I found that across the year, the amount of time we spent in any single problem context varied in length depending on the kind of mathematical progress we were making as well as on the calendar. The thematic "breaks" almost always happened when there was some kind of school holiday. For example, I commented in my journal that I thought we could have spent more time on "sampling and averaging," from a mathematical perspective, but because the winter vacation came at the end of December that unit got cut short. Four new students entered our class in the new calendar year, so we began a new unit when we returned to school in January.

Although I could easily map how much time we spent in each problem context, I did not yet have a representation of what mathematics we covered in those contexts. As I had commented in my journal, the problem contexts are a "list of activities, not topics or content." Naming the mathematics content that was taught in any given week or unit of lessons turned out to be much more difficult than charting the problem contexts in which we worked across the year. As we saw in the "grouping" lesson of September 28 (described in chapters 5, 6, and 7), multiplication and division and linear functions were all part of the content, and fractions might have been for some students. In the time-speed-distance unit (described in chapter 8), the breadth of concepts entailed in our work was even larger, and the boundaries among the kinds of content on the list would have been even harder to draw.

For each lesson of the year in my class, an observer addressed the question, "What was the substance of mathematical content—i.e., What specific topic(s), concept(s), or procedure(s) was (were) explored or discussed?" I searched the collection of these observation notes and found the days on which "multiplication" and/or "division" were mentioned. I see that work on multiplication and/or division was embedded in and related to many other topics, contents, and procedures across the year. (I include a sampling of those notes in appendix B to display the breadth of work on these topics as they arose again and again over the year.) Considered as "topics," multiplication and/or division were studied in my class in six different units, sometimes in the context of navigation, sometimes in relation to dividing up cakes for distribution among bakeries, sometimes as a key to understanding fractions, sometimes to find ordered pairs to link a graph with an equation. Overlaying this information on the chart of problem contexts across the year shows how the class revisited the study of multiplication and division and computational procedures for carrying out these operations repeatedly.

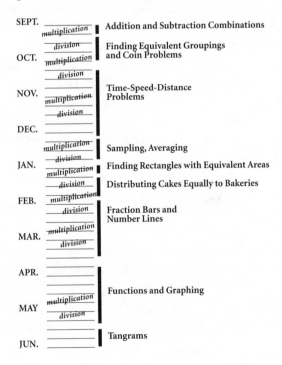

The topics we studied were, in some sense, the same across several different kinds of problems.

It is the teacher's responsibility to make progress through the curriculum in any kind of teaching in school. This analysis raises the question of what constitutes "progress" through the curriculum when students study by working on problems. Without some way of understanding how teaching aims to develop new learning in the intersection between topics and problem contexts, it appears as if I was simply teaching "the same thing over and over." I was not. I was also not repeating a single concept on higher and higher levels in a so-called spiral curriculum.

Teaching Topics as Connected Elements of the "Big Ideas" in a Discipline

The language of "topics" is commonly used to talk about the skills and concepts that are being taught and studied in school. My investigation of coverage in a series of lessons in the time-speed-distance unit suggests that something more is needed to understand the work of covering the curriculum by working on problems. While my students were doing multiplication and division in different problem contexts, they *were* studying aspects of these operations. But they were also studying something new in each context, namely, how those operations need to be tailored to the different constraints of different problem domains.[8] More importantly, perhaps, they were studying what *does not* vary in the mathematics across different conceptual and practical contexts. In order to understand the teaching I did to cover this kind of mathematical content, I needed a formulation of content that was more complex than a topic-by-topic list. Lists of topics, concepts, and procedures are only one way of looking at what is taught and learned when students work on problems. Fifth-grade topics like division and remainders, fractions and decimals, and rate and ratio, which we "covered" in the time-speed-distance unit, could also be considered as variants on a single "big idea."[9] They all go together to make up an understanding of one big idea, namely, multiplicative relationships.[10]

A fraction like ¾ indicates a particular multiplicative relationship between three and four. Four is one and one-third times larger than three. This relationship is what makes some fractions equivalent to other fractions, even though the numbers in the fractions are different. For example, ¾ is equal to ⁶⁄₈ and also to ⁹⁄₁₂ because all of these numbers indicate the same multiplicative relationship.

$$4 = 1\tfrac{1}{3} \times 3$$
$$8 = 1\tfrac{1}{3} \times 6$$
$$12 = 1\tfrac{1}{3} \times 9$$

In every case, the denominator (or number on the bottom) is one and one-third times larger than the numerator (or the number on the top). Another way to say the same thing is that the answer (or quotient) when you divide the top number by the bottom one is always the same.

$$3 \div 4 \ = .75$$
$$6 \div 8 \ = .75$$
$$9 \div 12 = .75$$

The numbers on the bottom get bigger as the numbers on the top get bigger, but the value of the fraction stays the same because the ratio between the top number and the bottom number stays the same. The big idea behind understanding equivalent fractions also applies to understanding why two fractions are *not* equal. Even though both ¾ and ⅗ involve three parts out of some whole, the two fractions are not equal because the ratio between the parts and the whole is different. In order to work with fractions competently, students need to use multiplication and division to study ratio as a multiplicative relationship.

In chapter 2, the class was studying the process of dividing 55 by 4 to find how far a car would go in 15 minutes at a constant speed of 55 miles per hour. At the end of that lesson, Ellie did a division and concluded that the car would go "13.3 miles." In her answer, ".3" indicates that "3" was left over when she divided. But this was an incorrect representation of the leftover, because the leftover was *three-fourths* of a mile, not *three-tenths*. The error arose because of a misunderstanding at the intersection of division and fractions. At the end of the lesson described in chapter 2, I knew that I needed to teach Ellie something about parts and wholes and how they are related to ratios using multiplication and division. I also knew that what I needed to teach her was going to have to stretch over several lessons and different problem contexts.

The Theory of Conceptual Fields

Gerard Vergnaud argues that, in order to learn mathematics, students must encounter relationships among concepts and topics in several different kinds of problems. In order to learn to operate in what he calls a "conceptual field," students need to figure out how to use different wordings and symbolisms for concepts and topics as they arise in different problem contexts. His way of defining mathematical concepts helps to explain the work involved in teaching these relationships:

> A single concept usually develops not in isolation but in relationship with other concepts, through several kinds of problems

and with the help of several wordings and symbolisms.... A conceptual field is a set of situations, the mastering of which requires mastery of several concepts of different natures. For instance, the conceptual field of multiplicative structures consists of all situations that can be analyzed as simple and multiple proportion problems and for which one usually needs to multiply or divide. Several kinds of mathematical concepts are tied to those situations and the thinking needed to master them. Among these concepts are linear and n-linear functions, vector spaces, dimensional analysis, fraction, ratio, rate, rational number, and multiplication and division.[11]

If we think of knowing mathematics only as knowing a list of individual, separate topics, the problem for the teacher in covering the curriculum is to give all of the students opportunities to study all of the topics one after another. But if, as Vergnaud argues, the growth of mathematical knowledge is more than a serial project of "concept development," then covering the curriculum involves more and different problems for teaching. Vergnaud observes that *research* on the teaching and learning of concepts must look at doing mathematics across different problem situations. The same holds for *teaching*. Learners only come to recognize the "invariance" among different situations as they analyze and work on problems in them as well as how several different concepts interact in solving a problem in a particular situation.

> One difficulty for researchers [on mathematics teaching and learning] is that a single concept does not refer to only one kind of situation, and a single situation cannot be analyzed with only one concept. Therefore, we must study conceptual fields.[12]

Analogously, one difficulty for teachers in teaching conceptual fields is that a single concept does not refer to only one kind of situation. Teaching must work across mathematical and practical situations, presenting and representing "big ideas" like multiplicative relationships. This kind of teaching gives students the opportunity to learn about what stays the same when fractions are used in different problems. It also give them practice with the language of rates, ratios, and fractions so they can study the different wordings and symbolisms needed to represent and solve problems in different contexts.[13] Using Vergnaud's idea of "conceptual fields" to look back at the chart on page 219 we could interpret the repetition of multiplication and division in different problem contexts across the year as an effort to work on the problem of teaching a conceptual field. Students worked on mathematics problems that involved them in using multiplication, division, fractions, and decimals in different problem contexts so that they could learn these topics and also study the big idea that relates them together.

Teaching Conceptual Fields and Teaching Topics Simultaneously

Although it made sense to me that students would learn mathematics by encountering "conceptual fields" in solving different kinds of problems, I was also responsible for teaching the topics in my school district's curriculum. I needed to assess what each of my students could do with multiplication, division, rates and ratios, fractions, and decimals, and decide which of these topics needed more studying by whom. I needed to monitor both students' understanding of conceptual fields and their mastery of conventional topics in ways that would take account of the differences in what they knew coming into the work as well as the differences in their accomplishments.

Cases of Teaching "Conceptual Fields"

To specify the problems of teaching mathematical "big ideas" while also covering the curriculum from a conventional topic-by-topic perspective, I now zoom in on two lessons that I taught two months apart but which focused on the same conceptual field.[14] In January my lessons were organized around a problem context in which students were given a quantity of cakes and a quantity of bakeries, and the problem was to distribute the cakes equally among the bakeries. There were leftover cakes, and they had to somehow be distributed. Students were challenged to interpret a decimal number that came up on the calculator when they divided the given number of cakes by the given number of bakeries. At that point, I organized their work so that they would not need to explore decimal notation to solve the assigned problems, but instead to work with halves, fourths, and eighths of cakes because these fractions were more appropriate to the context. In March, we returned to the interpretation of decimal notation using money as a problem context. Although the numbers to the right of the decimal point in a number like 44.44 are a fraction, and can be thought of as part of one whole, they also have a "place value" like the other digits. When we think of 44.44 as an amount of money, each of the fours in this number has a different value. The total is made up of:

> 4 ten dollar bills
> 4 one dollar bills
> 4 dimes
> 4 pennies

In posing problems that would have students working with quantities of pennies, dimes, and dollars, I taught the symbolic notation of the decimal system while we also continued our studies of fractions, multiplication, and division. In both the January lesson and the March lesson, the problem of figuring out the meaning of the remainder arose, and in order to solve it, students investigated the many concepts that contribute to understanding multiplicative relationships.

In the following two cases of teacher's and students' engagement with content, I describe and analyze the integration of teaching topics with teaching the mathematical structures that are invariant across mathematical situations. In each of the cases, the lesson involves talk about ratios in terms of part-whole relationships. Within the broad outlines of this talk, I insert topics that all students need to have opportunities to learn in the fifth grade. At the same time, I teach my class how those topics are related, both to one another within a given context and to a conceptual field that operates across the contexts. After the two cases are described, I identify the elements of the work of covering the curriculum in these cases, in a classroom where studying involves working on problems.

Zooming in on a Lesson in the Middle of the Year

The lesson I am about to describe occurred in the middle—literally—of the school year, lesson number 53 in a series of 105 hour-long lessons I taught to this class between September and June. Like the problem involving the car traveling at 55 miles per hour that was our focus in chapter 2, this problem had three parts, each of which implied a different way of working with the part-whole relationship. The Problem of the Day was:

Thursday, January 18

A delivery man has 111 cakes to distribute equally among 24 bakeries.

1) How many to each if only whole cakes?
2) How many to each if you can use half-cakes?
3) How many to each if all parts of all cakes are used?

In time-speed-distance problems, remainders needed to be expressed as minutes or fraction of an hour if the problem involved finding a time, or in fractions of a mile or feet if the problem involved finding distance. The context of this problem is different and so the way in which leftovers in a division are given meaning is different. Here, the "whole" is a simple cake, or one bakery. Unlike miles and hours, bakeries cannot be cut in parts. Cakes can be cut down to the smallest crumb, but such divisions are not practical. Cakes can be sold by the slice, however, so it is reasonable to talk in terms of halves, fourths, and eighths of a cake being distributed to bakeries. The mathematics of handling leftovers is different in this context, while the idea of ratio is constant across the two contexts. In this case of teaching, and the next, which involves dividing amounts of money, I examine the work that is entailed in teaching those similarities and differences.

In order to answer part 3 of the cakes and bakeries problem above, I anticipated that students would have already worked with whole cakes and half-cakes, and they would figure out that they needed pieces that were an eighth of a cake to make the complete distribution. (Each bakery needs to get 4 and ⅝ cakes.) To construct the problem, I first decided that in the end, each bakery would get some whole cakes and also ⅝ of another cake. Five-eighths is ½ plus ⅛. I chose the numbers of cakes and bakeries in the problem to make it come out this way. Working through each part of the problem, students would have to shift from distributing "half-cakes" in part 2 to working with wholes, halves, and eighths at the same time in part 3. I will examine the construction of the problem, some students' work on it, and a portion of the large-group discussion of the three parts of this problem to describe the teaching actions involved in covering both topics and structures.

Deciding What to Cover and What Not to Cover in a Problem Context

The specific numbers I used to design the problem on January 18 arose out of some work that students had done on a similar problem the day before. On that day, the problem was to divide 16 cakes among 62 bakeries. One student (Ivan) had used a calculator to do this problem, and asserted that each bakery would get "three point eight seven five cakes" based on reading the number 3.875 off the calculator screen.

I wrote in my journal after this happened:

> *1/17*
>
> *I want us to return to the question of whether or not bakeries ought to get anything besides whole cakes. I want to engage more kids in the kinds of "wanderings" that Ivan was doing as he sought to connect what was happening with numbers, on the calculator, to the idea of cakes being distributed equally to a number of bakeries.*
>
> *What if we "unpacked" the long division algorithm? Does that make any sense at all, now that calculators have taken over? One of the things I am intrigued with is that kids seem to use the calculator strategically rather than simplistically, indicating some ~~and~~ understanding of multiplicative relationships. This was certainly true of Ivan on Tuesday, and Candice—and I think a number of other kids—did*
> *18 x 16—too small 19 x 16 too large—*
> *a ~~am~~ similar kind of estimation as to what goes on with the calculator long division game.*

Students who had used the calculator to multiply as a way of estimating how many cakes each bakery would get were studying the relationship between multiplication and division. (There were sixteen bakeries. Try 18×16. Too small. Try 19×16. Too large.) That was an appropriate strategy and fruitful for studying multiplicative structures at this point in the year. But when Ivan used the calculator to divide, he got into territory he was not yet prepared to explore, and this was not an appropriate problem context in which to explore it. Using a number like 3.875 to solve the problem of distributing cakes requires understanding the connection between decimal notation and simple fractions, which we had not yet investigated.

When I speculated in my journal about "unpacking the long division algorithm" I was working with a topic-by-topic perspective on covering the curriculum, but I was also thinking about teaching the big mathematical idea that had initially come up in the time-speed-distance unit. The idea is how our perspective on what is "the whole" needs to shift when we do "long" division. To divide 73 by 6, for example, the first unit or "whole" we distribute is groups of ten. We distribute the seventy tens among six groups, and one ten is left over. The one that is left over becomes transformed from one whole ten to ten whole ones. It is then combined with the three ones we started with (in 73) and this gives us a total of thirteen ones to distribute. We can evenly distribute only twelve of those ones, by giving two to each group (6 × 2), and there is one "one" left. To continue dividing further, we could exchange that whole one for ten whole tenths, and distribute six of those tenths by giving one to each group (6 × .1). There are then four-tenths left.

$$
\begin{array}{r}
1 \\
6\,\overline{)73} \\
-\,6 \\
\hline
1
\end{array}
\qquad
\begin{array}{r}
12 \\
6\,\overline{)73} \\
-\,6 \\
\hline
13 \\
-\,12 \\
\hline
1
\end{array}
\qquad
\begin{array}{r}
12.1 \\
6\,\overline{)73.0} \\
-\,6 \\
\hline
13 \\
-\,12 \\
\hline
10 \\
-\,6 \\
\hline
4
\end{array}
$$

The unit with which we work changes across the computation. Each time we move over one place, we are working with a whole unit that is worth one tenth of the unit to its left. We could continue to divide by trading the leftovers for smaller and smaller units.

In order for Ivan and others in the class to figure out the meaning of 3.875 we would need to do this kind of "unpacking" of the long division algorithm to study how the size of the unit of cake we would be distributing to the bakeries changes as we move to the right. We would be doing a procedure to distribute whole cakes, tenths of a cake, hundredths of a cake, and so on. But this would be an absurd solution strategy, given the context in which the problem arose. There is no practical reason to divide cakes into tenths, and we certainly would not divide a cake into hundredths, particularly if it were to be sold in a bakery. The context of dividing cakes among bakeries would be better for looking at relationships among halves, quarters, and eighths as helpful ideas in carrying out a division with "leftovers." So instead of teaching students like Ivan to interpret the numbers on the calculator in relation to the long division procedure, I constructed a problem using numbers and stages that would focus students on halves, quarters, and eighths of cakes.

When I faced the problem of teaching students to interpret what they saw on the calculator, I needed to construct a sequence of work for my class. What I would have them study needed to make sense both in terms of the mathematical skills and knowledge I wanted to cover and the problem content in which I had set students to work. I wanted to get us into a place where we would be working with fractions more suited to the problem context but also be considering ideas about division and remainders. To do this, I needed to move my thinking about the mathematics from the calculator context through the context of place value as it plays out in the long division algorithm when there is a remainder in the context of cakes and bakeries. In the first stage of the problem, students were to focus on dividing up only whole cakes. Then they would study what happens when the unit shifts to half-cakes, and then let go of constraining the unit altogether to revisit the most open-ended and hardest-to-interpret solution, the one that comes with dividing up all parts of all cakes. We would come back to interpreting leftovers in division in terms of decimal numbers later in the year.

Connecting a Procedure for Long Division to the Problem Context

After constructing the problem for January 18, the next piece of work I did to cover the curriculum occurred at the beginning of the discussion. I had seen several students doing some form of the conventional long division algorithm in their notebooks in the time-speed-distance unit, so I did not want to ignore it here, even though it was not appropriate to get into decimals in this context. (During that unit, I had not ever put the conventional form up on the board, focusing more on the relationship between multiplication and division as a way into the topic.)[15] On January 18, after students worked on this Problem of the Day, I first showed them how the division or distribution would be conventionally recorded using the familiar algorithm if cakes were delivered to each bakery one a time. Then I showed how it would be recorded using the algorithm if *ten* cakes were delivered at a time. The cakes and bakeries context serves well here, because students can actually imagine and even draw the distribution. One group of students I am focusing on teaching here are those who, like Ellie, made drawings in their notebooks to distribute the cakes one at a time. (Ellie's chart showing "cakes gone" and "cakes left" records the relationship between division and subtraction as cakes are delivered one at a time to each of the 24 bakeries.) The numbers are large enough so that some form of procedure involving groups of cakes would make sense, but small enough to connect procedures and drawings.

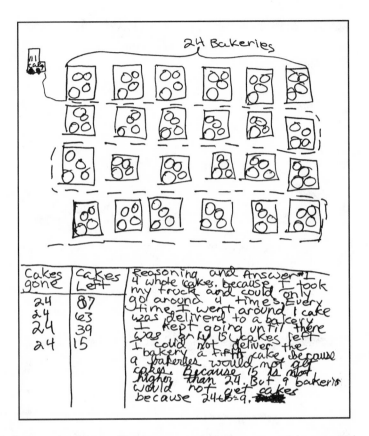

I used the standard long division procedure in my teaching to make a link between drawings and charts like this, and the steps in the standard procedure so that students might learn to use that procedure in situations where drawing would be impractical. I had chosen both the form of the problem and the numbers we would work with so that it would make sense to replace taking away *single* cakes for each bakery from the total as they were distributed with distributing *groups* of cakes at a time. That was the reason for making the number of bakeries large.

Lampert: In terms of long division here—if I just put the answer one up here [writing the "1" on the top],

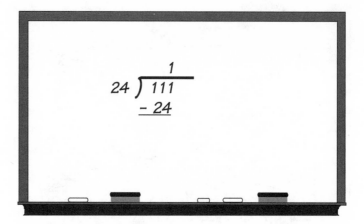

and I took twenty-four away [writing –24 under 111], that would mean I gave one cake to everybody.

If I put the answer ten up here [writing the "10" on top],

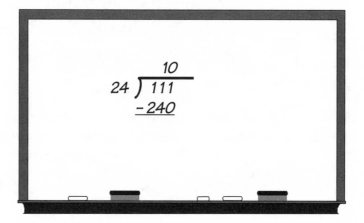

it would mean I would have to give two hundred and forty cakes out [writing "240" under "111"], and there aren't enough to do that, are there? There aren't enough to give everybody ten.

By making this comparison between "putting a one" and "putting a ten," I was able to link the steps in the procedure directly to cakes and bakeries to clarify the connections. I could show what multiplying 1 by 24 or 10 by 24, and then subtracting it from 111, would mean in terms of giving out cakes, or not. As I carried out the procedure, several students called out that there "aren't enough" to give each bakery 10.

Lampert:	How can you tell from this that there aren't enough?
	Charlotte?
Charlotte:	Because if you have a hundred and eleven cakes and twenty-four bakeries—twenty-four times ten is two hundred and forty, and that means two hundred and forty cakes, and you only have a hundred and eleven.

I next taught a matter of procedure that focused more on mechanics than on meaning. But there was also a topic from the curriculum in what I was teaching. The mechanics needed to be carried out in relation to knowing the relationship between multiplication and division.

| Lampert: | Okay. Now, what I see some people doing is something like this [writing the "1" on top in a different place] |

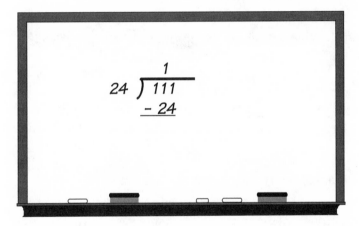

| | where they put a one here, and then they try to take away twenty-four? If you put a one in that place, that's the tens column. And so what you're saying is that each bakery gets ten cakes, and you can't, that doesn't work out. So when you use this long division thing you have to be really careful where you put your numbers if you want to communicate— |

The emphasis here is on the placement of the "1" above the 111. If it is placed above the tens place, it means ten cakes are given out even though it is not written as "10."

I then demonstrated how the answer to the first part of the problem (4 whole cakes) would be obtained using this symbolic system for recording the distribution of the cakes and how it leads to the conclusion that there are 15 cakes left over. I carried out the procedure on the chalkboard and as I did it, I talked about what I was doing in terms of distributing cakes. This was to show how to do the computation if a group of 4 cakes at once was distributed to each bakery. Twenty-four groups of 4 cakes use up 96 cakes. There are 15 cakes left over.

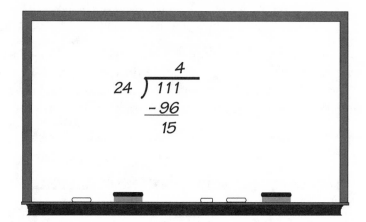

$$24 \overline{\smash{)}\begin{array}{r} 4 \\ 111 \\ -96 \\ \hline 15 \end{array}}$$

To close this part of the lesson, I asked several students to talk about what each of the numbers in the division represented in terms of cakes. If each bakery were given 4 cakes, 4 times 24, or 96 cakes, would be distributed all together. So we take those away from the 111 we started with, and there are 15 left over.[16]

Other Kinds of Distributions That Suit the Context

The next topic I introduced in this lesson was the notion of a "fraction" greater than one. (These fractions are sometimes referred to as "improper fractions" in lists of topics to be taught at the fifth-grade level.) I taught the symbols that would be used to represent such a fraction as well as words that could be used to talk about it. We had observed that there were such fractions in our work on hours and minutes in the time-speed-distance unit, but we had not directly investigated the relationship between fractions of a whole and quantities greater than a whole.[17]

The second part of the Problem of the Day on January 18 was an occasion to present improper fractions for study because the form of the solution that is called for is unclear. It could be either 9 half-cakes or 4½ cakes. Both of these solutions were discussed, and I challenged students to explain why they were equivalent distributions.

Lampert: How many to each if you can use half-cakes?
                   Dorota?

Dorota:	Um, I think it's nine.
Lampert:	You think it's nine?
Lampert:	And does anybody disagree? Charlotte?
Charlotte:	I think it's four whole cakes and one half.
Lampert:	Okay. Four whole cakes and one half. And when you said, Dorota, you think it's nine, did you mean nine wholes or nine halves?
Dorota:	Nine halves.
Lampert:	Okay. So we have two conjectures. Nine halves or four wholes and one half—

When Dorota says, "I think it's nine," she is using half-cakes as a unit of distribution. Charlotte's answer makes explicit that she is using two kinds of units (wholes and halves). I wrote "4½" and "9 halves" on the chalkboard next to part 2 of the problem, deliberately calling them "two conjectures" so as not to close down students' investigation of whether these two expressions would mean the same amount of cake. But then, before I said anything, Anthony raised his hand:

Lampert:	Anthony?
Anthony:	I think it means the same thing because four halves divided by two tells you how many wholes because two halves make up one whole. It means the same thing.

There are many ways I could have responded to what Anthony proposed, but I chose to focus on the symbols for writing nine halves as a fraction and the words for talking about it. I had heard some students, in talking with one another, refer to numbers like $\frac{9}{2}$ as "nine twos" and that seemed like it could lead to problematic confusions between multiplication and division.

Lampert:	Okay. So we could write nine over two, that's nine halves [writing $\frac{9}{2}$ on the chalkboard].
	This is something that we had talked about a little bit earlier in the year, that, it's kind of odd when you put a large number on top and a small number on bottom. But this is the way people in math would write nine halves. And then you could say that equals four and one half.
	Okay.

Now Karim raised his hand and "agreed with Dorota" that the bakeries would each get nine half-cakes. I asked him to explain why he thought that and he went on to explain how he had originally "thought it was eight" but changed his mind. He had "doubled" the 4 whole cakes each bakery had received in the first part of the problem, and thought this meant they would receive 8 half-cakes. When he talks about the "upper number" here, at first I do not understand what he is saying.

In asking the class to reflect on Karim's thinking, I see the potential for clarification by linking back to the study of "long division" and its relationship to multiplication. As with many other problems we had worked on, this one was designed so that the work on the later parts of the problem could build on work done on earlier parts, thus providing an occasion for making mathematical connections. Both Karim and Sam (who was trying to explain Karim's thinking) were attempting to make those connections, but as I had anticipated, their language for talking about the shifting relationships between parts and wholes was limited. I now had another chance to teach this big idea, here in relation to the topic of "improper fractions."

Karim: Because, like at first I thought it was eight because all that I have to do is double it twice.

Lampert: Ahh!

Karim: So I thought it was eight. But then I found out I was wrong—

Lampert: Why, how did you find out you were wrong?

Karim: Because I said to myself that twenty-four would stay the same but the upper number wouldn't, so it would change it, not make it twenty-four, but even if I did I would still have some left over, so I would be wrong.

I asked if anyone could explain what they thought Karim had been thinking. Sam told the steps he thought Karim had gone through which seemed to make it clear to him that the total number of half-cakes to go to each bakery would be nine. I asked for some further clarification of one of the steps in the procedure.

Lampert: Who else can explain what they think, um, Karim was thinking when he said it would be eight. Maybe some other people were thinking that too.

Sam?

Sam:	Well, what he what he did was he thought in number one, if you if you divide four into two pieces, four whole cakes into two pieces is eight halves but I want to say, maybe he didn't think about that last one.
Lampert:	What do you mean by that last one?
Sam:	Um, because the four and a half, because you had um a half um, because when you go you go up to ninety-six okay, and you do the regular—
	and that's four times, and you have to you have to uh—
Lampert:	Wait, wait, wait. I lost you. Where did ninety-six come from?
Sam:	Ninety-six, you start out twenty-four and then you forty-eight and then you go seventy-two and ninety-six. That's four cakes to each one.
Lampert:	Ah ha. Oh, right.

What Sam was talking about here was a link (similar to what Ellie had represented in her notebook) between multiplication and division, and a link between division and repeated subtraction.

When I asked Sam where "ninety-six" came from, I was providing the class with an opportunity to study how to connect a problem context and what is done with numbers. In his notebook, Sam had determined that 96 whole cakes (four 24s) would need to be taken away from 111 by adding groups of 24 until he reached a number less than 111, and realized he could not add 24 again without going over 111.

$$
\begin{array}{rl}
24 & \text{for the first bakery} \\
+\,24 & \text{again for the next bakery} \\
\hline
48 & \\
+\,24 & \text{a third time} \\
\hline
72 & \\
+\,24 & \text{a fourth time} \\
\hline
96 &
\end{array}
$$

He said in his notebook: "I +ed [added] 24 until I got to the closest multip. of 24 without going over 111. I figured out how many times I +ed [added] it."

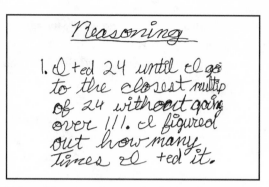

If you use 96 whole cakes out of a total of 111, there are 15 leftovers. Sam goes on to say what he did with the 15 leftover cakes:

Sam:	Then you got fifteen left over. So how did you, where is it you got to cut the cut the fifteen into halves and that gives you thirty.
Lampert:	Okay.
Sam:	And then after you get the thirty you take you give a one half to each one of them, and then you'd be left over with six.

Sam showed this procedure in his notebook, indicating that the 15 leftover whole cakes would yield 30 half-cakes. He takes 24 away from those 30, distributing 1 half-cake to each bakery, in addition to the 4 that have already been given out. This leaves 6 half-cakes still to distribute.

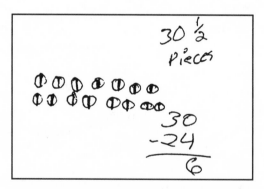

Lampert:	Okay. Good explanation. So whether you think it's nine halves or four wholes and one half, there's still six left.

Anthony, Karim, and Sam had all talked about "nine halves" and "four and a half" as equivalent and appropriate solutions to the problem of distributing cakes if you could use halves, although only Anthony talked about why they were equivalent. I still was not clear about what Anthony had meant about the "upper number" not staying the same, but at this point, Enoyat seemed anxious to make a contribution to the discussion. I had had a few interactions with him during the small-group part of the lesson and I wondered if my efforts to deepen his study of fractions had paid off, so I called on him.

Figuring out What Still Needs to Be Taught

One matter under study in the large-group discussion so far is a procedure for first determining how many half-cakes there are, and then distributing them. We now can work with half-cakes as a new kind of whole unit. But the way we speak about them also puts them in relation to whole cakes such that they are harder to talk about and the numbers associated with them are more complicated to perform operations on.

Lampert:	Now, the, the ones that are left, those six that are left. [Enoyat raises his hand.]
	Enoyat do you want to talk about that?
Enoyat:	Yeah. Um, see what I did when there were six left, um, I got one eighth, how I got that was I had one whole cake and then I divided it in half so it was two, then I divided it into fourths, so it was four, then I divided it one more time and I got one eighth.

Enoyat echoed what Sam had said about "being left over with six," and immediately began to talk about what the 6 leftovers would mean in terms of part 3 of the Problem of the Day (How many to each if all parts of all cakes are used?). Enoyat introduced "eighths" into the discussion on this day and into our work for the year. When we were working in the context of hours and minutes, we did not talk about "eighths of an hour." Eighths are not commonly used in that context. But here, when what is being divided up are cakes, it is common to cut the whole in half, and then cut the halves in half to get quarters, and then cut those in half to get eighths. It is the easiest way to get equal parts without measuring. Following this procedure does not necessarily indicate an understanding of what it implies for the solution of the problem, however. In this problem context, cakes and fractions of cakes need to be distributed among bakeries. Sometimes what are being distributed are whole cakes, sometimes half-cakes, and sometimes eighths of a cake. Each of these units has a relationship to the others and that relationship is not always made explicit in talking about steps in the distribution. I could not tell how close Enoyat was to understanding the solution, even though he had divided a cake into eighths.

One of the teaching problems that is particular to teaching "big ideas" like the part-whole relationship is assessing what students already understand and what they still need to learn, and doing this for many different students. Although there is no simple way of averaging their accomplishments, I need to steer the work of the class as a whole. Within that common journey through some mathematical terrain, I need to attend to who needs extra guidance and when they need it. There is no simple metric here as there is in teaching separate topics one after another, where what students have learned can be crossed off a list.

One part of the challenge is interpreting what students are talking about so that I can judge what they understand. But a more complex problem, with a sometimes confusing solution, is deciding when to ask them to be more explicit. On the one hand, such explicitness aids their study of mathematics and helps me to learn about them, but on the other, it is an intrusion into their reasoning process. The speaker may very well know quite clearly when he or she is talking about this or that unit of cake, and I need to figure out when it is appropriate to push beyond that understanding into a new level of work in the same conceptual field.

To get a better sense of who was understanding what, I picked up on something both Enoyat and Sam had asserted and used it to come back to an issue that a number of students seem to have been working on during earlier parts of the lesson. Both of them had said there were "six left" after the 30 halves had been distributed, and that these needed to be divided into eighths. Enoyat and I had talked during small-group time, and then he had said that the "six left" were 6 whole cakes. I was not sure from what he said in the large-group context whether he had changed his mind. The confusion here is not a simple matter of misspeaking. There *are* "six" left from the 30, and these 6 need to be distributed among the 24 bakeries. But they are 6 *halves* not 6 whole cakes.

This problem brings us to the heart of the difference between fractions and counting numbers. When we use counting numbers, we assume a one-to-one correspondence between each whole number and the things we are counting: apples, people, whatever. Fractions are different. The total quantity depends on what the unit is. Here, the "six" that are left are 6 *halves* or 3 whole cakes. To divide these whole cakes among 24 bakeries, each needs to be cut into 8 equal slices. But if we are starting with cakes already cut in half, the half-cakes only need to be made into 4 equal slices, each of which is ⅛ of the cake.

I taught here by drawing six deliberately irregular shapes on the chalkboard to represent what Enoyat had said and to highlight the possibility for confusion. I wanted everyone in the class to investigate the nature of the "six" that were left and think about how to divide them up among the bakeries. Then the problem to be solved would be how to answer the question as it was stated in the Problem of the Day: "How many to each if all parts of all cakes are used?" In order to answer that question in a way that would make sense in the context, we would need to be clear about what it was we were distributing.

> Lampert: Okay. Now I am a little bit confused here, 'cause I know a lot of people got this thing about one-eighth.
>
> But if there are six cakes left—
>
> and you want one two three four five six [drawing six irregular shapes on the chalkboard], and we have twenty-four bakeries—
>
> then it looks to me like you could just divide them into fourths.

I used contributions from students to develop the representation. First, I made six irregular shapes to represent the 6 leftovers after the half-cakes had been distributed. I then erased and clarified the shapes into six half circles and called them "six halves." Then I cut those halves in half, making a representation of "twelve quarter-cakes." Next I cut the quarter cakes in half again to make "twenty-four eighths" so we could distribute one-eighth to each bakery.

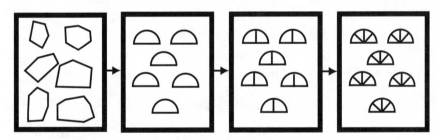

Once the representation of "twenty-four eighths" was up on the chalkboard in the form of half-cakes divided into quarters, I posed the problem as it was stated in part 3 of the Problem of the Day, "So how many to each if all parts of all cakes are used?" Several students had their hands raised, and I called on Shahroukh.

> Shahroukh: I think it should be five, like four and five-eighths.

Sam spoke next and agreed with Shahroukh. He explicated the reasoning he had done to arrive at his position, giving everyone another chance to study the relationships among multiplication, division, and fractions in this problem context.

Sam:	With those three leftover cakes all you have to do, there are six halves so all you have to do is put them in threes.
	And then like, what is it. There's twenty-four so you can just say that what times three equals twenty-four.
Lampert:	Okay and.
Sam:	AND that's eight, so you've gotta have, and if you can add um, what is it. An eighth to each one, then you're left with no eighths, so it's going to be a total of five-eighths. So four and five-eighths.
Lampert:	Okay. That's an important point that you made. Four and one-half plus one-eighth equals four and five-eighths. Okay. This one-half [pointing] could be thought of as four-eighths.

Sam agreed that each bakery would get "four and five-eighths," but then returned to his earlier train of thought rather than immediately commenting on Shahroukh's answer. He went on to explain, first why three leftover cakes would be distributed as an eighth to each bakery (because six halves is three cakes and *eight* times three equals 24), concluding with each bakery getting a *total* of five-eighths, four and five-eighths all together. I unpacked Sam's use of the word "total" to assert that "Four and one-half plus one-eighth equals four and five-eighths" and so that is what each bakery would get four whole cakes and five-eighths of a cake. Because it was conceivable that eighths of a cake could be sold as slices, this solution made sense.

Teaching Again in the "Same" Conceptual Field

Two months later, on March 14, I returned to the mathematics of interpreting fractions written in decimal form. I wanted my class to study how the placement of the decimal point in relation to the digits and the use of zero would affect the value of the number. I used this as an occasion to teach a conventional fifth-grade topic while also revisiting the conceptual field of multiplicative structures. I infused the lessons on decimals with talk and graphic representations that would focus attention on the relative value of "the whole." Moving back and forth between money and an area model of fractions, I supported talk about the common structure of ratio in both of these problem contexts.

Here I will briefly describe what we did on March 14, then analyze what we talked about on March 15. The first of these two lessons was devoted to collaboratively completing a chart and the second to commentary on what we had done the day before in terms of what it implied about relationships among fractions, decimals, multiplication, and division. After the commentary on what we had done the day before, students would be making their own charts in their notebooks to represent a similar set of numbers.

To begin the first lesson, I wrote some amounts of money on the board:

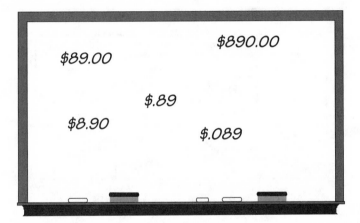

and next to these, I taped up a blank paper chart I had made on a large sheet of paper:

	pennies	dimes	dollars

I then said what we would work on together by filling in the chart, expressing each amount of money in three different ways: first, in terms of how many dollars it represented, then in terms of how many dimes it represented, and then how many pennies it represented.

We began with $890 as the "amount of money," and with student contributions and explanations, I filled in the dollars column with 890, the dimes column with 8,900, and the pennies column with 89,000. We then translated $89.00 into dollars, dimes, and pennies with little discussion. Then we worked on $8.90, and the challenge was how to express this as a mixed number in the dollars column as 8 whole dollars with some fraction of a dollar "left over." We talked about how $\frac{9}{10}$ of a dollar would not be a "real thing" but it was possible to write it mathematically. Our chart looked like this:

	pennies	dimes	dollars
$890.00	89,000	8900	890
$89.00	8,900	890	89
$8.90	890	80+9=89	$8\frac{9}{10} = 8\frac{90}{100}$
$.89	89	$8\frac{9}{10}$	$\frac{8}{10} + \frac{9}{100} = \frac{89}{100}$
$.089	$8\frac{9}{10}$	$\frac{8}{10} + \frac{9}{100}$	

The class ended early because it was a day for parent conferences. I said we would come back to this kind of work the next day.

I used the same chart in the next day's discussion to involve more students in exploring translations between common fractions and decimals to express remainders. I was teaching the topic of "remainders" yet again, but coming at it from quite a different direction than I had in the time-speed-distance unit in November or the cakes and bakeries unit in January. As fractions of hours can be expressed as whole minutes, fractions of monetary denominations can be translated into collections of smaller denominations. Depending on the denomination (e.g., dollars or pennies), the same amount of money can be expressed as a whole number (e.g., 90 cents) or a fraction (9 tenths or 90 hundredths of one dollar).

Although we never talk about fractions of a dollar other than halves and quarters, the way we write amounts of money uses decimal representations. Ninety cents is symbolized as 90¢ and also as $.90. The first representation gives the amount as 90 whole pennies, the second as $\frac{9}{10}$ of a whole dollar. Money is a very useful teaching tool because it is familiar and at the same time communicates the ambiguity of the unit in question. The teaching I did with the chart on the chalkboard connected students' familiarity with money to the mathematics of place value across the decimal point from whole numbers on the left to fractions on the right. We analyzed this the next day.

Linking Topics Together with a New Representation

I was trying to "cover" a conceptual field we had studied before and at the same time make curricular progress by bringing the same concepts to bear on a new situation. To do this, I needed to work again on finding out how much understanding students would have of the relationships within that set of ideas as it came to be used in this new context. Reba was not a regular participant in large-group discussions, and I did not have a good sense of her capacity to use fractions and decimals with understanding, so when she volunteered at the beginning of the discussion, I was eager to have an exchange with her.

I had begun the discussion with my own commentary on one of the entries in the chart we had made the day before, anticipating the chart students would make after the discussion was over:

Lampert:	Now I want to say one more thing about your chart. When you write the equivalence in pennies, dimes, and dollars, sometimes you're not going to have a whole dollar or a whole penny. So you'll need to have a fraction. Like remember yesterday. We had this one [writing $8.90 on the board next to the previous day's chart].
	We had eight dollars and ninety cents. How many whole dollars are in eight dollars and ninety cents?

It was at this point that Reba raised her hand.

Lampert:	Reba?
Reba:	Nine.
Lampert:	Nine whole dollars?
Reba:	Um, no eight.
Lampert:	Eight whole dollars?
	How do you know?
Reba:	Well, if, you um, the ninety, can't, well, you need ten more cents to be the dollar for the ninety. So if—

With this explanation, Reba was working on figuring out an essential multiplicative relationship: 100 cents makes one whole dollar. If you have less than

100 cents, you only have a *fraction* of a dollar. She used this idea to reason about the value of the decimal part of $8.90 in terms of part-whole relationships. I added the word "fraction" to what she said in my comment on her explanation, and asked questions that would move her to a different kind of representation of this quantity.

My teaching aim here was twofold. I wanted her to learn about decimal-fraction translations, and I wanted her to scrutinize the big ideas that were the foundation of the procedure we use to make these translations.

Lampert:	Okay, so we have eight whole dollars and then your challenge is to write this part of the money [pointing to the .90] as a fraction.
	What would you do with that?
	How would you write that part as a fraction?
	[to Reba] You said you need ten more cents to make a whole dollar.
Reba:	Uh huh.
Lampert:	When you think about that, how many parts are you dividing the dollar into?

Reba made use of my part-whole language to move between "needing ten more cents" and the idea that ".90" means "ninety out of a hundred." I asked her to explain her reasoning to give her practice with the language of the translation between whole dollars and whole cents, and cents as fractions of a dollar.

Reba:	The ninety is gonna be ninety out of a hundred.
Lampert:	How did you figure that out?
Reba:	Because there's a hundred cents in a dollar and there's ninety cents.

As I moved on to the next phase of this discussion, I could now make use of the links Reba had introduced among decimal place value, fractions, and the problem context of money. These links were important to study in their own right, and they were useful for making sense of the process of moving around among symbolic, verbal, and concrete representations of fractions.

Charlotte spoke next and added more interpretations and language to make sense of the connections among the representations, specifically linking "nine dimes," "nine-tenths," and "ninety cents." Donna Ruth used the unconventional phrase "ninety fraction a hundred" to refer to 90 hundredths, but the rest of what she said communicated that she had a reasonable way of thinking about that fraction.

Lampert:	Okay, what does anybody else think about that?
	Do you agree with Reba? Or disagree?
	Reba thinks it would be eight wholes and ninety hundredths.
	Charlotte?
Charlotte:	I agree with what she said and there's another way of writing it. You can write it nine-tenths.
Lampert:	Can you first tell why you agree and then tell why you would write it as nine-tenths?
Charlotte:	Okay. Um, ninety of a hundred because there is one hundred pennies in a dollar, so you divide it up into a hundred parts to see how much pennies there are. And you have ninety pennies. And so nine-tenths because you can divide a dollar into nine and you have ten dimes. And ninety cents is the same as nine dimes. Nine dimes.
Lampert:	Okay. Donna Ruth?
Donna Ruth:	I agree with Reba because ninety fraction one hundred is one hundred is a whole, so it um—
	If it was, if it was nine more, I mean if it was ten more then it would be nine dollars.
Lampert:	Ten more what?
Donna Ruth:	Ten more cents.

I added yet another twist to the transformations at this point, again to focus on the shifting nature of the whole. I pointed to the "$8.90" that I had written on the board and asked the class if it would make sense to say that meant "eight hundred and ninety cents."

I was both teaching and testing here, to see who had what degree of flexibility in moving around the field of multiplicative structures. Several students raised their hands and I called on Candice. Again, I responded to what she said using a word she had not used ("wholes") to attend to the invariance in the situation.

Candice:	Well, yeah, I think it is. Because, um, there's a hundred in one, a hundred cents in one dollar and eight dollars is eight hundred cents.
Lampert:	Eight hundred cents in eight wholes. What about the ninety?
Candice:	Well, it would be ninety cents there and ninety cents. So, it would be the same.

Saundra also had her hand up, and I asked her to comment on the same matter. She responded by moving the discussion into the variants that characterized the money situation: here we were dealing with bills and coins, not cakes or hours or minutes, and those objects had their own characteristics that would constrain the application of the mathematics.

Lampert:	Saundra what do you think?
Saundra:	Yeah, I guess it would be the same thing. The only difference would be the, the eight dollars is in bills and the rest of the ninety cents is just in pennies and quarters and things, but other than that it's the same.

I called on Shahroukh next, and his commentary was of a different sort, linking the concreteness of the monetary representation with part-whole reasoning and also with multiplication.[18]

Shahroukh:	Well, I agree with it because eight hundred and ninety is eight times larger than a hundred which is eight hundred and then you have ninety left, ninety out of a hundred, that's ninety cents out of a dollar. So you have exactly eight wholes and ninety out of a hundred.[At this point, I added $\frac{890}{100} = \frac{800}{100} + \frac{90}{100}$ to the chalkboard, near $8.90.]

In this conversation, the unit is "slippery" as it was when we were talking about whole cakes, half-cakes, and eighths of a cake.

In my responses to students' talk, I deliberately shifted the referent around from one whole being a dollar to one whole being a dime, and then a penny. For each amount of money, the quantity is constant, but the way it is expressed using the relationship between parts and wholes changes, depending on what is assumed to be the unit. Unlike cakes and fractions of cakes, these shifts are associated with the fundamental nature of our system for recording quantity using numbers wherein each "place" has a value ten times the place to its left and one-tenth the value of the place to its right. The digits that fill those places take on their value as multiples of ten or decimal fractions. Because our monetary system is built partially on the decimal system, it is a helpful representation for grounding the verbal and symbolic referents to the change in decimal units.[19] Students can ground their reasoning about a very abstract set of relationships in a familiar material as the commentary moves back and forth among these different kinds of talk.

Revisiting "Improper" Fractions in the Context of Decimal Numbers

In the cakes and bakeries lesson described above, we had to figure out the meaning of nine halves and its relationship to the division of cakes among bakeries. In the discussion of the chart of monetary translations, Connie brought "improper fractions" into this problem context as well. Continuing the talk about how to represent $8.90 with fractions, she said that it could also be an improper fraction—namely, 89 tenths. She explained her assertion by moving back and forth between the domain of fractions and the domain of money.

Next to $8.90, I wrote on the board what Connie had said, and then asked her to explain.

Lampert:	Eighty-nine tenths and eight dollars and ninety cents, you think are equal?
Connie:	Yeah, because ten-tenths equals one dollar and you can get eight dollars out of that and then you'll have nine-tenths left and nine-tenths equals ninety cents. So it's eight dollars and ninety cents.

Connie's contribution is a resource for me in covering the curriculum of mathematical big ideas. I can use her comment to assess her appreciation of the connections among topics, but I can also use it to teach other students about connections that might not have been apparent to them.

Enoyat volunteered to comment on what Connie said.

Enoyat:	Um, eighty-nine cents is the same thing as—
	Eight hundred and ninety-hundredths and eight dollars and ninety cents, because like what Anthony said, eighty-nine is, eighty-nine cents is, eight dollars and ninety cents is ten times and so it's eighty-nine tenths and eight hundred and ninety one-hundredths.

I added Enoyat's idea to Connie's on the chalkboard so as to make it available for the whole class to study.

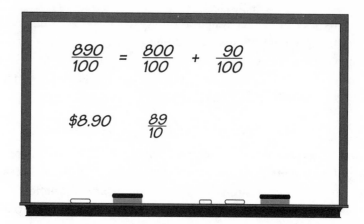

Enoyat used Connie's idea to study improper fractions in relation to the relationship between tenths and hundredths. He raised his hand and wanted to immediately reiterate the ideas in her assertion in terms of this other unit. We could have begun to talk here about how there were more hundredths than tenths because the pieces were smaller, but Sam was also eager to comment about what Connie said.

Working in Several Parts of a Conceptual Field at Once

The next student comment brought me a different kind of teaching problem: adding something new to the work on place value and multiplicative structures that we had not talked about in any other context. Sam had been interested a few days earlier in investigating the meaning of zeroes after the decimal point. Here he continued his investigation of when and whether they matter, and he talked about how zeroes function to indicate multiplication by ten.

In the teaching that I did in response to Sam's observation and in response to the students who spoke after he did, we see an extended example of the teaching work of moving around in a conceptual field, teaching several topics at once, and teaching the relationships among these topics. I needed to follow what students were saying in order to make a relationship between the mathematics of decimal numbers and their understanding of fractions, and I could not follow unless I was able to be at work in many parts of the field of "multiplicative structures" at once.

Lampert:	What do other people think?
	Sam?
Sam:	I think that it is because the eight hundred and ninety is the same thing as eight dollars and ninety cents. So you

take away zero from the numerator and denominator and then you have eighty-nine tenths and always like the same thing it's just multiplied by ten I think.

Lampert: Now there are some situations to which it makes sense to take away a zero and other situations in which it does not make sense to take away a zero.

What makes you think, Sam, that this is a situation in which it makes sense to take away a zero? [As I say this, I draw an arrow, connecting $\frac{890}{100}$ to $\frac{89}{10}$.]

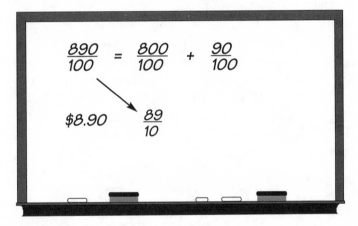

$$\frac{890}{100} = \frac{800}{100} + \frac{90}{100}$$

$$\$8.90 \qquad \frac{89}{10}$$

The next step in our study of the idea of the unit in the context of money took us into broader mathematical terrain as Sam began to use a language of "slices" and "cutting" to explain the meaning of the zeroes and why it made sense to him to work with them as he had done. Sam responded to my request for an explanation like this:

Sam: Well, that's just cut ten more each little slice from eighty-nine tenths, wait. I don't know how to—

The eight hundred and ninety-hundredths um are cut into each, what is it, each piece of the eighty-nine-tenths, each tenth and cut into ten pieces and make one with the eight hundred and ninety-hundredths. And the eighty-nine-tenths you're just multiplying it by what is it? Multiplying it by ten to get the number we're just multiplying, I mean like, cutting it, cutting into each piece into ten to get the eight hundred and ninety-hundredths.

The concrete referents to "slices" in Sam's comments made me think a different kind of drawing on the board would be an appropriate way to support the rest of the class in studying the new mathematics in his assertions. This is part of the work of teaching structures as opposed to teaching only topics. When I entertain two different representations of the same set of mathematical relationships (i.e., "slices" and coins), an additional focus of study becomes the similarities in the structure of the representations. I used the familiar pie representation to represent one whole, going along with Sam's language of "slices" and thinking that this representation might help clarify things for other students and help him learn to talk more clearly about the fractional relationships in his work.

The teaching problem I had to solve now was to make connections among the number symbols, the context of coins and bills, and this representation of parts and wholes as pies and slices. I needed to express these connections in my language and drawings in a way that would bring the rest of the class along into this new area of study. When Sam said, "cutting each piece into ten to get the eight hundred and ninety-hundredths," I imagine that he had begun with an image of 89 pieces that looked something like this representation of "89 tenths":

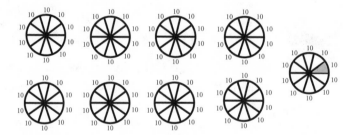

Each tenth of each "pie" that is shown here could be further cut into ten parts, making a total of a hundred parts in each pie. This is how Sam could claim that "eighty-nine-tenths" could be the same as "eight hundred and ninety-hundredths" by "multiplying."

In order to address the problem of continuing to teach Sam while also teaching the rest of the class, I put him in the position of judging my representation of his thinking.

Lampert: Okay, I'm going to try to draw a picture of what you said on the board.

Although I followed what Sam was saying, I thought I would need to break it down into several steps for consideration by the rest of the class.

I infused the commentary on my drawing with "facts" about fractions that were applicable to many such situations, like that all the parts needed to be equal. In this way I was able to teach topics in the curriculum at the same time that I was teaching about the big idea of multiplicative structures.

> Lampert: I'm just going to deal with the nine-tenths part for the moment, not the wholes, but the fractional part. In this circle there are ten pieces. They should all be equal, I tried to draw them as equally as possible.

What I drew looked something like this:

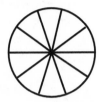

Following Sam's conceptual path, I then used this drawing to question others in the class about the meaning of the decimal numbers in terms of this representation.

> Lampert: How could I show nine-tenths on this circle?
>
>   Tyrone?
>
> Tyrone: Just shade in nine.

I followed Tryone's directions and shaded in nine of the ten slices, and wrote "$\frac{9}{10}$" next to what I had done.

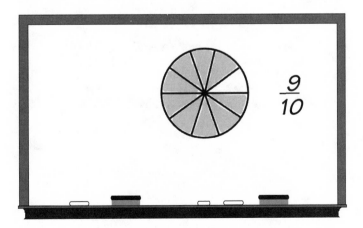

Then I asked the class how much the part that is not shaded in would be worth. Keeping what we were doing connected with the original problem context, Candice assumed the unit (or the whole) was a dollar and answered "ten cents" with that interpretation in mind. I picked up the connection and made it available to the whole class by writing it on the board under the drawing.

What I was trying to do here was to get a collection of different representations on the board so students could study both the anomalies in different problem contexts and how the representations were in some sense "the same." Sam's "pie" does not look anything like what a dollar would look like if we were dividing it into tenths. But it is the structure of the pie divided into slices that is the same as the structure of the dollar divided into units of "ten cents," or dimes. Although Candice and others spoke of each slice being worth "ten cents," I called each slice a dime to keep that relationship in the mix as well.

> Candice: It would be ten cents if the whole thing was a dollar.
>
> Lampert: Okay. It—
>
> Very, very good. If the whole thing and that's a very good condition, whole equals dollar, okay? [I put a label under the drawing.]

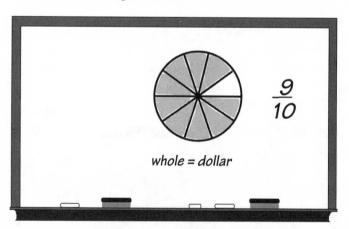

$$\frac{9}{10}$$

whole = dollar

> Then if the whole equals a dollar what each one of these pieces is—
>
> Students: Ten cents.
>
> Lampert: Ten cents. Okay? So I'm going to say orange pieces equal dimes. [The drawing had been made with orange chalk.]

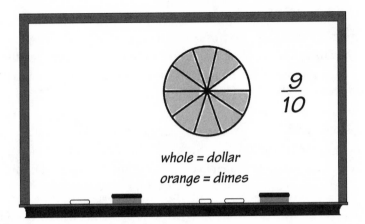

At this point I used the money referent to bring the class to the next part of Sam's explanation, where he took each of the tenths and cut them again into ten pieces to make hundredths.

Lampert:	Okay. Now, how can I show pennies on this circle.
	Oh, Tyrone, you want to say something before we move on to that?
Tyrone:	Um, it would be pennies if it was going to equal ten cents.
Lampert:	Excellent. Very good thinking.

Students Begin to Work with Structures as Well as in Contexts

Tyrone changed the frame of reference here. He used the circle I had labeled to represent a "dollar" and viewed it as being worth "ten cents." With this supposition, each slice would be worth a penny instead of ten cents. I was surprised at the sophistication of his assertion. What he did (and what several other students did in this discussion before and after he spoke) indicates a growth in understanding a big mathematical idea among several members of the class. He and the other students showed in their contributions that they were able to operate both *within* and *across* situations, taking account of both the variants and the invariance in multiplicative structures as they did so.

The "pie" I had drawn to represent what Sam said was meant to be worth a dollar, and each of its ten "slices" to be worth ten cents or a dime. Once I introduced dimes into the discussion, Tyrone made a speculation about dimes and pennies that expressed the basic idea of the common ratio that underlies place value in the way we write numbers. He said that if in the drawing the whole represented not a dollar but *ten cents*, then each slice would be a penny. We were still working on the part-whole relationships in interpreting fractions and decimals, but this time, students were taking the lead in that direction. It would be impossible to know whether they were actually "applying" what I had taught them earlier, but they were initiating the application of this idea in a new situation.

Candice had got us talking as if the whole "pie" was a dollar and each segment was ten cents. Now Tyrone was saying that if the whole pie was ten cents, each segment would be a penny. I decided to make a different circle, in a different color. I was challenged at this point to "direct the intellectual traffic" that was speeding around in my vicinity.

> Lampert: Alright. If I made a circle over here and I'll make this one red, and I had ten pieces and the whole equals ten cents then the shaded-in part would only mean nine pennies. [I make another drawing of a pie cut into ten slices, the same size but a different color.]

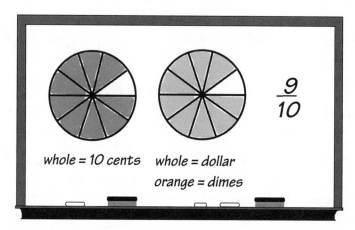

whole = 10 cents   whole = dollar
                    orange = dimes

$$\frac{9}{10}$$

By making the two circles the same size, I was deliberately making plain another anomaly—one that characterizes mathematical rather than context-bound representations. The similarity of the structures of the relationships between ten and one and between a hundred and ten is what is in focus here, *not* the comparison in size. The ratio 10:1 is equivalent to the ratio 100:10, just as $\frac{1}{10}$ is equivalent to $\frac{10}{100}$. These relationships are what give meaning to place value in our number system. We were working at the very heart of the concept of the fraction as a ratio, and the initiative to move us there had been Tyrone's comments on the diagrams.

Tyrone went on to make an even more profound assertion: that the parts of the pie could be dollars, and the whole ten dollars, or the whole could also be a hundred dollars, and the shaded-in part would be ninety.

Tyrone: It could be dollars then all of it equals ten dollars and be nine dollars, or a hundred, and ninety.

Lampert: Interesting. So what's important here is what you think the whole stands for, and that's exactly what Candice started out, when she said, if the whole equals a dollar then one piece is ten cents.

Tyrone was using the idea that the value of the pieces is variable in relation to the perspective one takes on the whole or "the unit."

What Tyrone did here was an example of what Hans Freudenthal would call "mathematizing": using a situation to get at its essential mathematical structure. Explicating how solving problems in a context contributes to learning mathematics, Freudenthal defines mathematizing as:

> turning a non-mathematical matter into mathematics, or a mathematically underdeveloped matter into more distinct mathematics. In mathematics instruction as I have in view, the context is, in the first instance, justified as an opportunity for the learner to mathematize it; mathematizing as a learning matter is an aim in itself.[20]

Although Tyrone is working in the context of money, and talks in terms of it, it is not money he is talking about. What he is talking about is the idea of ratio and proportion. He and the other students in this conversation have taken a mathematically underdeveloped matter and made it into "more distinct mathematics."

Common Contexts and the Work of Coverage Across Lessons

I teach to cover the conceptual field of multiplicative structures by having students work in a different problem context with different affordances and constraints imposed on the mathematics we can use. I expand and deepen students' experience with multiplicative structures by giving them opportunities to analyze them in different situations. Across situations, another level of "mathematizing" or making nonmathematical matters into situations for studying mathematics can be examined. Multiple situations are required for the mathematics to emerge; it is not in the situations but across them that the big idea of multiplicative structures comes to be understood. It is this abstraction of a mathematical idea from situations that makes it possible to use mathematics to solve problems in many different practical domains and to apply it to domains that are entirely novel.[21]

In terms of measuring whether and how the curriculum is being covered across the lessons, we see progress here in that students have initiated a representation to study the idea of the shifting unit. Sam introduces another representation with the same structure into the problem context of monetary exchanges. Tyrone expands Sam's contribution, focusing on the essence of the structure. Candice gets the conversation shifting between the cent as a whole and the dollar as a whole. And other students continue the discussion along these lines and pick it up the next day as they make charts of different values in decimal notation. In the overlap between learning the content and learning what is relevant to say in a mathematical discussion, Sam and Tyrone and Candice have produced some topics and connections among topics for their classmates to study. My role in supporting the relationship between the students in my class and the mathematics under study has changed as they have learned what to do to study mathematics using problems.

The ideas that we investigated in the context of dividing cakes among bakeries on January 18 and in the context of different units of money on March 15 could also be located on the map that I drew to represent the terrain of mathematics that we investigated in the time-speed-distance unit.

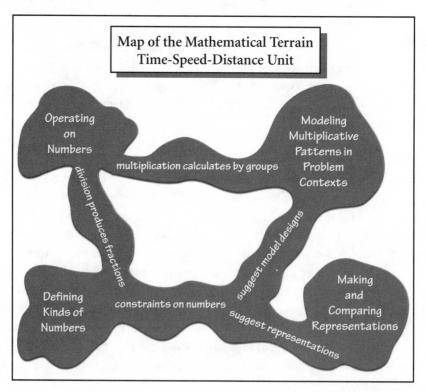

Map of the Mathematical Terrain
Time-Speed-Distance Unit

Operating on Numbers

Modeling Multiplicative Patterns in Problem Contexts

multiplication calculates by groups

division produces fractions

suggest model designs

Making and Comparing Representations

Defining Kinds of Numbers

constraints on numbers

suggest representations

The topics covered in all of these contexts are in some sense the same, but new "wrinkles" are added in each round of consideration. There is an increase in the level of conceptual detail when students contribute to discussions of these topics. These details, and the relationships among them, can be represented by elaborations of different parts of the map. In these elaborations, we see the topics of the curriculum and how they are related.

Arithmetic

From a mathematical perspective, the enlargement of the left side of the map displays more facets of students' work on the fundamental ideas and procedures in arithmetic while also showing how they fit in the field of multiplicative structures.

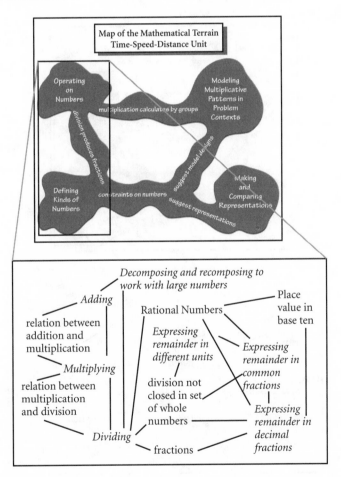

On the elaborated map, the terms in italics represent what students are learning to do, and the other terms, the concepts they need to think about to make sense of their work. Although arithmetic in school focuses almost exclusively on rules for calculation, its definition in the discipline of mathematics is more broad and conceptual. Arithmetic is the branch of mathematics that encompasses the study of integers, rational numbers, real numbers, or complex numbers under addition, subtraction, multiplication, and division.[22]

Mathematical Modeling

As students work on the mathematics of connecting or "modeling" (upper right on the map), they move back and forth between the concrete constraints of a problem context (like dividing up cakes to distribute to bakeries) and the constraints and affordances of arithmetic. Enlarging this part of the map, we show how students develop a more articulated set of connections among operations on decimals and common fractions.

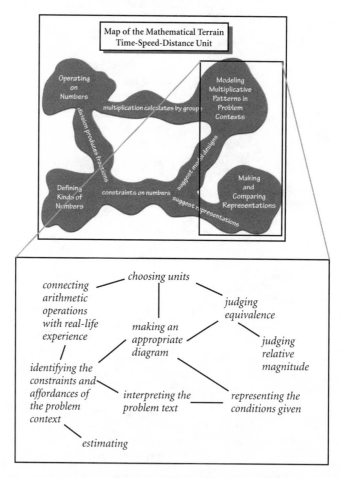

As the mathematics curriculum is represented in more and more detail on these maps, the problem of covering the curriculum can be seen as a problem of engaging students with an organic whole rather than with a set of discrete topics. The connections in these maps can represent connections in the mathematics, but they can also represent connections that a teacher can make from one student's work to another or from one lesson to another. If these connections are made explicit, the teacher can make use of them to teach both topics and conceptual fields.

Problems in Teaching in the Domain of Covering the Curriculum: "Invisible Work"

The purposeful long-term work of making connections among the topics that arise over and over again in problem contexts remains largely invisible to many classroom observers.[23] The work involved in raising mathematical structures to a level where they can be studied would be hard for someone to see if they were only looking for coverage in terms of getting through a linear series of topics one after the other. The topic-by-topic approach is the perspective most observers would bring to bear on trying to explain what I was doing in my teaching. The Scott, Foresman textbook series was still being used by most of the upper primary and middle school teachers in our district. If any of those teachers had come into my room during the lessons described in this chapter and tried to understand the teaching and studying they were seeing, they would have judged whether or not I was making progress in terms of where the content of subsequent lessons could be located in a list. They would have been likely to look at what I was doing and try to locate it somewhere in the customary sequence of lessons as I had done initially with the students' work in the time-speed-distance unit.[24]

In the Scott, Foresman teacher's guide, we are told that each topic is usually associated with one day's lesson, and there are not explicit connections from one lesson to the next.[25] Topics are embedded in chapters, and those are embedded in "units," but units are constituted by how many lessons they contain rather than by unifying themes or conceptual fields. As is almost uniformly true of such texts, a "lesson" appears on two facing pages, and its content is described in its title. The teacher's guide explains this structure as follows:

> The student's text has six units. Each unit contains three chapters. All lessons are on one page or two facing pages. The lesson format includes:
>
> - *a lesson title* that indicates the content of the lesson;
> - *teaching examples* that develop a skill and often begin with a motivational real-world problem;

- *exercises* that are graded from easy to hard, are often paired, and usually include applications with the same setting as used in the teaching examples.[26]

This organization is intended to give the teacher and the students a framework for identifying what pieces of mathematics are in focus in any particular instance of teaching and learning and a routine for moving through them.

Locating a lesson on an ordered list makes very clear where a class has been and where it will go next:

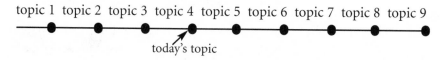

If the class is studying topic 4, for example, they will have "covered" topics 1, 2, and 3, and not yet encountered topics 5, 6, and 7. If the class did not "get" the material in the lesson on topic 3, the teacher would solve the problem by "going back over it again."[27]

Looking at the lessons described in this chapter through this topic-by-topic lens, what transpired might appear haphazard and confusing by contrast with the kind of mathematics lessons most of us remember. In those lessons, each day's studies were probably organized around a particular page in the textbook with a title at the top that said what topic it was about. In our collective memory, the teacher of mathematics worked a few examples of some procedure for computing or for solving a particular kind of "word problem," and the class was set to work on doing more of the same kind of problem. If most students in the class worked the page successfully, i.e., got the right answers, the teacher would go on to the next page the next day. If not, he or she would repeat the explanation of "how to do it" and the same routine would follow. The "smart" students might be working independently, several pages or even chapters ahead, having done these pages at some prior time.

In contrast to the familiar topic-by-topic approach, I worked on constructing lessons that were occasions for my students to investigate a number of different but related topics, and to investigate them repeatedly in different problem contexts. They worked in and across the contexts of relating time and distance when speed is given, of distributing cakes among bakeries under the condition that the cakes could be sliced, and of trading among different denominations of coins and bills to represent the same amount of money. In all of these contexts, I made both conventional and idiosyncratic symbols and procedures for working with multiples and fractions available so that students in my class could observe the connections and the differences in how these ideas are used in different contexts. In each unit of instruction, I made use of diagrams and charts to support students in characterizing and making deductions from patterns in the data that could be generated from the conditions given in the problem. Progress in this approach could not be seen until students had studied in several different problem-solving situations. With this experience, they could begin to identify the invariance across structures. One aspect of my work was giving them occasions when they could demonstrate this broad-based understanding of big ideas.

Teaching topics in a web of relationships while students work on problems involves four kinds of work:

- connecting ideas across problem contexts to build a coherent terrain for students to explore;

- elaborating ideas in the new context to add resources to students' repertoires;

- teaching conventional topics within frames of conceptual fields; and

- monitoring the growth of students' understanding and mastery of ideas and topics and tailoring choices about what to do next accordingly.

Each of these kinds of work can be further broken down into the actions that are taken to accomplish it.

To connect ideas coherently, I:

- mediate between the constraints of the problem context and the level of mathematics that students were able to perform with understanding;

- decide what to highlight from students' contributions to enable connections as well as coherence; and

- set boundaries on the problem context so that common structures across contexts would be more obvious.

To elaborate big ideas in new contexts, I:

- add more tools, e.g., calculator, number line;

- use different representations, e.g., linear vs. area models; and

- use common language, symbols, and drawings across contexts.

To teach conventional topics while working within the frame of conceptual fields, I:

- enable some of my students to be reviewing material that had perhaps remained unclear in an earlier set of lessons;

- add new and more sophisticated ideas to the mix for others to investigate;

- interpret representations created by students in particular problem contexts in terms of conventional representations; and

- adjust the content to the calendar and rhythms of the school year.

The work involved in monitoring students' learning will be elaborated in chapter 11.

The teaching actions listed here occur as the teacher builds on the interface between curriculum and instruction in interaction with students. Solving the problems of deciding when to infuse something new into the discussion, when to leave an investigation of an important idea and go on to something different, and how to adapt expectations to what one learns about students' capacities are all aspects of this element of teaching work. Teaching moves are made to address these problems in the context of actions that sustain students' engagement with topics and contents over the entire time they are in the class. Each time they meet a "big idea" like the relationship between multiplication and division, and engage in studying it, they are in some sense "studying the same thing over and over." But each different problem context requires new learning, since that idea needs to be adjusted to fit the constraints of the context and those adjustments result in an elaboration of understanding.

New Problems Raised by Reformulating Coverage in Terms of Conceptual Fields

In studying with problems, students and teachers do intellectual work to "construct bridges between the concrete and the abstract and between different ways of representing a problem or concept."[28] In this chapter, I have attempted to represent the work of maintaining a holistic perspective on big mathematical ideas while teaching conventional topics. But it is not only ideas that flow from one lesson to another across a school year in a particular class. Social connections also ebb and flow as my students get to know one another and I get to know them as mathematics learners. Individual personalities and relationships are not static, and these interact with the practices of teaching and studying ideas in a way that fundamentally shapes what I can teach and what my students can study and learn over time. Students and teachers are also working at constructing social bridges. In order to do the intellectual work that has been described here, they need to keep track of who talked in yesterday's discussion and who they will work with today, how they were feeling about what they produced last week, and what risks they are willing to take as we embark on a new set of problems.

In teaching and in studying with problems, mathematics flows from one lesson to another not by itself, but in the interactions and thoughts of the persons who make up the class. In these actions, the personal, the social, and the intellectual are inseparable. To work on the problems of covering the curriculum, I watch students and interact with them around mathematics, getting to know them as learners and doers of mathematics, every day of the school year. They watch and interact with one another over the same time frame. I learn from these interactions what I do to cover the curriculum. From inside of teaching, some of those interactions can be shaped more or less consciously. Others occur serendipitously. My teaching "agenda"—my work around what mathematics is to be taught and studied and how it gets taught and studied—is shaped by that information in several nested time frames: from what I do the next minute to what I do the next day or the next month. In the next few chapters, I take up this integration in the work of making mathematical connections while nurturing productive social relationships as a further elaboration on the problems of covering the curriculum using problems to engage students with big ideas.

10

Teaching Students to Be People
Who Study in School

To promote learning, every day and across the year, the teacher offers activities that make it possible for students to study: to read, to observe, to listen, to investigate, and to otherwise acquire the knowledge and skills indicated in the curriculum. To this end, teaching involves constructing tasks that engage students with new information and skills such as making schedules and seating arrangements. Teachers also can be said to "make" or "construct" *students* into resources that can be used to promote learning by teaching them to be the kinds of people who study in the classroom and who expect others to do so as well. Doing this in a school classroom carries several challenges. Students are in relationships with their peers as well as with the teacher. In my classroom, students were edging up on adolescence, they were in their final year of elementary school, there were a lot of them in a small room, and they were an unusually diverse group on every dimension imaginable. They did not choose to be in this class or in this school, or even to be in school at all.

Although some students show up at school as "intentional learners"— people who are already interested in doing whatever they need to do to learn academic subjects—they are the exception rather than the rule.[1] Even if they are disposed to study, they probably need to learn how.[2] But more fundamental than knowing how is developing a sense of oneself as a learner that makes it socially acceptable to engage in academic work.[3] The goal of school teaching is not to turn all students into people who see themselves as professional academics, but to enable all of them to include a disposition toward productive study of academic subjects among the personality traits they exhibit while they are in the classroom.[4] If the young people who come to school do not see themselves as learners, they are not going to act like learners even if that would help them to be successful in school. It is the teacher's job to help them change their sense of themselves so that studying is not a self-contradictory activity.

One's sense of oneself as a learner is not a wholly private construction. Academic identity is formed from an amalgamation of how we see ourselves and how others see us, and those perceptions are formed and expressed in social interaction.[5] How I act in front of others expresses my sense of who I am. How others then react to me influences the development of my identity. Influential interaction can take the form of talking and doing together, but it can also mean being quiet so that another person can concentrate. It can be as subtle as dressing a certain way in public or sitting in a particular posture to express solidarity. Because the relationships in a classroom occur among the same set of people, in a public setting, daily, and over a long period of time, they offer multiple occasions for self-expression and have a strong potential to influence self-perception.[6] What students are willing to do with one another and with their teacher in the public space of the classroom constrains their capacities to study and to learn. If a student does not see himself or herself as the kind of person who is going to learn, it seems unlikely that learning will occur. Even if such a person were tricked into acquiring some knowledge or skill, the chances that such learning would ever be used in public are probably slim.

On the surface, the work of teaching entailed here could be thought of as "classroom management" or "discipline." It is about what the teacher does to keep students on task, to keep them from "fooling around" or otherwise interfering with productive activity. But if we view students' productive or unproductive actions in the classroom as expressions of who they think they are, then classroom management merges with something that might be called "academic character education."

Teaching Intellectual Courage, Intellectual Honesty, and Wise Restraint

In this chapter, we look at problems of teaching that arise in the domain of influencing students to be the kinds of persons who are academic resources for themselves and for one another. To examine the work of teaching young people to be successful students, I consider two examples. The first is a study of my interactions over time with Richard. I begin with Richard in order to explain the teaching that I did leading up to the lesson-specific interactions described in chapter 2. There I described a teaching interaction I had with Richard in a lesson on rate in November. In that instance, Richard made a mistake in public, and I responded by pressing him to correct his reasoning. What I did in that lesson was risky, but the risk-taking needs to be explained as part of an ongoing stream of interactions with this student that began at the beginning of the year.

One of the hardest things to do in front of a group of one's peers is to make a mistake, admit one has made it, and correct it. Yet such a series of actions is an essential component of academic character. It defines the very nature of learning, for if we already knew everything we would never have to do such things. The second case is a study of my teaching Saundra, who also makes a mistake in front of her peers. The special problems for girls in maintaining an interest in mathematics while in the company of boys as they enter puberty are well known, and the teaching I examine in this instance is an effort to address those problems as a particular kind of academic character building. In the case of teaching Saundra, I also take up another kind of teaching problem, namely, structuring the use of manipulative materials so that all students in the class can use them for the serious study of mathematics.

In the analysis of teaching problems in these two cases, I look over the long term at the work that went into making relationships with Richard and with Saundra that would dispose them to study mathematics in my classroom. I was not doing this work with Richard or with Saundra because they were somehow unique or special or because they had more serious problems than other students did with learning in school. I was simultaneously doing the same kind of work that will be described here with all of the twenty-five students who came to my class on the first day of school and with the four additional students who entered in the course of the year. Each of the students in my class, whether extraordinarily competent or poorly prepared, presented teaching challenges as I aimed to support the development of his or her academic character. This work had to be done for everyone in the class.

The risk of public failure and its impact on relationships in classrooms is rarely acknowledged in the same text with analyses of how one makes progress in understanding the subject matter or increases one's skills in producing mathematical representations.[7] What we see in the teaching practice described in this chapter and in chapters 11 and 12 is that the work of maintaining productive relationships with and among students must include simultaneous attention both to academic identity and to progress. The fragility of individual identity in the school context is a problem for the teacher because it can get in the way of improving academic performance. In this domain, particularly, doing the work of teaching requires the cooperation of one's students.[8] If a student is unable to feel that it is safe to have and express ideas, or even to answer a simple question, then performance will not be improved. The work of establishing an environment in which students feel safe to do academic work with one another is a daily business requiring constant attention. In teacher lingo, we often hear of the importance of "being consistent" or "building trust." The goal of actions described by these terms is not consistency per se or even a trusting relationship, but a set of relationships that make it likely that students will engage in activities that will lead to learning.

At the same time the teacher is getting to know students and respecting who they are, she is trying to change them. She must accept and support each individual in order to build trust, and at the same time, make that individual over into one more inclined to study, to initiate the investigation of ideas, and to be identified as someone who will and can do what needs to be done to learn in school. For the student, taking on the "new" self that the teacher imagines is risky, and feelings toward the teacher for encouraging such risk taking may not be wholly positive.

In the work of teaching and studying as I have conceived of them, one must learn to practice what Georg Polya calls the "intellectual virtues" while reasoning in the presence of one's peers. He puts these virtues in the context of "the inductive attitude." Here, I am claiming that adopting such an attitude is essential to learning mathematics in school, and that such virtues can be taught in classrooms.

> In our personal life we often cling to illusions. That is we do not dare to examine certain beliefs which could be easily contradicted by experience, because we are afraid of upsetting the emotional balance. There may be circumstances where it is not unwise to cling to illusions, but [in the practices of learning and teaching] we need to adopt the inductive attitude which requires a ready ascent from observations to generalizations, and a ready descent from the highest generalizations to the most concrete observations. It requires saying "maybe" and "perhaps" in a thousand different shades. It requires many other things, especially the following three:
>
> | | |
> |---|---|
> | INTELLECTUAL COURAGE: | we should be ready to revise any one of our beliefs |
> | INTELLECTUAL HONESTY: | we should change a belief when there is good reason to change it… |
> | WISE RESTRAINT: | we should not change a belief wantonly, without some good reason, without serious examination[9] |

In the following two cases, I examine the problems for a teacher in making the classroom a place where these virtues can be studied and practiced by everyone.

Working up to Mathematical Risk Taking: Teaching Richard from September to December

Richard was new to our school in September, and he entered the class a self-declared mathematical bungler. In the exchange that I had with Richard on November 22, described in chapter 2, we saw him publicly making a mistake and publicly revising his thinking. Considered in isolation, what I did to teach Richard in that exchange could be seen as putting him at considerable social risk. In exposing his confusion to the class, I may have done more harm than good in my effort to help him to form an academic identity that both he and his classmates could accept and even value. It was the opportunity to work with Richard constantly over the course of several months that made it possible for me to teach Richard something about mathematics and about decimal numbers in our interaction on November 22.

Who Is Richard? Observing and Interpreting First Encounters

My work in making Richard into someone who would promote his own learning began with watching how he presented himself to me and to his classmates on the first day of school. In order to form a relationship with him, I needed to know who he thought he was. Richard came in the room on September 7 with a glint in his eye and a smile on his face. He moved easily around the classroom, bumping into people and furniture, until he found his way to the desk with his name on it. After he had been introduced to me as "the math teacher," Richard politely announced to Thom, his homeroom teacher, that he did not much "like math" and he had not been "very good at it" in the school he had attended before moving to our town. On the same day, Richard publicly presented himself to the class as both a risk taker and a person in need of some support if he was to engage in mathematical reasoning in front of his peers.

As part of our regular first-day-of-school routine, Thom set out to assign another student in the class to be Richard's "buddy." "Buddies" were a system that Thom used to orient new students to the school. Buddies were assigned to take new students to lunch and recess: settings where the teacher would not necessarily be close at hand if the new student needed advice or help. All of the other students who were new silently accepted the persons assigned to be their "buddies." Richard, however, responded to Thom's assignment of Giyoo as his buddy with a counterproposal. He said he wanted Ivan to be his buddy. He had met Ivan in his neighborhood during the summer, and the two had become friends.

As I was anticipating what I would need to do to be Richard's mathematics teacher, I thought it was worth noting that he spoke out in this way about his preferences. Richard was mildly challenging the teacher in charge, and it was the first day of school. This was a bold thing to do from one perspective, but sensible from another. Richard was asserting that he would feel more secure if he could hang out with someone he knew. He was not aggressive in his challenge to the teacher. He expressed his wishes in a calm and direct tone. I observed in this incident that Richard had the self-confidence to express his wishes to adults in a reasonable way. This kind of behavior was relevant to teaching him because I would be expecting students to challenge unreasonable ideas, whether they came from a teacher or another student.

Another relevant aspect of Richard's character became clear as we continued into the first math lesson. After Thom had taken care of assigning buddies and other matters pertaining to procedures for the first day of school, I asked the class if they could think of any ways they had used math so far that day. No one responded immediately, so I thought of an example. Before Thom had started assigning buddies, he had been working with the class to create a word web to define the word "buddy." He made a "web" to record their responses on the chalkboard that looked like this:

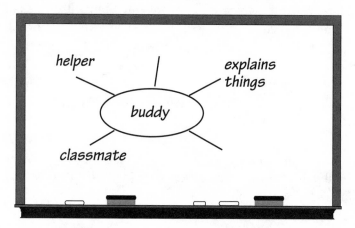

Students were directed to make a reproduction on paper, adding their own ideas to those shared with the whole class. I commented on the math in what they had been doing as they were trying to figure out where to write the word "buddy" as they laid out the web on their notebook pages. Then I asked a question to see what kind of language my idea might elicit.

> Lampert: What kind of a math—what kind of math do you think you would do to try to figure out where to write the word "buddy"?

Several students raised their hands, and I called on Ellie, who simply said, "Measuring." I asked for an elaboration on Ellie's comment, and again, several students raised their hands, including Richard. His contribution foreshadowed a theme that came up over and over again in both his spoken and written work: claiming to be able to do something but not to be able to "explain it."

Ellie:	Measuring.
Lampert:	Measuring is one. How would you measure—
	I didn't see anybody using a ruler so how could you measure it, if you didn't have a ruler?
	Richard?
Richard:	Well, you would see how much the, how long and how wide it is and. Um, I can do but I can't explain it.

What followed was my first effort to relate to Richard in a way that would support a change in both his competence and his sense of self. I took this opportunity to comment publicly on my expectations. I told the class, including Richard, about how we were going to do things this year with regard to "explaining." What I tried to teach Richard was that he would need to add explaining to his repertoire.

Lampert:	Okay, one of the things we're going to learn about this year is how to explain your thinking. So one thing, if you um, listen to how other people explain their thinking, that will help you to learn how to explain your thinking.

I did not tell Richard how to explain this answer on this occasion, but I took note of his reticence and I tried to give him, and everyone else, a clue about how to learn to "explain" as a way to study mathematics. And I communicated the expectation that everyone in this class would become a person who explains in public.

I continued to work at building my knowledge of Richard as a learner through watching and interacting with him in those early days of the year. When I was in a position to respond to what he was doing, I acted in a way that combined acceptance with an expectation for growth and change. I had a chance to do this in a discussion we were having about the math notebooks. I pointed out that the pages in them were made of "graph paper." I then asked students to describe the characteristics of that kind of paper. They talked about lines and angles. Shahroukh used the terms "horizontal" and "vertical." Shahroukh was a quiet and deliberate boy who had been at our school for several years and who had a well-established reputation for mathematical competence. He was tutored in mathematics at home, his parents were professionals who used mathematics, and he shared his expertise in lessons in an aggressive but usually tactful manner.

In the midst of this talk about what I thought of as "geometry," Richard asked me if graph paper was "better."

Richard: Is it better to have this paper than the other kind?

I turned the question back to him in a way that would continue the study of geometry, asking him to describe the characteristics of the paper. As he answered, I was able to learn that there were some ambiguities in his character, and that I might work to help him to enhance some aspects of his character and diminish others so he could become more intentional about his own learning. To begin to do that in this exchange, I identified him publicly as a person who could have ideas, and I gave him another opportunity to try to explain something. He immediately responded, using the terms that Shahroukh had introduced a few minutes before.

Lampert: Why do YOU think I got you this kind of paper for math problems?

             You must have an idea about that Richard. What do you think?

Richard: Well, it's got horizontal lines and vertical lines and it might be easier to write.

When Richard used Shahroukh's terms "horizontal" and "vertical" in his explanation he was doing more than taking on a new vocabulary. He was also taking on a bit of Shahroukh's academic character, allowing himself to be like him, and to let other students see that he could be so. But what he did was not wholly inconsistent with Richard's character. There had been something quite intellectually distinctive about his asking me why graph paper is "better." He exhibited curiosity, and it seemed as if he wanted everyone to know when something was on his mind. These were traits I thought I could build on to help him engage in mathematical studies.

Connecting with Richard to Support His Intention to Study Mathematics

During the first week of math lessons, I tried to learn what I could about how each of my students would express himself or herself in a classroom context, particularly when the focus was on doing mathematics. Some students raised their hands and had a lot to say about the problems we were working on. At first, Richard was not among them. I kept in mind what he said about himself on the first day, when he identified himself as not very "good at" or interested in doing math. On September 11, I took note of a

small glimmer of mathematical engagement, and on September 12, an out-
right expression of enthusiasm for working on the problem. Richard's
engagement on these occasions was semipublic. He was not hiding his
enthusiasm, but he was not displaying it in front of the whole class, either. I
needed to work at finding out what had caught Richard's interest so that I
could continue to structure the classroom environment in a way that would
keep him engaged.

On September 12, the problem was to find combinations of two two-digit
numbers that would add up to the sum of 51.

Richard rapidly produced several combinations and was heard to remark
"this is fun" and (somewhat sheepishly) "this is easy." There was something
in his voice that communicated both embarrassment and surprise. At the
end of the lesson, he asked me if he could take his math notebook home to
keep working. My effort to build confidence and trust by having students
reason about computations that were not arithmetically challenging to them
seemed like it might pay off with him.

One of my intentions in giving this kind of problem at the beginning
of the year was to learn about who would approach the problems strategically. I hoped the "easy" addition would not confound students' capacities to
reason about patterns and relationships.

The two pages of work Richard did in class looked like this.

Tuesday, september 12

Copy these into your notebook

These are Richard's first efforts, showing strategic thinking right from the start.

fill in the indifferent worm up to make these addition tru

Here he seems to be trying out a variety of combinations, perhaps thinking about what properties of numbers he could use to generate lots of combinations.

The work on the first page displays some strategic mathematical thinking. There is evidence of strategic thinking in beginning with 51 + 00 as the first combination, for example. Rather than beginning randomly, Richard makes use of the properties of 0. His second combination may reflect an effort to find the halfway point between 0 and 51, and the third combination builds on the first. Then we see some additions to 40, to 20, and to 10. This was an interesting and productive way to make use of the problem structure to study mathematics. I did not see anything like it in any other student's work that day. On the second page, Richard sets out to produce combinations to 51 in earnest. He seemed to like what he was doing well enough, even though it was clearly "math." What seemed to hold his interest was using patterns to produce more and more combinations. He had become involved in investigating a fundamental strategy in mathematical work, and he was using the problem as an occasion to practice his addition facts as well.

When I stopped to talk with Richard about what he was doing, I learned that it was going to take some work on my part to get him to go beyond generating combinations to making more general statements to explain how numbers work. I commented on our interaction in my journal:

> It really pleased me that Richard got so engaged, partly because I think his skills are weak + partly because Thom told me that he announced in class yesterday morning that he didn't like math. The skills part was confirmed today when I challenged him to figure out how many combinations he had, <u>not</u> counting by ones. He said he knew you could "count by threes and stuff like that" but that he "wasn't very good at it." So I said, Okay, let's have some <u>practice</u>, and I helped him count the ones he had in his notebook by twos. He had ~~turb~~ trouble with what to do after 18, 28, 38, and also what to do after 20, 30, 40.

Richard's self-identification as "not very good at" doing "stuff" like counting by threes, like his earlier claim that he could do something but not explain what he was doing, was something about him that I wanted to help him change. I saw that he had more competence than he was willing to own up to in public, maybe more than he knew he had, even when working in private.

What Richard had done on the first page of his notebook work suggested to me that he had the intellectual capacity to investigate mathematical ideas in a reasoned manner. There was a mismatch between what he could do and the way he portrayed himself. Assuming that if he saw himself as unable to explain and as "not very good" at mathematics then he would not try harder in class, I set out to make a relationship with him that would convey my sense of him as capable. I would hold up a mirror to him to show him what he could do whenever I observed him performing competently.

Using the Activity Structure of Lessons to Influence Richard's Sense of Himself as a Learner

Over the next week or so, I watched all of the students in my class to see how each of them would use the activity structure I had been making available to them to support the work of studying. I noticed that Richard would often begin class by copying the problem and then saying aloud, either to me or to another student, "What are we supposed to do?" The problems were designed to enable many possible entry points. He acted as if he was not able to find even *one*, and this was troubling. This was another thing about Richard that I wanted to help him to change. To be a resource in his own learning, he needed to be the sort of person who would make an interpretation of the problem and get going, not wait for someone else to tell him more explicitly what to do next. I offered small, relatively private encouragements along these lines. And then one day, I spoke to the whole class, publicly about my general expectations of everyone. What I said was set off by Richard's asking me what to do.

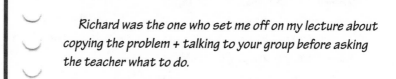

> *Richard was the one who set me off on my lecture about copying the problem + talking to your group before asking the teacher what to do.*

On September 26, I took a small, semipublic social risk, challenging Richard to take on a different sense of himself as a learner. Two other students seated near Richard were also having trouble getting going, and I decided to see if Richard would be an interpreter for them.

> Richard, Giyoo + Donna Ruth got going together after both Giyoo + Donna Ruth asked me → "don't get it, what are we supposed to do?" I took a chance on whether Richard could clear things up for them—and when I checked back they were all three "on task." It was a nice opportunity for them to learn that they don't need to depend on me to figure things out + for Richard to take a leadership role.

In this bit of teaching, I was shaping Richard's relationship with me and his relationship with his peers into ones in which he could confidently demonstrate his competence in figuring out what to do by himself or collaboratively with others in the class. Doing this would support his being able to study mathematics by working independently on the problems that were posed in the presence of his peers, providing an alternative way to be in the group. If I (or someone else) told him what mathematics to begin with to solve the problem, he would be missing out on an opportunity to study something that I had deliberately planned into the lesson.

I observed that Richard was tentatively able to make the transition from not being able to get himself going and publicly announcing his dependence at the beginning of many class periods to helping other students in his group start their work when called upon to do so. This was a significant change in the person he had presented earlier, to me and to his peers. On September 18, I reviewed the work in all of my students' notebooks, and I wrote the following positive assessment to Richard:

> 9/18
>
> Richard —
> Your work is very clear and neat. You are learning to see patterns in the numbers to help you think about the mathematics in these problems.
> Dr. Lampert

When the notebooks were returned to students on Monday morning with my comments, everyone eagerly looked to see what I had written. In order to gauge the impact of this act of teaching, I watched carefully to see who did what in response to my comments. Some students showed the comments to others, but Richard kept his private. Perhaps set off by reading this written assessment, which countered his image of who he was in math class, Richard began doing something teachers often refer to as "fooling around" with three other boys: Tyrone, Enoyat, and Giyoo. All of these boys were even less engaged with mathematics during the first two weeks of school than Richard had been. Keeping them on task required me to be nearby, if not more direct intervention. I do not know if Richard was embarrassed by my positive comments or if he started fooling around to prove to himself and to others that he was not the serious student that I wanted him to be. But I did know that this behavior was counterproductive and I needed to figure out how to change it.

Between September 18 and 28, there were many blank pages in Richard's notebook, and many pages where his work was incomplete, unreasonable, and inconclusive. On September 19, Richard did not write the problem that was on the chalkboard in his notebook and his work is of mixed quality. He demonstrated some strategic mathematical thinking and some competence with the arithmetic, but it came to a halt after a few computations and did not pick up again, suggesting that he had been distracted. Although he could have asked for help from his group, either he did not ask, or he did not get any help that he could use. He chose not to call his problem to my attention. I would need to watch more to see what was up.

The next day, I saw that Richard again did not copy the problem. He did some subtractions to arrive at the difference of 14, but he crossed out most of the experiments he did and what he wrote about them.

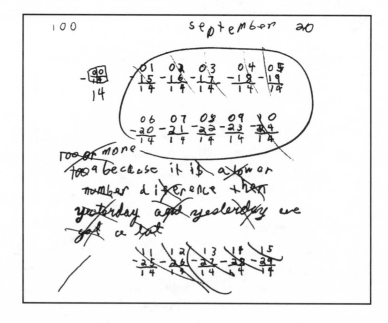

Although the symbolization of the subtraction is incorrect in the computations he crossed out, he did not cross out all of the incorrect ones. In terms of finding the absolute value of the difference, however, all of his work is flawless and makes good use of a strategic pattern to generate combinations. Even though it gets better toward the end of the week, the quality of Richard's work during this period seems very different from what I had been seeing before September 18. It is not clear what caused the change, but whatever it was, Richard was not engaged in the productive study of mathematics.

The next time I commented on Richard's written work, I wrote something very different:

> 9/24
>
> Richard —
> Please use every page in your
> notebook . Look over your
> arithmetic and make sure
> The numbers you are writing
> down are what you really mean.
>   Dr. Lampert

The unevenness of Richard's written work continued. So did the fooling around with Giyoo, Tyrone, and Enoyat.

Supporting Richard in Social Encounters with Structured Opportunities to Study

Making another move to enable Richard to work productively with his peers, I collaborated with Thom to change the seating arrangements. I was reluctant to make this move, because Richard needed to learn to be a student with everyone in the class watching. But I would get to that later. In the new arrangement, we moved Richard away from Giyoo, Enoyat, and Tyrone, and assigned him a seat next to Ivan and across from Yasu. I had observed both of these students to be regularly on task and to be helpful to their peers but not in a way that would be embarrassing. I had also seen them act self-assured, getting going with their own interpretations of the problems that were posed. Because Richard had identified Ivan as his friend on the first day of school, I would be experimenting with whether this relationship could support mathematical study in the classroom. Thom and I did not move Richard too far away from Giyoo and Enoyat, because the change we expected would have to happen in their presence as well. We did move Tyrone to the other side of the room. On the first day we tried this rearrangement, I wrote in my journal about how it worked:

> *What was going on in the rest of the class was more or less productive, except it went on too long. The new groups were getting established socially and there were some productive attempts as well as some social disasters. Shahroukh's attempts to <u>teach</u> (and he really did sound like a mini-teacher, not a teller), to <u>teach</u> a Tyrone were rebuffed. I don't know what Tyrone thought was going on, but he didn't like it. I'm sure he didn't like being separated from Giyoo and Richard and being aggressively involved by the class brain. Shahroukh was polite + appropriately didactic but aggressive + not terribly patient. I wonder if there's anything salvageable there?*
>
> *Yasu + Ivan both took up helping Richard + Donna Ruth who both were saying at the beginning: "I don't get it."*

Richard presented his more or less mathematically "helpless" self to his new neighbors, Yasu and Ivan. Unlike his earlier seatmates, however, they set about trying to get him engaged.

A few days later, I commented in my journal again on the general tone of interactions within the class, being cautious to attribute it to any teaching I had done, and taking note of the upcoming parent conferences.

> *After class 10/4*
>
> *It felt like a lot of consolidating was going on today, a bit like last Wednesday, but at a different level. Different sorts of participation, more engagement. I wonder how much of it has to do with the nature of the problem (<u>nobody</u> asked me an "I don't get it, I don't know what to do" sort of question), how much has to do with their feeling more settled in with one another, how much has to do with the fact that parents open house is coming up + they want to avoid us saying there are some problems with behavior (Tyrone, Giyoo, Richard, esp.)*

During October, I wrote progress reports to send to the parents of each of my students. This was the report that I sent home to Richard's parents at the end of the first marking period.

First Marking Period Report
MATHEMATICS
Grade Five

Name: Richard   Date: 11/4

Richard's engagement in mathematics has improved tremendously since the beginning of the school year. He is doing a much better job of paying attention, both to teacher-directed large group lessons and to small group activities, although he still needs to be occasionally reminded not to let himself be distracted. The substance of Richard's work has improved as well. He began the year with a lot of guessing, saying numbers and doing things with them without thinking about what he was doing. Now he is paying attention to patterns and using them to solve problems and thinking about what the numbers in a problem represent. He needs to work more on using drawings and diagrams to represent the information that is given in a problem, and his learning to do this is one of my major goals for him this year.

Richard has some trouble bringing the concept of place value (hundreds, tens, and ones) in numbers together with computational procedures, and at this stage that means he has trouble with borrowing in subtraction. He has a good sense of the concept of multiplication, however, and he is able to take large numbers apart, work on parts of them, and then put them back together in a mathematically appropriate way. Another goal that I have for Richard for this year is that he learn to transfer these good mathematical intuitions to performing more formal, abstract procedures correctly.

In this report, I tried to communicate my sense of the fragile but positive changes in Richard's disposition to work independently, in cooperation with his peers. He depended less directly on me to guide his work, at least on a few occasions. I hoped that this parent report would communicate to him that I had noticed.

On top of the substantively mathematical interactions I had with Richard in the first months of school, I used three teaching moves to deliberately intervene in his evaluation of his own capability: writing comments on his journal, rearranging his physical location in relation to other students, and noting progress in communicating with his parents. In each of these moves I tried to improve Richard's opportunities to study while leaving him a measure of freedom to express his "self" in the context of his relationships with his peers and with me. If his sense of himself as a learner of mathematics was going to change, it was not going to be enough for him simply to obey directions or depend on supportive peers. He needed to practice being competent in front of others without my intervention.

Observing Richard and His Peers as He
Tries on a Mathematically Studious Self

The discussion in which I asked Richard to revise his reasoning in front of the class described in chapter 2 occurred a few weeks after the parent reports were sent. The seating assignments had been changed again by that time, and now Richard was next to Shahin, a student who had joined the class just the week before. Shahin had a silly streak, but he also engaged vigorously in working on problems and he seemed adequately competent in doing arithmetic computations. Although Richard had been the one who needed a "buddy" to orient him on the first day, he was now more experienced at how to "do school" in this setting. Seated where he was, he was in a position to use his experience to teach Shahin.

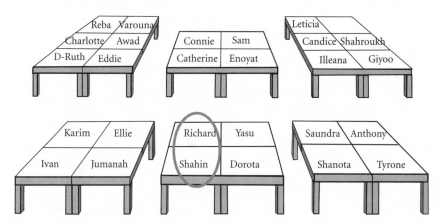

By making this kind of opportunity available to Richard, I intended to prepare him for somewhat less safe, more public performances of his understanding of what should be done to study mathematics in this classroom.

Before the interaction in the whole-group part of the lesson described in chapter 2, Shahin and Richard had had an extended independent conversation. They debated about how to figure out the distance that a car, traveling at 55 miles per hour, would go in half an hour. Sitting across from them, Dorota and Yasu worked together on a different approach to the problem. Although I was able to observe only bits and pieces of their conversation, I did listen at the time for how much mathematical study was happening. (Here I will use a recording of their collaboration to describe it in full for the reader.)

In their talk about their work on the problem, Richard and Shahin worked persistently but also seemed to be enjoying one another. They focused on various ways to compute half of 55. The social structure I had provided to support productive study in small groups deliberately placed responsibility on students for interpreting the problem in devising a solution strategy. These structures gave Richard the opportunity to respond as a sense-making critic to Shahin's rather frenetic activity. Richard could orient Shahin to classroom routines like using graphics to represent the problem without seeming to be a "wise-guy" or "smarty-pants," i.e., without being too arrogantly academic to be accepted as a co-worker by another, somewhat silly ten-year-old boy who was new to the class.

One example of Richard's efforts at appropriate mathematical self-expression occurred when Shahin attempted the conventional long division algorithm, but misplaced the numbers as he was doing various calculations. The first two steps in his procedure looked like this:

$$\begin{array}{r} 2 \\ 2\overline{)55} \\ \underline{1} \\ 45 \end{array} \quad \text{and} \quad \begin{array}{r} 22 \\ 2\overline{)55} \\ \underline{1} \\ 45 \end{array}$$
$$\text{then}$$

Richard questioned what Shahin was doing in his notebook.

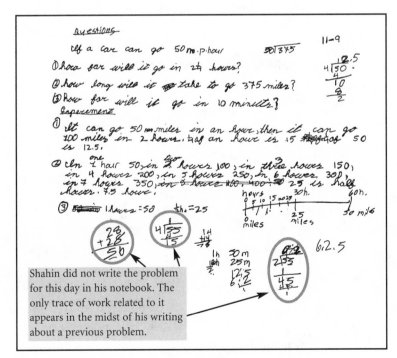

Shahin did not write the problem for this day in his notebook. The only trace of work related to it appears in the midst of his writing about a previous problem.

As Shahin talks, he listens, and finally says, "Yeah, but" as he attempts to bring both the problem context and the meaning of the numbers onto the table for study. Richard's alternative computations are approximate but sensible, whereas Shahin seems to be working through the procedure mechanically, not thinking about what it means in terms of the problem.

Shahin: Look, wait, wait, wait, watch this. Here, this page. Fifty-five divided by two, right? Equals to four bring down the one, this bring down the five, five minus one is four, forty-five divided by two is?

Richard: Forty-five divided by two?

Shahin: Uh-huh.

Richard: Is, um, twenty-four.

Shahin: Okay, twenty-four, twenty-four times two?

Richard: Forty-eight.

Shahin: Okay, how about twenty-two? Twenty-two times two equals forty-four, forty-four, it's um, it's remainder one. Four hundred, four hundred twenty-two, remainder one. So that means that you don't count the—

Richard: Yeah, but first—

At this point, Richard calls Shahin's attention to the representation of the trip on the journey line in his notebook, indicating where half of an hour-long journey would be marked.

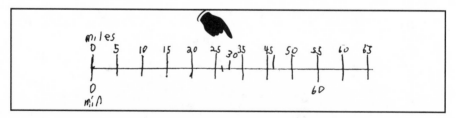

What Richard did here made it possible for him and Shahin to work together productively to try to straighten out their solution. When Shahin says, "But we're talking about fifty-five miles," Richard moves closer to the solution, first reiterating that it is half of 55 they need to find, then starting that process by finding half of 50. He takes on the role of explainer and directs Shahin in how to work on the problem.

Shahin: But we're talking about fifty-five miles.

Richard: Okay, half of fifty-five? Half of fifty is twenty-five.

Richard goes on to estimate half of 55 more and more accurately, finally arriving at 28. Shahin is distracted from what Richard is saying by a computation that he had carried out earlier to produce the answer "twenty-two."

Richard: Okay, half of fifty-five? Half of fifty is twenty-five.

Shahin: No, what's half of fifty-five?

Richard: It's like twenty-eight.

Shahin: No.

Richard: Yes.

Shahin: No, it isn't.

Richard: Yes, it is.

Shahin: Wait, where did I do that?

Richard: Twenty-six.

Shahin: Wait, tell me how did I get this then. If it's supposed to be twenty-eight, how did I get this then.

Richard: I don't know how you got it.

Shahin: Wait. How do you know it's twenty-eight? Twenty-eight, twenty-eight, twenty-eight plus twenty-eight is six and four, five, fifty-six, fifty-six. It's twenty-two.

Richard: Twenty-two? Twenty-two? Twenty-two?

Shahin: Where would twenty-two be on this then?

Richard: Twenty-two would be about here. Except you—

Richard said "twenty-eight" first, but then revised to "twenty-six." Shahin continued to question Richard as if he had not revised, asking him again how he knows it is "twenty-eight." And Richard questioned Shahin's "twenty-two." Richard tried out the solution that Shahin was preoccupied with (i.e., 22) on the number line, but he did not seem to be satisfied with it.

At this point the camera turned away from Richard and Shahin, and the next piece of evidence we have about Richard on November 22 is the record of his participation in the large-group discussion recounted in chapter 2. A key element in our exchange during that discussion is his estimation that ¼ of 55 is 13.5, which he arrives at by taking half of twenty-seven. What he did then seemed to follow a pattern that had been established in his interactions with Shahin.

An Expanded Picture of Teaching Richard About Division and Decimals

The teaching I did during the discussion in response to Richard's efforts can now be explained as a piece of practice that extended across time and across relationships. In the incident from the whole-group discussion that followed his work with Shahin, Richard made a confused assertion, and he made it in front of the whole class. He revised his assertion to "thirteen and a half or thirteen point five" and while he and I talked about that, several other students bid for attention. My action-answers to the questions I asked about what to do to teach Richard (and the class) in chapter 2 can now be seen as part of a continuous, deliberate stream of *inter*action with Richard. His performance in front of the class can be seen in terms of its continuity with his engagement in teaching and being taught by Shahin.

When we put an expanded frame around what Richard did and what I did in the large-group discussion on November 22, teaching practice in that instance can be seen as both temporally and socially connected across the members of the class and across the previous several weeks. In that large-group discussion, I and some of the students in the class were teaching Richard by our reactions to his initial speculations, but what we were saying to him about his abilities to reason were not only expressed in the words and actions of that moment. They were part of a long-established conversation. The duality of my accepting Richard's estimate and at the same time inviting a revision is a practical action. By doing this, I express my ambivalence about how much to praise and how much to push this student based on what I had been doing to teach him since I met him in September. I was teaching Richard to respect himself as the kind of person he was when working with Shahin. I wanted to help him to become a person who could make sense of mathematics and initiate working on it in the company of his peers in school. Simultaneously, I was working to structure the situation so that he could save face with his peers and maintain his integrity as both a serious student and a funny, lively, ten-year-old African American boy. I did similar work across the year with Giyoo, Enoyat, and Tyrone, some of which is documented in the following chapters.

Integrating Academic Character into Preadolescent Social Life: Teaching Saundra to Think and to Reason

In the next example, we look at the work of teaching Saundra, who asserts during a lesson in February that five-sixths and five-twelfths go with the same point on the number line. The teaching that I do in response to Saundra's assertion is directed toward getting her to reason about the mathematical implications of what she has asserted. At the same time, it is oriented toward keeping Saundra interested in doing mathematics and toward forming some of the girls in the class into a group of intellectually supportive peers.

Saundra is a biracial girl who looks, and sometimes acts, like a teenager. Like most of her classmates, she is only ten years old, but unlike most of the other girls in the class, she is preoccupied with her appearance, talks a lot about popular music and movies, and flirts with boys.[10] When she has a choice about who to hang out with in the class, she chooses other girls who sometimes look and act similarly adolescent (Ellie and Candice). These three girls often dress alike, in clothes that one might see teenagers wearing in popular TV shows. Their conventionally adolescent behaviors are not necessarily antithetical to the development of an identity that includes reasoning things through in public. But the research I had read on girls and math, and my own experience as an adolescent girl who wanted to study math and also be socially acceptable, made me aware that I need to work to keep students like Saundra publicly engaged.

The incident that provoked the teaching under analysis here occurred in the kind of lesson in which academic competence and a student's sense of self as a learner are particularly closely related. It was at the end of a unit and the class activities were organized to make it possible for students to demonstrate what they had learned. A lesson at this stage of instruction can be an occasion for students to make explicit what they have studied and learned or it can turn up new confusions. If a student is still struggling with familiar ideas at the end of a unit, the experience can be taken as a message about identity. Students who do poorly on assessments are likely to think of themselves as "not good at math" and give up trying to learn it.

All year, I had been trying to organize activities in which Saundra could see herself as mathematically competent.[11] She was sometimes disdainful of her less sophisticated classmates and reticent about showing much of an interest in her studies. Both Saundra's public engagement in studying mathematics and her private activity were sporadic. Some days her notebook writing is tight, focused, and effusive and there are many diagrams, while on other days, we find very little evidence of constructive work. She took me by surprise one day in late January when she told me after class how much she liked what we were doing in math. This was unusual behavior, not only for her, but also for ten-year-olds in general.

A particularly problematic feature of Saundra's written work up to this point had been the lack of self-conscious analysis of how she arrived at her conclusions. She liked to do the activities, it seemed, but when she wrote about her thinking about mathematics she described it as a kind of mysterious intuition rather than logical reasoning. In working on the problem of finding combinations of coins that would add up to one dollar in October, for example, Saundra produced pages and pages of possible combinations. She also wrote about a pattern that she observed when she discovered she could "go by twos," but went on to say, "I don't know how I did. I just did." About another pattern, she said, "I just don't know how I found it."

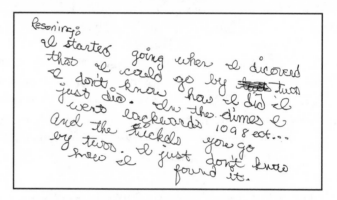

I wrote in her notebook in response to this work:

> You need to try to explain
> your thinking more clearly. Try
> to pay closer attention to *how* you are
> doing something *while* you do it.

I continued to write such comments in Saundra's notebook all through the winter, but she rarely wrote anything under "reasoning." She continued to just state her answers to the questions posed in the problem and next to them she would write something like, "I just think it" or "I hope this is right." In this notebook entry, for example, she underlined "think" and "hope" as if to convey the importance of these processes, but she does not make the effort to explain why she thinks or hopes that what she does makes sense.

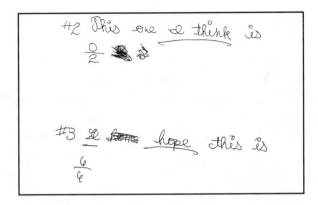

Saundra's participation in whole-class discussions was similarly uneven and did not usually include explanations of what she was doing or thinking. In a lesson on February 7, however, a high level of engagement in that day's activities led Saundra to perform in front of the class. She even got up from her seat and took the initiative to come to the chalkboard to show what she meant when it was unclear to me and to others in the class. Because she participated publicly in the way she did, she gave me an opportunity in that lesson to work with her on her reticence about reasoning. In teaching her on February 7, I was trying to clear up her confusion but at the same time allow her to continue to feel (and other students to see) that she could be the sort of person who could think something through and reflect on why it was "right" or "wrong." The problem context for Saundra's participation that day was different from anything we had done so far that year. We were working with Fraction Bars, and she seemed to particularly like the physical quality of the procedures for solving problems with these materials. As with the case of Richard, we need this larger frame to explain the work of teaching Saundra to take responsibility for her own learning by being intellectually more courageous.

Another Context for Studying Fractions:
Adapting Commercial Materials to Classroom Culture and Curriculum

Doing mathematics with Fraction Bars involved manipulating a set of rectangular cards, all the same size, but different colors, and observing the structure of the cards in relation to the numbers and operations they were designed to represent.[12] The Fraction Bars come with a book of activities that introduce students to the features of the material by having them compare and order the Fraction Bars and align them with numerical symbols, linear models of fractions, and fraction names. Then students use the Fraction Bars to represent and compute additions, subtractions, multiplications, and divisions of fractions. I believe that the opportunity to do mathematics with these physical materials was what enabled Saundra to become a more active learner during January and February.

At the beginning of a unit on comparing fractions to decide which is larger or if they were equal, each pair of students received a set of Fraction Bars (represented here by a drawing in Anthony's notebook) to use between them to work on the problems.[13] The set included a total of thirty-two one-by-six-inch rectangular bars made from colored cardboard including:

three "blues," representing no halves, one-half, and two halves;

four "yellows," representing no thirds, one-, two-, and three-thirds;

five "greens," representing no fourths, one-, two-, three-, and four-fourths;

seven "reds," representing no sixths, one-, two-, three-, four-, five-, and six-sixths;

and thirteen "oranges," representing no twelfths, one-, two-, three-, four-, five-, six-, seven-, eight-, nine-, ten-, eleven-, and twelve-twelfths.

The activities in the Fraction Bars book did not specify any particular social structure or task structure that the teacher and students were to use with these materials. Part of my work was to make the activities in the book into structured tasks for my class, adapting them to what these particular students needed to study and to the routines I had established. I also needed to decide how long the students would spend on each activity, what order to do them in, and which ones to leave out. And I needed to connect the mathematics we would work on using the Bars with what students had studied in previous lessons and with what I intended to teach in the future. These are all acts of teaching that cannot be taken care of by finding a good material or a book of activities.[14]

The decision to use Fraction Bars was a shift in the media of engagement and communication. I used them because I wanted to attract more students like Saundra into more intense mathematical studies than I had been able to do with drawing, writing, and discussion. At the same time that we started to use the Fraction Bars I made a change from work in groups of four to work in pairs. The seating arrangements remained the same, so pairs of partners could easily see one another's work across the table, and students were expected to continue to use their notebooks individually to record conjectures, experiments, and reasoning. But because two people had one set of Fraction Bars between them, the kind of collaboration that was required was more direct than what they had been doing in their "groups of four." Arranging for productive work to happen in a pairwise arrangement was a teaching action aimed at supporting the development of all of my students as intentional learners. I thought pairs of students sitting across from one another would be more likely to present their thinking to the class as a set of ideas they shared because the pairs had developed their solutions to the problems with one set of Fraction Bars between them. It would also make it easier to distribute, keep track of, and clean up the materials in pairs. Choosing one particular partner for each student gave me more control over the ways in which I could use my students to offer other students opportunities for study. By now I knew my students well enough to make specific pairings for specific reasons.

Using manipulative materials with ten-year-olds (especially prematurely sophisticated ten-year-olds) is a personally and socially sensitive venture. Such materials are often thought by students to be for younger children or for those who don't "get it." At the upper elementary level the expectation is that only students who cannot operate with words and symbols need to use concrete materials. Deciding that my whole class would use the materials meant that I had to figure out a way to make them appealing to self-conscious preadolescents and have them be viewed as serious academic tools, not as toys or as something for students to do if they could not do the "hard math." I needed to present the Fraction Bars as necessary for the study of fifth-grade-level mathematics so that all of my students would consider what we were doing to be appropriate for their age and stage in life. I did this by posing the Fraction Bar problems in the same structure of conjecturing and explaining that we had been using since the beginning of the year.

The Fraction Bars would be used in my class for investigating the nature of numbers between zero and one. At the beginning of the Fraction Bar book, problems were posed in terms of "finding matches" for one or another of the Fraction Bars, e.g., "Which Fraction Bars match with the one-half bar?" Or "Which kinds of Fraction Bars don't have any matches with one-third?" Matches could be demonstrated physically by placing Fraction Bars with the same amount "colored in" next to one another, like this:

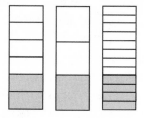

With matching Bars like these in front of them, students could be asked to name the fractions (two-sixths, one-third, and four-twelfths) and indicate their equivalence using number symbols ($\frac{2}{6} = \frac{1}{3} = \frac{4}{12}$). The area model, the words, and the number symbols all have the same mathematical structure, but they have important differences that students would need to observe.

I used these kinds of problems to involve students in studying the characteristics of equivalence in the domain of rational numbers. For example, the Problem of the Day on January 30 was stated like this:

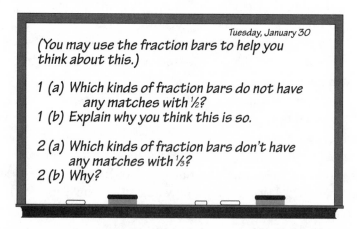

Tuesday, January 30

(You may use the fraction bars to help you think about this.)

1 (a) Which kinds of fraction bars do not have any matches with ½?
1 (b) Explain why you think this is so.

2 (a) Which kinds of fraction bars don't have any matches with ⅓?
2 (b) Why?

By using the term "kinds of Fraction Bars" I intended to give students some latitude about the extent to which they would use the physical characteristics of the Fraction Bars to reason through the problems. They could answer question 1(a) by referring to the color of the Fraction Bars that will not match with one-half, as in "The yellow Bars will not have any matches with one-half." Or they could say something as abstract as "The Fraction Bars that represent numbers whose denominator is odd will have no matches with one-half."

The creators of Fraction Bars avoid the complexity of the idea that two fractions with different numbers in the numerator and denominator can be equivalent by using the term "matches" to describe them. For example, one-half and two-fourths are "matches," although the numbers that are used to indicate the common ratio in these fractions are not "the same." I wanted my students to investigate why some Fraction Bars "matched" although the numbers associated with them were different. I used many of the problems in the book that came with the Fraction Bars, but I adapted them to continue the emphasis on finding patterns, drawing and writing to experiment with ideas, making conjectures, and providing reasoning for assertions that I had initiated at the beginning of the year.[15] I presented the problems in the Fraction Bars book in the Problem of the Day format that had become routine for this class, so they appeared similar to the problems we had been working on and cued students to use the same structure for their work together. Students used the Fraction Bars to generate not just physical arrangements or verbal descriptions of what they saw, but also explanations about "matches" or equivalent fractions in problems.

Connecting Work with Manipulative
Materials and the Study of a Conceptual Field

Although this chapter is about the work of teaching as it aims to build students' academic character, we cannot understand the teaching actions related to that goal apart from the mathematics in which the class was engaged. We were working on studying fractions, and what we were doing was intended to help students do better at later work on adding, subtracting, multiplying, and dividing with numbers in fractional form. There are fundamental ideas that my students needed to understand in order to know what quantity any particular fraction signifies, whether it is written with numbers, displayed in an area model, or described using words. Deciding which of two fractions is larger or if they are equal is fundamentally a matter of understanding what quantity each fraction signifies, and the decision needs to be consistent across representations. Knowing what quantity a fraction signifies is necessary if you are going to use procedures for adding, subtracting, multiplying, and dividing fractions in a way that makes sense in different problem contexts.

In an area model like Fraction Bars (or the pies and slices we had been using to figure out what different decimal numbers signify), "pieces" or parts of a whole represent fractions. At the same time, the pieces themselves are units that can be counted, and the parts need to be counted to compare the representations of two fractions. When the size of the whole is kept constant as it is in the set of Fraction Bars, the pieces need to be of different sizes to represent different kinds of fractions. A piece that represents "one-fourth," for example, will not stand for the same quantity as a piece that represents "one-third," if the size of "the whole" is kept constant. This is true and it is also confusing because in both one-fourth and one-third, we are talking about *one* piece.

My class studied the importance of the size of the pieces in relation to a constant whole by figuring out what "matches" could be made in the collection of Fraction Bars, and they investigated how these matches would be signified with words and numbers. They also worked on deciding which of two fractions represented by two Fraction Bars was larger and explaining why. Students could work on figuring out whether three-twelfths was larger than, smaller than, or equal to two-sixths, for example, by comparing the Bars that represented those fractions:

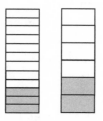

Even using the Fraction Bars, this is not a simple problem because both the size and the number of pieces that are shaded on each bar must be considered. The right-hand Bar in the illustration above has more of its area shaded in, but it only has *two pieces* shaded in, where the left-hand Bar has *three*. Because what we are talking about here are different-sized parts of a whole, this is a situation in which "3" stands for *less than* "2."

In an area model of the meaning of fractions, when the size of the unit or "the whole" is held constant, two kinds of counting are required to know which is larger or whether two Fraction Bars represent the same quantity.[16] To order Fraction Bars you need to take account of how many pieces each is cut into as well as how many pieces are "colored in." In the realm of counting numbers, we would not say "2" was larger than "3," no matter what we were counting. But a Fraction Bar with two pieces colored in can represent a quantity that is larger than that represented by one with three pieces colored in if the two pieces represent two-*sixths* and the three pieces represent three-

twelfths. We would say that a group of five apples and a group of five oranges both contain the same quantity of fruit, but we would not say five-*twelfths* is the same quantity as five-*sixths.* Two different characteristics of each Fraction Bar or each fraction-written-as-a-number need to be considered and related in order to make the decision about which is smaller or larger.

To study this anomaly in comparing fractions, I gave my class this problem on February 6, reminding them that in Fraction Bars, "the largest number is represented by most colored in":[17]

> *Tuesday, February 6*
>
> **CONDITION: If largest number is represented by most colored in**
>
> **PROBLEM:**
> 1. *Choose any ten Fraction Bars from your pile.*
> 2. *Put them in order from smallest to largest.*
> 3. *Write the fractions in order in your notebook.*
> 4. *Write your reasoning.*

What the class is supposed to be studying by doing all the parts of this problem is how the area (i.e., Fraction Bar) representations of fractions (answer to task #2) relate to their numerical (symbolic) representations (answer to task #3). If students chose ten Fraction Bars randomly to do the problem on February 6, as they tried to line them up in order, they would sometimes come across two Fraction Bars that represented the same quantity, and thus could not be "put in order from smallest to largest." Some students found a way to cope with this issue and others ignored it. This problem raised an issue that led to the design of the next problem and to the exchange with Saundra that challenged me in teaching her to maintain her intellectual integrity.

To confront the representation of equality, I decided that in the lesson on February 7, we would line up fractions along a number line. Within this problem context, we would be able to take on the question of how two different numeric symbols representing different numbers of pieces on the Fraction Bars (e.g., ½ and ¾) could be associated with the same point on the number line. The Fraction Bars could be used as an additional representation of the fractions, helping students to think about what it means for two fractions to be equal.

Relating to Saundra's Mathematics in the Social Context of the Class

The notebook work done by Saundra and other students on February 6 provides some background for my decision to use the number line in the closing lesson of the "comparing fractions" unit on February 7. As the class worked on the previous problem, the discussions between partners and among students at the same table were lively and everyone was involved in the task. In what they wrote about their work in their notebooks, most students made reference to their use of the Fraction Bars to investigate the order of the fractions, and some made actual drawings of the Fraction Bars they used. We can see from their notebook work where their studies are concentrated, and what issues are left unresolved to be encountered in the next day's discussion.

In her notebook, Saundra says she used the "area shaded in" on the Fraction Bars to order the ten fractions she and her partner picked out on February 6, but she does not draw them as part of her explanation. She does not take on the problem of comparing two different numbers with the same amount colored in (e.g., ⅔ and ⅘).

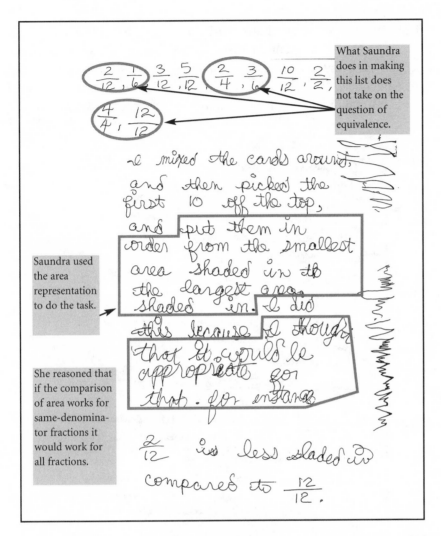

What Saundra does in making this list does not take on the question of equivalence.

Saundra used the area representation to do the task.

She reasoned that if the comparison of area works for same-denominator fractions it would work for all fractions.

$$\frac{2}{12}, \frac{1}{6}, \frac{3}{12}, \frac{5}{12}, \frac{2}{4}, \frac{3}{6}, \frac{10}{12}, \frac{2}{2},$$

$$\frac{4}{4}, \frac{12}{12}$$

I mixed the cards around, and then picked the first 10 off the top, and put them in order from the smallest area shaded in to the largest area shaded in. I did this because I though that it would be appropreate for that. for instance

$\frac{2}{12}$ is less shaded in compared to $\frac{12}{12}$.

Saundra's list suggests that she thinks one-sixth is larger than two-twelfths, that three-sixths is larger than two-fourths. It also suggests she thinks that two-halves, four-fourths, and twelve-twelfths are to be ordered according to how many pieces are in the whole (with twelve-twelfths having the most pieces, and therefore being the largest). Saundra uses an odd linguistic construction to elaborate her reasoning when she says, "I did this because I thought that it would be appropriate for that." Her use of the pronouns "it" and "that" in the same sentence make it very hard to know what she is thinking.

Unlike Saundra, Dorota draws the Bars to show her reasoning, but she does not grapple with equality, either. Three-thirds and six-sixths are equivalent, but she lists them in order one after the other, suggesting they range from "smallest to largest." Perhaps she is assuming that six-sixths is larger because it has more pieces. In contrast to Saundra, Dorota uses more nouns to describe the connection between what she did and what she thought.

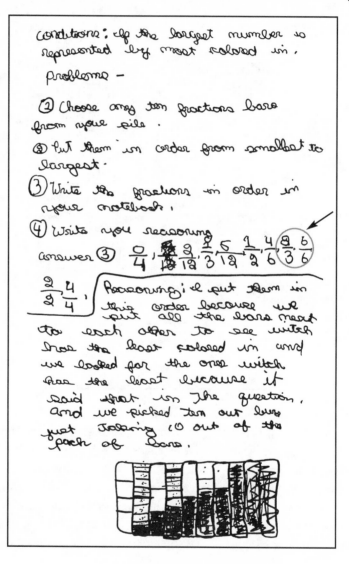

Catherine does not draw the Fraction Bars, but she uses two other representations to think about their relative magnitude: a number line and pie-shaped area models.

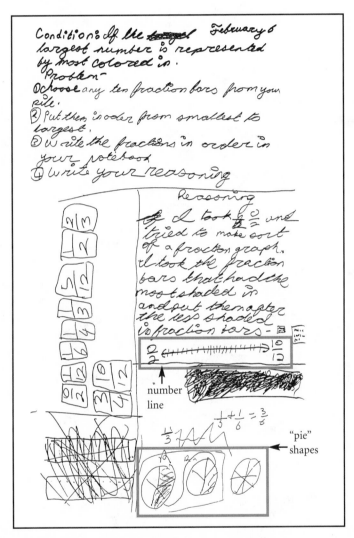

number
line

"pie"
◄── shapes

Catherine links the linear representation directly to the area model when she says that the ones with more shaded in "come after" the "less shaded in" Bars. Because of the Fraction Bars she picked, deliberately or by chance, the question of equality does not arise for her.

Charlotte's work is strongly strategic from the outset and also avoids the question of how to represent equivalence. She picks out only *twelfths* from the set of Fraction Bars. Those are the only kinds of Fraction Bars of which there are ten of the same kind. Having done that, she only has to put the numerators in numerical order.

42-6

Condition: If the largest number is represented by most colored in.

Problem -
① Choose any ten fraction bars from your pile
② Put them in order from smallest to largest
③ Write the fractions in order in your notebook.
④ Write your reasoning.

EXPERIMENTS

① ② ③ ④

REASONING
③ $\frac{1}{12}$, $\frac{2}{12}$, $\frac{3}{12}$, $\frac{4}{12}$, $\frac{5}{12}$, $\frac{6}{12}$, $\frac{7}{12}$, $\frac{8}{12}$, $\frac{9}{12}$, $\frac{10}{12}$

④

REASONING
③ $\frac{1}{12}$, $\frac{2}{12}$, $\frac{3}{12}$, $\frac{4}{12}$, $\frac{5}{12}$, $\frac{6}{12}$, $\frac{7}{12}$, $\frac{8}{12}$, $\frac{9}{12}$, $\frac{10}{12}$

④ I picked the 12ths because there are at least 10 fraction bars that 12THS on them. This is the These are the only set of fraction bars that have at least 10 fraction bars of the same kind. I know $\frac{1}{12}$ is the smallest and $\frac{10}{12}$ is the largest because $\frac{1}{12}$ has only one piece colored in and $\frac{10}{12}$ have 10 pieces colored in. Which ever fraction bar has the the smallest least colored in and whatever fraction bar has the most colored in has the is the largest. It works for all the ones in between the smallest and largest, too.

③④. See if you can X put all the fraction bars in order.

REASONING
$\frac{0}{4}$ $\frac{1}{12}$ $\frac{2}{12}$ $\frac{1}{6}$ $\frac{3}{12}$ $\frac{1}{4}$ $\frac{4}{12}$ $\frac{2}{6}$ $\frac{1}{3}$ $\frac{5}{12}$ $\frac{6}{12}$ $\frac{3}{6}$ $\frac{2}{4}$ $\frac{1}{2}$ $\frac{7}{12}$
$\frac{8}{12}$ $\frac{4}{6}$ $\frac{2}{3}$ $\frac{9}{12}$ $\frac{3}{4}$ $\frac{10}{12}$ $\frac{5}{6}$ $\frac{11}{12}$ $\frac{2}{2}$ $\frac{3}{3}$ $\frac{4}{4}$ $\frac{6}{6}$ $\frac{12}{12}$.

Unlike all of these other students, Ellie shows by drawing and labeling that she *has* studied the problem of two equal fractions being represented by different numbers. She does not complete a written explanation, but she connects the one-fourth Bar with the three-twelfths Bar, and writes under them that they are the "same thing." She does a similar representation for six-sixths and two-halves. She puts boxes around the fractions that represent the same number above the Fraction Bars.

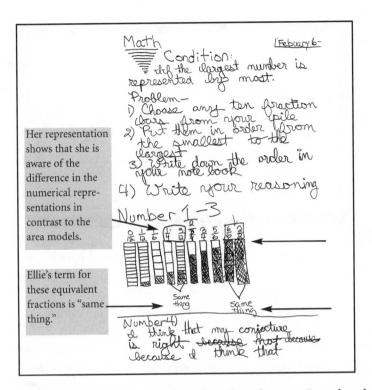

Her representation shows that she is aware of the difference in the numerical representations in contrast to the area models.

Ellie's term for these equivalent fractions is "same thing."

I have included work from several students here because I used such work to construct my teaching later in this lesson and in the next lesson. The variations in approaches showed me what I would have to work with in a discussion. They also exhibit what it is that Saundra is either not able to do or does not choose to do in the way of elaborating her reasoning. Although I could see that Ellie clearly confronted the problem that I had wanted to discuss, I also knew that the kind of relationship she had with Saundra would make using her work in the discussion difficult.

Checking Engagement and Understanding to Prepare for a Discussion

As students finished ordering the ten Bars they picked out from their sets in the lesson on February 6, I challenged them to go on to order all of the Bars. Most students were engaged in this task when the class came to an end and picked it up again the next day when they came in and sat down. To prepare for the summative work I wanted to do using the number line on February 7, I taped a long piece of white paper on the chalkboard and drew the number line on it with a focus on the part between 0 and 1.[18]

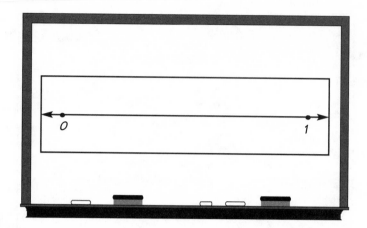

I did not plan to record our work directly on the chalkboard because I wanted to produce a more permanent representation that we could come back to in the future.

I also wanted a more formal sort of record of what students could do at this point. Rather than having them work in their individual notebooks according to our daily routine, I gave each pair a sheet of plain paper with a similar line printed on it, with directions and a space for both partners to write their names.

Locate the numbers
associated with each
Fraction Bar on this
number line. Work with your partner.
Write in your notebook why you think what you did makes
sense.

Name_____

Name_____

0   1

I thought that having one number line between them would spur them to figure out together where to put the fractions on the line, teaching them to study by talking about the various representations of quantities between 0 and 1. Unlike the notebook pages, the paper I handed out was not already measured out with a "graph paper"–type grid, so students would have the additional challenge of dividing up the line appropriately. I used this unusual task structure because I saw this lesson as an occasion for bringing some kind of closure to our work on using the Fraction Bars to study how fractions can be placed in order. Students would work both as partners, on the worksheet, and as individuals in their notebooks writing their reasoning.

In between students' working independently and the whole-class discussion on February 7, I noticed that although most students were still working with their partners, a few in the back of the room had finished and were playing games like tic-tac-toe in their notebooks. They were also talking and laughing in ways that were distracting to students who were still working. I commented on who had been involved in this in my journal.

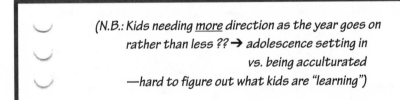

> *a few of the kids who were done started playing tic-tac-toe with their partners, or this game of "boxes"; ⊥ ⊥ which I remember playing a <u>lot</u> in fifth grade! Varouna + Saundra were doing this, as were Sam, Kumar, Connie + Dorota.*

I wanted to get Varouna, Saundra, Sam, Kumar, Connie, and Dorota back to focusing on the Fraction Bars before I stood up at the front to record our work on the number line. Reflecting in my notebook after class, I saw their need for more direction in this matter as part of a general trend in the class, which I attributed to "adolescence setting in" and I knew I would need to work on keeping academics on their minds along with social concerns. As social concerns began to dominate, I worried about how to keep track of what my students were learning about how to study.

> *(N.B.: Kids needing <u>more</u> direction as the year goes on rather than less ?? → adolescence setting in vs. being acculturated —hard to figure out what kids are "learning")*

Although students like Richard were learning to adopt more of an academic persona during lessons, there seemed to be a counterforce operating as they were developing physically and socially and becoming more interested in socializing with one another. The six students I mentioned in my journal (including Saundra) were all seated in the same part of the room. They were three of the sets of "partners" for the Fraction Bar activity. I wanted to get them re-engaged with the mathematics in the lesson before I took on the whole class for discussion.

Standing near the back of the room where most of the "off-task" activity was going on, I picked up a pile of Fraction Bars that were not in any particular order, and I picked one randomly out of the bunch. I held it up, looked toward the group that was disengaged and asked if anyone could tell me where it would go on the number line. Candice, who was making a diagram, looked up from her notebook and volunteered that the Bar I was holding was "one-sixth." Meanwhile, just behind her, Saundra was trying to get the attention of Tyrone as she fanned out her set of Fraction Bars (which she had arranged according to color) and fluttered them in front of her face. She turned around and tapped Connie on the shoulder. Connie turned around. It is hard to interpret Saundra's gestures at this point. She might have re-engaged in the study of fractions and started looking in her fan for the red "one-sixth" Bar and asking Connie to help her find it. But it is equally likely that she could have been showing off her colorful fan to another friend, making no connection to the content in the lesson.

While I was watching this, Reba was telling me how to cut the number line between 0 and 1 so that I could find the point for ⅙. I turned aside from that work and said to Saundra, "Saundra, are you paying attention?" I deliberately used a question to address Saundra, inquiring about what she was up to rather than assuming she needed to be told to pay attention. I was trying to make it possible for her to use my exchange with Reba as a way to get back to her studies if such a direction was needed. She might have turned to me and said, "Yeah, I am trying to find our one-sixth Bar. I know it's here at the beginning of the reds in my fan." But she remained silent and turned around to watch what I was doing with Reba. Reba was trying to explain that the best way to put the fractions on the line was to break the line into twelfths before you start, because all of the Fraction Bars could be equated with twelfths.

Now, several students were talking at once, and I was making my way toward the front of the room to use the chalkboard. At this point, Saundra and her partner, Varouna, were saying that like Reba, they also began by marking off the line in twelfths. Loudly enough for everyone in the class to hear, Saundra added another assertion about the "other ones," going beyond just talking about the twelfths to asserting that that five-twelfths and five-sixths would go at the same place on the number line. She said she and her partner put ⅚ "under" ⁵⁄₁₂ to label the same point. She seemed to be trying to present evidence that she had indeed been paying attention.

> Saundra: And then the other ones we put beneath them where we put, like under five-twelfths we put five-sixths.

The class was not yet in "whole-group discussion" mode, and my next action could be to make Saundra's assertion open to public discussion, or not.

I considered how rare it was for Saundra to address me or anyone else in the class in the public forum of a whole-class discussion. That she had done so on this occasion was both an opportunity and a challenge. The problem I had posed that led to the talk about cutting the line between 0 and 1 into twelfths was where to put *one-sixth*. Now Saundra was talking about five-sixths and saying it went "under" five-twelfths. Saundra had not said that five-twelfths and five-sixths were equal, but she did say that they go at the same point on the number line. I knew several students in the class would disagree.

Addressing the Problems of Teaching Saundra in This Context

Saundra's assertion presents me with teaching problems in several domains at once. The solutions to these problems are contradictory, presenting me with multiple dilemmas to be managed. Some of the teaching problems I need to address in the exchange described here are particular to this moment and this situation, and others are problems that have been requiring my attention since the beginning of the year. I need Saundra to learn the correct placement of fractions on the number line. I need her to understand why five-sixths is larger than five-twelfths. And at the same time, I need her to learn to think of herself as a person who can study and explain her mathematical reasoning and that she can do it in school, where her peers are watching everything she is doing.

Saundra's placement of the fractions ⅚ and ⁵⁄₁₂ on the number line was not correct. If I only wanted her to place fractions in the correct order, I could have told her she was wrong and how to place them correctly. But in order to know what and how to teach her about the meaning of fractions so that she could work with them in other ways, I needed to know what she meant by putting these two fractions at the same point on the number line. In order to teach her how one decides whether something is right or wrong in mathematics, I needed to get her to examine the meanings of the representations and symbols she was using and reason from assumptions to conclusions. But if I got her to talk more about this now, I would also have to consider what effect the judgments of her peers would have on her sense of herself as mathematically able. If Saundra thinks that five-sixths and five-twelfths are equal, I am going to have to find a way to get her to think differently while allowing her to save face in front of her classmates on the occasion of one of her few public performances. Whatever I do will be intended to teach her, but also to teach other students in the class, both about the mathematics and about what sort of person Saundra might be as a classmate.

What I do next is to deliberately slow down and simplify the discourse to give Saundra time to think, and perhaps to revise, what she had said about five-sixths being at the same place on the number line as five-twelfths. My talk here is intentionally very explicit so as to model the ways in which she and other students might talk about what they are doing and thinking. Making things move more rather than less slowly here is a risky move, because some students are obviously ready to move on to more challenging work. I put aside five-sixths for the time being and first ask Saundra to tell the class where five-twelfths would go on the drawing. She tells me and she tells the whole class that it is "hard to explain" where five-twelfths goes. I say to her, expressing my sense of the purpose of our being together in this classroom somewhat more directly than I usually do, "That's why you're here so you can learn how to do it."

In response, Saundra gets up from her chair at the back of the room and comes up to stand next to me at the chalkboard, a rare but not out-of-line action for a student to take in this class. Pointing to the number line on the board, she counts, starting with the mark for zero-twelfths, and she points to each hash mark as she goes: "one, two, three, four, five." She stops on the fifth hash mark, points, and says, "Here."

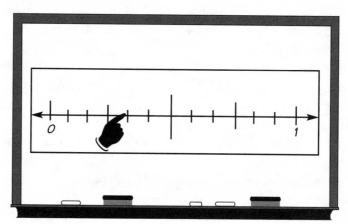

I write "⁵⁄₁₂" above the spot she has pointed to and ask her to explain why she put ⁵⁄₁₂ there.

I had asked Saundra to perform the relatively simple task of finding five-twelfths on the number line in front of the class as a way to deflect other students from judging her assertion that five-sixths would go in the same place as five-twelfths. But Saundra makes my work more complicated by making another problematic performance. She had claimed that five-sixths "goes under" five-twelfths (i.e., at the same hash mark) on the number line and now she was saying that ⁵⁄₁₂ goes with the mark that indicates ⁵⁄₁₂ (having counted the point representing 0 as "one-twelfth"). Now there are two matters on which her classmates are likely to disagree. Students all around the classroom are talking to one another, and several have their hands raised, bidding for the chance to speak.

To teach here, I need to act in a way that will maintain the tension between supporting Saundra and instructing her, and in instructing her, teaching her the correct placement and teaching her why it is correct. And I need to not only do that myself but guide others in the class to do it as well. I want whatever I do to express my expectation that Saundra will take this seriously and have the courage to perform her reasoning publicly. I also want her to know that I will help her if she needs help to make the new and unfamiliar connections among the Fraction Bars, the number line, and the words and symbols that name the fraction in front of the class. To build Saundra's mathematical competence, and at the same time maintain her academic self-confidence, I must now work like an air traffic controller, keeping all of the planes that are trying to come in for a landing from crashing into one another. To do this, I need to manage the multiple selves that Saundra and I bring to this encounter, as well as managing the multiple mathematical topics that surround the two issues that are now on the table and the other students and their ideas.

I worked with Saundra at the chalkboard on the placement of $\frac{5}{12}$ before inviting anyone else to speak to the class. Together we made a quick revision and got the line labeled so that $\frac{5}{12}$ was repositioned on the fifth hash mark after 0. What is on the board as a result of my work with Saundra so far is:

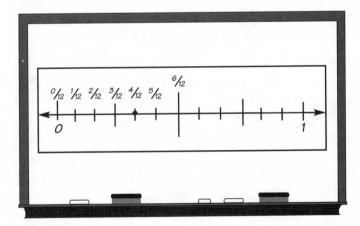

At this point, I might have introduced a question about where $\frac{1}{2}$ goes, since that would give everyone another familiar benchmark before taking on the question of where to place $\frac{5}{6}$. But before I could do anything else, Saundra, still standing next to me at the front of the room, moved on from placing the twelfths to tell the class more about the second part of her earlier assertion. She said, "And then we went to sixes," and continues, "and we put those underneath where they go." Several students raised their hands again, and some like Shahin, who is right at the front of the room, jumped around in their seats to attract my attention to their disagreement with what was happening.

I first called on Charlotte because I had observed a pattern of respectful consideration in the way she responded to other students in the class when she disagreed. She is perhaps the most sophisticated in the class in her use of the English language to describe and reflect on her actions. Charlotte travels with a very different set of girls than Saundra, and she often still wears her hair in pigtails. I don't imagine that she is the sort of peer that Saundra would seek to identify with, but I know she will respond to Saundra's situation with sensitivity, perhaps providing a model for some others of how to disagree.

Charlotte did as I expected she would, and chose to comment on the aspects of Saundra's performance that she agreed with and not to comment on the confusion around the placement of $\frac{5}{6}$. By "agreeing" with Saundra, she gives Saundra a social resource to work with in forming a sense of herself as someone who can be productively engaged in reasoning about mathematics.

Lampert:	What do other people think about that?
	Charlotte?
Charlotte:	I agree with Saundra where she has the twelves because the first mark that she marked which was zero-twelves, and then the next one is one-twelfth and so you keep going in order and then you plus.

After Charlotte spoke, I called on two more of the many students who had their hands up to indicate they wanted to respond to what Saundra had said. Karim also agreed with Saundra's placement of $\frac{5}{12}$ and supported his assertion with a logical argument deriving from the location of $\frac{6}{12}$ at the halfway point between 0 and 1. He claimed that because five-twelfths is one-twelfth less than six-twelfths, and six-twelfths is the same as a half, then $\frac{5}{12}$ must be associated with the hash mark one space to the left of $\frac{1}{2}$. I responded by emphasizing the location of $\frac{1}{2}$ between 0 and 1 on the number line on the board, and label it "$\frac{6}{12}$." So far, no one is taking on a disagreement with Saundra's placement of $\frac{5}{6}$.

Next, I call on Shahroukh because he has been anxiously waiting to speak. I think I can predict what he is going to say, and I am not sure it will be helpful to Saundra, but I need to balance his need for attention and self-esteem with my other responsibilities. As I expected, he commented definitively on the incorrectness of Saundra's placement of ⅚ and ⁵⁄₁₂ at the same place on the number line. Using evidence that sounded like a reference to areas colored in on the Fraction Bars, he asserted that "Five-sixths *has to be* ten-twelfths [because] *ten-twelfths* has the equal amount as *five-sixths*." (The area of five-sixths on a bar is the same as the area of ten-twelfths on a bar, so they cover an "equal amount.") And to further impress whoever is listening and can understand the relatively advanced logic of what he has to say, he adds a comment on the appropriateness of cutting the line in twelfths:

> Shahroukh: And I think that um, the reason it's cut into twelfths I think is the best way because um, half, third, fourth, and sixth can all be placed um, in the place where the twelfths are, twelfths mark.

My problem now is to use what Shahroukh has contributed to further the development of mathematical thinking in the discussion so that he knows his participation and understanding are valued, while at the same time continuing to make it safe for Saundra to try to explain why she did what she did. Although Saundra also divided the line into twelfths, she does not have the facility with fractions represented as relationships between numbers that would enable her to get much out of Shahroukh's disagreement with her position on the placement of ⅚.

Because several students were using the twelfths as reference points, and because I wanted more shared information available to process Shahroukh's assertions, I slowed the pace again to get all the twelfths labeled along the number line before returning to Saundra's problematic assertion. I again began the labeling process by making a dot at ⁷⁄₁₂ and proceeded to get all the rest of the twelfths labeled, calling on three girls and one boy to assist in the process. I said the word-name of each fraction after the student said it, and wrote the symbols for it next to the spot where it belonged, setting up a pattern for further ordering and labeling that I hoped Saundra would recognize.

| Lampert: | Okay let's just uh, take this one step at a time. What number goes with this dot? [pointing to the dot I made at ⁷⁄₁₂] |
| | Right here. |

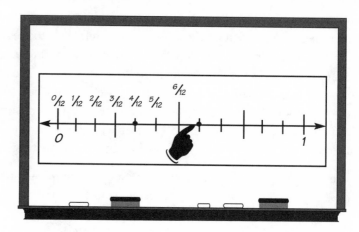

Lampert:	Yasu?
Yasu:	Seven-twelfths.
Lampert:	Seven-twelfths.
	It's sort of very crowded here, but what number goes with this dot [moving my finger to the next hash mark on the line]?
	Donna Ruth?
Donna Ruth:	Eight-twelfths.
Lampert:	Okay, eight-twelfths.
	And with this one here [moving to the next]?
	Ileana?
Ileana:	Nine-twelfths.
Lampert:	Nine-twelfths.
	And with this one here [moving to the next]?
	Enoyat?

Enoyat: Ten-twelfths.

Lampert: Ten-twelfths.

What is on the board now is:

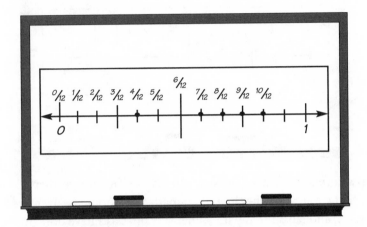

Using the routine established at the beginning of the year to take some of the emphasis off of getting the "answer" and put more of it on reasoning, I next identified the potential disagreements with Saundra as two "conjectures" that were on the floor for consideration. I hoped my detailed work on labeling the line would give Saundra some more time and more information to use to think about her placement of ⅚. I also intended that the participation of a wide range of students would give her the confidence to see herself as someone who could continue to be engaged.

Lampert: Now what, what Shahroukh just said is that he thinks
               five-sixths should go together with ten-twelfths [writing
               ⅚ above ¹⁰⁄₁₂].

               And Saundra and Varouna's conjecture that five-sixths
               should go together with five-twelfths [writing ⅚
               above ⁵⁄₁₂].

I circled the proposed alternatives.

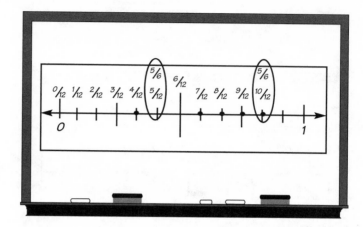

I next propose to the class that we try to resolve the disagreement. I also announce that we are near the time when math class should be over. I repeat the conjectures, and label them with students' names as I have done in the past.

Lampert: So, why don't we try to resolve that one.

And that's what we'll, that's where we'll end up with today.

See if we can—this is um, five-sixths should go with ten-twelfths, this is Shahroukh's conjecture [putting a ring around these two fractions, and labeling them with Shahroukh's name].

And five-sixths should go with five-twelfths, that's Saundra and Varouna's conjecture [putting a ring around these fractions, then labeling them with Saundra's and Varouna's names].

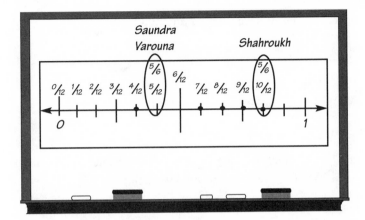

Lampert: Now, if you agree or disagree, remember that your job is to convince other people that you're being reasonable one way or the other.

This last remark reminded students to be careful in disagreeing with their peers, without calling attention to Saundra's particular vulnerability in this regard. I tried to suggest that it would be equally legitimate to disagree with Shahroukh.

Building Socially Acceptable Intellectual Supports for Saundra

I am holding on to the possibility that Saundra will change her mind before the class is over and that she will do it with intellectual honesty. But I also recognize that it will now take even more courage for her to change her mind in public, and that support from some others in the class might make her more willing to do so. I would not accomplish what I set out to teach if she changed her mind only because Shahroukh said she was wrong. I call on Reba at this point, who has also indicated she disagrees with Saundra. I do this to place Reba between Shahroukh and Saundra, to soften Shahroukh's authority. I want to teach Saundra that there are other people in the class she can identify with besides Shahroukh or the "smart boys." She does not have to be unusually articulate or knowledgeable, or a boy to participate productively in the study of mathematics. Reba identifies with Shahroukh as she disagrees with Varouna and Saundra, and she includes her partner, Jumanah, in her assertion. But her explanation is not clear. It seems to be an observation of the number patterns in what she can see on the board rather than a reasoned conclusion based on what these numbers mean, either in terms of Fraction Bars or the number line.

Lampert:	Okay, Reba what do you think?
Reba:	Um, I agree with Shahroukh.
Lampert:	Why?
Reba:	Um, well, me and her did at least, okay.
Lampert:	Um, Shahin be quiet.
Reba:	Um, I don't um, understand how Saundra and Varouna put five-sixths in with five-twelfths.
Lampert:	Okay, we'll give them a chance to explain.

Reba is addressing her remarks to me and to Saundra and Varouna, not saying they are wrong, but that she does not understand how they did what they did. I ask her to explain what she did to add to what they have to think about. Her "explanation" is not tied to the Fraction Bars.

Lampert:	But why don't you tell me why you agree with Shahroukh.
Reba:	Um, five, five is half of ten, right?
Lampert:	Uh huh.
Reba:	And twelve is half of six.
Lampert:	Nope. No, twelve is not half of six.
Reba:	Six, six is half of twelve.
Lampert:	Okay.
Reba:	And I think that's, they, um, that's how both of those should go together. But, I, um, I don't understand how that Varouna and Saundra worked together.

Now I have at least three pressing agendas. I need to bring the class to a close because it is time for recess. Shahin is very anxious to say something to me and the class and when he is anxious he gets silly and distracts other students. And I am still hoping Saundra will revise. I turn to the Fraction Bars to try another route to having Saundra recognize that ⅚ and ⁵⁄₁₂ would not go at the same place on the number line, and also to give Reba a concrete representation to link to the numbers she was talking about.

Lampert:	Here's five-sixths, this is what five-sixths looks like [holding up the five-sixths Bar].

Does anybody have five-twelfths in their hands? [I take the five-twelfths Bar from Karim.] Remember who I took it from so I remember to give the right thing back. [I hold up the five-twelfths Bar next to the five-sixths Bar.]

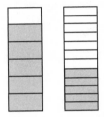

Okay, now visually, if you look at these two Fraction Bars, you have five-sixths, and five-twelfths, what could you say about them?

What do you see?

I want to proceed carefully to avoid the possibility that someone might come down hard on Saundra for what they might perceive to be her continuing confusion about how to use the number line to represent order. I imagine that if anyone embarrasses her for making a mistake, it will be a disincentive for her to ever try anything like this in public again. But I do want to set the groundwork for her to revise her placement of ⁵⁄₁₂ "under" ⁵⁄₆. I am simultaneously trying to build a case against Saundra and have her be able to take the other side of the argument with integrity.

As Catherine speaks in the next part of the discussion, I try to convey that I can see why what Saundra did might have made sense. I take positions in the discussion that I imagine Saundra might take, saying for example that "They both have five" when Catherine says five-sixths and five-twelfths "don't match." I am hoping that the language that Catherine uses in response to what I say will become available to Saundra as a resource for her own reasoning.

What I am trying to do here is to connect the area representation of these fractions on the Fraction Bars, the word-names of the fractions, and their placement on the number line. At the same time I am trying to connect

Saundra with other students in the class so that she might take up their way of talking and reasoning about fractions. As I did when I labeled the twelfths, I use other girls—Catherine, Dorota, Ileana, and finally Ellie—to reason about the comparison of the two fractions with me. Ellie is Saundra's most often chosen pal during recess and after school. Her explanation follows the same logic as the one Karim gave earlier, but makes a direct reference to the Fraction Bars.

Lampert:	Catherine?
Catherine:	They don't match.
Lampert:	What do you mean they don't match. They both have five.
Catherine:	Yeah.
Lampert:	So what do you mean they don't match?
Catherine:	Five-sixths is—has bigger pieces and five-twelfths has smaller pieces and five-sixths, um the pieces are too big so they are higher then five-twelfths, the pieces are smaller so they are lower.
Lampert:	Okay what do you think Dorota?
Dorota:	The red one has more colored in.
Lampert:	Okay. What does that mean?
Dorota:	That, um, they—

Anthony and Shahin are sitting between me and Dorota and they are talking to one another and waving Fraction Bars around. I try to calm them down and keep Dorota talking.

Lampert:	[to Shahin and Anthony] You know you guys are being very distracting to me and a few other people.
Dorota:	They don't match at all.
Lampert:	Why?
Dorota;	Because they're suppose to be colored in the same amount to—have the same amount.

We cannot hear all of what Dorota says on the tape. In my response to Dorota's argument based on the Fraction Bars, I see an opportunity to make plain the conventional assumption that Fraction Bars with the same amount colored in should go on the same place on the number line.

Ileana immediately picks up on where I am trying to go and refers back to the quantity represented on the red Bar (five-sixths) as "taking up more space." We cannot hear what Ileana says, but I use "okay" to indicate that I am following her argument and also use it as a marker for the rest of the class to give her argument careful attention.

Lampert: And what does that have to do with the number line?

Ileana: Um, it means—

Lampert: Okay.

            Okay, so you think the ones, your idea, your reasoning is
            that ones that have the same amount colored in should
            go at the same point on the number line.

Before I have a chance to ask Ileana to repeat her reasoning, Ellie jumps into the conversation and disagrees with her. I ask questions that are intended to get Ellie to be very explicit in expressing her reasoning.

Ellie: I think it's five-sixths because five-sixths has more
            colored in than five-twelfths.

Lampert: What is it that you think is five-sixths?

            Because we have a number of things going on now.

Ellie: The red one.

Lampert: The red one is five-sixths.

            So you are saying.

            The question that I asked Ileana is which is the bigger
            number?

Ellie: I think it's five-sixths.

Lampert: Why?

In answer to my query, Ellie gives the explanation that is similar to what Karim said earlier. To get the whole filled in on the five-sixths Bar, you need one more (sixth) to fill it in. To get from five-twelfths to a whole, you need seven more (twelfths). Her logic is visually linked to the appearance of the

Fraction Bars that the class has been working with for several lessons. In what she is saying here, she is using the different units of measure: a sixth, a twelfth, and a whole Bar, and she holds their relationship in play throughout. She does not say anything about the fact that the twelfths pieces are half the size of the sixth pieces.[19] (Her line of argument would not work if we were comparing five-sixths and *ten*-twelfths.)

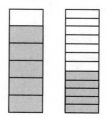

Ellie: Because um it has um five, well there's only one more to be in the whole, and on five-sixths there is seven more to be in the whole.

Lampert: You said on twelve, five-twelfths there's only one more to be in a whole and on five-sixths there's seven more to be in a whole.

Ellie: Oh.

    On five-sixths there's one more and on five-twelfths there's seven.

Lampert: Now, that's an interesting piece of evidence that Ellie just said.

    She said this one's closer to a whole [holding up the five-twelfths Bar].

    What do other people think about that?

Several students had their hands raised. We were several minutes into recess. At this point, it felt like I needed to take the risk of giving the floor to Shahin. He explained why he agreed with Ellie, and he expanded the argument on a crucial point: *the size of the pieces.*

Shahin: Because I think five-sixths is the biggest pieces, that is, bigger pieces and has the most colored in. And uh, I think five-twelfths is the smallest because, just because five doesn't mean it's the same because the pieces count. And it's less colored in.

Before I dismissed the class, I wanted to return to Saundra and Varouna and find out what they had been making of all this. Varouna speaks first and uses only number-names in her assertion, making no reference either to the Fraction Bars or to the number line.

Lampert:	Varouna and Saundra?
	What do you think?
	About this discussion?
Varouna:	Um, I—
Lampert:	I couldn't hear what you said.
Varouna:	I'm still with five-sixths that goes with five-twelfths because six is half of twelve and five and—
	Um, five and—
	Oh, and I go with five-sixths go with ten-twelfths.
Lampert:	Why?
Varouna:	Because six goes into twelfths and five goes into ten.

From a mathematical perspective, Varouna seems to be accepting the truth of two statements that contradict one another. Five-sixths goes with five-twelfths *and* five-sixths goes with ten-twelfths. The reason that she gives for the first assertion is similar to something that Reba said, but she does not finish. Maybe she pauses because she recognizes that in order to finish she would have to pair 5 with 10 and not with 5 (as in 6 is half of 12 and 5 is half of 10 and therefore, five-sixths goes with ten-*twelfths*). I try to revoice what Varouna said, linking the numbers more explicitly with an operation. I gesture around the pairs of numbers that have been said to be the same: first ⅚ and ⁵⁄₁₂, then ⅚ and ¹⁰⁄₁₂. Even though everyone seems anxious for the lesson to be over at this point, I continue to hope for clarification.

Lampert:	It's true that five goes into ten two times and six goes into twelve two times.
	But the question is: are these the same number [pointing to five-sixths and five-twelfths] or are these the same number [pointing to five-sixths and ten-twelfths]?

Varouna does not answer and I turn to Saundra:

Lampert:	Saundra, what do you think?

I wait what feels like a long time for Saundra to answer, but she remains silent. I then make yet another effort to respect and rescue Saundra, but she again makes herself vulnerable to the judgments of her peers. Again, I try to communicate that *if* you are paying attention to the number of pieces, it could be reasonable to conclude that ⅚ and ⁵⁄₁₂ "go together." I also try to make the implied contradiction explicit.

> Lampert: There's a good reason to put these together because they both have five and so you could say this is one-sixth, two-sixth, three-sixths, four-sixths, five-sixths.

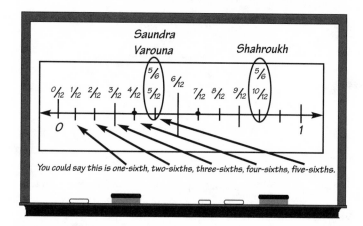

You could say this is one-sixth, two-sixths, three-sixths, four-sixths, five-sixths.

Making the connection between pieces of the two Fraction Bars and hash marks on the number line, I again count along the hash marks that are marked with twelfths, this time calling them "one-sixth, two-sixths, three-sixths, four-sixths, five-sixths."

Saundra Defends Her Actions While I Teach Reasoning

Such a counting strategy would imply that ⅚ (one whole) would have to go on the same place as ⁵⁄₁₂, at the halfway point between 0 and 1. But Saundra does not reason about the contradiction. She simply concurs that "that's what we did."

> Saundra: [interrupting my counting] Um huh, that's what we did.

In her response, "what we did" stands in for a reason and obviates the need for any further explanation. Because she is describing an action rather than evaluating contradictory assertions, she does not see a need to change her mind. I then ask her what she *thinks* about labeling those same points as twelfths, counting along by pointing.

Lampert:	And if you're counting twelfths you could say one-twelfth, two-twelfths, three-twelfths, four-twelfths, five-twelfths.
	What do you think about that?

She does not answer with a description of her thinking. She finds it acceptable to answer my question by saying "I don't know." Instead of knowing what she thinks or thinking about what she knows, she talks again about "how we *did* it," and "how we *arranged* them."

Saundra:	I don't know.
	That's how we did it though.
	That's how we arranged them.

Now I play out the implication of their arrangement that I was hoping she would see and be able to articulate: if you follow this algorithm for labeling the points on the number line, then the placement of the fractions that are equal to one whole becomes problematic.

Lampert:	That's how you arranged them so you, and so then that—
	I mean that this would have to be six-sixths [pointing to the halfway point, labeled ⁶⁄₁₂]?

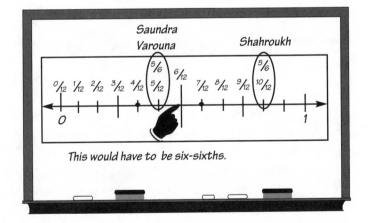

Saundra:	Um...
Lampert:	Is that right?

Saundra watched what I did, and disagreed. She says, again describing an action, that she and Varouna put ⁶⁄₆ "down at one."

| Saundra: | Um... We put six-sixths at one, down at one. |

I was trying to give Saundra the time and social space to reason. There is a visually represented contradiction in what she has done indicated by all of the space between where she put 5/6 and where she put 6/6. But she remains silent, and several other students continue to bid for attention. I then dramatize the contradiction, explicitly calling it to Saundra's attention by using the words "way over here" and walking along the distance on the chalkboard.

Lampert: So, five-sixths is over here [pointing to the spot labeled "5/12"],

And six-sixths is all the way over here [walking down the chalkboard to exaggerate the distance, and pointing to the hash mark labeled "1"]?

Is that right?

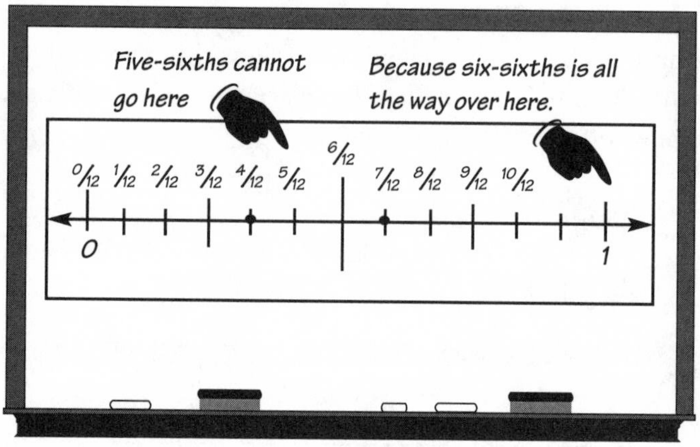

At this point many students start talking audibly, and hands go up all over the room.

With this set of exchanges, the lesson had gone on well into recess time. The weather was awful outside, so I was not overly concerned, but I knew many students were watching the clock. But many were also watching Saundra and me and bidding to say something. I decided to give Shahin another turn to speak and then bring the discussion to a close. Shahin gave another explicitly logical explanation for why 5/6 could not be "under" 5/12, at the same point on the number line. He referred to the diagram on the board and asserted that *three*-sixths would go at the halfway point, along with 6/12, and if 3/6 went there, then 5/6 could not go to the left of it.

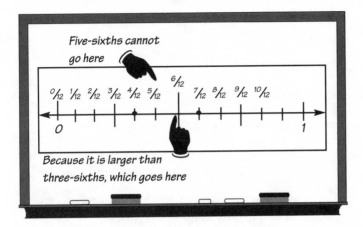

There were now several different arguments that contradicted what Saundra and Varouna had done (Shahroukh's, Reba's, Ellie's, Shahin's using the Fraction Bars and Shahin's using the benchmark ½, and mine, using the implication that ⅚ and ⁵⁄₁₂ would have to both be at the one-half mark).

Varouna raises her hand, and when I call on her, she says she wants to revise, but her communication expresses defeat and concession rather than understanding. She is not able to use any of the representations or language that have been generated to give a reason why she revises.

Lampert:	Okay, um, Varouna?
Varouna:	I want to revise.
Lampert:	Why?
Varouna:	Because—

Here Varouna pauses for several seconds and the class is silent, but obviously antsy, ready to go to recess.

Lampert:	You want to think about it some more?
Varouna:	Umhum.

Saundra indicates that she is ready to talk. She gets up and sits on her desk top, something that is not generally allowed in this class except in very unusual circumstances. By doing this she is making her position even more public. I had announced that it was time for recess, so there was a different, less formal mood in the class. Saundra uses her "bully pulpit" to say she wants to revise, but then she goes on to give a substantial justification for "how we did it" concluding that "it could be either way." At this point, the class becomes rowdy, partly in anticipation of recess, but also, perhaps, because I am not the only one who has been hoping that Saundra would change her mind.

Lampert:	Saundra?
Saundra:	Well.
	I want to change my,
	I want to revise and the reason is because, um, we had written them like how the number order they went.
	We weren't thinking of, um, how, how even they were, up next to each on the Fraction Bars.
	So I mean, I guess really it could be either way.
Lampert:	Okay, Varouna, do you want to add something?
Varouna:	No, I'm not ready.
Saundra:	And it could be that way because they match up or because the numbers are the same. It could be that way.
Lampert:	Okay, five minutes outside.

When I dismissed the class, there was a lot of talking and shouts of "disagree!" could be heard above the din.

Saundra's statement, "That was how we did it," and her continuing to maintain that "It could be that way" posed a dilemma for me, both in the moment and in my long-term relationship with Saundra. On the one hand, she had been intellectually courageous. She performed her understanding publicly and maintained her dignity. She seemed to indicate that if she had been thinking about "how even they were, up next to each on the Fraction Bars" she might have placed the numbers on the line differently. On the other hand, she did not admit that the conventional labeling system would make any more sense than the one that she had adopted. Her conclusion was that either you could pay attention to the numbers in the numerators of the fractions (which would put $\frac{5}{6}$ and $\frac{5}{12}$ at the same place) or you could pay attention to whether the Fraction Bars related to the numbers at the same point on the number line "match up." Reasoning mathematically, one would have to conclude that there is a contradiction between these two approaches, but this did not trouble Saundra.

I dismissed the class for a short recess without any closure on Saundra's assertion. I knew we would be continuing to study fractions, and I would come back to these ideas with Saundra and Varouna. But in my long-term relationship with Saundra, I had more to grapple with than teaching her about fractions. If I were going to continue to teach her, I could not go on letting her be the sort of person who presents herself as not knowing what she thinks, not thinking about what she knows, maybe not either "knowing" or "thinking" at all, but simply "doing."

Problems of Practice in Teaching Students to Be People Who Study in School

At this point, given the two cases I have chosen to present, it may seem to the reader that it is the less competent students who need to be taught to have "academic character." I could have chosen any student and written a case study of these kinds of teaching problems, but space in this book is limited. Those who were more competent, like Shahroukh and Charlotte, produced different but equally difficult challenges. Teaching them was often a matter of convincing them that they still had more to learn, that I was capable of teaching them, and that the reasoning of all of their classmates was worthy of their intellectual consideration.

Three related kinds of teaching problems are associated with academic character building for all students. The first is doing what it takes to know students as mathematics learners, with all of the personal complexity they bring to that work. In the above cases, we saw teaching addressed to this problem being performed in several ways, including:

- building up knowledge of students over time and in different kinds of situations, so as to be able to appreciate the ambiguities and contradictions in their personalities;

- watching how students use the activity structure (i.e., seating arrangements, notebook use, etc.) and modifying it when it is not working to support intellectual courage;

- assessing the social environment to get a sense of what it would mean to "start small" and designing opportunities to take semipublic social risks; and

- putting students in positions where it is safe to reveal aspects of themselves that may or may not be academically acceptable in a classroom setting.

These actions are subtle and often indirect. Many of them are intended to elicit behavior that students may not consider socially acceptable. By making it safe for students to behave in the ways they think they should gives me a basis for figuring out what I need to teach them. In the work of getting to know students, the effort must be ongoing, for if teaching is successful (or even if it is not) people change over time rather than in any single instance of interaction. As students differentiate themselves, they try on different character traits by acting in public, and it is this fragile self-definition that the teacher is getting to know.

As the teacher is getting to know students, a second problem for teaching is influencing who they can become by structuring opportunities for each student to construct an identity among his or her peers that includes the disposition to study school subjects in the way they are to be studied in a particular class. Young people in school are moving from being determined by their families of origin to shaping their own characters in relationships with their peers and other adults. Many of those relationships develop in interactions that occur in classrooms.

As we saw in the above cases, specific actions that can be taken to address this problem include:

- giving students private, written feedback that recasts them in a light that is somewhat different from the self they express in class in public, and watching how they respond to it;

- designing intellectually challenging tasks that are at an appropriate developmental level, i.e., not perceived to be "babyish" by students;

- giving students opportunities to exhibit academic character in settings where I will protect them from their peers making fun of them, directly by not allowing it and indirectly by modeling respect;

- taking account of what effect parental sanctions might have on students, working in concert with parents but not "ganging up on" students, giving them a little more space than their parents might give them to develop their social/public personality;

- being aware of who identifies with whom among their classmates, and structuring the situation so that those identifications lead to productive developments in each student's academic character; and

- being a "mirror" for students, reflecting back to them the competence they express and showing it to others discretely.

By making the classroom into a place where students can be themselves and also study in relationship to the other people, the teacher is making students into people who can accept being studious, in all of its manifestations, as part of their public character.

Finally, the teacher builds academic character by deliberately being a particular kind of person with students. As professional actions are taken, the teacher faces the problem of expressing what it can mean to be an adult who both respects others and places high expectations upon them. The teacher addresses this problem by being a person who respects and nurtures academic character, while also recognizing that such a character might be difficult for ten-year-olds to enact in school. By exhibiting personal complexity in her own behavior, the teacher can foster the growth of each student's identity in such a way that it can include being an intentional learner, while allowing the student to maintain other valued character traits that might otherwise be seen to be in conflict with doing well at school. In the work I have described in both examples, my work as a teacher included shaping my own public self both to exhibit and respect academic character and intentional learning and also to respect the ways that these particular ten-year-olds have of being in the world.[20] I need to model an obvious seriousness about the study of mathematics, but I must do it in a way that students could see to be within their grasp and within their self-definitions to emulate.

The kinds of teaching problems that have been investigated in this chapter might not need to be a part of teaching in circumstances where teachers and students come together one-on-one or when students know what they want to learn and how to learn it. But when teaching occurs in schools, these problems are some of the most challenging elements of the practice. Besides being a social environment that not everyone assumes is about learning, the classroom has characteristics that put social and personal stress on both teachers and students.[21] When students move from home and community to school, they generally move from a situation in which they interact with only a few people who know them very well to a situation in which they must interact with a large number of relative strangers for many hours every day. Whether their home and community relationships are productive of a disposition to study or not, these relationships are familiar, and they are few. In the classroom, relationships are many and the people with whom they are to be formed are relatively unknown. It is rare in the United States for classes of students to stay together with one another from one year to the next, and even more rare for students to stay with the same teacher.

In September, everyone in a class is setting out to make new alliances and identify new adversaries. Moreover, all of the young people are in competition with one another for the attentions and assistance of a single adult. Learning how to interact in public, in productive ways, with large numbers of other people, in close quarters, is stressful, even for adults who have presumably more experience doing it. When one is in competition with those people for scarce resources, the difficulty of maintaining productive relationships increases. And escaping bad relationships in the classroom is hard; it is likely that most of the people who are there in September will still be there in October, and in November, and even in January, and the following June.

In addition to the challenges of making relationships in classrooms, students must face the fact that being in school carries with it the expectation that they will change. When the school year finishes in June, a student should be walking out of the classroom a somewhat different person than he or she was in September, not only in the sense of knowing more, but also in terms of acquiring social maturity. Who one is in a relationship—the funny one, the verbally aggressive one, or the silent observer—makes the responses of others more predictable. Becoming more serious, or quieter, or a more active participant so as to become a more productive student will bring about a change not only in oneself, but also in how others respond. To a large extent, what that change will be is unknown. For a student, losing the familiar version of oneself, the version that walked in the door in September, means striking out into unknown territory. The familiar self knew how to handle relationships, even if the strategies so employed were not necessarily productive of learning. With a change toward academic engagement, one may win new friends and more praise from the teacher or a parent, but one may lose friends as well.

For the teacher, the work of establishing and maintaining productive human relationships in the classroom occurs with the understanding that it is the teacher's responsibility to assist students in changing themselves over time and to define the direction of that change. Because of the close quarters in which teachers and students work with one another, and the immature character of school learners, teachers must be occupied with socializing students. It is the teacher's job to help students become increasingly fit for working productively in the constant company of many others of the same age who they are not at liberty to choose. David Cohen, in an analysis of the work of teaching, observes that teaching, like social work, organizational development, and pastoral counseling is a "practice of human improvement."[22] Cohen reminds us that trying to change others is risky business, and the risk is compounded with the assumption that students in school may also be trying to change themselves to comply with teachers' or parents' expectations. The expected change covers multiple overlapping dimensions of the person's identity. The aim of teaching is both to improve each student's knowledge and skill and to improve his or her disposition to use school as a setting in which to learn.

11

Teaching the Nature of Accomplishment

Teaching and studying are activities that aim toward a goal. In society writ large, there are many different perspectives on what that goal ought to be. Students construct their ideas of progress out of what they know of these perspectives. In the classroom, the teacher has the opportunity to teach students something about what counts as accomplishment in that particular setting. This means teaching them about what they should be trying to learn, as well as how to measure their progress. On the surface, it appears that progress is being made when the ratio of right answers to wrong answers goes up or as pages of work are completed. More substantively, progress could be conceived of as a development from not knowing something to knowing it, from not being able to do something to being able to do it. Accomplishment would then mean becoming a person with more knowledge and improved skills. From this perspective, it becomes important to define the knowledge and skills that are worth having.

Accomplishment in the Classroom

Students cannot be said to make progress in learning unless they acquire some knowledge or a degree of skill that they did not already have.[1] In the small society of the classroom, where everyone's progress is open to public scrutiny, students have the opportunity to investigate how they are doing in relation to others in acquiring skill and knowledge. What they learn in such an investigation cycles back either to motivate or to suppress their interest in attempting to make further progress. In this way, students' perceptions of their own accomplishments can be either a resource for teaching or a constraint on what teacher and students can do together.[2]

The image of progress as a shift from not knowing to knowing, taken together with the complexities of the class as a small society and the subject matter as a web of related ideas and tools, presents the teacher with several problems to address in working with a school class to define progress:[3]

- Demonstrating Knowledge and Skill
  One set of problems in the domain of teaching about progress arises from the fact that learning in school depends not only on students acquiring knowledge and skill but on their learning when and how to use knowledge and skill so as to demonstrate their acquisition to

others. In an academic setting, in order for others to know when knowledge and skill have been acquired, a student must be able to communicate appropriately about what he or she knows in terms that are understood in that setting. In my classroom, a student would need to be able to represent ideas and strategies in words, drawings, or manipulations in such a way as to convince others that these ideas are being used in ways that make sense. So I would have to teach students to do those things if I were to find out if progress was being made. And I would have to teach students that doing such things was an indication of their progress.

- Multiple Dimensions of Competence
  Mathematical competence is complex and multidimensional. As we have seen, sometimes the capacity to make drawings of an idea precedes being able to use that idea in making a correct computation. A student may be able to solve a problem but not to talk about why the strategy used to solve it is appropriate. Being able to use an idea in one context might not carry over to other contexts. This means that there are multiple dimensions of progress on which students can be ahead of or behind their peers. And it also means that they are sometimes ahead of or behind themselves. What a student knows and is able to do does not simply add up to a larger and larger amount as the days go by. Progress is not a unilateral leap forward. So I would need to teach students to see competence as multifaceted and complex.

- Different Starting Points
  Everyone in a school class does not begin at the same starting point. How much progress is made depends on where someone starts. On all of the dimensions of knowing, students in the same grade start at different places, even though the whole class starts the school year more or less together, beginning the same grade on the same day. Some students come from different schools, and almost all from different families. They bring different resources and experiences. Communication and representation of progress within the class needs to somehow take account of these variations, both among students and within each student on different measures of accomplishment. I would have to teach students that progress can mean different things for different people and different things at different times for the same person.

- Public Progress

    Progress from not knowing to knowing in the classroom is largely public. Unless everyone in a class acquires the same knowledge and skills at the same time, the class becomes divided into recognizable "haves" and "have-nots." If having some kind of knowledge or skill is valued, then those who do not have it are in a less desirable position than those who do.[4] This status inequality can have an impact on how and whether students can work together and what they contribute to one another's academic character, and thus on the resources available to the teacher in providing opportunities to study. So I would need to teach in a way that the public demonstration of competence did not become a restraint on students' interest in making further progress.

These problems, like those analyzed in the previous chapter, involve teaching students to be the sort of people who will study productively in school. In this chapter, I investigate teaching problems that arise in this domain of practice at the level of work with the whole class. In chapter 3, I examined teaching the whole class in terms of the construction and maintenance of a classroom culture. Putting and keeping such a culture in place can create resources for both teaching and studying. Here I focus on constructing two additional resources for teaching that operate at the level of work with the whole class: formal assessment and teaching to the misunderstandings behind common errors. Using my journal reflections, I focus a wide-angled lens on elements of my practice that address academic character building in the context of the complex, public nature of progress in school.

In the kind of teaching that I was trying to do, the challenges of letting students know what they had learned and what they still needed to work on were exacerbated. Measuring and communicating progress was made more complicated by my aim to teach all students and to teach them at a high level of mathematical engagement. Evaluating students' work could not be a simple matter of marking answers right or wrong and giving each student a score. I needed to develop a testing and grading scheme that would communicate something about the complexity of what mathematics students were learning, or not. Whatever I did would also need to communicate what students were supposed to be learning. An appreciation of the nature of progress is required if students are to form intentions to learn that are appropriate to accomplishing learning goals along multiple dimensions in an environment where performance expectations include using, representing, and communicating one's knowledge.

A Quiz on Fractions as a Resource for Teaching About Accomplishment

Quizzes and tests are administered to the whole class at the same time, while each student works alone, in relative privacy. In their conventional form, such assessments communicate the assumption that everyone is supposed to know and be able to do the same things at the same time in the same way. If these kinds of assessments are to be used in a setting where students are also supposed to learn about the complexity of competent performance, they must be deliberately designed and discussed in these terms. In the instance of teaching that I will describe here, I was trying to teach the complexity of competent performance by the way I responded to student work on a quiz.

At the end of February, my students and I were about two-thirds of the way through the school year we would spend together. We had been working with the Fraction Bars for about a month. We used the Bars to work on what it means for one fraction to be larger or smaller than another, when fractions could be said to be equal, and how to record and understand what happens when you add one fraction to another. On February 26, I gave a quiz on this material, structured so that students would work alone and in silence for a whole class period. The quiz had six problems on three pages:

Name _____ Date_____   page 1

Put these fractions on the number line

$$\frac{2}{3} \quad \frac{2}{12} \quad \frac{4}{4} \quad \frac{3}{12} \quad \frac{5}{6} \quad \frac{1}{6} \quad \frac{1}{2}$$

Experiments:

What fractions written as numbers would go with these fraction bars?

Which fractions in this collection would be "matches" on the fraction bars? Write them in the box with equal signs between them.

$$\frac{4}{12} \qquad \frac{6}{12} \qquad \frac{5}{6} \qquad \frac{2}{3} \qquad \frac{5}{12} \qquad \frac{1}{3} \qquad \frac{1}{2} \qquad \frac{4}{6}$$

Experiments:

Prove that $\dfrac{3}{12} = \dfrac{1}{4}$

Prove that $\dfrac{1}{2} + \dfrac{1}{4} = \dfrac{9}{12}$

Find the sum of $\dfrac{1}{6}$ and $\dfrac{1}{2}$

How many fractions are there that are equal to $\dfrac{3}{4}$? How would you find them? Explain your thinking.

Identifying Common Mistakes

Most of the mistakes students made on the quiz were concentrated in the area of addition. There were two problems on the quiz that were designed to assess how students would think about adding fractions with "unlike" denominators based on what they had learned about the meaning of the numeric symbols for fractions. In one, the task was to "prove" that an indicated sum made sense.

$$\text{Prove that } \quad \tfrac{1}{2} + \tfrac{1}{4} = \tfrac{9}{12}$$

In the other, the task was to find a sum.

$$\text{Find the sum of } \quad \tfrac{1}{6} \text{ and } \tfrac{1}{2}$$

What I was testing for with these problems was whether students would use an area model derived from our work with the Fraction Bars or any other appropriate representation to make sense of the numbers as they carried out the operation of addition.

Several students disagreed with the sum that was stated in the "proof" problem and asserted instead that "½ + ¼ = ⅖." They explained their answers by stating that "1 + 1 = 2" and "2 + 4 = 6." Some students used the same procedure to "find the sum of ⅙ and ½," arriving at the answer "⅞." Ivan's work is typical of students who proceeded in this way:

In the first problem, Ivan made an assertion that was counter to the one he had been asked to prove. This seemingly self-confident move made me wonder how he (and others who did the same thing) perceived his own mathematical competence. Ivan claimed that he was "thinking" here, and he did not think "$\frac{9}{12}$" was right because he added the "ones" on the top to get "2" and on the bottom, he added 2 plus 4 to get 6, arriving at the number we would call "two-sixths."[5] The mathematical confidence that underlies "thinking" as a self-defined reason for doing something is desirable. But if, as in the case of Saundra in chapter 10, it is not based on knowledge of the conventions of mathematical interpretation and on appropriate evidence, it cannot be taken as an indication of competence. I wanted students to learn to reason in ways that also took account of the conventional meanings for mathematical symbols.[6] In calling attention to such a mistake, I worried that I would deflate a level of confidence I had worked hard to establish. Although I had the teacher's power to respond to work like this by simply "marking it wrong," I recognized a potential conflict between the positive development represented by a mathematical self that has the confidence to make a counterassertion and the recognition that what students like Ivan had done represented a fundamental misunderstanding about the meaning of numbers written as fractions. Ivan said he was "thinking" and that was a good thing. But what did it mean to him "to think"?

I worried about what effect it might have to judge the work of students like Ivan in the presence of other students who had demonstrated a more solid understanding of how fractions work. If students like Ivan genuinely believed that what they were doing was mathematically appropriate, what effect would it have to simply tell them they were wrong? I wondered in my journal about the mismatch between their perceptions of their competence, and mine.

> *The gaping question in my mind is whether they perceive themselves the same way I do: I don't think so. i.e., the kids who did ½ + ⅙ = ⅖ probably think they know how to add fractions. <u>Math</u> problems like this are simply <u>not</u> an occasion to say "I don't know" whereas if you asked kids to tell about the Civil War + they didn't know anything about it they'd probably leave it blank rather than doing/writing something, whether it has meaning or not.*

My concern about whether students knew that what they were doing did not make sense was connected with my goal of teaching everyone that they could understand and do mathematics by using their own powers of reasoning. They were doing something, and doing it confidently. They didn't just leave the item blank, nor did they communicate that they knew they were confused. Yet they were operating on fractions in a way that did not make sense.

What they were calling "thinking" was not what I would call mathematical reasoning. I needed to teach them what these words might mean in terms of the performance I expected from them. Seeing this as a language problem is a different way to construe a knowledge deficit than simply to say that these students did not know a rule for how to add fractions with "unlike denominators" or that they did not have the skill to follow such a rule.

Using Public Reasoning as a Teaching Tool

Because of my dual concerns about developing content knowledge and self-image, I made a plan to have the whole class work again on one of the addition problems from the quiz the next day. Having observed that more than one but not all students had used the same inappropriate procedure, I structured the work of the class in a way that would have everyone not only studying strategies to do and explain the addition, but also studying the process of convincing or being convinced by others in their group about a way to add fractions that would make sense. I did not pass back the quiz papers or otherwise identify the particular students who had made the nonsensical assertion that $\frac{1}{6} + \frac{1}{2} = \frac{2}{8}$. I did not mention the Fraction Bars. I planned the lesson in my journal, noting that I would give special attention to reviewing the routines for students revising their reasoning.

What to do on <u>Tuesday</u> ?

Small group:
    conjecture on test $\frac{1}{6} + \frac{1}{2} = \frac{2}{8}$
      agree, disagree, why?

large group
    discuss that and finish   } may
      eighths number line   not
        from Friday.   get to
                        this
                        til Thurs.

give back quiz—first discuss letter grading
    + collect   with Thom
    again?
    no→xerox
      for folders.

> *Wed* →
>   *no teaching because*
>   *of parent conf.*
>
> *Tuesday—On Board:*
>
> > *Some people conjectured on the quiz that*
> > $$\tfrac{1}{2} + \tfrac{1}{6} = \tfrac{2}{8}$$
> > *Do you agree or disagree?*
> > *Write your reasoning.*
> > *Try to convince your group of*
> >   *what you think.*
>
> *Review—write reasoning*
>   *discuss*
>   *revise reasoning if necessary*
> *also* → *Bathroom procedures.*

I explained the lesson structure to the class as follows:

Lampert: I gave you this problem to do today because a lot of people wrote this on their quiz [indicating the conjecture that is on the chalkboard].

Not everybody—but a lot of people—

So I thought we needed to think some more about why that did or didn't make sense.

In "thinking some more" together about these fractions, I hoped students would have an opportunity to teach other students as they tried to convince one another that what they were doing made sense. It would be anyone's choice about whether to "own up to" having made the erroneous conjecture. By structuring the discussion in this way, I would not set myself up as the final arbiter of right and wrong mathematics. Instead, I would use public reasoning to create an environment in which there could be lots of ideas in the air about why $\frac{1}{2} + \frac{1}{6} = \frac{2}{8}$ would not make sense.

The most common argument I heard students making to one another during class on March 6 was that the sum of one-half and one-sixth could not be $\frac{2}{8}$ because two-eighths was smaller than one-half. If you are adding something to one-half, the result needs to be bigger than one-half, not smaller. These students were clear that $\frac{2}{8}$ means two parts out of eight, where the whole is the same size as the one against $\frac{1}{2}$ and $\frac{1}{6}$ are being measured. They were reasoning about the addition in ways that also took account of the conventional meanings for mathematical symbols. As Leticia put it:

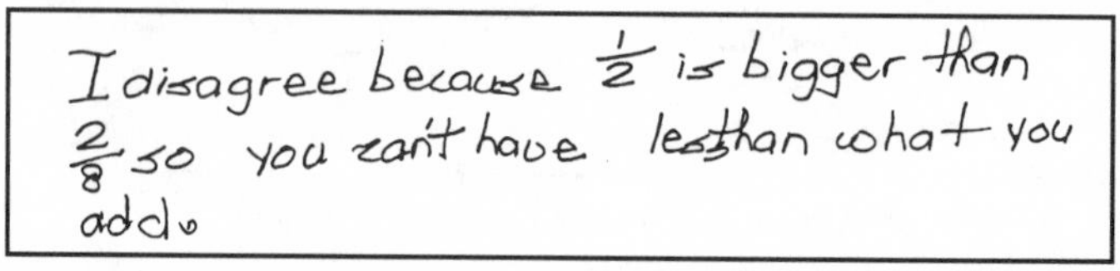
I disagree because ½ is bigger than
2/8 so you can't have less than what you
add.

To further support the idea that the sum had to be something other than $\frac{2}{8}$, several students, like Charlotte, drew Bar-like diagrams in their notebooks as a way of constructing an argument that might convince their peers:

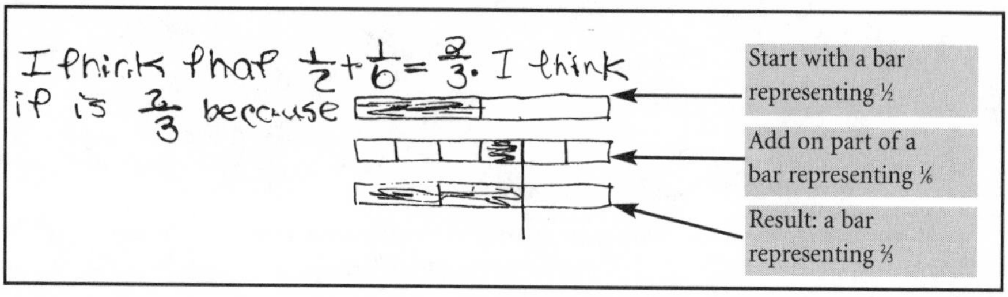
I think that ½ + 1/6 = 2/3. I think
it is 2/3 because
Start with a bar representing ½
Add on part of a bar representing ⅙
Result: a bar representing ⅔

Using the graph paper grid on the notebook page, these students were able to make accurate area drawings to compare the areas.

Other students proved that the sum of $\frac{1}{2}$ and $\frac{1}{6}$ could not be $\frac{2}{8}$ by using procedures they had learned from family or other teachers to add fractions with unlike denominators by finding a "common denominator" and transforming the addends into appropriate equivalents. Candice, who had come in September from another school, did this:

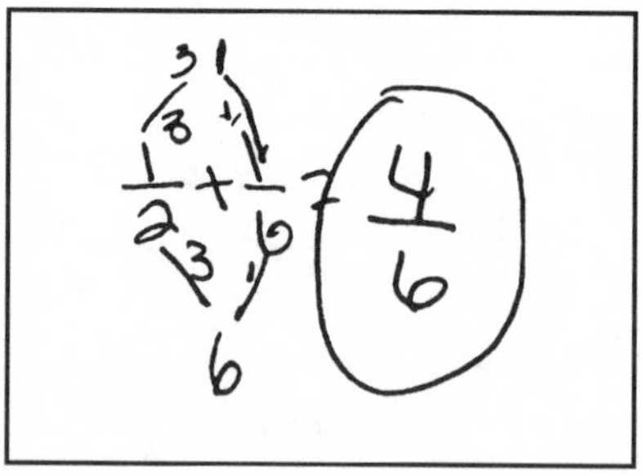
4
6

She then asserted that four-sixths was equivalent to two-thirds. Although she used a symbolic form that did not communicate the meaning of the fractions or the operation, her written text explained that she had changed $\frac{1}{2}$ to its equivalent, $\frac{3}{6}$, and then added that to $\frac{1}{6}$.

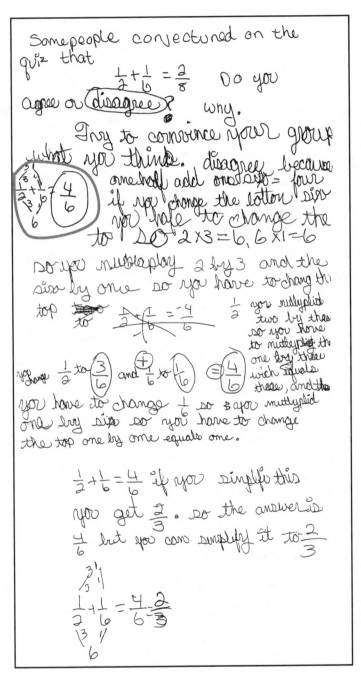

Some people conjectured on the quiz that

$$\frac{1}{2} + \frac{1}{6} = \frac{2}{8}$$ Do you

agree or (disagree)? why.

Try to convince your group what you think. disagree because one half add one six = four if you change the botton sixs you have to change the to so 2×3=6, 6×1=6

so you multaplay 2 by 3 and the six by one so you have to chang th top to $\frac{1}{2} + \frac{1}{6} = \frac{-4}{6}$ $\frac{1}{2}$ you mullyplid two by thee so you have to multyplig th one by three wich equals three, and the you have to change $\frac{1}{6}$ so afor multyplid one by six so you have to change the top one by one equals one.

$\frac{1}{2} + \frac{1}{6} = \frac{4}{6}$ if you simplfy this you get $\frac{2}{3}$. so the answer is $\frac{4}{6}$ but you can simplify it to $\frac{2}{3}$

$$\frac{1}{2} + \frac{1}{6} = \frac{4}{6} = \frac{2}{3}$$

While this work was going on, many of the arguments that could be heard in small groups around the room for why the answer to the addition could not be two-eighths came from students who had interpreted the symbols correctly on the quiz. Those who did not reason correctly on the quiz could listen to these arguments and figure out what made sense without having to associate themselves with their errors on the quiz. No one needed to know who had done it right and who had done it wrong.

Opportunities to Publicly Reflect and Revise

Tyrone left both of the addition items blank on the quiz and expressed considerable frustration at the time, crumpling the page on which those problems appeared. But after working with his group on the problem the next day, he explained to me (and said he wanted to tell the whole class) what he was now thinking about it. It was close to the end of the period when he spoke in the discussion and he was talking fast. The first time he "disagreed" with $\frac{1}{2} + \frac{1}{6} = \frac{2}{8}$ in front of the class, the explanation he gave was hurried and jumbled, and he began with several misstatements. I tried to slow him down and get everyone's attention because I could tell that he had a kernel of good reasoning to share with the class, and he was thinking in logical steps from evidence to conclusion.

Tyrone:	[speaking very quickly] I disagree because um, one-sixth is the same as one-fourth like size. And one-fourth is smaller than one-half and one-sixth is than one-half. If you add anything to one-half, like one-sixth, it will go over, and two-eighths, I mean two-sixths, it's already smaller.
	So it can't add up to be two-sixths.
	If—
Student:	What?
Lampert:	[to the class] Let's just be quiet.
	Tyrone's getting a little bit confused because we're getting close to the end of time and he's trying to do it fast. So if you would just be polite and listen and let him try to say what he is trying to say, I think he'll get it right.
	[to Tyrone] Okay.
Tyrone:	One-sixth is the same as.
	What is it?
	One-twelfth.
Lampert:	Is one-sixth the same as one-twelfth?
Tyrone:	No.

Lampert:	No.
	I didn't think so.
Tyrone:	[slapping his hand against his forehead as if frustrated]
Lampert:	Tyrone, what you told me before was—
	This was the conjecture.
	[circling the conjecture from the quiz on the chalkboard]

Tuesday, March 6

Some people conjectured on the quiz that

$$\left(\frac{1}{2} + \frac{1}{6} = \frac{2}{8}\right)$$

Do you agree or disagree?
Write your reasoning.
Try to convince your group of what you think.

Tyrone:	[now speaking very loudly] Two-eighths.
	Two-eighths.
	Two-eighths.
Lampert:	What's the same as two-eighths?
Tyrone:	One-fourth.
Lampert:	One-fourth. Okay.
Tyrone:	Two-eighths is the same as one-fourth.
	One-fourth is smaller than one-half.
	One-sixth is smaller than one-half.
	Two-eighths is smaller than one-half.
	And if you add one-sixth to one-half and two-eighths is smaller than one-half.
	So if you add one-sixth to one-half it couldn't be two-eighths because two-eighths is smaller than one-half.

Lampert: Excellent.

                Excellent.

                Excellent.

                Excellent.

        [Many students applaud.]

Other students showed evidence in their notebooks of having been convinced, or at least unsettled by a similar logic. Ivan had asserted on the quiz that the sum was ⅜ and not ⁹⁄₁₂. His notebook page for the lesson following the quiz reveals that he began class with one way of thinking and ended with another.

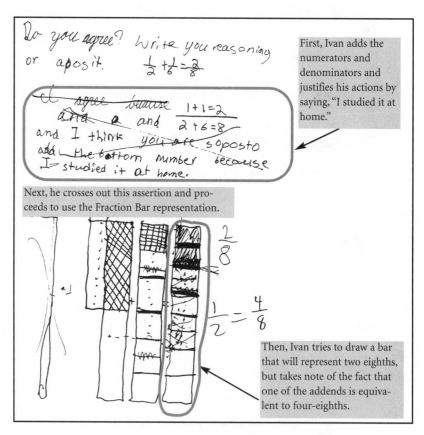

First, Ivan adds the numerators and denominators and justifies his actions by saying, "I studied it at home."

Next, he crosses out this assertion and proceeds to use the Fraction Bar representation.

Then, Ivan tries to draw a bar that will represent two eighths, but takes note of the fact that one of the addends is equivalent to four-eighths.

Ivan does not go so far in this work as to find the sum of one-half and one-sixth, but he is studying the problem here by trying to make a bar that matches what he claims he "studied at home." Using his drawings to investigate the addition of fractions, he could have perceived that ⅜ is too small to be the sum of ½ and ⅙.

Reba also presented a different way of thinking about the problem in her notebook than what she had done on the quiz. She was working with Candice, whose notebook page (p. 339) showed the integration of studying that she had done the year before about making equivalent fractions with our work with Fraction Bars. Using a new idea she seems to have picked up from Candice, Reba's resolution of the conflict between her earlier thinking and the new evidence she encounters is partial, like Ivan's. Reba used equivalent fractions written as numbers, and she wrote about what she did in words that are similar to the words used by Candice, but there is not enough in what she wrote to know how she was interpreting the symbols and operations.

> I disagree because $\frac{1}{2} + \frac{1}{6} = \frac{2}{8}$ because
>
> $\frac{1}{2} + \frac{1}{6} \times$ does not $= \frac{2}{8}$ this is white I did
>
> $\frac{1}{2} + \frac{1 \times 1 = 1}{} = \frac{4}{6}$ and $\frac{4}{6} = \frac{2}{3}$
>
> $\frac{1 \times 3 = 3}{2 \times 3 =}$
>
> $3 + 1 =$ $\frac{1}{2} + \frac{\textcircled{0}}{6} =$
>
> simplifide frist I did 6 in a factor tree 6a and I did 2
>
> $1 \times 6 = 6$ $2 \times 3 = 6$ to figure out 6
>
> so I times it by 3 $1 \times 6 = 6$ but $\frac{1}{2}$ I took the 3 and times it by 1 = 3 and Remember when I put 6 in the factor tree then I took the 1 and the 1 because the factor tree of 6 is $1 \times 6 = 6$ and this
>
> $1 \times 1 = 1$ and $3 + 1 = 4$ and when I got $\frac{4}{6}$ and $\frac{4}{6}$ is simplafi to $\frac{2}{3}$ is simplitfi fou $\frac{4}{8}$ $\frac{8}{12}$ is simplifed to $\frac{4}{6}$

Candice's work showed more clearly than Reba's the equation of ½ with ³⁄₆, and then how she added that to ⅙. Based on what I saw in her notebook, I wondered what Reba would do with the denominators in an addition problem if we had another quiz. Like Ivan, she was able to make use of the social and intellectual resources available to her in the class to study something more about how to work with fractions, but her expression of understanding was incomplete.

Tyrone, Reba, and Ivan were all able to use this lesson after the quiz to revise their thinking without reference to what they had done on the quiz. When I subsequently returned their papers, these students (and their classmates) would have this experience of public, reasoned revision to put alongside my evaluation of their quiz work. They could use the two together to judge the nature of their own competence. From the teaching perspective, I had solved some problems and exacerbated others with this post-quiz lesson. On the face of it, the students who had not performed competently on the quiz made mathematical progress during the lesson. The problem and the way I had structured their activity with it were resources they could use to restudy the same material and learn from that work. But because of the public and collaboratively constructed nature of their competent performances, I was still left with a gnawing concern about how to proceed in my teaching given the different levels of private, individual performance on the quiz. I will take up these problems in chapter 12.

Making Grading a Resource for Teaching

A formal assessment like a quiz could be thought of as a one-way communication from students to teacher about what they know and are able to do, working alone and in silence. It can also be thought of the other way around, as a way for the teacher to communicate to students about what kind of performances demonstrate competence. In the conventional system for grading a quiz, each problem is considered to be more or less "right" or "wrong" and a total score is computed based on the ratio of right to wrong answers. Whether in the form of a percentage, a raw number, or a letter grade, this total score enables students to rank themselves at the top, middle, or bottom in relation to the other students in the class. The conventional approach to grading makes it a kind of "zero-sum-game" in which there have to be winners and losers unless everyone gets everything right. Because of my effort to convince all of my students that they could learn mathematics, I did not want to give some of them an excuse to stop trying.[7] I wanted my students to learn not only that everyone could learn mathematics but also that there was more to knowing mathematics than simply getting the answer right or wrong.

A Grading System That Represents Complexity

To represent the complexity of students' progress in a way that would make it available to them as something to study, I avoided using a clear-cut grading scheme. Instead, I considered their work on each problem, giving credit, partial credit, extra credit, or no credit. I did not give an overall grade to each paper. I awarded partial credit to a student's work when he or she showed an appropriate representation of the information given or demonstrated some sensible reasoning. I awarded extra credit very selectively to identify exceptionally notable performances of understanding on particular problems. I wrote in my journal about this scheme, and how my judgments of performance on the quiz interacted with what I saw students had been able to do in class.

> ### *Grading the quiz from Feb. 23*
>
> *I decided to give credit (C), partial credit (PC), no credit (NC) or ~~extra~~ extra credit (EC) for each question. I was not consistent across papers—i.e. I gave some kids extra credit for the same work that other kids got just credit for if I thought it represented a special accomplishment for that student— this kind of an assessment means that what I see on the quiz is evaluated interactively with what I see in the class, which is harder to document, but necessary to take account of.*

In my journal, I also recorded the assessment of each question for each student.

	1	2	3	4	5	6	7
Giyoo	PC	C	PC	C	PC	NC	NC
Jumanah	PC	NC	PC	EC	PC	NC	NC
Tyrone	C	PC	PC	C	NC	NC	PC
Enoyat	PC	C	C	EC	NC	NC	C
Saundra	NC	C	C	EC	PC	PC	NC
Reba	PC	C	NC	EC	NC	NC	C
Shahin	PC	C	PC	C	NC	PC	C
Donna R.	NC	PC	PC	C	NC	NC	PC
Ileana	PC	C	EC	C	PC	NC	PC
Varouna	NC	PC	PC	NC	NC	C	PC
Catherine	C	C	PC	C	PC	NC	C
Ivan	NC	NC	NC	NC	NC	NC	PC
Candice	EC	C	PC	C	PC	C	C
Anthony	C	C	C	EC	C	C	EC
Connie	C	PC	C	C	EC	EC	C
Martin	C	C	C	C	C	C	EC
Yasu	C	C	C	EC	C	C	EC
Charlotte	C	C	C	C	C	C	C
Ellie	EC	C	PC	EC	C	PC	EC
Dorota	EC	C	PC	C	C	C	C
Shahroukh	C	C	C	EC	EC	C	EC
Leticia	EC	C	PC	C	C	PC	C
Awad	PC	PC	C	EC	EC	PC	C
Karim	EC	C	C	C	PC	NC	C
Sam	C	C	C	C	C	C	C

I explained my grading scheme to the class based on my assessment of the extent to which their work "made sense." I deliberately did not use the words "right" or "wrong" or "partially correct" because these seemed too simplistic for labeling the variations in their performances. These were words I had heard students use in talking with one another, but as much as possible, I directed public talk about performance toward a different kind of vocabulary.

Lampert:	On your quiz there were a lot of questions.

For every question, if you did something that made sense, I gave you credit. If you did something that did not make sense, it says NC [tracing the letters with her finger in the air] next to it, which means no credit. No credit for doing things that don't make sense.

I then explained how I wrote "PC" for partial credit "if part of what you did made sense" and "EC" for extra credit "if you did an excellent job of explaining your reasoning." Students then asked various questions about how I used the system, and talked among themselves about it to translate my scheme into their own terms. My scheme was puzzling, as expressed in this exchange with Dorota. (We cannot hear Dorota's question, but my answer suggests she wanted to know how the "highest" performance on the quiz would be graded, if there were to be an overall grade.)

Lampert:	You either got credit, no credit, part credit, or extra credit for every question.
	Dorota?
Dorota:	Well, what is the—
Lampert:	Well, if you got extra credit on every question that would be the highest. But if you got credit for every question that would be like getting an A.

In grading the quiz, the use of "extra credit" and "partial credit" was my tool for communicating the complexity of progress to each student. I used these grades on almost every paper. Simply getting credit for all of the problems would earn you the equivalent of an "A" if grades were being assigned, while getting "extra credit" on a particular problem was a special kind of recognition.[8]

I include some examples of how I used this grading scheme here to clarify these distinctions for the reader, but I did not display these comparisons to my class. I was careful to hand back papers to students in such a way as to make my communications to each student as private as possible.

Extra Credit

I awarded "extra credit" on the quiz for two kinds of performances: those in which students demonstrated that they could use multiple means of representing their understanding and move back and forth among these representations, and those that demonstrated that students had made progress toward a more complex kind of understanding from a starting point of being able to competently follow a rule.

When Shahroukh, for example, came to my class in September, he was already very facile with using numerical manipulations for finding equivalent fractions. He had expressed frustration when he was challenged to connect these manipulations with representational systems of equivalence like the area model of the Fraction Bars, communicating a sense that he thought doing the numerical manipulations competently was "enough." I needed to find a way to communicate to him what he had learned. On his quiz, he demonstrated progress toward using an area model to communicate the meaning of his numerical manipulations.

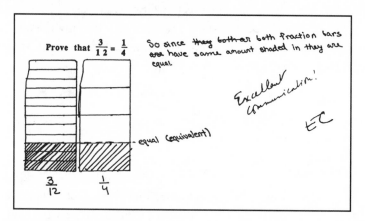

I deliberately labeled what Shahroukh had done here as "excellent communication" because what I had been working to have him learn in the weeks prior to the quiz was how to translate his numerical-symbolic understanding into the terms of the area models so that he could use his knowledge to solve problems in more diverse settings and to interact with others in collaborative work.

Although they did not begin the school year with the same level of competence in manipulating numbers in symbolic form as Shahroukh, both Saundra and Ellie went even further in using an area model to explain the ideas behind their reasoning about equivalence. They both articulated the essential relationship between fourths and twelfths that underlies the numerical-symbolic expression of equivalence; namely, that every "one-fourth" piece contains *three* "one-twelfth" pieces. Saundra numbers the twelfths "1," "2," and "3" to show how the twelfths count up in relation to the fourths.

This was indeed a strong indication of her learning, given what I had experienced in my interaction with her over the number line a few days before.

To represent the same iterative operation in working on this problem, Ellie says, "there would be three pieces every time the fourth was divided."

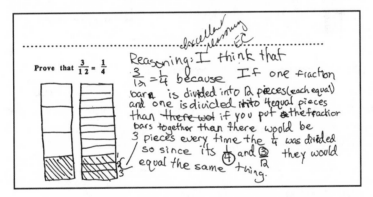

Ileana also used drawings of "pieces" to identify equivalent fractions, creating drawings of an area model based roughly on the Fraction Bars. This was an unusually expansive independent performance for Ileana. Throughout the winter term, she had worked in constant collaboration with other students, usually watching while others used the bars to investigate fractions, and she demurred from participation in whole-class discussions. When she did volunteer, she spoke very softly and used few words. I considered her well-elaborated graphic experiment on the quiz to be an "excellent" indication of her progress in her understanding of fractions, and told her so with my comment.

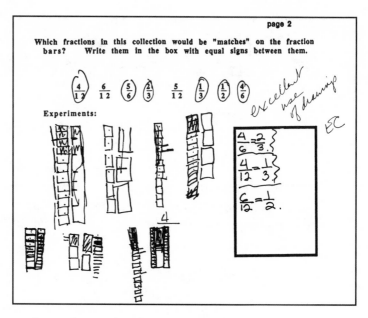

Among the students who demonstrated that they could use more than one representation for addition or equivalence, Connie worked both with numbers and with the area model in her experiments, moving easily back and forth between them at all stages of the solution.

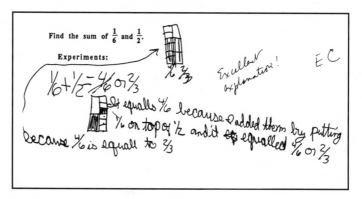

Similarly, Dorota uses twelfths and the area model to figure out where the Fraction Bars would be placed on the number line.

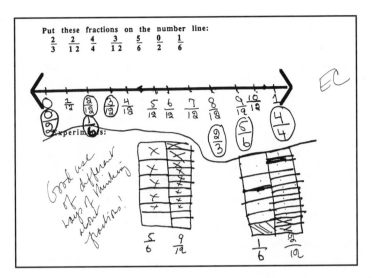

In all of these examples of work that were awarded "extra credit" on the quiz, students were communicating to me that they were making progress on several dimensions of mathematical performance at once. In my grading, and in the comments I wrote next to their work, I attempted to communicate with them about the special nature of their competence and its value.

Credit

"Credit" was awarded for competent performance. In stating to the class that getting credit for all the problems was adequate to get a grade equivalent to an "A," I intended to communicate that work at this level was good enough to indicate that students were doing well in fifth-grade mathematics. No credit, or partial credit, on any question, was not good enough. I reflected on this way of thinking about the grading of the quiz in my journal when I recorded an exchange I had with Tyrone after I handed out the papers. Tyrone had received credit for his work on two of the quiz problems, partial credit on three, and no credit on two. In an exchange with me after he got his paper back he tried to judge how "good" his results were based on this information. I told him that his scores "could be better" and he responded by asking if what he had done was "good enough." I wanted him to know that I expected him to do well enough to get credit for *every response*.

> Tyrone: if I only got 2 Ns is that good?
>
> M: could be better
>
> T: <u>good enough?</u> good?
>
> M: not good enough unless you get all Cs

Examples of creditable performances include Anthony's work on placing fractions on the number line:

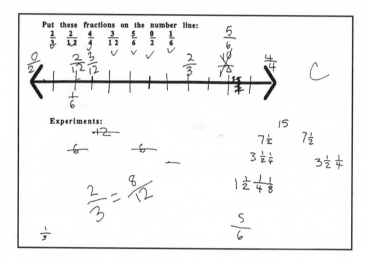

Charlotte's work on the addition problem:

and Martin's:

Charlotte shows the addition with drawings of area models and Martin with equivalent fractions.

In contrast to the "extra credit" performances, these students do not move around among multiple domains of communication and representation. Of course, I wondered if they would have done this if I had made it an explicit part of the problem, but I was more interested in finding out on the quiz which students would intentionally make use of several different ways of thinking in their work on fractions without any prompt from the teacher.[9] In awarding these fully competent performances credit, I wanted to acknowledge that they were correct. The "extra credit" performances were not more correct, but I wanted to acknowledge that they were special.

Partial Credit

An example of a performance that showed reasoning in terms of an appropriate representation of the given information but did not follow through to a reasonable solution was what Candice did on the "proof" problem. She does not connect her representation with her numerical-symbolic work on the quiz, and so her performance was awarded partial credit.

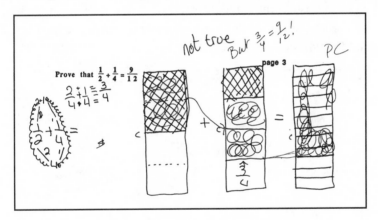

Candice seems to have a strategy for using an area model to reason about addition, but because she does not connect what she did with the Bars to the procedure she did with numbers, she concludes that the addition is not true, even though her diagram seems to illustrate that it is true. Part of what she did made sense, enough to demonstrate that she had some understanding of the meaning of the fractions. But her conclusion "not true" does not make sense because it is inconsistent with her diagram. I wrote "PC" next to her work, and the comment "But ¾ = ⁹⁄₁₂!" to indicate exactly where I thought her sense making broke down.

On his quiz paper, Kumar also made an effort to use the Fraction Bars to represent what one-half and one-fourth would mean in terms of an area model of fractions, and what it would mean to add them. But his representation does not show the sum as the total area comprised by the amounts shaded in on the two Bars he places end to end.

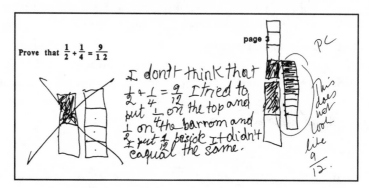

I circled a part of his diagram and wrote next to it, "This does not look like ⁹⁄₁₂." My purpose was to focus his attention on precisely where his reasoning broke down.

Giyoo's response to the same question does not use Bars at all, but indicates some knowledge that the "bottom numbers" must be the same if you are to add the numbers on "top."

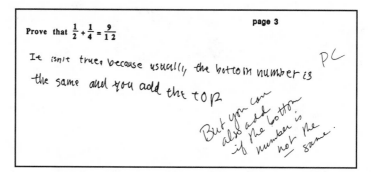

Since he had done some work in class where he simply added numerators and denominators, no matter what they were, this was an indication of progress in his understanding and use of fractions. In an effort to provoke his thinking, I wrote in response that fractions with different bottom numbers could be added.

Saundra's work on the other addition problem includes several different kinds of experiments, one of which is an accurate drawing of an area model for the two addends. She writes several sums in number-symbolic form, and after each she writes a question mark, indicating that she is not sure how to connect the area models of the two given fractions to the operation of addition. What she writes in these symbolic additions does not make sense, and there is some indication that she knows that because she put question marks next to her answers.

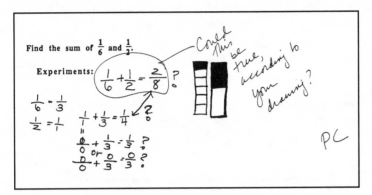

With my comment, I tried to indicate the importance of the drawing in Saundra's work.

No Credit

Ivan's work on the additions on the quiz (p. 334) is an example of the sort of work that received no credit because it did not attend in any way to either the meaning of the fractions or the meaning of the operation of addition. One of the answers on Reba's paper provides another example of this kind of work:

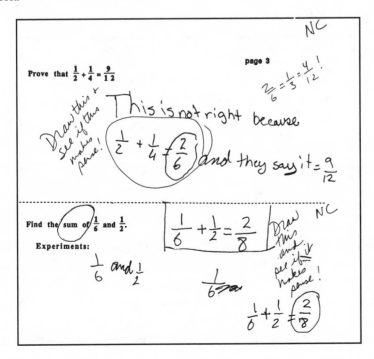

On Reba's quiz, I gave no credit for these performances, but in the comments I made next to her work, I left it up to her to draw a representation of what she had asserted so that she could see for herself if it would "make sense."

The preponderance of "no credit" judgments on the quiz work were on the problems having to do with addition. A few students were unable to work with fractions in a sensible way in other parts of the quiz, like Varouna, who received no credit for her work on the number line:

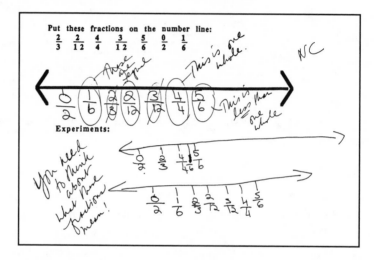

and Jumanah, who did not correctly match numerical symbols with the area models that were given:

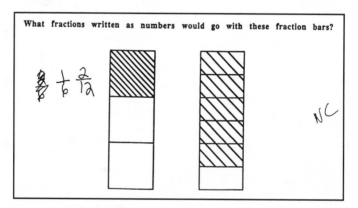

Although "partial credit" and "extra credit" could be used as tools to express the different kinds of learning trajectories that students were on in different domains, the "no credit" performances, especially on the addition problems, seemed to set some students off from the others in a more obvious way. They had not learned to use the meaning of numbers written as fractions, they had not learned to use drawing as a way to test their assertions, and they were confident enough in their operations and interpretations to challenge a statement they were asked to prove.

Problems in Teaching the Nature of Progress

To address the teaching problems that arise in the domain of giving meaning to "accomplishment" I used several actions that were also used to achieve other instructional goals. These include:

- speaking and writing deliberately using words that define accomplishment in this classroom context, and

- designing social structures in which students have the opportunity to teach and learn from other students, in this case, about the nature of accomplishment.

To examine the work of teaching students in a whole class across time what it is to be mathematically competent, I have described and analyzed these practices in connection with the work of formal assessment, grading, and responding to common errors.

As with many of the other practices I have examined in this book, work in these arenas involves using language very deliberately to name what students are doing and what I am doing. Using words like "credit" and "no credit" instead of calling what students do "right" or "wrong" and indicating that it is possible to be partly or especially competent with "partial credit" and "extra credit" is more than a matter of using a technical, context-specific vocabulary. It is a resource for teaching that can be used to convey a system of meaning around what is valued and how performance can be differentiated to indicate progress, or not. Using such words does not guarantee that students will adopt either the words or their meanings, but it does give them an opportunity to consider a different, more complex way of thinking about their accomplishments and about what they still need to learn.

Also familiar by now is the use of students to teach other students. The particular focus here is on how such teaching functions in the face of common errors. Instead of identifying those students who made the error as a group that *does not have* something that the rest of the class *does have*, I teach by making the common error into an opportunity for all students to study mathematical reasoning as well as fractions. This enables all students to re-engage with the mathematics of the problem without identifying themselves with the "have-nots." Avoiding such an identification has benefits for both those students who made the error and the students who performed competently. It communicates to everyone that competence is more than an individual possession; it also develops interactively in use. Because the grading on the quiz was ambiguous and even inconsistent, students could not easily peg either themselves or their peers as "good at math" or "not good at math" and act accordingly. Yet the system I used did make it possible for everyone in the class to investigate those circumstances in which making sense was valued, and for individual students to find out more about what a performance looked like if they were not making sense.

Remaining Problems for Teaching

Given the way teaching and studying in a class like mine must be organized in school, it is difficult to avoid the risk of some students experiencing public failure on the same tasks at which others succeed. This would be true even if no quizzes or tests were given, since everyone can see what everyone else can and cannot do most of the time. But formal assessments more directly convey the common hurdles over which everyone in a given class is expected to jump. I used my grading system and class discussion of common errors to counter the tendency for such standards to discourage and diminish students' academic self-confidence, but I was still left with the question of what to do about the students who had failed to take account of the meaning of numbers written as fractions when they attempted to add them.

I summarized my reaction to the quiz results in my journal, worrying about the diversity of levels of performance.

> *After the quiz—Feb. 24*
>
> The quiz results present me with the diversity of levels of understanding in the classroom: not only understanding content, but understanding whether + how to make sense of content.
>
> The weakest area on the quiz was in <u>adding</u> fractions: more kids than I want to admit added <u>denominators</u>. Well → we didn't really spend much time on adding fractions, <u>but</u> if they got anything out of the lessons on the meaning of fractions, they wouldn't do that, no? It <u>is</u> interesting that one way this came up was that I asked them to prove that $\frac{1}{2} + \frac{1}{4} = \frac{9}{12}$. I suggested that this was a <u>true</u> statement, and some kids had the <u>confidence</u> to say it was not true, offering the proof that $\frac{1}{2} + \frac{1}{4} = \frac{2}{6}$.

Following this summary, I reflected on what I thought the most challenging teaching problem was in this circumstance.

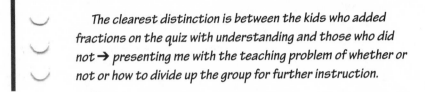

The clearest distinction is between the kids who added fractions on the quiz with understanding and those who did not → presenting me with the teaching problem of whether or not or how to divide up the group for further instruction.

As we saw above, some of the students who had not performed competently on the quiz were able to rethink their assertions in the context of small-group and whole-class work. But as our work in this problem context was about to end, their understanding of the meaning of the fractions seemed too limited to serve them in doing additions of all sorts and doing them independently. At the same time, several students in the class had demonstrated a thorough understanding of the meaning of the fractions we had been working with, and were able to use that meaning in appropriately operating on the fractions with addition on the quiz. I would need to decide how to continue to teach these two different kinds of students in a way that was consistent with the kind of "revisiting" of big ideas described in chapter 9.

Formal assessment, grading, and responding to common errors are elements of practice that highlight the differences in what students can do. Even if it is possible to avoid starkly communicating about those differences in public, they become the basis for further teaching. As I had observed in my journal, one obvious possibility would be to group students for instruction according to the differences in their performances. Students might be grouped based on some general assessment of their achievements, or they might be grouped for specific instructional needs. Sometimes choices about grouping are made outside the purview of the individual teacher, but often it is a resource that a teacher can use when it is deemed to be appropriate. In the chapter that follows, I take an extended look at the problem domain of grouping the class for instruction, beginning with actions I intended to take after the quiz on fractions, and investigating the work I did around this issue across the entire year.

The fractions quiz on February 26 gave me a different kind of look at my students. I saw them not only as individuals, but also as a class in relation to the mathematics I was teaching. I saw a static representation of what they could do, rather than the dynamic interactive performances that occurred in regular lessons. On the quiz, some of my students were able to use what I had been teaching them, together with whatever they knew before coming to my class, to make independent judgments about the meaning of fractions and apply that to the operation of addition. Others were not. I wondered if I should take the class apart and teach them in groups according to these differences.

From the beginning of the year, I had kept the class together and related to everyone as if they could be competent all of the time.[1] This was not an ideal arrangement, but grouping for instruction according to variations in accomplishment would mean changing the nature of my relationships with my students and changing students' relationships with one another. At least for some students, I anticipated that grouping would change what they were willing and able to do because it would change their sense of themselves as learners. The practice of grouping students according to their mathematical accomplishments, as demonstrated only by their performance on a quiz, was a practice that I had seriously mixed feelings about. There might be some additional and different teaching I could do within that sort of organization, but I knew from working with these students and others that understanding and skills were not stable. Sometimes they performed competently, sometimes not. Whom they were working with mattered, as did how the problem was formulated. And I am sure there were many other things that affected what they could and could not do on any particular occasion. If I were to give another quiz on the same content, the results might be quite different.

One problem I faced in teaching the whole class together was adjusting instruction to the kinds of variations among my students' skills and knowledge that were demonstrated on the quiz. But an equally challenging problem was adjusting to these variations *within* each student's performance. My students were not uniformly competent or incompetent, and across the class, the variations in their strengths and weaknesses did not follow any simple pattern. Of those who did not perform competently on the quiz, some had been able to contribute productively in small-group problem solving, and had been heard to say things in whole-class discussions that suggested a level of understanding that was not apparent on the quiz. Other students sometimes performed competently on tasks like computation, but were not always good at explaining their reasoning or representing relationships among ideas. From one problem context to another, students had different degrees of success with using the same mathematics. Such within-student variations undoubtedly exist in all classes, but they became a much more obvious problem given the kind of teaching I was trying to do. Because I expected my students to study mathematics by working with problems and to bring a complex web of mathematical ideas to bear on solving them, students who might otherwise be academically unsuccessful had opportunities to use their knowledge and display their understanding.

But then there were the quiz results to consider. Even though I could appreciate the complexity of students' knowledge and how it might be demonstrated in the classroom, I also recognized that *all* of my students somehow needed to learn *not* to routinely add the numerators and denominators as a way to add fractions with different denominators. I could teach them that this procedure was "against the rules" and they could probably memorize an appropriate procedure. But I knew, from experience with these and other students, that such teaching was not likely to result in competent performance over time. I suspected, for example, that someone had tried to teach Ivan to operate according to the rules, and it did not "stick" when he tried to perform the additions on the quiz. If he and everyone else in the class were going to continue to further mathematical studies, they would all need to know why it does not make sense to add unlike denominators and be able to figure out how to add fractions.

In this chapter, I analyze the problem of teaching all of the students in my class to understand fractions so that they can figure out that adding denominators does not make sense. Using the fractions quiz results as a reference point, I describe the teaching work entailed in analyzing the differences in skills and knowledge in my class. From that point, I then move backward and forward to examine my practice in relation to differences in performance across the year. I analyze the work of tailoring social and intellectual environments to accommodate differences, while at the same time expecting a high level of mathematical performance from all students. I consider the elements of practice that come into play as I respond to the "moving target" that is presented by many-faceted assessments of what a class knows and is able to do.

Elements of Teaching in Understanding Variations in Achievement

One kind of practice I needed to do here was to better understand the problem. What were the variations in students' accomplishments? What were the dimensions of competent performance? How many students were demonstrating particular kinds of errors? A second kind of practice I needed to do was to imagine concretely how I might restructure the social environment so that I could anticipate what the consequences of different forms of instruction might be with this class.

Getting to Know Students as a Whole Class

In chapter 5, I described the work of getting to know students as individuals. Here, the work I describe is similar but also different, because I am trying to get to know the class as a whole. To do this work following the fractions quiz, I portrayed the array of students' performances in my journal as a way to help me think about the problems I would be facing.

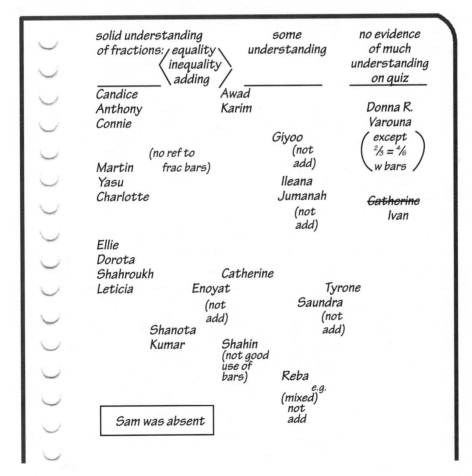

This was not a simple ranking of competence. Next to students whom I placed somewhere in the middle (having "some understanding"), I used shorthand to specify difficulties, like using "not add" to indicate that they did not use their understanding to work on the addition problems. I indicated that Martin had not used any representations besides number symbols, and Shahin did not connect representations to the work he did with numbers.

I wrote in my journal about an idea for what I might do with the students who had not used their understanding of fractions to work on the addition problems: I would "confront them with the evidence." But I faced a dilemma in trying to do this in the setting of the whole class, because I did not want to make their deficiencies something for everyone else to investigate. I considered whether I might be able to take these students aside and work with them privately, in a socially safer environment than the whole-class setting.

> *My pedagogical ideal in this case would be to confront kids with the evidence, i.e.:*
>
> $\frac{1}{2} = \frac{6}{12}$ *on the fraction bars*
>
> $\frac{1}{6} = \frac{2}{12}$ "   "   "   "
>
> $\frac{1}{2} + \frac{1}{6} = \frac{8}{12}$ *or* $\frac{4}{6}$ *or* $\frac{2}{3}$
>
> *I'd like to be able to do that <u>without</u> the kids who already understand it as an audience.*
> *How can I organize that to happen, given the constraints on my teaching in Thom's class?*

The essence of the problem I was facing was this: If I divided the class into different groups at this point in the year based simply on how students did on the addition problems on the quiz, I thought I might be able to solve some of the teaching problems that had been gnawing at me. But doing this would mean I would have additional work to do. I would have to figure out how to engage some groups in working independently while I worked with others. I would have to figure out a public explanation for the grouping, even if it was tentative, and explain it in a way that did not cause some students to lower their expectations of themselves in relation to their classmates. I would have to manage new and different kinds of social configurations because of the routines I had already put in place to support work in heterogeneous groups. I knew that different social issues would arise if the groups were to become homogeneous, rendering obsolete the organization of instruction that had been more or less adequate to manage differences in gender, race, ethnicity, and social class among the students.

Evaluating Alternative Kinds of Instructional Organizations

Although much of the work of coping with students with diverse knowledge and skills needs to be done face to face with the students themselves, a substantial part of the work on this problem is speculative: What would I anticipate might happen if I did "this"? What if I did "that"? What would I need to do in conjunction with any kind of social restructuring to maintain other parts of the instructional environment and classroom culture? Considering all of the issues in the mix, I worked in my journal to imagine concretely an appropriate instructional environment, taking account of the constraints of the daily schedule and my other responsibilities. I did many "thought experiments" to articulate for myself the possible consequences of various approaches to reorganization. I needed to be especially careful because my potential to teach serious mathematics to all of the students in my class (and their disposition to study it) was at stake.

I began to devise a strategy for managing the dilemmas I was facing. I thought I might teach lessons to the whole class on a new topic, one that did not highlight students' differing appreciation of the meaning of fractions. And then I would come in at some other time during the day and work with small groups while others did assignments. I reconsidered time, space, student's identities, and social dynamics in the mix with ideas I had about what mathematics I could teach this class. I began to think about some mathematical problem contexts to use to teach the whole class that would be new for everyone.

How would I organize the large-group activities so that kids could move in and out of it? I don't really want to do that. What I want to do is find something new to teach the large group → functions + graphing!
and then do the small groups at a separate time.
What if I did large group everyday from—well, would
it be better right after ^ lunch recess? or at the end?
I never get out of there before 2 anyway it seems.
What if I did small groups from 12:55 to 1:20 or so, and then a large-group lesson? I could do the small group 3 days a week, giving me a little more time in the morning?

> *How would this ability grouping affect the*
> *dynamics of the class as a whole? I think the ^ would* effect
> *be minimalized if I kept the class as a whole*
> *on separate topics like functions + graphing.*

Working with the Larger Context in Which the Class Operates

Next, I contemplated sharing my ideas about how to reorganize mathematics instruction with Thom, my collaborating teacher. I would need his cooperation to carry out the mechanics of any changes I wanted to make. Before class the next day, Thom and I discussed a tentative "grouping" plan and agreed it could be put in place after the vacation. For some "regular" lessons on functions, Maya Math (a part of the "Voyage of the *Mimi*" curriculum), and geometry, the whole class would remain the instructional unit. For other topics, instruction would occur in small groups of students who needed the same kind of help with fractions and decimals.

> *Thom + I had a bit of time to talk at recess about the*
> *grouping problem. He felt that it would be appropriate to*
> *work with kids at different levels. What we came to was*
> *that I would teach a regular lesson on functions, Maya*
> *Math, or geometry + then spend time with a small group*
> *on fractions + decimals. I will do fractions + decimals*
> *with the whole class from now til spring vacation. After*
> *vacation, I will do functions + graphing ala <u>Real Math</u> +*
> *while I am working with a small group each day, Thom will*
> *do some CSMP booklets with the rest of the class.*

I thought I might work with different groups on different days in response to what they had done on the quiz. The CSMP (Comprehensive School Mathematics Program) booklets would be familiar to my students because they had worked in them in fourth grade, and the mathematical tasks they presented were engaging and worthwhile, both different from and complimentary to what we had been doing. The fifth-grade CSMP booklets were available on a shelf, and both Thom and I had used them in other years. So a tentative plan for teaching students in groups was in place and could begin after spring vacation, in a few weeks.

Looking with a Wider Lens at Teaching to Differences

To act on teaching fractions in March, I needed to consider what had happened with other content at other points across the year when differences in students' accomplishments became obvious. I pulled back from speculating about what to do next and looked at patterns in what I had done so far in response to students' diverse and unstable levels of performance. This "pulling back" is a strategy I used to teach, as well as one I use here to analyze the work of teaching. To figure out what to do about differences in students' skill and understanding, I needed to fit whatever I was going to do in March into the continuous stream of teaching I had done so far that year. To be consistent and learn from my experiences, I would need to take a retrospective look at what I had done so far about differences, and how students had responded.

Yearlong Accommodations to Differences in the Class

In choosing to teach fifth grade in a school where there was only one fifth-grade class, I had knowingly taken on the full spectrum of ten-year-olds in the neighborhood. With one exception, I did not have access to any special services for students who might have been identified as having special needs in mathematics. Some students in my class did receive special help in learning English as a Second Language, and others were tutored in reading. In the one case where I was offered special education services, the school counselor had tested a student in my class and found her to be "educable mentally retarded." The assumption was made that she could not function in a "normal" fifth-grade mathematics class and the counselor suggested she be taken out of the room during my lessons to do other activities. I asked the principal if she could stay with my class for a time and have her participation monitored. I continued to expect her to work on the same problems that everyone in the class worked on. She seemed happy to do so, and was observed to contribute productively in both small- and large-group activities.

Starting in September, I had taken account of different dimensions of competent performance and of the instability in students' knowledge and skill across contexts by choosing Problems of the Day in which all students could be engaged. As I described in chapter 4, I used such problems to make it possible for students to perform in different ways with different kinds of competencies, alone and in discussions with their classmates. In the beginning of the year, I reminded myself that being able to "get into" a problem at many levels was a basic criterion for choosing the Problem of the Day. I wrote about this in my journal on September 10.

> *I've been trying to decide about how to handle the first*
> *day →work individually on a problem coming in from lunch*
> *recess for sure, to get that routine in place. Problem*
> *needs to be one that can be represented on the board—*
> *and it should be a problem that leads to some*
> *hypotheses about patterns and relationships, but also*
> *one that people can get into at many levels.*

I followed up these thoughts in my journal on September 11, recognizing that I had not succeeded in my initial attempt to choose a problem that would make it possible for students to use different knowledge and skills to engage serious mathematics. There are many aspects of teaching that seem overwhelming in the first week of school, but I chose to comment particularly on "the diversity of students' capacities on all levels." The students in this class were different in the arithmetic skills they brought to their studies, and they were not equally good at composing reasonable mathematical arguments.

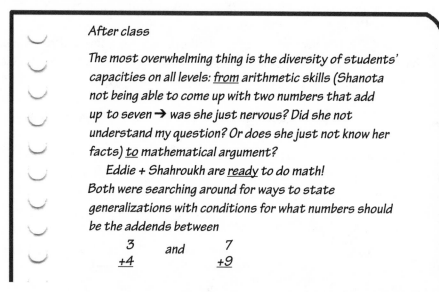

> *After class*
>
> *The most overwhelming thing is the diversity of students'*
> *capacities on all levels: from arithmetic skills (Shanota*
> *not being able to come up with two numbers that add*
> *up to seven → was she just nervous? Did she not*
> *understand my question? Or does she just not know her*
> *facts) to mathematical argument?*
>   *Eddie + Shahroukh are ready to do math!*
> *Both were searching around for ways to state*
> *generalizations with conditions for what numbers should*
> *be the addends between*
>
> $$3 \atop {+4}$$ *and* $$7 \atop {+9}$$

In this reflection on the first lesson, I had considered two different dimensions of mathematical competence, and I observed that students varied on both of these dimensions and they were not always congruent.

More Differences and More Participation

In December, I wrote again that I was challenged by how many different kinds of understanding and skill could be brought to bear on the work we were doing. At that time, students were working on a multistep sampling problem that engaged them in studies of multiplication as well as in speculative reasoning based on mathematical evidence. I had printed out the steps in the problem on a worksheet because at this point in the year, our lessons were often disrupted by last-minute changes in the preholiday schedule.

Suppose you know that there are 23 classes of students at Kellogg School, and suppose you walked into the third grade and counted 28 in that class.

1. How many students would you think there were in the whole school?
   Experiments: (Draw a diagram if it will help you think about this.)
   Conjecture:
   Reasoning:

2. Now suppose you walked into a first-grade room, and there were 17 students in that class. Would you change your mind about how many students were in the whole school?
   Experiments:
   Conjecture:
   Reasoning:

3. If you could look into one other classroom to refine your estimate about how many students were in the class, which one would you want to look into?
   Why?

This series of problems engendered broad participation and at the same time brought out more different kinds of mathematical performance.

After class 12/8

This class turned up an interesting range of thinking about sampling → given knowledge about one classroom, students used a variety of techniques to make projections about the whole school. The problem allowed several levels of entry and students (most notable: Ileana + Varouna who had not heretofore been engaged took an active role in the discussion) ①Dorota, Varouna + Ileana used a very literal approach to projection: they drew a map of 23 classrooms, imagined the various grades and (presumably based on their

> *knowledge of the situation at our school) they speculated about how many children would likely be in each room, and then added them up. I wonder how or if they used the information given in the problem (that there were 28 kids in the third grade)—it may be that they used it to assure themselves that the "Kellogg" school was pretty much like other schools they knew about.*
>
> *② Another approach, which could be construed as a kind of opposite approach, was taken by Candice + Sam, and quite a few others. This was to take 28 (the no. of kids in the one classroom you visited) + multiply it by 23 (the number of classrooms). Tyrone did this + got "messed up" on the multiplication. I hadn't really thought about this as an opportunity to teach kids something about the meaning of the multidigit multiplication algorithm, but I did take that opportunity, because it was a good representation of the mathematics.*

A few days later (December 14), working on another sampling problem, I again noted that students with different kinds of knowledge and skills were able to be "obviously actively involved"; not only were they doing the work, but they were doing it in ways that clearly expressed their engagement.

> *Obviously actively involved today were: Yasu, Sam, Shahroukh, Karim, Saundra, Varouna, Ivan, Connie, Anthony, Candice, Shahin, Martin, Dorota, Eddie, Charlotte, Reba, Enoyat, Ellie, Ileana*

And I said something similar again on January 8 during work on the cakes and bakeries problems (described in chapter 9):

> *Lots of kids were obviously engaged in this activity; many different levels, but most of them productive.*

On January 30, I was interested specifically in the different kinds of mathematical argument that emerged in a whole-group discussion:

> *Some kids are very much at the specific level, some at the level of generalization + some in between. The speech I made was, I think, intended for the kids in between who are "pushable" toward more general thinking: Sam, Ivan, Karim, Awad, Candice, Enoyat, Ellis, Charlotte, Connie, Shahin, Yasu, maybe even Shahroukh.*
> *Solidly in the generalization camp now is Martin.*

On this occasion, I tried to tailor my instruction to the variations I observed, "pushing" students who seemed ready to study something new, without separating these students from the others.

With this retrospective look, I was able to see more precisely how the Problems of the Day that I assigned to the whole class represented a continuing effort to give every student the opportunity to learn the big mathematical ideas embedded in the work. As we saw from the comparisons among many examples of student work from the lessons of September 18 (chapters 5, 6, and 7) and January 18 (chapter 9), they chose their own strategies for working on the problems, they investigated different mathematics, and I assisted in those investigations. Before I did anything about reorganizing the class for instruction, I needed to be reassured that indeed, there was evidence of students' learning across a spectrum of accomplishment, even though they were studying different mathematics.

Figuring out What to Teach in March and Whom to Teach It To

Having taken a broad view of the problem of differences in accomplishment and the practices I had been using to address it, I returned to figuring out what to do next about the problem posed by the results of the fractions quiz. After the quiz, there were a few more classes before spring vacation. I had imagined that I might start teaching students in separate groups after they came back from the break. Meanwhile, I hesitated to do anything special with the students who had not used an understanding of fractions to do the additions on the quiz. No matter what I did after the vacation, I needed to teach a lesson at this point that would allow me to learn more about who needed to study what.

I decided to revisit a problem we had worked on before the quiz. The problem had involved ordering ten different fractions, all with a denominator of 8, on the number line. Some of the fractions were smaller than one whole, and some were larger. The larger numbers had been included to connect work on fractions with work on multiplication and division. There are no Fraction Bars to represent eighths, so if students wanted to use an area representation to compare, they would have to construct it themselves. The inclination of particular students to do this (or not) would give me some further insight into the capacities of students to make sense of the symbols for fractions.

Revisiting and Revising: The Problem of Remainders

The Problem of the Day we had started working on the week before was this:

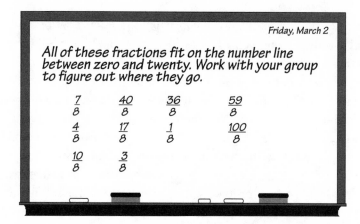

Many students had correctly lined up these fractions, using the order of the numerators, but most had not taken account of how close together or far apart they would be on the number line. So when I returned to the problem following my analysis of the quiz results, what I put up on the board was this:

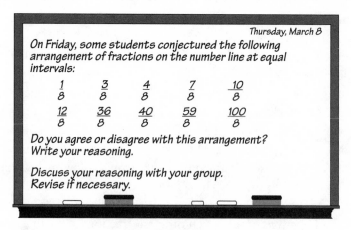

As with the discussion of adding denominators right after the quiz, I was using the whole class here as a "reasoning community" to manage instruction because several students had made a common error.

During the discussion of where to put the eighths, I first placed some whole-number "benchmarks" on the number line to help with the placement of the fractions, discussing these placements with the class.

Then when we came to discussing the placement of $^{100}\!/_8$, the class agreed that it should be to the right of 10 on the number line. But the problem was: How far to the right? To address this problem, we needed to return again to the study of what to do with the remainder in a division. We got into this mathematics because someone suggested dividing 100 by 8 to find out how many eighths are in 100 eighths. We found that there were 12, with a "remainder" of 4:

$$8 \overline{)\, 100} \atop \begin{array}{r} 12 \\ -96 \\ \hline 4 \end{array}$$

The discussion then focused on the problem of what to do with this "4" in relation to the placement of $^{100}\!/_8$ on the number line.

The wide participation of students with different dispositions and different levels of competence in solving this series of problems surprised me.

> We got partway into the issue of dividing to find the whole number or mixed number equivalent of an improper fraction. The person who said $^{100}\!/_8$ was near 12 (Sam; I think) said that made sense because 12 x 8 was near 100 and 13 x 8 was too big. He (Sam) later came back + said that $^{100}\!/_8$ was exactly 12 ½ and we went off into figuring out why that might make sense. This turned out to be a discussion about <u>remainders</u>: some people thought 100÷ 8 is 12 remainder 4. So then the question ~~beca~~ became why 12 R 4 is 12 ½. Someone brilliantly explained that the 4 leftovers were <u>4 eighths</u> and not 4 wholes. I think that it was Martin. Then Tyrone said something about how that "made sense"— "if you were thinking about it in terms of math and fractions and stuff." ➔ INTERESTING: when I pursued it, he could not go more deeply + he got frustrated, but there was a terrific indication there that he was picking up some elements of discourse.

Revisiting and Revising: The Problem of Grouping for Instruction

From the perspective of the problem of whether and how to "group" students in my class with different levels of accomplishment on the quiz, this entry in my journal about the lesson on March 8 is notable because it describes a substantive mathematical exchange among Sam, Martin, and Tyrone. These were three boys with widely varying knowledge and skills on several different dimensions, and substantially different personalities. If I were to teach those students who had problems with fractions on the quiz separately, this kind of collaborative study of remainders would not be possible.

Martin had entered my class in January, having come from a school where he had been placed in the "gifted and talented" program. He was very proficient in doing calculations of the most advanced sort, but he had almost no experience with reasoning about why one or another calculation was appropriate in a given problem context. Sam came to our school from a large school in Detroit in late September, and often remarked how the mathematics he did at his "old school" was quite different from what was done at our school. He said he had done no work prior to fifth grade on fractions except in their decimal form. In my class he did every problem that involved fractions by using a calculator to turn these numbers into their decimal equivalents. Tyrone was not good at performing conventional mathematical tasks. He almost never wrote in his mathematics notebook. He had come to our school a few days after the beginning of the year from a rural school in the South. His reading level and his level of computational skill were both very low. He also had something of a reputation as the class troublemaker. He rarely talked in large-group discussions, and when he did it was hard to interpret his reasoning. I was amazed that Martin, Tyrone, and Sam would collaborate in developing a solution to the problem of the leftover "4" and in constructing an explanation of why that solution made sense. Their collaboration brought a new and interesting aspect of the mathematics of fractions to the class. And because each of these boys needed to learn something different, this was an efficient way to teach them, together.

I wrote further in my journal that day about the high level of engagement in studying important mathematical ideas among other students who had demonstrated distinctly different levels of accomplishment on the quiz. Varouna, for example, had shown little understanding of fractions on the quiz. Yet there was obviously some understanding there, or she would not have been able to explain the relationship between twelve-eighths and thirty-six-eighths and place them accurately on the number line.

3/8 after class .

Today I feel like underline{everyone} was engaged + learning something. Martin and Shahroukh were making significant contributions at their level. Varouna, Giyoo, Awad → all were engaged in the issue of how much "space" was between the numbers. Varouna very clearly explained that $^{12}/_8$ was farther away from $^{36}/_8$ ~~and no~~ than it was portrayed on the number line. + then Giyoo said it was $^{24}/_8$ away. Awad was drawing on what he + his group had done on Friday, but both he + Ellie complained about the difficulties of writing down their reasoning about underline{why} they disagreed with the number line.

I had made some notes during class about what different students were worrying about, ending with a record of conjectures made by two students, Sam and Ellie, in the large-group discussion. In this somewhat cryptic journal entry, I noted several different kinds of performances of understanding in the March 8 lesson. They ranged from Donna Ruth's assertion that 9 times 12 could not be 104, to Sam's proportional reasoning and equalizing fractions, to Dorota's, Tyrone's, and Karim's moving back and forth between common fractions and their decimal and percent equivalents.

This mix of ideas, from this mix of students, was an opportunity both for me and for my students to study the complex meaning of competent performance. It would never have happened if I had immediately grouped the class according to how they performed on the quiz. I wrote at length about what I learned about my students from that lesson.

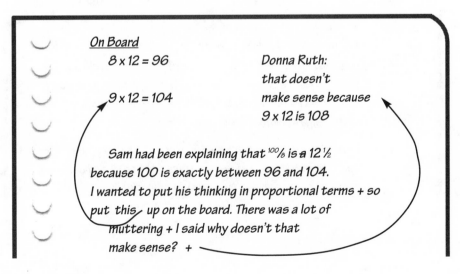

On Board

$8 \times 12 = 96$

$9 \times 12 = 104$

Donna Ruth: that doesn't make sense because 9×12 is 108

Sam had been explaining that $^{100}/_8$ is a $12\frac{1}{2}$ because 100 is exactly between 96 and 104. I wanted to put his thinking in proportional terms + so put this up on the board. There was a lot of muttering + I said why doesn't that make sense? +

> *So I gave a speech*
> *about how knowing your facts helps with*
> *math.*
> *Meanwhile: Sam had been saying he constructed a*
> *multiplication table for 12½. I put ~~2½ × 12~~ 12½ × 2 = on*
> *the board, but then we went elsewhere.*
> > *at 1:39, Dorota brought up that she had figured*
> > *out 12½ × 2 → that it was 25.0 because 12½ = 12.5*
>
> *Me* <u>why?</u> *~~Sam~~ :*
>
> > *Karim ½ = .5 = .50*
> >
> > *Tyrone = and it also equals 50% and ⁵⁄₁₀*
>
> *me* <u>why?</u> *½ = .5*

In this journal entry, the most surprising player is Donna Ruth. She had performed very poorly on the fractions quiz, and rarely made a contribution to whole-class debates. Yet on this day, she made a statement accompanied by reasoned evidence about why a particular assertion could not make sense. She was able to see herself in a more complicated way, and other students were able to regard her differently as a result.

A Tentative Solution to the Problem of Differences

We continued to work on fractions and decimals for several more lessons before the vacation. On March 14, I wrote:

> *Two interesting things about this [lesson] were ① that I*
> *was operating with different kids at different levels and ②*
> *that several kids "conjectured" in the more formal sense of*
> *the terms about <u>why</u> the pattern was evolving the way it*
> *was: Sam, Anthony, Shahroukh.*
>
> *Several kids were not involved + I wonder what they were*
> *thinking: ~~but it was not to~~ but it was not that certain*
> *<u>kinds</u> of kids (as in ability levels) were involved.*

> *The whole lesson seemed to flow a lot more smoothly*
> *than I expected it to.*
> *I put the dollar amounts up on the front board + asked*
> *kids what they thought — and one thing that is certainly*
> *different in this classroom culture is that a very vague*
> *question like that gets responses that are substantive*
> *and worth building on.*

Between March 8 and 14, the whole class had investigated decimals and fractions using money as a context, and they had done that fruitfully at many levels, together. (This work is described in chapter 9.) I abandoned my plan to group some students for lessons on fractions.

March 14 was a significant watershed in my thinking about the problem of how to manage students' diverse knowledge and skills. From the quiz until that date, I had been contemplating the radical step of dividing the class into groups after spring break. I had been planning how I would do that. But after what I observed between March 8 and 14, I renewed my commitment to the idea that keeping all of my students together would be the most productive way to work. The actions that I performed to teach during this period in relation to the problem of diverse levels of accomplishment were to *hesitate* and to *deliberate*, while learning what I could about how my class could operate in whole-group discussions to study fractions.

Managing Teaching Problems with New Mathematics and New Resources

Although I decided to keep the whole class together through the spring, I was not free of the teaching problems raised by the different levels of mathematical competency in my class during that term. In April, I was out of school for a week to attend a professional conference, and then there was a week of school vacation. When I joined my class again after this two-week hiatus, I prepared to begin working in a new problem context. I wanted to choose a direction that would give students the opportunity to study important mathematical ideas but would not depend on their being able to operate competently on numbers written as fractions. At the same time, I needed a context that would present them with some situations in which the meaning of fractional numbers could be further investigated with new conceptual and representational tools. I hoped that more collaborations like those I observed in March would grow out of this work. This would strengthen the understanding of the students who added denominators on the quiz so that they could reason that such an approach to adding these kinds of numbers does not make sense, and everyone would study some new mathematics.

"Functions and Graphing" was a topic in the fifth-grade curriculum that would be new to everyone, and therefore it would surface fewer differences in the knowledge and skills that students brought to their studies. It would also be a context in which I could pose problems at multiple levels of competence with numerical computation while providing an opportunity to study a big new idea, namely, the essential connections among the representations of the relationship we call a "function."

> *Returning from 2 weeks away: where to begin?*
> *I've decided to do functions and graphing because*
>
> > *it seems appropriate to start something "new" at this juncture*
> >
> > *The year is going by much too quickly*
> > *+ I want to fit this topic in*
>
> *I want them to feel that they are learning something new and important, learning how to do something they didn't know before: function rules, ordered pairs, graphs, slope, y intercept, + the relationship among all these things.*

I also decided to add a new twist to the way the class was organized. "Functions and Graphing" was a unit in a textbook—*Real Math*—that I had used before with fifth graders.[2] I thought that using some pages from this textbook would be an interesting variation on Problems of the Day.

New Material Resources: Using a Textbook

The "Functions and Graphing" unit in *Real Math* began by introducing students to something called a "function machine" as a representation for a "function rule" that would operate on input numbers and produce output numbers. The following page[3] from *Real Math* introduces the operation of the function machine, and shows a way to represent the relationship between inputs and outputs as a list of number pairs.

Suppose you put a number into this function machine. The machine will add 5 to it. We say that the function rule for this machine is +5.

If you put a 3 into the machine, 8 will come out.
If you put a 5 into the machine, 10 will come out.
Copy and complete this chart for a +5 function machine.

(+5)	
In	**Out**
3	8
5	10
7	▪
9	▪
11	▪
13	▪

From *Real Math* by Stephen S. Willoughby, Carl Bereiter, Peter Hilton, and Joseph Rubenstein. Copyright © Open Court Publishing Company 1981. Reproduced with permission by The McGraw-Hill Companies.

Like a fraction, a function is a mathematical relationship. The relationship in a function is defined by a rule. When the rule is applied, some operation or operations on an "input" number (usually symbolized by "x") produces another number, the "output" (usually symbolized by "y"). Studying functions as a mathematical tool is not just a matter of finding the outputs for given inputs as we had done with time and speed, cakes and bakeries, or length and width. In these contexts, the problems involved students in finding outputs for given inputs, using information about how the input and the output were related. Now the problems would involve determining what kind of relationship exists between *sets* of inputs and outputs, observing patterns in those relationships, and representing them in different ways.

New Mathematical Representations as Resources

The same function can be represented in three different ways: by a *rule* that relates the output numbers to the input numbers, by a *list of pairs* of input and output numbers, all of which will have the same relationship (called "ordered pairs"), and by a *graph* that shows all of the possible pairs.[4] For example, these are three representations of the same simple function:

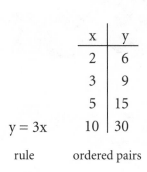

x	y
2	6
3	9
5	15
10	30

y = 3x

rule   ordered pairs

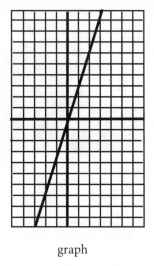

graph

The connections among these representations, as well as the representations themselves, are important tools in solving mathematical problems because they represent powerful patterns. It is possible to see from the table of ordered pairs, for example, that all the y-values are three times their corresponding x-values. We can tell how steep the line on the graph will be from the equation and from the table of ordered pairs. To find the graph from the table, we need to look at the patterns in the way the y-values change in relation to the changes in the x-values. In the table, when x "goes up" by one (from 2 to 3), y goes up by three (from 4 to 6), when x goes up by two (from 3 to 5), y goes up by six (from 9 to 15), and when x goes up by five (from 5 to 10), y goes up by fifteen (from 15 to 30). The pattern here is that the increase in y is always three times the increase in x.

What is represented in each of these forms of the function is the invariant ratio that links functions with fractions. The ratio "works" for any pair of values. For example, if y = 3x and I have an x-value of 100, the y-value will be 300. From x = 2 to x = 100, x goes up by 98. From y = 6 to y = 300, y goes up by 294. The ratio between the changes—the ratio of 294 to 98—is still 3 to 1. We always can see the same pattern in the slope of the line no matter how big we make the graph: it is always "tilted" so that it goes through the squares on the grid by going "up three, over one":

I thought that studying graphs like this would strengthen students' competence in working with division and fractions and at the same time give them an opportunity to learn something new. I designed opportunities into the lesson for everyone to study connections between functions and fractions as a way to keep the whole class together and also respond to differences in their accomplishments in the domain of fractions.

Moving on to New Ideas While Attending to Continuing Problems

The *Real Math* text uses the language of "function machines" to introduce the idea of functions, and then introduces the symbols "x" and "y" for the input numbers and output numbers. After they work on some exercises applying the rules of different functions to given sets of input numbers, the text presents students with a riddle whose answer can be found by using a function machine to break the code. I used these text pages as a resource to exert a leveling influence on the class. The terms and symbols were new, but what students were to do with them did not make challenging performance demands.

Everyone in my class worked without interruption on both the exercises and the code-breaking activity.

> I walked around the room, interacting with different groups on different topics + levels. I haven't done that for a long time, and it felt good: it felt like a way to see what was going on + do a little teaching here and there that would take the emphasis <u>off</u> of performing in large group.
>
> By the end of the period, most kids were on the riddle, so the timing came out just right for nearly everyone. No one was able to totally race through it and doodle and no one was totally "stuck" and the worksheet seemed to give them good substance for group interactions. At the end, there was "a learning" →
> people knew what an ordered pair was

My remarks here represent a mix of satisfaction that, indeed, everyone was actively engaged in studying something "new" and my continuing concern with adjusting my pedagogical problem solving to different levels of accomplishment.

After a few days of teaching the class how to operate within the framework set by the *Real Math* text, I began to construct Problems of the Day that would give them the opportunity to study the mathematics in what they had been doing. On April 17, the students were to complete these tables of ordered pairs:[5]

7. x +7 → y

x	y
8	■
30	■
■	27
6	■
■	107

8. x ×6 → y

x	y
3	■
■	54
10	■
■	48
7	■

9. x −3 → y

x	y
■	5
■	10
■	9
24	■
3	■

10. x ×7 → y

x	y
7	■
0	■
10	■
■	14
■	21

11. x −4 → y

x	y
■	15
■	21
■	72
■	3
■	19

12. x +6 → y

x	y
■	25
■	35
■	45
■	55
■	65

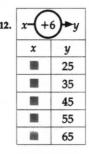

13. x ×10 → y

x	y
■	100
■	200
■	300
■	400
■	500

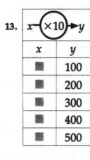

14. x −10 → y

x	y
■	100
■	200
■	300
■	400
■	500

Find the function rules before you complete these charts.

15. x ? → y

x	y
2	■
■	20
6	12
0	■
12	18

16. x ? → y

x	y
100	■
3	3
2	■
7	■
25	25

17. x ? → y

x	y
3	9
20	60
5	15
■	27
■	30

18. x ? → y

x	y
6	0
20	■
5	0
31	■
12	■

From *Real Math* by Stephen S. Willoughby, Carl Bereiter, Peter Hilton, and Joseph Rubenstein. Copyright © Open Court Publishing Company 1981. Reproduced with permission by The McGraw-Hill Companies.

The task in this set of tables is to find the missing values and to indicate the "function rule" in the circle at the top of each table. The first problem I gave students following this page of work directed them to look back over what they had done to fill in the tables of ordered pairs, and write about patterns.

I noticed a wide variation in what students chose to write about and in the extent of their analysis, but there was a uniformly high level of mathematical thinking going on. Writing about "number 16," Awad, for example, notes that the differences in the x-values vary in the same way as the differences in the y-values. Awad observes that if the function rule is "x 1" ("times one") then "you get the same number as you started on."[6]

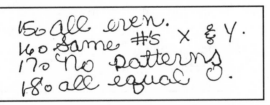

Patterns

Number 16 has a pattern because the function rule is X1. The X number is 8 so the Y number is also 8 because X1 means you get the same number as you started on. 100×1 equals 100. 3 times 1 equals 3. 2 times 1 equals 2. 7 times 1 equals 7, and 25 times 1 equals 25.

I noticed a pattern in number 12. The X numbers go by 10 and the Y numbers go by 10 also. The numbers in the X side are 29, 39, 49, 59. On the Y side the numbers are 25, 35, 45, and 55. Also the X numbers go 2, 3, 4, and 5.

Saundra's observations are much more abbreviated, but no less mathematically appropriate.

15. all even.
16. Same #'s X & Y.
17. No patterns.
18. all equal.

Charlotte's observations are similar to Saundra's mathematically, although her language for communicating her reasoning is more expansive.

> THINGS I SAW
>
> 18. All the answers are zero. This is because if you take any number and put it into 0 groups you will ~~actey~~ always have an answer of zero.
>
> 16. All the numbers remain the same when they go in and come out. If you put any number into a group of one you will have only one group with the same number in that one group, that you started with.
>
> 15. All the numbers are even because all the numbers all ready given were all even and you have to add an even number to all those numbers which will give you another even number because even + even = even.
>
> 14. All the out numbers are multiples ~~o~~ of 100. This makes all the in numbers just ten more than ~~you~~ the out number.
>
> 13. All the out numbers have ~~just o~~ one more zero than the in number. This is because if you multiply anything by ten you just add a zero to the number.

Giyoo's work is somewhat different. He makes a generalization about all functions. He uses the word "mathematics" here to mean the arithmetic operations of addition, subtraction, multiplication, and division using specific numbers, as in "when I couldn't figure one of them out, I tried many [operations]" and "if one [operation] works for both of them, [then] the rest of them are the same pattern."

> I think I learned some patterns. Because when I couldn't figure one of them out I tried many mathmatics. Especially on the last one I couldn't figure it out. But my group ~~told~~ look at the 2 numbers told me to that are facing each other. like 6 --- 12, ~~_____~~ 12 ---- 18. If ~~it~~ one mathmatics work for both of them, rest of them are same patterns.

These work samples represent the engagement of students in thinking about functions across the different categories of accomplishment that had emerged from their work on fractions. Although they vary in linguistic sophistication, they are remarkably similar in their level of analytic observation.

Graphing as an Even More Powerful Equalizer

As the text began to engage students in analyzing and making graphs of functions, the activities focused their attention on the idea that the points corresponding with the ordered pairs generated by a function rule would fall on a line. Reading graphs was something students had done in social studies and science lessons, but the mathematics of graphing points on the Cartesian plane was new for everyone. Relating the three representations of a function—the function rule, a set of ordered pairs, and the graph—was a substantial piece of new mathematics for everyone as well. Again following the lead of the text in posing a Problem of the Day, I challenged students to describe patterns in different graphs and in how the graphs related to the rules and tables of ordered pairs.

The range of students involved in this graphing work was again noteworthy. In the first part of the journal entry below, I identify two groups of students: "the advance troops" and those who "they could easily bring along." Students in the first category were actively studying what difference it would make on a graph if something was added to the x-value to produce the y-value, how the "tilt" of the line was affected by the number you multiplied "x" by to get "y," what would make the line tilt "upward" or "downward," what functions would make the line go through the intersection of the two axes, and other such fundamental ideas in analytic geometry.

> _Those_ are the main issues on the table that I'm familiar with, and they are primarily issues for Sam, Shahroukh, Anthony, Charlotte, Martin, Dorota ➜ these are the "advance troops" and I think they could easily bring along Awad, Ivan, Ellie, Yasu, maybe Kumar, maybe Shahin, Tyrone, certainly Connie (she is more private, but perhaps should also be an advancer), maybe Candice + Saundra. In many ways, I think my role in bringing these kids into the discourse is the most crucial + the most potentially productive.

The advance troops[7] are students who are deeply engaged in studying the mathematics of linear functions. They worked on this at home and came into class the next day with new ideas to share, bubbling enthusiastically about these ideas while other students took their seats. (These students had also performed so well on the fractions quiz that I worried about what might be "left" for me to teach them.) In taking responsibility for teaching all students, I had to work at keeping these kinds of students from becoming disengaged by making sure that something was always available to challenge them.

My role with the second set of students that I named here was different.[8] In this mathematical domain, the leaders are not relying as much on their relationship with me to have a positive sense of themselves as mathematical performers. But among the potential followers, there are several students who are on the edge, not sure they want to be good at math or even good at school. I saw my role with these students in the functions lessons as "crucial" and potentially very productive. My sense of responsibility here has to do with promoting the kind of personal growth and development that I described in chapter 9. By keeping the class together, they could learn mathematics and a sense of mathematical efficacy from their peers as well as from me.

In the two sets of students I have described so far, I have accounted for sixteen of the twenty-eight students now in my class. I went on to write about a "third set of kids" and what I thought I had been teaching them in the context of this work on functions and graphing.[9] These were the students I worried about most throughout the year, wondering if I was being responsible by keeping them together with the rest of the class.

> *I am more satisfied in this unit than in others that a third set of kids is learning something new and valuable because the subject matter includes new <u>tools</u>—and they are operating in an atmosphere where they can get a sense of how these tools might be used to really <u>do</u> mathematics. I'd love to get some interview data that probes <u>very carefully</u> what all this graphing + functions stuff <u>means</u> to: Giyoo, Reba, Donna Ruth, Jumanah, Leticia, Catherine, Shanota, Varouna + Ileana.*

Although I had divided the class in thirds in terms of their performance in the work on functions and graphing, the lines between the groups were not clearly drawn. Nor were they drawn according to a single standard of competent performance. Perhaps the strongest factor in my decision to avoid making the class into groups was my shifting judgment about who belonged where in these groups.

> *The lines between the thirds are fuzzy to me,*
> *especially for the first ⅔ I described. In terms of more or*
> *less public ~~but~~ and more or less skilled, but <u>evidently</u>*
> *intentional learners, I'd include (going around the room)*
> *Kumar, Sam, Charlotte, Dorota, Awad, Ivan, Ellie,*
> *Martin, Enoyat, Shahin, Karim, Candice, Shahroukh,*
> *Anthony, Tyrone, Connie: what I mean is that there is*
> *<u>evidence</u> that these kids have a productive and creative*
> *mathematical epistemology by now. I might also include*
> *Ileana + Catherine, but their tool repertoire is so severely*
> *limited it's hard to judge. I'm intentionally not including*
> *Yasu here. Her privacy is counterproductive.*

What I mean here by a "creative and productive mathematical epistemology" is that the students I listed all had demonstrated some disposition at this point in the year to make sense of mathematics and to use opportunities to study it in productive ways.

Acts of Teaching for Working with Diverse Skills and Understanding at the Whole-Class Level

In order to teach my whole class the content of fifth-grade mathematics and give them the disposition to study it, I employed problem-solving practices that included both deliberation and interaction, including:

- choosing and using activities that make it possible to array members of the class on different spectra of accomplishments;

- clarifying the possible variations and dimensions on which students might vary;

- evaluating the consequences of alternative instructional organizations;

- considering and responding to the larger school context in which the class operates;

- articulating continuing patterns in my responses across the year to students' diverse and unstable accomplishments;

- using those patterns to create a consistent "next move";

- choosing new mathematical topics that will present a more equal set of challenges to everyone in the class;

- choosing resources that all students can make use of to study; and

- making tentative changes in the social organization of instruction and observing the consequences.

These practices were intended to address two kinds of problems: variations in accomplishment among all students in the class and variations within each individual student's accomplishments over time.

In relation to the problem of diverse performances on the quiz, the most fundamental immediate action that I performed was to hesitate. To identify "hesitating" as an active form of teaching seems counterintuitive. But to pause in the face of uncertainty is a strategy for addressing teaching problems when it gives students an opportunity to study. In the analysis in this chapter, my hesitation gave my students the opportunity to explore their own mathematical competence. And it gave me an opportunity to learn more about how to teach them. Accompanied by deliberation and observation, hesitating at this point in the year contributed to the solution of some of my teaching problems. Perhaps it could be seen as sidestepping these problems, but from another angle, it enabled me to come at the problems in a fresh way and it enabled my students to productively re-engage with important mathematics.

Confronted with students who do something like adding denominators after they had been actively studying the meaning of fractions for weeks—as I had been with the quiz results—I could have concluded that these students would never learn to reason and represent their thinking in ways that would enable them to understand mathematics. Or that they would at least never learn that until they learn to do basic computation. I could teach them a rule and hope they remember it until they finish fifth grade (when they become the responsibility of some other teacher). But mathematics is so much more than rules, and that was something I also wanted all students to learn. It seems important to teach all students that mathematics is complex, and also to teach them that they are people who can learn it. I certainly do not claim to have figured out either for myself or for anyone else what to do about the diversity of knowledge and skills that present themselves in any school class. What I have attempted to display here is the work of my learning, from day to day, how to teach serious mathematics and intellectual courage to my whole class in the face of diversity.

13

Teaching Closure

The close of the school year comes because of where you are in the calendar. Its arrival has nothing to do with the time it takes a class to understand complicated ideas and acquire important skills. In this chapter, I examine the problem of ending a year of teaching, a year of relationships between students and the subject they are studying. Before our time together was over, I needed to teach my fifth graders what they had learned and what they were now able to do, and to see that for myself. I wanted them to finish the year with a solid and coherent sense of the big mathematical ideas we had worked on. And I wanted to give them an opportunity to demonstrate what they had learned about how to study mathematics. To do this, I needed to provide occasions for them to "perform" their skills and understanding[1] while coping with the inevitable end-of-the-year irregularities in the schedule and the social excitement that comes with transitions. As the year came to a close, I planned to teach lessons around problems that would make use of an amalgamation of the skills and ideas that had occupied our attention across the year to represent some kind of a conclusion to our collective story.

The school year began to end for me in March. At that point, I took account in my journal of how many teaching days were left in each week, and how they would be configured across the calendar. I could see that the late spring would be full of disruptions in the regular schedule. To do the work of concluding the year, I needed to balance students' engagement in studying mathematics with a respect for the necessary social rituals.

Mar 6–9	Parent conferences—miss Wed.	3 days
Mar 13–16	Parent conferences—miss Tues.	3 days
vacation week—miss this week		
Then there is April—		
April 3–6 Fri.—records day		3 days
April 10–13 Good Friday, no school		3 days
April 24–27—miss 3 days—New York		
May 1–4 Wed.—field trip to statehouse		4 days
May 8–11—trip to middle school		3 days
May 15–18—observers		4 days

	May 22–25—Wed. Safety picnic	*4 days*
	May 29–June 1—Thursday, no teaching	*4 days*
	June 5–8	*4 days*
	June 13—last day of school!	

Starting right after spring break, the routines put in place in September and maintained throughout the year to support students' learning would begin to be significantly disrupted. There would be field trips to finish projects they were working on in other subjects, whole-school musical and cultural productions, visits to the middle school, and parties and picnics of various sorts. These were the predictable disruptions. I knew there would also be many last-minute changes in the daily schedule.

In addition to disruptions in the schedule, the students would be excited by their anticipation of a big change in their lives. My class would be finishing not only fifth grade, but elementary school. The kind of place they would be going to school next year would be very different and so would the kinds of people that they would have in their classes. Our neighborhood elementary school was one of the smallest in town, and one of the most diverse, whereas the middle school would have sixth, seventh, and eighth graders from half of the schools in town and from many more affluent families. It was in a large building on a busy street. In middle school, the days and the classes would be structured differently. Students would move from room to room and have many more teachers across the day, and if they continued in our school district, their classes would be tracked according to "high," "middle," and "low" academic ability. All this would be happening simultaneously with the profound personal issues that arise as one leaves childhood and enters adolescence. The class would make their orientation visit to the middle school in the first week of May, and I was sure it would make a lasting impression as they began to see themselves in that setting.

I constructed my teaching in the last several weeks of school to take account of this anticipated transition while also intending to give students and myself an opportunity to see what we had accomplished together over the year. From April 5 to May 22 I taught the unit on functions and graphing. At the end of that unit, I built in several opportunities for culminating performances. One was a pair of lessons in which students worked on a new kind of function problem that would bring many different topics into play. Another was a unit on plane geometry, focusing on new content but showing my students and I what they had learned about how to study in my class, no matter what the content. The geometry unit turned out to be much shorter than I had hoped because of disruptions in our schedule. But it did provide an opportunity for consolidation and closure because it demonstrated how students could transfer the reasoning and communicating they had learned to do into a substantially different mathematical realm rather quickly. Finally, on the last day of school, we made a collaborative representation on the chalkboard of all the things we had done together, and each student wrote a letter to a potential new neighbor about what he or she should do to study mathematics in my class. I hoped all of these experiences would solidify the key elements in the lessons I had been teaching all year into something called "fifth-grade math" that students could bring with them into other settings.

Providing an Opportunity for Students to Demonstrate Acquired Knowledge and Skill in a Conceptual Field

With three weeks of school to go, I wanted to finish the "Functions and Graphing" unit and leave time for another short unit on geometry. The year was clearly winding down, and many "end-of-school" social activities were starting. Although I thought it would be preferable to teach a "culminating lesson" on the last day of school, I knew that June would not be the time for serious and sustained investigation. So I designed the culminating lesson to end the unit on functions and graphing, just before our third and final quiz at the end of May.[2] Like every other lesson, I wanted the last lesson on functions to involve a set of activities organized around a problem that was both accessible for all and challenging to everyone. But I also wanted it to pull together the connected set of ideas we had worked on in different contexts throughout the year. All year I had been struggling to keep the group together while having all students engaged in studying new mathematics. At the year's close, I wanted to push our work as far out on a mathematical limb as I could without letting anyone fall off, so that both my students and I could see what we had accomplished.

Making Something New into an Occasion for Consolidation

Over several weeks, we had been investigating functions like these:

$$y = x + 3$$
$$y = x - 9$$
$$y = 4x$$
$$y = x \div 5$$

by making and analyzing tables of ordered pairs and graphs. But we had not yet studied a function where you would obtain the y-value by using more than one operation on the x-value like:

$$y = 4x + 3$$

"Composite functions" like this are harder to derive from a table of ordered pairs than the simpler kinds of functions that we had been working on. Finding the pattern that links the x and y values in a table of ordered pairs representing a composite function requires a mix of arithmetical manipulations and number sense, but as it is discovered, the result weaves together a whole set of important ideas.

To teach with this kind of problem at the end of the functions unit would amalgamate the studies we had done across the year of multiplication, division, ratio and proportion, and fractions. I would also be able to use this kind of problem to hold students' end-of-the-year attention because although it is arithmetically challenging, it has the flavor of code-breaking and the built-in incentives that go with figuring out a puzzle in competition with one's peers. I wrote my plans in my journal:

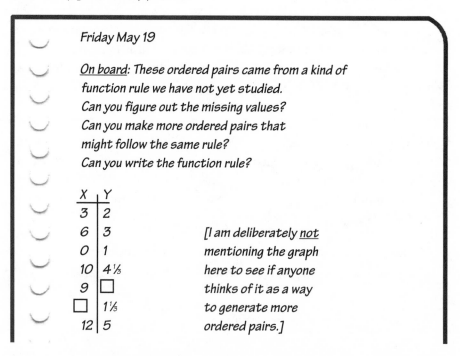

Friday May 19

<u>On board</u>: *These ordered pairs came from a kind of function rule we have not yet studied.*
Can you figure out the missing values?
Can you make more ordered pairs that might follow the same rule?
Can you write the function rule?

X	Y
3	2
6	3
0	1
10	4⅓
9	☐
☐	1⅓
12	5

[I am deliberately <u>not</u> mentioning the graph here to see if anyone thinks of it as a way to generate more ordered pairs.]

The function rule I wanted my students to find from this partially completed table of ordered pairs was y = x ÷ 3 + 1. In designing this problem, I very deliberately chose which ordered pairs I would include and which I would leave with a "missing value" to make the problem accessible and yet challenging at many levels. I wondered if it would occur to anyone to make a graph as a way to represent the relationship in the table and find the missing pairs.

Doing the Mathematics of Anticipation One Last Time

As I designed the culminating problem, I needed to consider both the mathematics I wanted it to address and the steps students might go through in solving it, as I had with every other problem they had worked on during the year. But for this problem, I especially wanted to design in a series of steps that would reveal how the many different mathematical ideas we had studied could be connected. Considering the social challenges I was facing, I needed to make sure there were steps toward a solution that could be done by everyone in the class, quickly enough for everyone to stay engaged, even if the classroom environment were somewhat hectic.

Given the kind of practice with number-work that had preceded this lesson, I anticipated that students might begin to work on the problem by first paying attention to the ordered pairs that involved only counting numbers. (The others are shaded in the following table.)

x	y
3	2
6	3
0	1
10	4⅓
9	☐
☐	1⅓
12	5

At this stage, the problem to be solved is to find the y-value when $x = 9$.

x	y
3	2
6	3
9	☐
12	5

Looking for patterns in the counting-number ordered pairs (3, 2), (6, 3), (9, ?) and (12, 5), I anticipated that students would notice that the x-values "go up" by three as the y-values "go up" by one. Using this pattern they could figure out that the missing y-value was 4.

If students were to graph the function using only the counting-number ordered pairs that were given in the table, they would have another way to find the missing value.

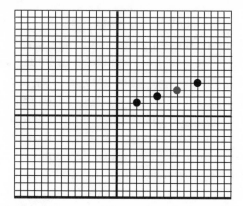

Using what they had been recently studying, they could use the graph to recognize the "slope" of the line as "over three, up one," and so, the missing y-value is at the point $(9, 4)$ where $y = 4$. Both of these approaches would follow on work we had been doing with simple functions.

Once the "4" was placed next to the "9" in the table of ordered pairs,

x	y
3	2
6	3
0	1
10	4⅓
9	[4]
☐	1⅓
12	5

and the nearby ordered pairs rearranged in order of ascending x-values—$(9, 4)$, $(10, 4)$, $(12, 5)$—students might notice that the x-value "11" was not on the table. Using the graph or using number sense, this might then lead to inserting the ordered pair $(11, 4⅔)$. Following this line of reasoning, the result would be a table like this, which would display the y-values between 4 and 5, and showing the pattern of the y-value increasing by ⅓ each time the x-value increases by 1.

x	y
9	4
10	4⅓
11	4⅔
12	5

This would lead, I thought, to their unraveling the "code" linking the x-values to the y-values. The intricate relationship between multiplication and division and between division and fractions, and what all these relationships imply about the rate of change (which translates into slope on the graph), all come into play in figuring out the pattern and finding the missing values.

Collaborative and Competent Performances of Understanding

Although the work got off to a slow start, everyone became engaged after a few minutes, individually and with his or her group. During class, I wrote some notes in my journal as I watched my students perform. I reflected both on students' mathematical accomplishments and on the social problems of working with them at the end of the year.

> *During class: May 19*
>
> *Dorota and Awad both asked: Is there one function rule*
> *for the whole thing?*
> *Catherine + Yasu talking quietly—no one else talking for*
> *about 10 minutes into class.*
>
> *(need to discuss the: "work by yourself, then discuss"*
> *vs. "discuss, then revise by yourself" routines →*
> *my teaching is a continual experiment with*
> *which is better for which kids)*
> *At 1:35:*
> *There is a lot of frustration with the problem*
> *but most of it is being handled positively*
>
> *Even Saundra right now is productively engaging with her*
> *group. What is going on with her? I feel as if I could learn a*
> *lot if she would tell me about it.*
> *As far as I can see, no one has tried a graph yet (1:50)*

After class I added more reflections, taking note of what a wide variety of particular students had done with the problem. I include a lengthy excerpt from my journal notes here to illustrate both the variety and the number of students engaged and how they were studying composite functions. The way in which ideas traveled around the room during this class was a combination of end-of-the-year frenzy and students' learned capacity to make use of one another's thinking.

It was very quiet at the beginning of class as people wrote down what I had up on the board. I went to Ellie + Kumar and spoke quietly to them about "behavior problems" from yesterday.

After a few minutes (they came back <u>late</u> from lunch, so this was like about 1:15 or so) there began to be moans + groans and requests for hints. The most well-articulated question was whether all of the ordered pairs fit the <u>same</u> function rule.

Ivan asked me a question I couldn't figure out the meaning of—it was something like "Could it be a negative?" I tried to get at what the "it" was, and it seemed like he wasn't sure himself, but it was something like "what you do to the x value to get y." I said do you mean "subtract something?" and he said "<u>no</u>, a negative."

As far as "hints" go, Martin asked if it was a "combination" of things that you did to y, and Awad wondered if it had something to do with dividing by three because of the y value of 1⅓. With or without my working to make them public, these questions + how I responded to them became part of the "ideas in the air."

absent: (Sam)

Later when I asked Kumar, Charlotte + Dorota to explain what they did, how they figured out the rule, Candice explained how she heard <u>this</u>, + then heard <u>that</u> as she was trying to figure it out and used what she heard to develop her ideas.

In the group of Martin, Catherine, Enoyat, Varouna, and Shanota there was a lot of excitement which I could not quite make out, but it seemed to be collaborative, at least among Yasu, Catherine and Martin (at an earlier point, Varouna had called me over + explained something she had been thinking that had to do with the first two ordered pairs. She had her hand over the rest of the ordered pairs, but what she had done was to compute the <u>difference</u> between the y and the x value for each ordered pair—but she was not consistent in whether she went from x to y or from y to x. She + Shanota were <u>active</u>, but it is unclear how much they were <u>with it</u>.)

<u>Catherine</u> came up after class to tell me that she wanted to spend time on Tuesday discussing this problem because she likes the problem + it's hard, it's unusual, not like just multiplication or division or addition, but it's "shifted times three."

1	0
2	3
3	6
4	9
5	12
6	15
7	18
8	21

shifted times 3 ↓

this was more articulate I think, than anything Martin said about it

Martin was <u>so</u> pleased with himself for figuring this out. He described it to me in the most animated way: "first I saw this + then I saw that,

The social and intellectual quality of students' performance on this occasion served as a suitable culmination of our efforts on both fronts. It was an occasion for students to consolidate and display what they had learned in the course of the year, both about math and about how to study math in school. Martin's admission that he was challenged, while I could observe that he was also interested, was particularly satisfying to me, since I had been working at finding something that would challenge and interest him for many weeks. In addition, he was happily working to collaborate with all of the students in his group, a few of whom had been able to keep up with him on figuring out this problem.

Evidence of Accomplishment in Student Work

On Monday, I put the table of ordered pairs with the missing values up on the board again, along with some very explicit instructions about what students were to do.

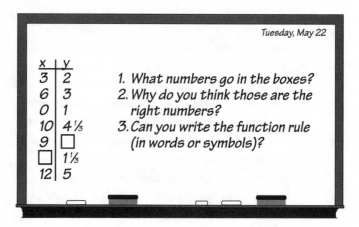

The students' notebook work from this lesson was an additional performance of understanding, more private and personal than the whirl of ideas that went around the class in the lesson before. It confirmed their abilities to both substantively communicate about those ideas and maintain their idiosyncratic strategies. To add a special note of seriousness to their productions on this day, I told students that I would be collecting their notebooks. In addition to their work on the quiz, I would take what they wrote about their work on this problem as an indication of their mathematical learning about functions and graphs. I directed them to work in their groups on the table of ordered pairs, on producing more ordered pairs that would fit the rule, and on constructing a graph. But I also told them that before the end of class, they were to each write their own reasoning about the function rule in their notebooks. As it had been at every point throughout the year, the range of student work was daunting, but it was also a satisfactory ending to both the unit and the year. The students' work on this problem demonstrated their mathematical, personal, and social development, and how these were integrated in competent performance.

Awad began with experiments that used addition to investigate the multi-plication and division of fractions.

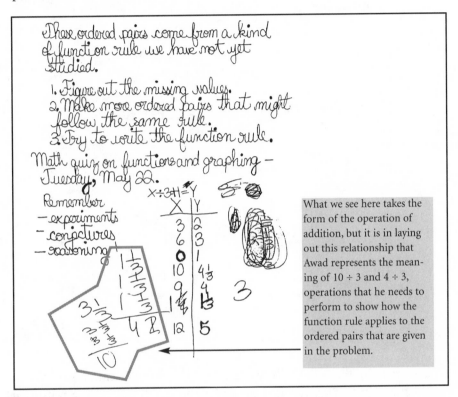

These ordered pairs come from a kind of function rule we have not yet studied.

1. Figure out the missing values.
2. Make more ordered pairs that might follow the same rule.
3. Try to write the function rule.

Math quiz on functions and graphing — Tuesday, May 22.

Remember
– experiments
– conjectures
– reasoning

What we see here takes the form of the operation of addition, but it is in laying out this relationship that Awad represents the meaning of 10 ÷ 3 and 4 ÷ 3, operations that he needs to perform to show how the function rule applies to the ordered pairs that are given in the problem.

He then formalized these calculations into a more organized representation of how the composite function operates on each input number: first divide the x-value by three, then add one to the result.

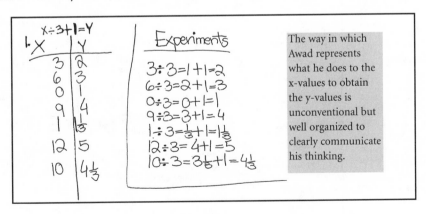

The way in which Awad represents what he does to the x-values to obtain the y-values is unconventional but well organized to clearly communicate his thinking.

Ellie made a similar representation of the operations on x to find y in each ordered pair, but hers was in the form of a "diagram" that although it is idiosyncratic, indicates the order in her work.

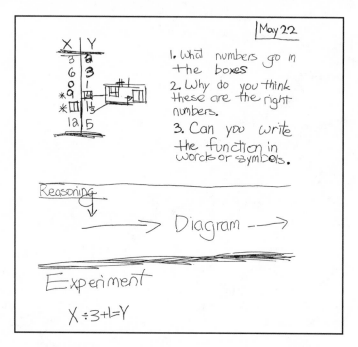

It is interesting that Ellie calls her function rule a "suggested function rule conjecture," indicating the way in which she has taken up the norms of reasoning in the class.

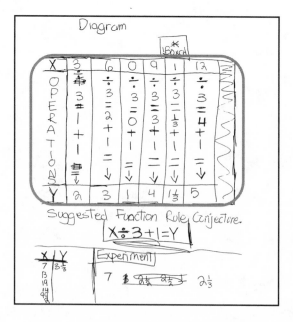

Anthony's work pages from these two days are a much more playful representation of his thinking and the way he engaged in studying composite functions.

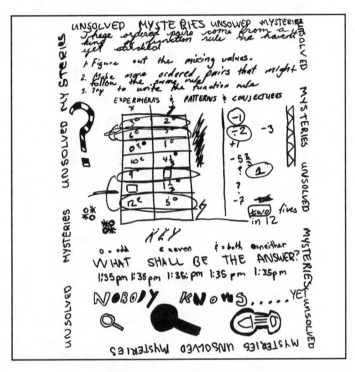

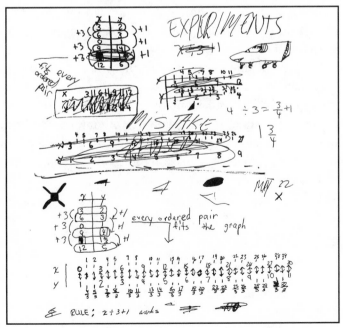

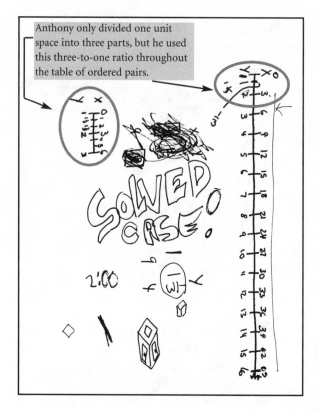

Anthony only divided one unit space into three parts, but he used this three-to-one ratio throughout the table of ordered pairs.

In his experiments, Anthony used a number line that harkened back to the time-speed-distance unit, placing the x-and y-values in relation to one another along a single linear dimension. Although unconventional, it does seem to have been the key to his group's thinking through the problem as we see from what Connie wrote (p. 403).

Connie's work documents not only mathematical development, but also the development of her capacity for collaboration and for communicating about the processes involved in mathematical studies. Connie attributed the "breaking of the code" in her group to Anthony, but her written explanation of the problem-solving strategy they used was more verbally expansive than his. At first, we see her rejecting Anthony's graph, at the bottom of her first page.

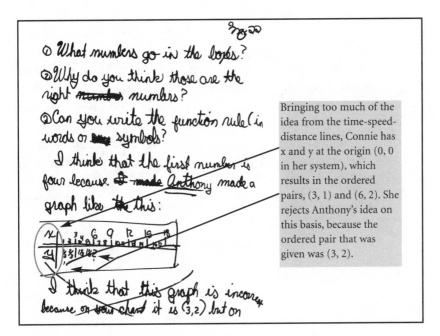

① *What numbers go in the boxes?*

② *Why do you think those are the right numbers numbers?*

③ *Can you write the function rule (in words or symbols?*

I think that the first number is four because it made Anthony made a graph like the this:

I think that this graph is incorrect because on your chart it is (3,2) but on

> Bringing too much of the idea from the time-speed-distance lines, Connie has x and y at the origin (0, 0 in her system), which results in the ordered pairs, (3, 1) and (6, 2). She rejects Anthony's idea on this basis, because the ordered pair that was given was (3, 2).

On her next page of work, Connie revised and acknowledged Anthony. Connie's graphical representation shows the three-to-one relationship between the y-values and the x-values. Going further than Anthony to show how the number line connects to the calculations, she filled in all of the fractional values of y that correspond to the whole number values of x.

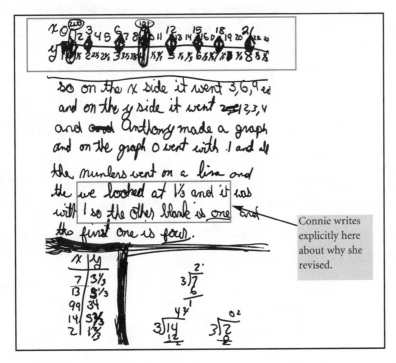

so on the x side it went 3,6,9 ...
and on the y side it went 1,2,3,4
and Anthony made a graph
and on the graph 0 went with 1 and all
the numbers went on a line and
the we looked at 1⅓ and it was
with 1 so the other blank is one and
the first one is four.

> Connie writes explicitly here about why she revised.

Tyrone and Jumanah were in the same group as Connie and Anthony, and the transcript of their work suggests that they were active participants in reasoning and communicating about the function rule and how it worked. But Tyrone did not record any of his thinking in his notebook, and Jumanah simply said that she figured out that "4" was the missing number in the first problem, and that the second missing number was "different." She had written very little in the way of "reasoning" all year, and I took her use of the words "I think" here to be a positive indication of the development of some mathematical efficacy.

> Reasoning: I think that my reasoning is 4 on the first missing number. second missing number is 4 like the same different from the first one.

Dorota's writing from the lesson of May 22 also represents an integration of studying mathematics and studying the collaborative process. She recorded how her group divided up the task of finding the function rule: "All of us [tried] to find a part of the question (problem) [then] we put our ideas together." She went on to describe what "we" did until her group found the function that worked for all of the ordered pairs.

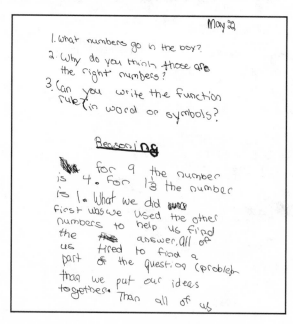

> May 22
> 1. What numbers go in the box?
> 2. Why do you think those are the right numbers?
> 3. Can you write the function rule (in word or symbols?
>
> Reasoning
>
> for 9 the number is 4. For 13 the number is 1. What we did first was we used the other numbers to help us find the answer, all of us tried to find a part of the question (problem) than we put our ideas together. Than all of us

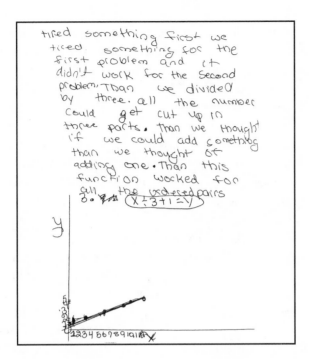

In terms of the similar use of "ideas in the air" by groups and neighboring students, it is noteworthy that Candice, Donna Ruth, Saundra, and Yasu also recorded their thinking similarly, as did Charlotte, Awad, Ellie, and Ileana. These collaborations are illustrated on the seating chart by arrows connecting students who acknowledge one another as the source of their ideas.

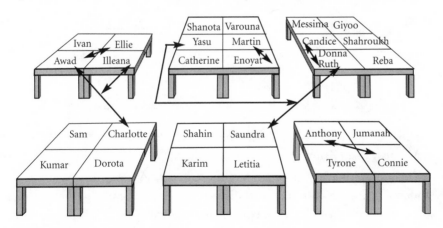

The movement of ideas around the class in the lessons of May 21 and 22 was one demonstration of what students had learned about how to study mathematics. Their notebook work indicates a development toward a kind of collaboration that both draws on the thinking of others and creates unique interpretations. What students did here is similar to the kind of "citation" of sources that is seen in more mature academic work.

Providing an Opportunity for Students to Demonstrate What Has Been Learned About Studying Mathematics

Following the culminating lessons on functions and graphing at the end of May, I made use of whatever class time I could get in June to teach a unit on the properties of plane figures and their relationships to one another. Despite the shortness of time, or perhaps because of it, I was able to turn these lessons into another substantive opportunity for students to display what they had learned about how to study mathematics. With the support of some concrete materials and a well-defined task, they were able to jump right into reasoning about relationships among shapes without much direction from me. Because we were in the last few weeks of school, I chose to work in ways that were even more different from what we had been doing in September through March. We would be working on a different kind of geometry, moving away from analyzing graphs on the Cartesian plane to analyzing the properties of two-dimensional figures. We would use tangrams, a set of simple polygons with commensurate sides that can be assembled to form other polygons worthy of investigation.

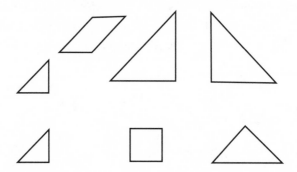

Using Concrete Objects and Competition to Hold on to Mathematical Attention

These physical objects were a tool for supporting continuity and interest. Students had more than the usual distractions to interfere with their studies, and the schedule of classes was far from regular. But we continued to do serious mathematics with these objects, not simple games. The geometry of polygons was a context in which to consolidate what we had been teaching and studying about the process of "knowing mathematics." This was a domain in which students could make assertions about shapes, agree or disagree with one another, and then make arguments to explain their reasoning. Students could bring physical objects to the reasoning process, but the patterns of interaction I had worked to establish since the beginning of the year could also be maintained.

Another resource I drew upon to make these lessons into a serious conclusion to the year was a set of clearly defined tasks to be done individually. We began the unit with students each making a set of tangrams from a square of construction paper. After a day of using the pieces of the set for an informal discussion of the properties of the shapes that composed the tangram square, I drew heavily on the guidelines for working with tangrams in Robert Baratta-Lorton's *Mathematics: A Way of Thinking.*[3]

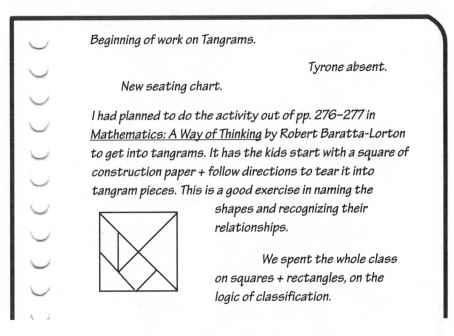

Beginning of work on Tangrams.

Tyrone absent.

New seating chart.

I had planned to do the activity out of pp. 276–277 in <u>Mathematics: A Way of Thinking</u> by Robert Baratta-Lorton to get into tangrams. It has the kids start with a square of construction paper + follow directions to tear it into tangram pieces. This is a good exercise in naming the shapes and recognizing their relationships.

We spent the whole class on squares + rectangles, on the logic of classification.

The activities in this book were easy to pick up on the spur of the moment, both for students and for me, so they could be used whenever I could get hold of a few minutes of teaching time. I had used activities from this book in other years, and I knew I could rely on them to engage my students and engage them substantively, even at this frantic time of year. They would also serve to keep me going along a structured and coherent mathematical path in the midst of organizing field trips and picnics.

Conversation using the mathematical terms for the pieces and making assertions about their inherent relationships grew out of the activity of making the tangrams from rectangular pieces of construction paper. I informally directed students' talk toward reasoning about the relationship between squares, rectangles, and other polygons. In this way, familiar vocabulary was reviewed and new logical problems were investigated. There were many opportunities to study the properties of different shapes as I directed students to generate definitions for each kind of piece and place them in a classification scheme. Even though the tone of the talk was more casual than our "large-group discussions" had been, it was substantive and filled with evidence for assertions. I used those assertions to make a "string picture"[4] on the chalkboard that represented the importance of specifying the properties of different shapes.

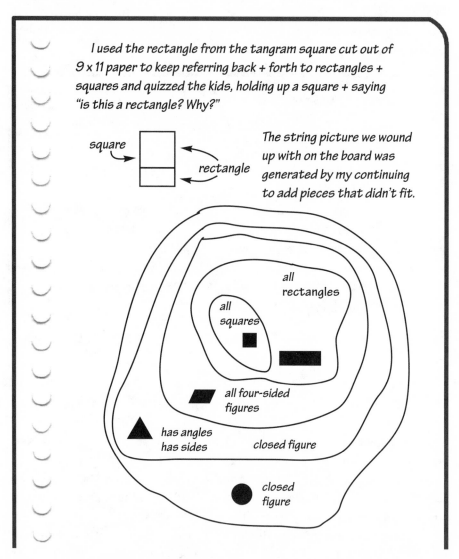

I used the rectangle from the tangram square cut out of 9 x 11 paper to keep referring back + forth to rectangles + squares and quizzed the kids, holding up a square + saying "is this a rectangle? Why?"

square

rectangle

The string picture we wound up with on the board was generated by my continuing to add pieces that didn't fit.

all rectangles

all squares

all four-sided figures

has angles
has sides

closed figure

closed figure

The vocabulary here was mostly familiar, although the more formal terms like "trapezoid" and "parallelogram" had been available to only a few of the students.

To minimize chaos, I had students working either alone with their own sets of manipulable materials or in whole-class discussions. They were not to work with partners as they had using the Fraction Bars. They could consult with those sitting nearby, but the assertions they would make would be their own. Both the design of the problems that I posed and the provision of a set of tangrams for each student were intended to help "keep the lid on," maintaining a somewhat informal end-of-school arrangement, but also supporting productive study.

This excerpt from *Mathematics: A Way of Thinking* exhibits the kinds of help I was able to get from Baratta-Lorton for the second lesson in the tangrams unit:[5]

LESSON 20-2

TANGRAM PUZZLE

PURPOSE:

To provide practice in assembling shapes with the puzzle pieces; to allow each person to succeed in assembling shapes

MATERIALS:

1. Tangram puzzles
2. Unlined paper
3. Scissors
4. Yarn

In the previous lesson, some students may not have been able to reassemble the square with their puzzle pieces. This lesson is designed to provide them practice in assembling a variety of shapes with their puzzle pieces while allowing each to control the level of difficulty at which he or she is working. Thus, each student has the opportunity to complete a task and feel successful.

Teacher: I have drawn a matrix on the overhead and a larger version on the bulletin board. I will help you begin to fill in both matrixes.
Can you make a square using one tangram piece?
Student: Yes.
Teacher: Show me how.
Student: This piece is one piece and it's a square.
Teacher: Okay. Since you can make a square with one piece, I'll write "yes" on the overhead underneath the square and across from the one.
Johnny, would you please trace the square onto a piece of paper, cut it out, and pin it up in the appropriate space on the bulletin board . . .

	□	△	▭	▱	◁
1	YES				
2					
3					
4					
5					
6					
7					

From *Mathematics: A Way of Thinking* by Robert Baratta-Lorton. © 1977 by Dale Seymour. Used by permission.

The sample conversations between teacher and students in the book sounded a lot like what my students and I had been doing to study mathematics, so I knew that this would be an appropriate end-of-the-year activity. It would keep students involved because they would have a chart to fill in to keep track of their findings, and there was an element of competition, but the work also involved doing substantive mathematics, like using the idea that all the squares that could be made with the tangram pieces could also be listed on the chart under the rectangle column.

Solving a Student-Generated Mathematical Problem

On the fifth and last day of this unit, the problem for investigation was whether two of the tangram pieces could be joined to make a hexagon. The form of the problem was mathematically formal, involving definition and proof. Several students, having experimented with a number of combinations of shapes to complete their charts, declared that it was impossible with this set of shapes to make a hexagon with two pieces. Several students were beginning to formulate explanations for why it was not possible when Martin exclaimed, "I did it!"

What he produced looked like this:

I saw in what Martin had done an opportunity to teach many different aspects of plane geometry. If it had been earlier in the year, I could easily have diverged from the structured path set by the book and gone off into a whole new unit on angles and polygons. It was frustrating for this to happen when there might be only one more class period left. I lamented that it was the end of the year.

Thursday June 7

Oh—I wish it were not the end of the year!!!

A __wonderful__ discussion developed today from Martin's invention of a hexagon out of a rectangle and a parallelogram

The class's discussion of whether Martin's figure was or was not a hexagon ranged over several important geometrical relationships and demonstrated the need for precise definitions and assertions. I wrote some notes in my journal about who had talked about what:

> *Yasu, Charlotte, Shahin, Shahroukh, Anthony, Sam, Connie, Dorota, + Candice were active in a discussion of the <u>angles</u> in this figure—how to measure them, what their relationships might be, etc.*
>
> *Yasu, I think—or was it Charlotte—had asserted that a four-sided figure had angles summing to 360° because it was made out of 2 triangles each having 180°.*

Central to the discussion was the relationships among the angles in the figure Martin had constructed. There were speculations about which angles had to be equal and why, and about the difference between internal and external angle measurement. Important arguments grew out of the idea, suggested by Yasu or Charlotte, that any four-sided figure could be divided into two triangles, for example:

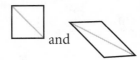 and

And so we could use what we knew about the angles in triangles to sum up the angles in Michael's hexagon. In a single class hour, the amount of material that we covered was enormous, the use of evidence and reasoning was intense, and the level of participation across the class was very high. Socially and linguistically, the lesson was climactic in that many students participated, and a wide spectrum of students exhibited confidence with reasoning and giving evidence. My work at this point, having constructed the occasion for this performance, was to stand back and let it happen.

On a day when we might have been cleaning up the room or even legitimately escaped to the playground, we had done some of the most serious mathematics of the whole year, with the broadest participation. Although the discussion was playful and wide-ranging, it had a structure similar to that found in formal mathematical proofs. Many students were invested in whether Martin's shape could in fact be called a "hexagon." It mattered in this circumstance that there were differences between interior and exterior angles, and so ideas like this could be studied without my intervention. Although

I was regretful that we did not have more time to spend on plane geometry, I was amazed at how much of it came into this single discussion.

Celebration, Coda, Reprise, and Farewell

On the day before the last day of school, Thom and I took our class to a local park, where we all ran around in the early summer sun and ate sweet, cold treats. My journal entry that day was brief:

June 12

Volleyball + popsicles

Our final class meeting the following day was more formal. During the time of day when we usually held math class, I began the lesson by having students make a "clustergram" to capture our shared understanding of what the year had been about and represent it on the chalkboard for everyone's consideration. Students called out things that they thought described some aspect of our work, and I arranged their ideas in a web. I was using this form of activity because it was one that the class had used on many occasions to investigate many different topics, in language arts, science, and social studies lessons, beginning with the clustergram on what it means to be a "buddy" they made with Thom on the first day of school and continuing throughout the year. I copied the results of this activity into my journal after class.

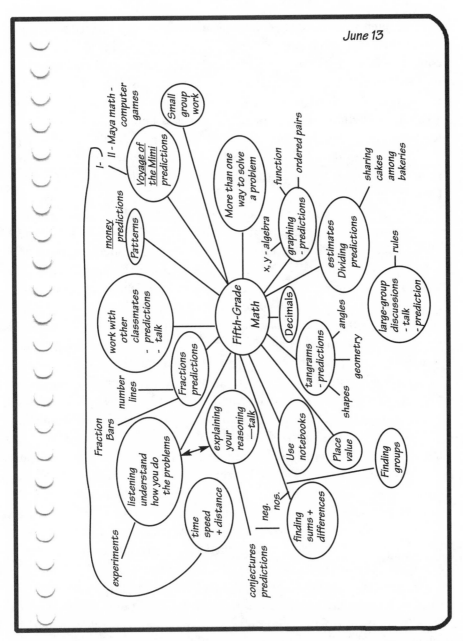

June 13

After we completed the class clustergram, I posed students a problem—not a mathematics problem, but a pedagogical one. In order to have a more individualized record of their thinking about studying mathematics in school at this point, I asked them to write a letter to a ten-year-old who might move in next door to them during the summer, and who would be in my class the following year. I told them to describe what we had done, and offer this (hypothetical) student advice.

In chapter 3, I argued that "My teaching cannot proceed without some complementary actions on the part of the learner." I included the student-content relationship in the model of teaching practice, and I explained that the work of establishing and maintaining that relationship was fundamental. In this and other chapters, I have described actions that students learned to associate with studying mathematics in my classroom, and what I did as a teacher to initiate and support those actions. The letters that my students wrote on the last day of school to their hypothetical new neighbors portray something of what *they* would say about what they learned about how to learn in my class.

Learning from classroom lessons—what I have called "studying"—is a skill that students must acquire if they are to succeed in school in any kind of classroom.[6] What is to be learned about studying is often conceived as a collection of "techniques" or strategies.[7] Some scholars have argued that different subjects require different methods of learning.[8] In a classroom where the content is taught by having students work on problems and by discussing and evaluating their solutions, what must be learned includes both strategies for learning and a new perspective on what is to be learned. When I asked students to write privately about what they might imagine telling a ten-year-old who would move in next door to them during the summer, I asked them to tell this student what he or she could expect to be doing to learn mathematics in my class. I told them not to worry too much about spelling and grammar, and because it was the last class, I did not ask them to revise. Even the essays from students just beginning to learn English as a Second Language were quite substantial, and I include several examples of essays here as illustrations of what different students found to be worth mentioning about the year and about the way lessons in my class were structured. A few students used "the lesson" as the time span for organizing their writing about what happens in this class. Others ranged their descriptions over the year, and some did both.

I begin with Saundra's essay as a follow-up on my analysis of my work with her in chapter 10.[9] She is notably explicit about working on problems with "many, many solutions" and about what to do if you want to "change something."

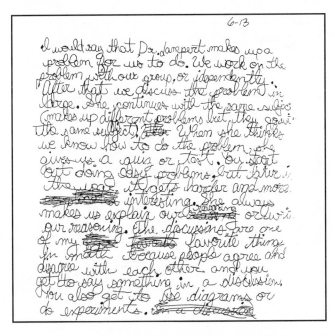

Awad writes about first working with "our group or independently" and then discussing the problem in the whole class. He sees the year as moving from working on easy problems to working on problems that are "harder and more interesting."

Enoyat portrays the year as progressing from "not being used to giving reasoning" to a point sometime later when "it makes sense."

June 13th 1st day of

Math

I would say that when Dr. Lampert first started with us we had to learn how to give our reasoning and people weren't use to that but now it makes sense. In the beggining of the year we also had to learn that there is more than one way to solve a problem no-matter if you are adding, subtracting, multiplying or deviding there is more than one way to solve a problem.
We also did all different kinds of stuff like deviding same as sharing we had a couple of problem doing with deviding or sharing cakes into bakeries. Then we started doing fractions with the fraction bar and throw out the whole year have been doing patterns. In the end of the year we were working on functions and graphing them it also made sense. working in our groups.

Leticia recounts a topic-by-topic description of the year, during which "we learn a lot of new things not just one."

MATH   Page ①

June 13th

I think first I will say that we learn lot new things not just one. And also that we just dont do The work and turn it in. we discuss it in our class. And also that when we discuss it and a person got patterns or something that he/she recognize in math that the problem that we are working on. And thats the problem we are going to work on the next day, Dr Lampert will ask you if you disagree or agree.

In the beggining of the year we started on mini computer. Well its not the kind that other teachers do its the kind when you add. Like this And you're trying to find patterns.

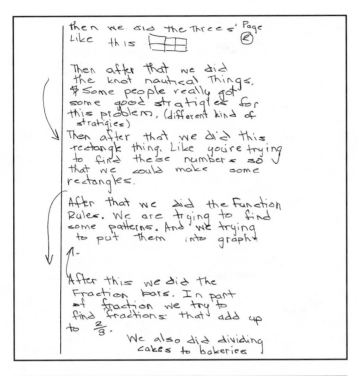

then we did the Threes' Page
Like this

Then after that we did
the knot nautical Things,
& Some people really got
some good stratigies for
this problem, (different kind of
stratigies)
Then after that we did this
rectangle thing. Like you're trying
to find these numbers so
that we could make some
rectangles.

After that we did the Function
Rules. We are trying to find
some patterns. And we trying
to put them into graphs

After this we did the
Fraction bars. In part
of fraction we try to
find fractions that add up
to $\frac{2}{8}$.
        We also did dividing
        cakes to bakeries

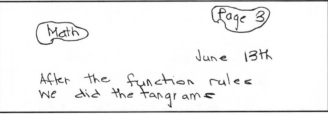

Math   Page 3

                    June 13th

After the function rules
we did the tangrams

Some students wrote only a line or two, but what they chose to write about
is telling; for example, Giyoo lists some math topics and vocabulary, and says
"If they didn't understand I would draw picture[s]."

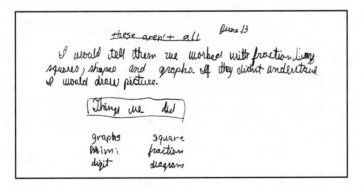

these aren't all   June 13
I would tell them we worked with fraction, diny
squares, shapes and graphs. If they didn't understand
I would draw picture.

    Things we did

    graphs   square
    mini   fraction
    digit   diagram

Tyrone writes about how as well as what we studied:

> Math and talk and work with others. We do
> places value, fractions, graphing. We were video
> taped. We studied knots miles ph. We learn Math
> words

and Shahin lists problem contexts and focuses on the use of the notebook for writing reasoning.

> Math
>
> 6-13
>
> I would say that "we were working on m.p.h,
> fractions, graphing, and tangram. And we have been
> watching a vidieo called "The Voyage of the Mimi."
> We have a3 notebook that we write the problems
> in. You have to give your reasoning also. After
> that we discuss what we did."

Ivan elaborates on the processes of agreeing and disagreeing and explaining to study math.

> June 13,
>
> I would say that
> we studied fraction we
> divided, timesed, added and
> we subtracted. I explaned
> my idas about what I
> think the answer is
> for a problem. Then we got
> together as a class and
> discosed what our answer
> would be some people would
> disagrey with some ideas
> then they nded to explane
> why they disagrey with that
> idea, and they need to explan
> what they agrey with. If they
> agrey they ned to explane
> your ideas on why do
> they agry. You ned to think
> on a probbe for about half
> an hour. We worked on
> thing like tangrams, MM, CM, things
> like the weigh, and the lenght.
> We had a program called
> the Voyge of the Mimi
> we quid watch on TV.
> We studied things like speed,
> time distance. We graph
> things'. We nded to work with
> with other people. There are
> rules for large group.

Shanota described how various elements of the classroom environment came into play:

> Math   June 13
>
> I think if the new student who will be in fifth grade next year I think I says likes in Dr. Lampert's Math we did like after the lunch is finsh and the resses is finsh we look at the chalk board and the a math problem that we have to solve and we our on not book and we write down what is on the clack board. If you have a question ask you group first if your group doese not no what the answer of your qustion is ask Dr. Lampert's and all that is time speed distance, graiping, fraction and fraction bar, small group works, more then one way to solve a problem, large group discussions, tangram and ther more that we stady

Candice took a more rhetorical and differentiated approach to the assignment:

> Math   June 13
>
> First I would ask him/her. in your class last year did you ⒶA explain your reasoning and talk with others in your class. or did ⒷB you just do your work and not desuic it any thing and just works independent. which one
>
> If said Ⓐ
>
> then this class would preaty much like it you work with others kids in the class when you get an answer it is never wrong till you dicusse it. you always explain your reasoning you usualy do diferent things everyday. look forward to be having her she is realy fun

> If said (B)
>
> Well this class will be much different. In this class you give reason for everything your answers are never wrong entill you discuss it. You do all different things. I will leave the rest for you to find out I just want to tell you to look forward to having a very good year and have lots of _fun_.

In this final assignment of the year, all of the students who wrote these letters found it important to mention not only mathematical topics but also the social and personal aspects of teaching and studying content in my class. The integration of the social and the intellectual was part of the content to be studied and learned in my class, and these letters gave students and I an opportunity to see what had been accomplished in that domain.

Teaching to Bring Closure to the Year

Practice in the classroom at the end of the school year is at the same time playful and serious. Perhaps both students and teacher take certain liberties precisely because they recognize that they are not likely to see one another again after the last day of school, although they have been together every working day for nine months. Work at this time of year can be more experimental because one need not anticipate that its consequences will reverberate for months or weeks or even days. If a lesson falls apart on the last day of school, one need not pick up the pieces and try to regain coherence. The end of the year is paradoxically a time when one must work at being serious, keeping the lid on even more tightly until it is time to take it off altogether and say goodbye. Summer is suddenly upon us with the emancipation it symbolizes in our part of the country (from coats and boots, and from walls and doors, as well as from the more or less constant supervision of grownups). But until that final bell rings, many children and one adult must continue to exist together in cramped quarters for several hours at a time.

I addressed these problems with both the form and the content of the problems I gave students to work on in the final weeks of school. The composite function problem:

- amalgamated several big ideas we had been working on across the year, both so that students would have a sense of what they had learned and so that they would be able to explore fundamental connections among these ideas;

- challenged the students in a more conventional "puzzle" format so as to engage their attention when many distractions were present; and

- communicated to everyone in the class that they might be able to continue to study mathematics in its more abstract forms.

The tangrams problem had some similar elements in that it was also a kind of puzzle, but it contained new mathematics. The problem was more than a review of by now familiar ideas. Although we had talked about polygons and angles, I had not posed problems in such a way as to require students to clarify definitions of geometric figures and to recognize what elements of those definitions were essential to making logical assertions about their relationships. The activity was also cumulative in that students used reasoning tools that they had developed in the realm of number theory to apply to the classification of geometric shapes. Their performance at making, challenging, and defending conjectures in this unfamiliar mathematical domain was a representation of what they had learned about determining the right answer in any realm of mathematics, and it signaled a development in their capacity for independent judgment.

The letters that my students wrote on the last day of school suggest that the social resources that are available to me as a teacher may be at their maximum point at the end of the school year: I know what to expect from my students, and they know what I expect from them. The intellectual resources, in terms of the ideas and skills students bring to their learning, are also maximized. That is as it should be if students have learned what I have made available to them to study. At the same time, the thing I need most—more *time* with my students—is not available. What is done is done, what is taught is taught, what is learned is learned, and there is nothing more that can be done. Along with the problems of teaching students at the end of the year, I have the problem of teaching myself to cope with the inevitable unmet goals and with the melancholy of ending relationships nurtured over nine months of almost daily interaction.

An Elaborated Model
of Teaching Practice

In all of the chapters of this book, I have moved back and forth between investigating the work of teaching with problems and analyzing the problems in teaching. In chapter 3, I drew upon a familiar three-pronged model of teaching practice to suggest that the work of teaching is done in simultaneous relationships with students, with content, and with the student-content connection, while students do the complementary work of making a relationship with the content to learn it.

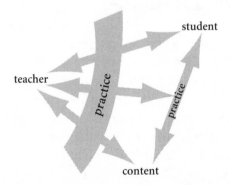

Elements of the work of teaching, I argued, occur along the arrows that make up the model, in the interactions where relationships develop. Actions taken by the teacher in these relationships simultaneously connect her with students and with content as she addresses the problems of practice.

Some of the problems of practice I have investigated are problems that every schoolteacher needs to address: setting up the room and making a schedule, planning lessons, working with students while students work independently or in small groups, instructing the whole class at once, linking lessons over time, covering the curriculum, helping students get motivated to study, assessing whether progress is being made, managing diversity, and bringing the year to a close. These problems are solved within the teacher-student-content triangle, differently in every classroom, in ways that take account of the resources available and constraints on action in the moment. As Ted Sizer wrote in his study of high school teaching,

> The character of this triangle is subject to change, varying from
> pupil to pupil, teacher to teacher, subject to subject, day to day,
> even minute to minute. Change any one of the triangle's members

and the others have to shift to accommodate, or even to break apart…. As long as schools are for learning, no relationship within them is more important than this triangle. That these triangles vary for different people, subjects, and times makes the task of providing constructive schooling an extraordinarily complex and subtle business.[1]

From the perspective of an insider to the practice of teaching, I have made an effort to unpack some of the complexity and subtlety of which Sizer speaks.

I have also tried to understand the special problems and practices associated with a particular kind of teaching. Because I was trying to teach *with* problems, I faced teaching problems particular to that approach: convincing students that everyone can do mathematics problems, teaching students how to learn mathematics by doing problems, connecting topics within conceptual fields and problem contexts, making the social environment safe for revising ideas, and organizing coherent lessons. By considering solutions to these problems in conjunction with solutions to the more common problems of practice, I have tried to investigate how teaching with problems can be done in an ordinary school classroom.

In the previous chapters, my analysis of the common problems and practices of classroom teaching, as well as my efforts to examine teaching with problems, have been framed by the three-pronged relationship among teacher, student, and content. But these investigations also suggest several ways in which to elaborate the basic triangle to move closer to an adequate model of the complexity of the work. In this final chapter, I first take up elaborations on the triangular model that would apply to teaching practice across grades, subjects, and instructional approaches given the universal features of classroom interaction. Then I consider elaborations that might help to explain the additional complexities of trying to teach mathematics with problems in schools.

The Problems of Teaching over Time in a Whole Class

There are several fundamental characteristics of teaching and studying in classrooms that are evident in the description and analysis of the work but are not well represented in the triangular model of practice. *For one, classrooms are always full of students, while the model shows the teacher working with students one at a time.* The need to relate productively with students "en masse" constrains the work of connecting students with content in ways that it would not be constrained in a one-on-one relationship. It causes more problems for classroom teachers to solve than they would face if they met each student one-on-one. But working at teaching in a classroom crowded with learners also makes it possible for a teacher to connect students with content using actions that could not be taken in a one-on-one tutorial.

In classrooms, students have relationships with one another over content. When they act in the public space of the classroom, they also teach one another, deliberately or not. By structuring relationships among students to support appropriate learning, a teacher in a classroom can add to her practical resources. A teacher can also ignore what students teach one another, but even if she chooses not to address the problem of structuring student-student interaction, she is constrained in teaching individuals by the fact that everything everyone says and does in the classroom is more or less public. To some extent, whatever the teacher or a student does or says to another individual can be observed by others, and so is also an occasion for them to learn something. Because relationships among students in classrooms provide an arena in which all teachers can work to solve problems of practice, they need to be represented in a model of the work of teaching.

In addition to the social setting in which classroom teaching occurs, we also need to take account of the time frame in which teachers and students make relationships with one another and with content in school classrooms. The time over which teachers relate to students and to content adds more complications to the basic model, and more resources and constraints to practice. *In the classroom, both social relationships and relationships with content have a history and project into future encounters.* Students make connections and relationships across lessons, and the teacher can deliberately try to structure them to support learning, or not. Teachers can choose to ignore the problem of making connections and relationships across lessons. But if the teacher takes on the problem of using these over time to support learning, she must do the additional work of understanding the persons in those relationships as they change over the course of the time they are together, and also take account of how relationships develop over time. She must provide tools for students to use to connect ideas from one lesson to another in ways that are appropriate to the subject matter under study. In this way, time can be used as a resource to connect students with content. By attending to the development of relationships with students over time and by attending to the connections among ideas that evolve in those relationships, the teacher can use them to support learning. The teacher, the students, and the content in the triangular model are not static entities; they change over time, and so does the work involved in making relationships among them. This dynamic aspect of practice also needs to be represented in a model of the work of teaching.

Social Complexities of Practice

Because interactions over content can occur with different students simultaneously, the teacher must work at maintaining a usable relationship with many students at once. As relationships with more students are added to the model, the practice-arrows multiply, as do the problems the teacher needs to address and the resources she has at her disposal.

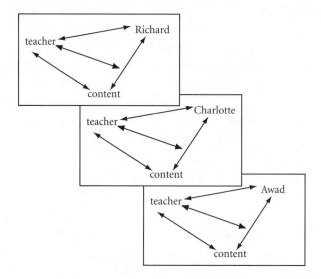

But there is only one teacher, and because she works in the public space of the classroom, her actions must address the content in relationships with more than one student at a time. What might be separate triadic relationships with each student in another kind of setting need to be integrated into a unified representation. The teacher has working relationships with individuals and with the groups of which they are a part, and these develop in the same set of interactions. For the model to reflect the social complexity of the classroom, it needs to look more like this:

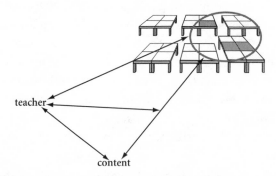

But even this version is not adequate, for students also have relationships with one another over content. Students sometimes deliberately teach one another in moments of interaction. But working with peers can also mean something more than directly interacting with them; it can mean identifying with them based on a relationship built up in another context. It can even mean a student's imagined sense of agreement with another person in the class based on a perceived commonalty. In all of these ways, students teach one another. The work of teaching is to structure those interactions to be productive of academic learning. A teacher can make better or worse use of the relationships that students have with one another and better or worse use of various groups within the class as targets of instruction. But because it is possible to use them as resources, the model needs to represent the work entailed in doing so.

To complicate these social matters further, all of the teacher's interactions with individuals and groups during lessons occur in the more or less public setting of the classroom, with everyone in the class able to see and hear most of what goes on. Practice-arrows go not only to each student and to groups of students, but also from the teacher to the class as a whole.

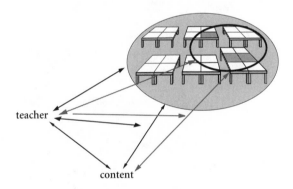

Just as the teacher can make use of her relationship with a small group or with another student to teach, she can make use of the class as a whole. She can use the class as a resource by making the environment quiet enough for everyone to hear everyone else when that is appropriate, and by getting the class organized to start and stop a particular activity in concert with one another. So there must be practice-arrows from the teacher to each student, from the teacher to groups of students, and from the teacher to the class as a whole, and work goes on along all of these arrows at the same time, in the same actions.

Temporal Complexities of Practice

The social and intellectual relationships in the classroom in which the content is taught and studied develop across many days and weeks and months, from the first day of school in September to the last day in June. The teacher and the class are together for an hour more or less every school day. Actions taken by the teacher in relation to individuals and groups are thus continuous, not only with what happens immediately prior, but with the entire history of relationships with all of the students in a class and all of the curriculum, across however many lessons the class has shared. To represent this continuity, the model needs another practice-arrow, one that moves through relationships over time.

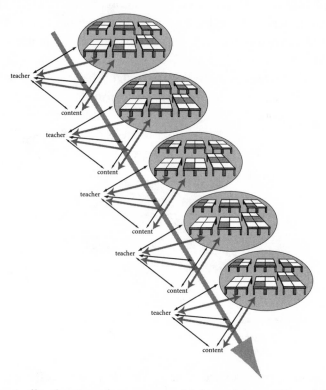

Most typically, the time frame over which teaching and studying occur in class is the school year. Some students come and go, of course, and there is the occasional need for a teacher to leave a class midstream. But the familiar unit of teaching begins in September and ends in June.

The memory of the teacher and the memories of the students, as well as their anticipations of where they are going, separately and together, in the near and longer-term future, contribute to the knowledge that informs how the teacher and students manage relationships with content in any particular moment. Again, the teacher can make use of individual and collective memory and anticipation, or not, but how memories and anticipations are managed affects what can be learned. If a teacher is to use the continuity of relationships with students productively to engage everyone in studying worthwhile content, she needs to work over time at managing relationships with each individual student, and with groups of students (e.g., students who talked a lot in class, students who had poor calculating skills, students who were sitting near one another, etc.). At the same time, the teacher must manage relationships with the multiple images of mathematical ideas that are the focus of these many communications.

Finally, the model must be complicated temporally to acknowledge that the work of teaching does not usually occur in just one class. Other practice-arrows need to go across classes, and sometimes, across subjects. For elementary schoolteachers, there are several subjects to be taught to the same groups of students across the year. This means that there are different content areas within which the teacher will be forming working relationships with individuals, groups, and the class as a whole. For secondary teachers, there are often five or six different groups of students with whom working relationships must be established.

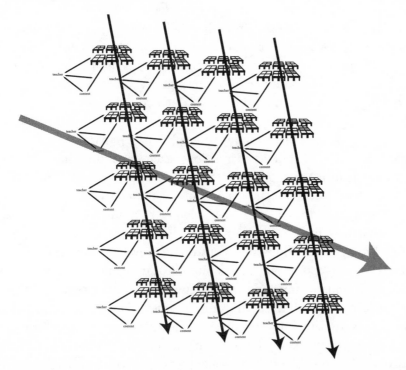

Many teachers at the boundary between elementary and secondary levels also teach different groups, although they may teach several subjects to the same group. The most complex arrangement, of course, would result if a teacher were teaching a different class and a different subject at each hour of the day, a situation that is not unknown in some schools.

Practice as Zooming in and out, Temporally and Socially, to Address Teaching Problems

In chapter 3, I suggested that a photographic metaphor would be useful for developing a method to analyze the large volume of records of practice I had accumulated to document a year of teaching and studying in my classroom. I return to that metaphor here, not to represent practice, but to explain it. To do the work of teaching, the teacher in the classroom also needs to do something akin to zooming in and zooming out, acting simultaneously in both "the big picture," across time and across relationships, and in moment-by-moment interactions with individual students. To solve the problems of teaching "this content" and teaching it *now*, as well as building up ideas over time, to teach "this student" as well as every other student, the teacher must be constantly readjusting the lens through which she sees both students and content. The readjustment is not just about multiple levels of *seeing*, however. The teacher's *actions* must zoom in and out, from individuals to groups and back again, from the whole class to a pair of students who disagree and back again, from constructing a drawing on the chalkboard to constructing a whole unit of instruction and back again. These actions must be, at the same time, both narrowly convergent and widely panoramic, and everything in between. And, they must often converge on more than one focal point.

The importance of the "zooming" metaphor here is that actions in narrow contexts are embedded in broader actions taken across time and across students; practice in the moment is not carried out separately from larger exploits. Every teaching action, no matter how narrow its intent, has an impact on shaping the complex set of ongoing relationships aimed to enable every student in the class to learn mathematics over time, and conversely, those ongoing relationships are a constraint on every action. As the teacher "zooms in" and "zooms out" across multiple dimensions, she can make use of different units of time and social networks as resources to make more kinds of teaching possible, and the units of time and interaction in which the work occurs overlap. This is the quality of teachers' work that makes it difficult to judge what is going on from any sample of the work, like watching only one lesson a week or monitoring interaction with only a few students over time.

Without the complications of the model elaborated here, the establishment and maintenance of relationships with students, as individuals and as groups, in the moment and over time, remain an invisible aspect of practice. Yet it is clear that these relationships are not simply nice to have, they are fundamental resources that are used in getting the job of teaching done. Like nurses who make it their business to know patients and their families because to do so is good medical practice, teachers who maintain productive, long-term intellectual and social connections with their students are working toward their professional aims.[2] The work that is entailed in maintaining these relationships is not something a teacher does because she has a friendly disposition, but because she is identifying and sharpening the essential tools of her trade.

The Complexities of Content in Teaching with Problems

Because I was doing a particular kind of teaching in the practice that I portray in this book, I needed to solve problems in my work that do not necessarily arise in other kinds of teaching: convincing students that everyone in the class could solve mathematics problems, teaching students how to learn mathematics from solving problems, connecting topics within conceptual fields and across problem contexts, and organizing coherent lessons while opening them up to build on student thinking. Like the problems common to all kinds of teaching, these needed to be addressed in different units of time and in different social configurations.

The fundamental difference between teaching with problems and other kinds of teaching revolves around the nature of the content and what it means to study it in school. *As it is enacted in classroom relationships while students work on problems, the content is more than a series of topics.* When students engage with mathematics in a problem, *the content is located in a mathematical territory where ideas are used and understood based on their relationships to one another within a field of study.* In its simple form, the three-pronged model can represent teaching topics, but it does not represent the work a teacher must do to support students in understanding mathematical connections in terms of the big ideas in which topics are embedded. The model needs to represent conceptual fields as content and the making of deliberate connections among the ideas in those fields as a key activity of teachers and students.

If it is to represent the work of teaching with problems, the content corner of the teacher-student-content triangle also needs to include more than topics and conceptual fields. *Students need to learn how to learn mathematics with problems while also learning to "do school."* When teaching of the sort I have described occurs in school classrooms, the teacher has to teach students how to investigate big ideas while also teaching other kinds of content that the romantics among us wish did not have to be taught, like sitting still, listening quietly, and the like. If students are to study mathematics by discussing solutions to problems using mathematical discourse in a school classroom, *they need to be taught to behave with a particular sort of academic "civility."* Inventing and maintaining routines to teach higher-order social norms is one way to address this problem. Schedules and seating charts are another. Especially when classroom interaction with content involves students taking intellectual risks in the company of their peers, confronting the regular and predictable frustrations that come with working on ill-structured problems can easily deteriorate into social chaos if students are not also learning to manage interaction. If the social management gets preference over the mathematical work, however, the consequences are equally problematic.[3] *Solving the problem of teaching students how to study goes hand in hand with teaching them that they can learn by studying with problems,* or what I have called "academic character building." In addition to representing relations with conceptual fields and the topics within them, the model must show relations among teacher, students, and these other kinds of "content."

Complicating the Model with the Nature of Subject Matter in Solving Problems

Stepping back from the problems of establishing and maintaining productive relations with and among students over time, we now look more closely at the complications that can enter into teachers' and students' work as they interact with content as it is used in solving problems. Looking back at the teaching in chapter 2 with a list of fifth-grade topics in mind, the content in my exchange with Richard could be described as "dividing to find mixed numbers."

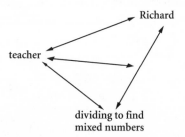

The problem was to find out how far the car, traveling at 55 miles per hour, would go in 15 minutes. Because 55 is not divisible by 4, some whole number of miles and a fraction of a mile would need to be found to express the distance traveled. The focus of instruction in this kind of division at the fifth-grade level is the remainder—what does it mean in the context of the problem? And how is it to be symbolized as a number? In relation to this content, Richard was working not on 55 divided by 4, but on 27 divided by 2. He had simplified the problem somewhat by working with smaller numbers, but he still faced a problem with how to handle the remainder and what it means. My work with Richard needed to occur in relation to the connection he had made between 55 divided by 4 and 27 divided by 2. Working with my own understanding of the mathematics in the strategy he engaged, I would find a way to teach him about the topic of "dividing to find mixed numbers."

When a topic like "dividing to find mixed numbers" is encountered by a teacher and a student in the context of devising and defending a strategy to find distance when time and speed are known, the topic is taught and studied in solving the problem. In the context of such work, the boundaries between this topic and other topics in mathematics are blurred. In work on problems, the aspects of mathematics that have been separated into topics for organization into school curricula are encountered as the unified whole that gives them meaning. It is only because they have been distilled out of a compound and arranged into a list of discrete terms that we now know them as separate entities. The "compound" that is the curriculum of big mathematical ideas is more than a mixture of component parts; it is a new and different thing to be learned.[4]

To teach these ideas, the teacher draws on her knowledge and relationship with mathematics to articulate the connections among topics in communications with students. It is that work I now seek to represent in relation to the instructional triangle. In chapter 8, I used this map to display the mathematical terrain we were exploring in the time-speed-distance unit:[5]

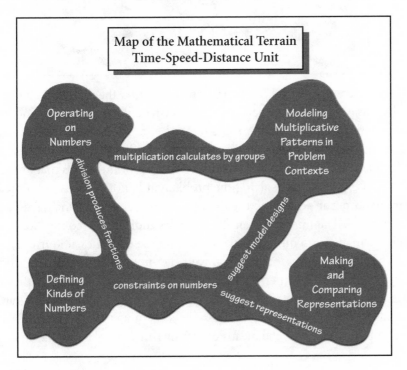

The challenge of representing the teaching of topics while also teaching their connections in conceptual fields is a matter of figuring out how to use this map in relation to the three-pronged relationship among teacher, student, and content.[6] I examine several possibilities here, and choose one that seems to model the nature of this work from the perspective of teaching practice.

We might represent where Richard and I "go" on this map to find the mathematics he needs to study by placing teacher-student-content triangles in particular successive locations and drawing lines from one to the next.

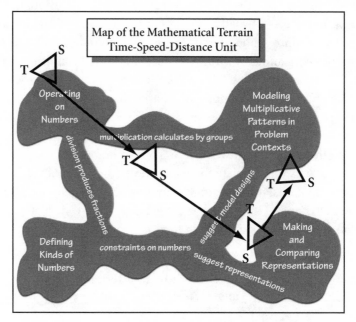

In this representation, the topics are arrayed around the map instead of in a straight line. The content vertex of each instructional triangle points to a mathematical "place" where a topic might be located. These are the places where the teacher and student go, one after another, together. The teacher and student move according to the identification of the topics that are relevant to interpreting and solving the problem at hand. There is not a predetermined order in which the topics at the content vertex of the triangle are encountered. The lines between the triangles indicate the connections that might be made from one point to another on the educational journey.

Although this representation of traversing the content shows connections from one topic to another in the content on the map, it suggests that the travelers on a mathematical journey only visit one place after another, rather than also encountering the connections as something to study. It emphasizes the stopping points, not the means of getting from one place to another. The teacher may have a perception of how the places visited are related to one another, but as the instructional triangle is portrayed in this representation, the student only sees one place after another. Places come one after another in a line, like geographic destinations rearranged for drivers on a "Triptik."[7] This representation is adequate for the part of teaching and studying that focuses on single topics. But in teaching and studying with problems, representing and communicating about connections among ideas and the larger fields in which those connections are situated are also an essential piece of the work. Moving the content vertex of the instructional triangle from one point to another on the map does not adequately represent this part of practice. That vertex needs to point to the connections and to the whole map as well.

One example of such a multidimensional vertex would be the connections in the content represented by the journey line I drew during work on the time-speed-distance problems. On November 20, we used this representation, which I constructed on the chalkboard.

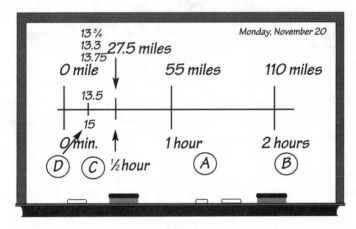

The continuous work of making this diagram in relation to students' contributions to the discussion did not happen in mathematical places associated with single topics; rather, it was constructed to help us relate to the *entire mathematical terrain* of multiplicative structures, and have a discussion about it. To specify the subject matter at the vertex of the instructional triangle in a way that represents what mathematics is being taught and studied, I cannot simply use points on a line, even if the direction of that line is not predetermined.

Another problem with the point-to-point journey-on-a-line representation of teaching work arises if we acknowledge that all students do not go to the same places in the same order. Nor are they necessarily in the same place at the same time. We might portray where some of the students were in their studies at a particular moment in the discussion like this:

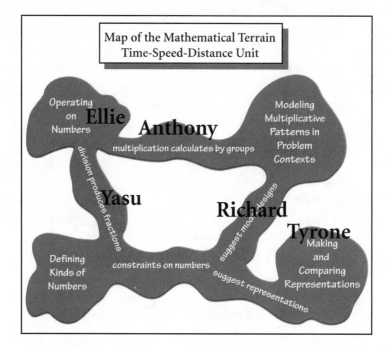

But if we do this we are left with the problem of where to put the teacher. The work entailed in managing this diverse set of mathematical investigations all at the same time needs to be represented in the model. If the work of the teacher were represented as following several students along variable but linear paths, she would have to be in several "places" at once. There would be no indication in such a model of the work of maintaining coherence among the representation of the mathematical ideas in play so that they can be studied in a discussion among different students and across time.

From the point of view of the teacher attempting to teach mathematical connections as well as conventional topics, it makes more sense to represent the "content" that is part of the triad as the whole terrain of a conceptual field rather than as a point on that terrain. Rather than representing the teacher's work as many overlapping, sequential step-by-step trips through multiple single topics, it is more accurate to portray it as teacher-student and student-student engagement with multiple, connected topics simultaneously.

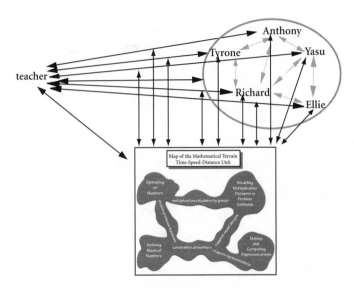

Coherence in communication about ideas depends on both the teacher and the students relating to mathematics in a holistic way as they simultaneously investigate individual topics in the curriculum. The practice-arrows must go not only from the teacher and the student to separate topics as they do in the map on page 434, but also from the teacher and all of the students to the mathematical terrain as a whole.[8] Although they are not illustrated here, the practice-arrows also need to go not only to different individual students, but also to different, dynamically constituted groups of students, up to and including the group that is the whole class.

Complicating the Model with Additional Content: Teaching Students to Get Knowledge out of Their Work with Problems

As my students invented and defended solutions to problems with their classmates, they were engaged with studying something else—something that encompassed their work with both individual topics and conceptual fields. They were using and investigating the "discourse rules" of the discipline. As they used these rules to decide what was true and right and useful in relation to the problems they were working on, they could decide what would count as legitimate "knowledge" at the same time that they would acquire new knowledge.[9] I needed to teach them to do that, and also to maintain a classroom culture in which mathematical discourse would be regularly practiced in the context of working on problems. This way of "doing school" produced additional intellectual and social problems to solve, but it also made additional teaching resources available. The discourse rules of the discipline could be used as tools for doing teaching if they could support the development of knowledge out of a process of reasoning about mathematical relationships. By making it possible for students to reason about mathematics, the teacher uses discourse to produce learning. The routines for interaction (like conjecturing and revising) that I taught at the beginning of the year and the patterns of interaction that I enforced throughout the year to maintain academic civility are examples of this kind of practice.

For students to study the discourse of mathematics, I needed to teach them to reason about why the ideas and processes that are known to the field are legitimate. I also needed to teach them that they were capable of reasoning from what they already knew to acquire new mathematical ideas. Doing this required opening up the assertions that were made in mathematics lessons to questions about whether these assertions made sense. Encouraging students to put more than one assertion on the table for discussion is a strategy for providing them an opportunity to practice mathematical argument and to study what works in such an argument as convincing evidence. In the course of developing and evaluating arguments for or against an assertion, the ideas and processes in the domain are taught and studied simultaneously with teaching and studying the rules of discourse. When the answer becomes "known" or a strategy is "learned," it is through this process of discussing what makes sense and why.

Using mathematical discourse in the communications between teachers and students, and among students, puts ordinarily taken-for-granted rules and definitions into the mix of ideas that students must reason about. So one of the problems of teaching is deciding what to present as accepted or conventional knowledge, and what to open for redefinition or debate.[10] Because students are engaged in discourse that is intended to create and refine mathematical knowledge, both the record of knowledge and the rules of discourse are necessarily modified and enriched by their use in the classroom context.[11] This means the teacher needs to do the work of deciding when to incorporate situationally constructed rules and meanings into the conversation and examine their implications, and when to simply remind students of the conventional rules and interpretations.

Additional challenges arise for the teacher because the classroom is not the only place where such negotiation about conventions takes place. As a "body of knowledge" mathematics does not stand still.[12] The matter of what mathematicians and users of mathematics count as acceptable tools, terms, concepts, and discourse practices is sometimes a difficult matter to pin down. Outside as well as inside the classroom, mathematics is a dynamic entity. As uses are found for conventional ideas, those ideas are shaped into new ones. As theory develops, new discoveries are made and new rules emerge for how to determine which discoveries should be accepted as shared knowledge.

Because teaching mathematical discourse as a way to study and learn is both social and intellectual, this work is represented in the instructional triangle along the practice-arrows from the teacher to the students as well as along the practice-arrows from the teacher to the content. Because learning how to acquire new mathematical knowledge while working on problems enters into the actions a teacher takes with students, individually and as a class, we must add another practice-arrow and a content vertex that encompasses mathematical as well as social content. Because students use the discourse they study in classroom interaction to produce knowledge of topics and conceptual fields, a ring around both the class and the terrain map represents this content.

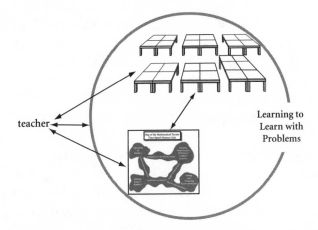

An example of the complexities of practice that I am trying to represent here is found in the teaching I do in the lesson described in chapter 2, when Ellie chooses to interpret "13 remainder 3" as "13 point 3." She had carried out the division of 55 by 4 like this:

$$\begin{array}{r} 13 \ \text{R}3 \\ 4 \overline{\smash{)}55} \\ \underline{-4} \\ 15 \\ \underline{-12} \\ 3 \end{array}$$

In what she said about the answer to this division, Ellie represented the leftover "3" at the bottom using the symbol that we recognize as a "decimal point," but she did not use this symbol the conventional way. The nature of her error is complex, and it takes us into questions of why something is or is not true in mathematics. To account for the leftover in her answer, Ellie should have considered what the "3" would mean in relation to the number she had divided by (i.e., 4). To equate "point three" with a remainder of 3 when you are dividing by 4 suggests that it means "three-fourths." But in the conventional number system currently in use in the United States, the "point three" in 13.3 always means "three-tenths." I could have gone in the direction of accepting Ellie's unconventional use of "point three" and worked with the class to play out what this would imply for how we use the number system.

Yasu did something like this when she disagreed with Ellie and said her answer of "thirteen point three" for a time of 15 minutes could not be right because if it were doubled, it would be "twenty-six point six." (The car goes at a constant speed, so it goes twice the distance in twice the time. We had already established that the car went 27½ miles in half an hour, so it could not go 13.3 miles in 15 minutes as Ellie had asserted.) What Yasu was doing here was using mathematical discourse to teach Ellie something about why we have agreed to the convention that 13.3 must always mean thirteen-and-three-tenths. Other meanings would lead to complications in the number system that would make it difficult to use in problem contexts. Yasu did not explain the meaning of the decimal numbers, but she did create a convincing argument for why Ellie's use of these symbols would lead to a contradiction.

Ellie and Yasu's exchange was an occasion for them to practice mathematical reasoning and an opportunity for other students to see what was involved in doing that. In order for everyone in the class to study discourse, I needed to teach not only the norms of discourse, I also needed to teach students to "do school" in a way that would make this discourse possible. They needed to be quiet, polite, and patient so that the discourse could happen and be educative. I needed to teach them that listening to their peers was a way to learn. In a setting like this, these are academic virtues, not just ways to manage life in a crowded classroom. They are essential behaviors for students to learn if they are to work together to practice and demonstrate mathematical reasoning in the context of solving problems, and so they must be represented at the content vertex of the instructional triangle.

Zooming in a Different Dimension

Structuring classroom interaction so that Ellie could do what she did and Yasu could do what she did in response, and so that others could watch and listen, was a practical strategy that I could use to manage teaching big ideas and curriculum topics, while also teaching the discourse of mathematical invention. It was a way of using the problem context as a source of reasoned explanations so that students could work on assessing their own and one another's assertions while using and learning arithmetic. And, it was a way to teach Ellie not only how to do long division and what to do with the remainder, but also that these are processes that are supposed to make sense.

While I was "zooming out" in the content terrain to include these multiple aims in my teaching, I was simultaneously "zooming in" on Ellie and Yasu and on specific topics like division and decimal numbers. Using the problem context to structure the discourse in this way positions Ellie's studies of what to do with the remainder in the entire long history of how our decimal number system came to be based exclusively on multiples of ten and why that system is the one that we live with today rather than others that were tried and abandoned. My work here includes encouraging Ellie and Yasu to disagree, protecting their relationship, and clarifying the meaning of decimal numbers. Having a positive relationship with Yasu is not irrelevant to whether Ellie will be able to make progress as a mathematical thinker. I also needed to protect both Ellie and Yasu from unproductive conflict. Letting Yasu say why Ellie was wrong sets up a social problem that Ellie and Yasu will need to cope with. If Yasu comes off as "good at math" and Ellie as less competent, then others in the class could conclude from this exchange that Ellie or Yasu is more or less desirable as a friend.

As I do in the social sphere, I must teach on several levels at once in the content sphere. Zooming in and out on content is also a way to do the simultaneous teaching of discourse, conceptual fields, and topics. Adding a representation of this zooming in and out on content to the model allows us to portray complexities in teachers' work that would otherwise remain invisible.

The Complexities of Teachers and Students as Actors in the Work of Teaching

The model I have so far developed portrays the teacher, the class, and the content as if they were static entities and their only existence was within the classroom walls. Indeed, this is where the teaching and studying of academic content happens. But *the persons that teachers and their students are in the classroom develop from life experiences much broader than those they can have in that setting.* The problems that teacher and students face, the resources that are available to them to solve those problems, and their capacity to use those resources are all constructed out of a mixture of what they experience together and the life experiences they bring with them into the classroom. As I have examined practice in the previous chapters, I have noted over and over the importance of getting to know my students. Part of what I needed to know was how the character they brought with them into the classroom would interact with everything else in the learning environment. But I needed to recognize that character is not consistent and static. At times they might be influenced by parents and at other times by peers or by television. I needed to know and work with that character, and try to add academic virtues to what students would be willing to be, in school.

As I got to know my students I was also getting to know myself. As I taught, I was regularly investigating my own mathematical understandings as well as my character and my social skills, and what I could do with them in lessons. This was not just a matter of reminding myself of what I knew; it also entailed figuring out who I should be with my class. In doing my work, I used aspects of my intellectual and personal character in relation with my students to teach them. Like that of my students, my character is not static, nor is it internally consistent. It is influenced by what I do outside the classroom as well as by what happens as I teach.

Teaching with the Complexities of Human Character

Each of the three elements of the triangular model needs to be displayed in relation to the broad and shifting frames of influence on both teacher and students in order to adequately represent teaching practice. All of the practice-arrows I have so far discussed go between people who have different personalities on different occasions, depending on the varying strength of different influences. The teacher must work to keep up with students' varying states of mind and of feeling and act accordingly.

In all classrooms, character comes into play in acts of teaching and studying. But it is up to the teacher to know and use her own complicated self and the complicated identities of students as tools of practice. As with other resources of practice, the teacher can ignore who she is and who her students are, or ignore the changes in her own and students' characters from one situation to another. Or she can accept character as a given and not try to shape it to make the learning environment productive for everyone. The actions of teachers and students in relation to one another and toward the material under study are variously shaped by their personal histories and by present social circumstances. But teachers and students are free to "act back" on their circumstances; what they can do together is not fully determined by where they come from. Will, as well as experience, comes into play in any interaction with content.[13] If it is her intention to do so, the teacher can find ways to make use of what students bring to support students' opportunities to learn. She can structure both her interactions with students and the environment in which they are working in an effort to influence their intentions. These elements of the work must also be accounted for in any model of teaching practice.

This analysis leads to a more elaborate representation at each of the three vertices of the instructional triangle. I have argued that the teacher addresses multiple problems with a single action. The teacher also integrates multiple selves into her professional identity, using different aspects of her character to address different kinds of problems.

The teacher is always one person, acting, but she is not always the same. Similarly, students bring multiple ways of being themselves into the classroom.

As these complicated selves come in contact with the content to be learned in the classroom, they bring external influences into the mix as well:

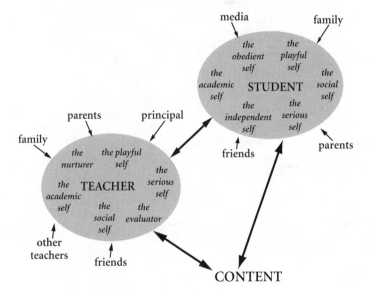

Complicating these vertices complicates what must happen along the practice-arrows connecting persons and content. Considering the various influences on their actions, it is easy to see how teachers and students might bring a multiplicity of intentions, meanings, and values to every interaction with content. It is the teacher's work to design those interactions so that they have a chance of producing academic success.

The Complex Character of Content

In conjunction with the people in the classroom, the curriculum brings influences from outside the classroom to the teacher's work. Just as the teacher's relationship with any single student is complicated by that student's place in a network of social relationships, her work with content is complicated by its placement in the web of forces that shape it. Although content is filtered through the persons of the teacher and the students in a particular class, what is made available for students to learn is not a simple matter of the individual preferences of the participants, expressed willy-nilly as they interact. The process of curriculum determination is set in a public institutional context, influenced by textbooks, standardized tests, methods texts, supplementary curriculum materials, and the teachers' professional preparation. These are influenced in turn by political and cultural forces.

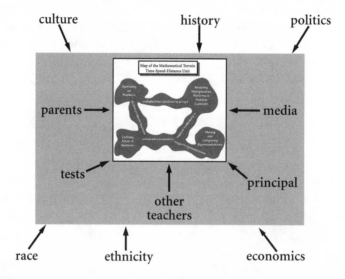

The multiple influences on content enter the classroom in various ways, but as a practical matter, they must be managed in communication between teacher and students as they express those influences, either overtly or in the subtleties of everyday interaction. Students both learn and create the local and public significance of what they are doing as they construct talk and writing to express their ideas to teacher and peers. In most U.S. classrooms, this involves a negotiation of meaning among individuals and groups of different status and cultural backgrounds. And the meaning that must be negotiated involves fundamental assumptions about what it is we are doing here in this classroom, "anyway." The teacher's work—as it is performed along the teacher-content arrow and along the arrow that connects the teacher with the relationship between the student and the content—includes interpreting and managing the multiple influences on content while engaging in multiple kinds of relationships with students.

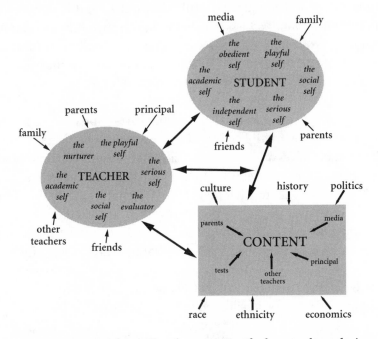

But we cannot stop there. To take account of what teachers do in practice, the diagram that shows all of the influences on who teachers and students are and what the subject matter is must also be extended into different social configurations and across time. It needs to be integrated with the first elaboration of the model (p. 429), for teachers, students, and content, and the influences upon them, grow and change over time. The powers that influence what is in the curriculum, what the teacher worries about, and what interests students are always there, but they are not always the same. As persons who act to accomplish their aims together in classrooms, teachers and students are not internally consistent or static. As they change from day to day, the work of the teacher includes adapting to those changes.

I do not claim that these elaborations of the representation of teachers' work to include the complexities of character are anything like a full explanation of how people in any setting come to act the way they do. My purpose is only to indicate that in a representation of the work of teaching, we cannot neglect the complicated characters of the people doing the work or the influence of relationships they have outside the classroom. We cannot neglect the complications of the persons who work in classrooms in a representation of teachers' work because if the *teacher* neglects them, she forfeits valuable resources of practice. For example, I needed to take account in my teaching of the fact that students do not uniformly come to school with a sense that mathematics is something that can be learned by all students through the act of studying.[14] Parents, the media, and peers influence what students think they are supposed to be doing in a mathematics class, and students express identities that are more and less productive of learning. But for communication in the classroom to be a productive and safe opportunity for mathematical study for all students, and for it to be a resource that the teacher can use, everyone needs to be able to engage in productive social interactions with their peers and with the teacher.

Making those interactions happen becomes part of the work of teaching, and this is where the multiple selves of the teacher come into relationships with the multiple selves of the student. Teacher-student interactions become a part of the content as students try to learn whether and under what conditions it is safe to talk about what they think. Taking the kinds of intellectual risks that are entailed in arguing about assertions and examining assumptions is something that must be taught and learned.[15] For each classroom that they enter, students also need to learn new routines and participation structures.[16] For some this content will come easily because who they are supposed to be in the classroom will match who they are at home or in other social settings. For others, it will need to be explicitly taught.[17]

Navigating in the Complicated Terrain of Teaching with Problems

For the teacher, working in relation to multiple, complicated, and changing students and multiple, complicated, and changing contents may be compared to navigating an unwieldy ship on a large and tumultuous body of water. There are shifting winds and current to take account of, there are obstructions that are not obvious, and sometimes it is foggy. With the appropriate tools and knowledge, you can usually determine where you are, where you need to go, and where everyone else is in relation to where they need to go, but not always. Some of the elements in the teacher's working environment are stationary, but many are moving, fast, and in all different directions. As the teacher acts in such an environment, she looks around and ascertains where things are in relation to her and in relation to one another and how they are moving. Maybe if we take account of all the dimensions on which teaching is complicated, it is more analogous to being an airline pilot or the navigator of a submarine than to being a ship's captain.[18] In order to make a move in *three* dimensions, one needs to look up and down as well as left and right, and forward and back, to locate the relevant objects in the environment, many of which are themselves moving across all of these dimensions as well. As more problem domains are added, the teacher's working environment takes on more dimensions and the work navigation gets more and more complex.

The problem space in which the teacher works is full of ideals to be realized, full of worthy destinations. To make it possible for the teacher to realize these ideals and get to these destinations, students and their relationships with one another must be employed as resources to complement the resources the teacher brings and the objects that are physically available in the environment. In the best of all possible worlds, these multiple resources could be orchestrated to produce learning for all of the students all of the time. In the actuality of teacher's work, however, the practices intended to realize these ideals are often incompatible. In this sense, the classroom is a microcosm of the larger social world. In the words of William James, "The actually possible in this world is vastly narrower than all that is demanded; there is always a pinch between the ideal and the actual which can only be got through by leaving part of the ideal behind."[19] As we investigate the practice of teaching, we must ask, which part? Can rules be made a priori to help teachers decide what goals to sacrifice and what goals to satisfy?

James concluded that such rules might be helpful but intuitions about the immediate situation will be more so. "For every real dilemma is in literal strictness a unique situation; and the exact combination of ideals realized and ideals disappointed which each decision creates is always a universe without precedent, and for which no adequate previous rules exist."[20] His words presage what Ted Sizer said about teaching, quoted at the beginning of this chapter. Plans are brought to the teaching situation that relate teacher actions with desired outcomes. But these plans do not suffice to determine what a teacher will do or should do in the course of instruction.[21] Because teachers work in a web of social relationships, and because they and their students have multiple and changing intentions, they must weigh uncertain evidence and make moment-by-moment choices about how to proceed, continuously creating what James called a "universe without precedent."

Because teachers are personally present over time in classroom situations where conflicts arise, they have the capacity to alleviate conflicts using strategies that are unavailable to those intervening in practice from the outside. Because I was teaching in ways that enabled me to learn more, both about my content and my students, I was able to develop more resources for coping with conflicts in my practice. The elaborations in the teacher-student-content relationship that I propose suggest something about how multiplicity and conflict might be managed. Like other elements of the work of teaching and studying, the management of conflict takes place continually over time as well as in particular moments of interaction. It takes place one-on-one and in different social configurations. So work toward a goal can accumulate. The teacher can put off one set of intentions while working on another, and know that there will be another chance to act on those intentions that were put off. Another student might do what a teacher cannot do in a particular instance if the appropriate patterns of interaction are in place.

As the relationships in the work of teaching are made more explicit in each elaboration on the model, the problems a teacher faces in practice and the resources available to solve those problems both increase multiplicatively. And in the end, each set of complications must be integrated with the others, for the teacher must do it all, and all at the same time. If the elaborations of the teacher-student-content relationship I have represented in each part of this chapter could be integrated, we could see the many practice-arrows along which the teacher works. And I have surely not identified all of them. Even as I know the model must be further revised and elaborated, I recognize that this endeavor is dangerous because it forces us back on the question of whether teaching—especially teaching with problems—is an impossible task. I hope that this book has gone some distance toward showing not only that such teaching is possible in school classrooms, but also *how* it is possible to manage the myriad relationships involved in doing it.

Complete Transcript of Large-Group Discussion on September 28

Lampert:	Okay, how many people are finished with A, B, and C? How many people are finished with A? How many people are finished with B? So C is the problem that a lot of people are still working on.
Student:	I haven't done my reasoning.
Lampert:	Okay, what I think we'll do now that I know more or less where everyone is, is to have a discussion to see what you think goes in these boxes, and why you think it.
	Now, I want to remind you of moving from small-group to large-group rules. That means that things are going to be going on up here on the blackboard, so if you're not seated in a position where you can see the blackboard you might want to turn around.
	Okay. Who has something to say about A?
	Richard?
Richard:	I think that if, A, is twenty-two. Groups.
Lampert:	Okay, so twenty-two groups OF twelve equals ten groups OF six.
	Can you explain your reasoning about that Richard?
Richard:	Because, I timesed twelve and ten. Twelve times ten equals twenty-two.
Lampert:	Ten times twelve—
	Or tw—, I'm sorry, twelve times ten is like this. Is that how you did it?
	Okay, now I want to remind you that this means twelve groups of ten.
	This means ten groups of twelve.
	If I have ten groups of twelve—

One of the things that I came around and did with some people is to draw a picture that would help you to reason about these problems. Twenty-two groups of twelve, you could draw as a twelve, a twelve, a twelve, and so on until you got twenty-two of them. Or you could even put little X's in the circles like I did yesterday with the paper clips. Twenty-two groups of twelve seems to me like it would be quite a lot of stuff, if I did twenty-two of these.

But let's look at ten groups of six for a minute. Six, six, six, six, six.

How do I know that I have ten groups of six there without counting them? Ellie?

Ellie: Because you made um, on the top you made five of them, but, you made five rows on the top and you just made a line exactly like that on the bottom.

Lampert: Okay, that's the story of a mathematical shortcut. I only had to count the first row of five and then I gave each one of them a partner and that gave me ten groups of six.

Now let's count by sixes here.

Students: [along with Lampert] Six, twelve, eighteen, twenty-four, thirty, thirty-six, forty-two, forty-eight, fifty-four, sixty.

Lampert: That's our six times table. One group of six.

Eddie and Awad you should be looking up here.

One group of six is six. Two groups of six is—

Students: Twelve.

Lampert: Three groups of six is—

Students: Eighteen.

Lampert: Four groups of six is—

Students: Twenty-four.

Lampert: Five groups of six is—

Students: Thirty.

Lampert:	Thirty, and now I can do the same thing. If this much is thirty, how much is the whole amount going to be? Leticia?
	Sixty.
	So I have ten groups of six here. Now, Richard, what do you think about this twenty-two groups of twelve thing?
	What if I had just ten groups of twelve? How many would that be?
Richard:	I don't know.
Lampert:	Okay, let's do the top row. Twelve plus twelve is twenty-four, plus twelve is thirty-six, forty-eight, sixty. Now if the top row is sixty, how many am I going to have altogether? Richard?
Richard:	One-twenty.
Lampert:	One-hundred and twenty. Now this is ten groups of twelve. Richard what do you think about your idea of twenty-two groups of twelve?
Richard:	It's wrong.
Lampert:	Is it too big or too small?
Richard:	Too big.
Lampert:	Okay, so we have to make this lower. Can it be ten?
Students:	No.
Lampert:	Why not? Who can explain why not? Karim?
Karim:	Because it won't be like, if you times ten and twelve then you times ten and six, they won't be both the same answer.
Lampert:	Okay, so whatever I have on this side has to be the same as what I have on this side.
	So it seems like it said ten times twelve is going to be a little bit, or maybe even a lot, too big.
	What do you think?
	Charlotte?
Charlotte:	You could find out that if you tried ten times twelve, that it would have to be five times twelve, because what we did was

we counted by twelve the top row and then we added sixty, and sixty, and it came out to sixty. Then you know that only the half the ten would be sixty. Half of the ten groups of twelve.

Lampert: So you're basing what you're saying there on what we just did. When we counted all these, we got up to, Donna Ruth, what did we get up to on the top there?

Donna Ruth: We got up to sixty.

Lampert: Okay, and that is really exactly what we want because we have ten groups of six over here and that's sixty.

So what number should go here? What do you think?

Yasu?

Yasu: Five.

Lampert: Five groups of twelve.

Can somebody please explain why it should be five groups of twelve?

Leticia?

Leticia: Because ten times six is sixty. Five times twelve equals sixty.

Lampert: So ten groups of six, the arithmetic we can do for that is ten times six, and the arithmetic we can do for twelve, is five times twelve.

But if you don't happen to know what five times twelve is, you can do it another way.

Tyrone, can you explain another way if you don't happen to know five times twelve? What else could I do?

Tyrone: Add twelve, five times.

Lampert: Add twelve, five times. Okay. One, two, three, four, five times twelve. Two, four, six, eight, ten, twel—

Two, four, six, eight, ten carry the one. One, two, three, four, five, six. Five times twelve is sixty. Okay?

Shahroukh?

Shahroukh:	I think—
	The reason I think it's correct is because twelve groups of five is sixty. And ten groups of six is sixty, too, so they're both equivalent.
Lampert:	Okay, that's good.
	That's what we're trying to do here. Equivalent and equals mean the same thing. Another way you could think about this problem and use a drawing to help you think about it is to look at your ten groups of six. How could I make a group of six into a group of twelve? What sort of regrouping could I do here that would help me to think about groups of twelve?
	Donna Ruth do you have some ideas about that? How could I make these into groups of twelve?
Donna Ruth:	You get two sixes and um—
Lampert:	Okay, two sixes.
	Now what do I have inside the brown circle there?
Donna Ruth:	I don't know.
Lampert:	Ileana, what do I have inside the brown circle?
Ileana:	Twelve.
Lampert:	Twelve. Six and six. How many times can I do that here? Altogether? Connie?
Connie:	Five.
Lampert:	Five times. So I make groups of twelve out of my groups of six. Drawing a picture, it's not really a picture, it's sort of a diagram and I heard you talking about diagrams in science yesterday, helps you to think through the problem. So when I see you being stuck and not being able to make any progress, or if I see your thinking being confused, I'm going to ask you to draw a picture because that is something that is very important to do in mathematics.
	Tyrone turn your chair around and sit on it properly please.
	Okay, so that was problem A.

	How about problem B? Um, Enoyat? What do you have for problem B?
Enoyat:	I have thirty groups of two equals fifteen groups of four.
Lampert:	Okay, does anybody have something different for problem B? All the people who raised their hands have that in their notebook?
	Who can explain it? So that everybody could understand why—that's true. Awad would you like to try to explain it?
Awad:	Okay. Since thirty times two is sixty and you have to find how many groups of four, is in sixty, then so, I did fifteen times.
	I tried, I tried um, a few numbers to see which one would be.
Lampert:	Okay, you could try four times ten and that's forty and that's not big enough is it? Or you could try twenty and that's too big. Four times ten is forty and four times twenty is eighty. What does this tell you about the answer? If you tried these two experiments what does it tell you to try next? Connie?
Connie:	Fifteen times four.
Lampert:	Why fifteen?
Connie:	Because it's between ten and twenty.
Lampert:	Okay, you want to pick something that's going to give you a number between forty and eighty, so you pick something that's in between ten and twenty. And when you try fifteen it comes out to be sixty. Sixty is right in between forty and eighty too. Numbers have all these kinds of nice relationships that help us reason about them.
	Yes, Candice? Sorry, Charlotte.
Charlotte:	Um, another way you could think of it is if you knew fifteen plus fifteen equals thirty, and thirty plus thirty equals sixty, so fifteen groups of four would be right.
Lampert:	That reminds me of what Tyrone said before. Which is, fifteen, fifteen, fifteen, and fifteen. These two together make thirty, and these two together make thirty. So when you put these two together they make—
	Again, reasoning about relationships in numbers.

Now, problem C I know a lot of people didn't get to. Why was problem C more complicated than problems A and B? Candice?

Candice: 'Cause C has two numbers missing.

Lampert: Something groups of seven equals something groups of twenty-one. Okay.

Now, some number of groups of seven is going to equal some number of groups of twenty-one.

What do you think? Anthony?

Anthony: There are many possibilities in that. Like it could be three groups of seven equal one group of twenty-one. It could be six groups of seven equal two groups of twenty-one.

Lampert: Okay, excuse me. Richard and Tyrone and Giyoo, would you leave the room please? Wait out in the hall for me and I'll speak to you after class.

I'm sorry, could you repeat that please?

Anthony: There are many possibilities, like it could be three groups of seven and one group of twenty-one, or it could be six groups of seven and two groups of twenty-one. You can just double it all the time.

Lampert: What does anybody else think about that? What do you think Shahroukh?

Shahroukh: I think he's right and that pattern would keep on going.

Lampert: Why does that work?

Three groups of seven equals one group of twenty-one? Six groups of seven equals two groups of twenty-one.

What do you think? Candice?

Candice: Because three times seven equals twenty-one, and twenty-one ones equals twenty-one, and that means six times seven equals forty-two, and twenty-one two times equals forty-two.

You can go on.

Lampert: If I do three times seven I get twenty-one, and that's one group of twenty-one. Shahroukh?

Shahroukh:	You can keep on adding three on this board. Like it could be nine times seven equals sixty-three and three groups of twenty-one, and you can keep on adding three on this board and keep on adding one on that board. So, you can go on forever.
Lampert:	So, let's just test that out though. I'm going to write the answers to these multiplications then and this colored chalk here, although this one's a little bit bigger, let's see. Three times seven is twenty-one, I am just putting this in here and one times twenty-one is twenty-one. On this side, then next I have six times seven, which is—
Students:	Forty-two.
Lampert:	Forty-two, and on this side I need two groups of twenty-one is forty-two. Sorry. I just wrote a mistake on there.
	So two groups of twenty-one—
Student:	Forty-two.
Lampert:	—is forty-two.
	Now, what would the next one be? Connie?
Connie:	Seven times nine?
Lampert:	Okay, but since I'm writing it this way and I want to follow a pattern, I'm going to write nine times seven. And what's nine times seven?
Connie:	Sixty-three.
Lampert:	Okay nine times seven is sixty-three. Now on this side we're going to have what?
	What should that be?
	Donna Ruth?
Donna Ruth:	Three times twenty-one?
Lampert:	And what is three times twenty-one?
Donna Ruth:	Sixty-three.
Lampert:	Let's try to practice a little mental multiplication. Three times twenty is twenty plus twenty plus twenty. That's sixty.

Three times one, that's pretty simple, is three.

So, three times twenty-one is going to be sixty-three.

So I get the same thing on both sides.

What should be the next problem on this side? We had three groups of seven, six groups of seven, nine groups of seven. Yasu?

Yasu: Twelve groups of seven.

Lampert: Twelve groups of seven. Twelve groups of seven I can get by doing twelve times seven. Now, again, what's the mental multiplication here?

Twelve can be broken up into two parts.

Ten and two.

What's ten times seven? Varouna?

Varouna: Seventy.

Lampert: Seventy.

What's two times seven? Leticia?

Leticia: Fourteen.

Lampert: Fourteen. If I have seventy and fourteen, what's twelve times seven?

Seventy and fourteen. Donna Ruth?

Donna Ruth: Eighty-four.

Lampert: Eighty-four. The tens have to go up by one, and the one becomes fourteen. Gotta start doing these things in your head.

What's the problem I need on the other side of over there? Reba?

Reba: Four times twenty-one.

Lampert: Okay, four times twenty-one.

Again, what's four times twenty? Reba?

Reba: What?

Lampert:	What's four times twenty?
Reba:	Four times twenty is um, eighty?
Lampert:	Eighty. And then four times one is—
Reba:	Eighty-four.
Lampert:	So four times twenty is eighty, and four times one is eighty-four.
	So it comes out the same. Okay. Let's see.
	We'll do one more.
	What's the next problem on this side? Connie?
Connie:	Fifteen times seven—
Lampert:	Okay, fifteen times seven. Now we have fifteen, break it up into two parts. Ten times seven is—
	Ivan what is ten times seven?
Ivan:	Seventy.
Lampert:	And five times seven?
Ivan:	Thirty-five.
Lampert:	Thirty-five. Now I need to add in my head seventy plus thirty-five. Well, seventy plus thirty is a hundred. Plus five is a hundred and five.
	And on this side what's the problem?
	Candice?
Candice:	Five times twenty-one.
Lampert:	Five times twenty is—
	Five times twenty—
Candice:	The answer is a hundred and four, I mean a hundred and five.
Lampert:	Okay, the answer is a hundred and five, but I wanted you to practice taking these numbers apart. Five times twenty is what? Five times twenty.
Candice:	Forty, no.

Lampert:	Five times twenty plus twenty plus twenty plus twenty plus twenty.
Candice:	It's a hundred.
Lampert:	Five times one is—
Candice:	Five.
Lampert:	So that's how I get one-oh-five. So it seems like this conjecture that you can keep on going works.
Varouna:	You missed ninety-five there.
Lampert:	I missed ninety-five where? Where does ninety-five go?
Varouna:	Four times twenty is eighty, four times one is four so it's eighty-four—
Lampert:	Excuse me, only one person can go to the bathroom at a time. Sorry.
Varouna:	But at five times twenty you say you have a hundred and five instead of ninety-five.
Lampert:	What's five times twenty? Twenty, forty, sixty, eighty, let's go.
Varouna:	Oh. A hundred.
Lampert:	Okay? Ivan?
Ivan:	When you said five times twenty, here's an easier way to do it. Just time five times two would give tens and add one more zero.
Lampert:	That works for all of these doesn't it? Four times two is eight, so four times twenty is eighty. All of those.
	Good reminder. Okay, Charlotte? And then we need to stop.
Charlotte:	You can also follow a pattern after you started, after you get going a little bit by the tens go up by two and the ones go up by one and you can get the answers pretty quickly in your head. Because the tens keep going up by twenty, and the ones keep going up by one.
Lampert:	Well, I can't really let that one go by. What's the next answer going to be?

Dye:	Wait a minute Dr. Lampert. No, no we can't have this going on. No, people are going to be figuring out math in their heads now. They're not going to be practicing their times tables. I can't give a hundred-and-sixty-five problems, what's going on here? Oh no, this is big trouble. You mean, Charlotte, you can tell me what, six, what would it be now—
Lampert:	Six times twenty-one without even figuring it out—
Dye:	Without even figuring it out. You could tell me the answer for six times twenty-one?
Students:	YES.
Lampert:	Why Karim? Why do you say anybody could?
Karim:	Because it's pretty easy.
Lampert:	What is it about these numbers that makes it so easy?
Karim:	Well, first thing you know is it's going by twenties, and the ones place is going by ones.
Lampert:	Okay, so if the tens place is going by twenties, what should it be next?
Karim:	It should be one-twenty.
Lampert:	One-twenty. And what goes in the ones place, Yasu?
Yasu:	Six.
Lampert:	Six.
	Two, four, six, eight, ten, twelve—
	One, two, three, four, five, six. Okay.
	Do you see any patterns like that on this side?
Students:	Yes.
Lampert:	Same pattern. The answers are the same. Anthony?
Anthony:	Look at it from the left side it's three, six, nine, twelve.
	On the right side it's one, two, three, four, five.
Lampert:	That's right. These numbers go up by, in groups of three. There are a lot of interesting patterns here and one of the

things that we are going to be studying a lot this year is patterns like this. And this is a kind of mathematics that will move us into working on a topic in math called algebra.

This is called, what we're doing here is talking about a function.

And what that means is that what you put in this box determines what you have to put in this box.

As soon as you pick what goes in this box, you can't put any old thing in this box, can you? They're related.

There are lots of possibilities, but you can't put this one together with this one can you?

Student: No.

Lampert: You have to put this one together with this one.

They all have partners.

So the partner for six is going to be two. And the partner for nine is going to be three.

What? Suppose I put twenty-one in this box? Oh that's too easy. Everybody would know that right off the bat.

Let's see. Suppose I put twenty-seven in this box. Donna Ruth?

Donna Ruth: Nine.

Lampert: How did you figure it out?

Donna Ruth: Because—

Lampert: Okay Donna Ruth thinks nine. And, am I, I know I shouldn't be going over but I can't—

Donna Ruth: I think it's four.

Lampert: You think it's four.

Okay. First you thought nine then you thought four.

Ivan, what do you think?

Ivan: I think it's four or, three point nine, wait um I think it's four, call on someone else.

Lampert:	Okay. I want everybody to look at the pattern that we got here. The relationship between these and see if you can use that pattern to reason about what goes in that box. There's a relationship between the numbers over here and the numbers over here. And I want to see if you can use that relationship.
	Okay I want to hear from Yasu, Shahroukh, and Donna Ruth. What do you think Yasu?
Yasu:	I think it's nine.
Lampert:	You think it's nine. Shahroukh, what do you think?
Shahroukh:	I think it's nine.
Lampert:	You think it's nine.
	Donna Ruth, what do you think?
Donna Ruth:	I was going to say a pattern. I see a pattern.
Lampert:	Okay, but do you think it's four or nine?
Donna Ruth:	I think it is four.
Lampert:	You think it's four.
	Okay, now, can you explain your reasoning?
	And then I'll have Yasu and Shahroukh explain their reasoning.
Donna Ruth:	Because four times seven is twenty-eight minus one more is twenty-seven.
Lampert:	Okay, but, one of the things I want you to think about here, is this means twenty-seven times seven.
	And this means four times twenty-one.
	That's what that means.
Donna Ruth:	I think it's nine.
Lampert:	Why?
Donna Ruth:	Because I agree with Shahroukh.
	Why, I don't um—
	'Cause nine times three is twenty-seven.

Lampert:	Why does that matter?
	Can you explain why that matters Shahroukh?
	She said nine times—What did you say Donna Ruth, he didn't hear you.
Donna Ruth:	Nine times three is twenty-seven.
Shahroukh:	I don't think that has to do anything with it. Why I got um, nine at the end, was because one hundred and five, you get nine on the end, so what you have to do, you have to go over the five on that side, okay when you add—
	Let's say we had five, when it would be six, it would be eight in that digit, when we had seven it would be one, when we had eight if would be four, and when had nine it would be—seven.
Lampert:	Okay, so you're reasoning on the basis of the last digit. Seven times seven is forty-nine so the problem has to end in nine, so this has to be nine times one.
	Does anybody know what Donna Ruth means when she say, "Because nine times three is twenty-seven?" What do you think Charlotte?
Charlotte:	I thought, I think that maybe she was thinking nine in the box, and then times seven is twenty-seven groups seven of equals twenty-seven which is in the first box in the problem.
Lampert:	Yasu?
Yasu:	I think she meant like um, if you look in the left one it's—
	By three and then if you multiply nine times three it will be twenty-seven.
Lampert:	I think that if you look at these numbers—
	What happens?
	The number over here. Anthony?
Anthony:	Times three all the time?
Lampert:	It's always three times bigger than the one over there, is that what you were thinking, Donna Ruth?

Donna Ruth: Yeah, and um, and it's like even and odd.

Lampert: That's true too.

Okay, I think we really need to stop now. Let's have the pens collected and have you put your notebooks in your desk please.

Lesson Topics in a Sample of Lessons
in Different Problem Contexts Across the Year

Date	Lesson Topics Identified by the Observer	Problem Context
9/25	Combinations of integer pairs of at most two digits whose product is twelve; discussion of patterns and ways of telling that a student has found all combinations; use of new vocabulary interwoven with practice of multiplication facts	Multiplicative Grouping and Coin Problems
9/27	The lesson focused on the understanding of multiplication via grouping and regrouping objects.	Multiplicative Grouping and Coin Problems
9/28	The lesson continued the theme and the same sort of problems as the previous day in grouping and multiplication.	Multiplicative Grouping and Coin Problems
11/2	• relationship between speed, time, and distance • division (explored in small groups) • functional relationships	Time-Speed-Distance Problems
11/8	• relationship among time, speed, and distance • concepts of time, speed, and distance • multiplicative nature of problem solution • what do you do with the remainder/part of whole unit of measure	Time-Speed-Distance Problems

Date	Lesson Topics Identified by the Observer	Problem Context
11/14	• multiplication used to test conjectures; counting by 10s on the time scale and the trial number on the distance scale; going beyond repeated addition to multiplication	Time-Speed-Distance Problems
11/21	• fractional parts of an hour • estimation to the nearest whole number, nearest one decimal place • multiplication by 9, repeated addition of 9	Time-Speed-Distance Problems
11/28	• fractions (within the context of a time-speed-distance problem • use of division to compute number of feet traveled in a specific amount of time • repeated halving of an interval to get closer to 10 minutes • counting by ⅛s (the fraction of a mile corresponding to 5 minutes) • ⅓ of 2 miles vs. ⅔ of 1 mile	Time-Speed-Distance Problems
1/8	• area • factors/multiples • patterns • rectangle • role of multiplication with respect to area	Constructing Equivalent Rectangles
1/9	• area • rectangles • orientation • role of multiplication in area • relationship of division to multiplication • fraction and decimal multiplication/ division through use of calculator	Constructing Equivalent Rectangles

Date	Lesson Topics Identified by the Observer	Problem Context
1/11	• area/rectangles • multiplication/area • using a chart to organize information • role of conditions in solving a problem • strategies for finding 1½ of a quantity	Constructing Equivalent Rectangles
1/16	• division with remainders • fractions (wholes as halves) • estimating	Cakes and Bakeries Problems
1/19	• adding fractions of unlike sizes (halves, fourths, eighths) • equivalent fractions • multiplication • equating fractions to decimals • reciprocals: addition/subtraction, multiplication/division	Cakes and Bakeries Problems
1/24	• use of multiplication/estimation to help schedule time usage • possible proportions; i.e., looking at data to determine if proportional relationship exists	Cakes and Bakeries Problems
2/7	• ordering fractions and placing them on a number line • equivalent fractions • division	Fraction Bars and Number Lines
2/16	• ordering fractions; meaning of larger (in relation to "closer to one") • relating fraction denominator to number of spaces on the number line • connections between fractions and division	Fraction Bars and Number Lines

Date	Lesson Topics Identified by the Observer	Problem Context
2/16 (cont.)	• patterns between numbers of spaces and lines on the number line • multiples of numbers in the denominator	
2/21	• patterning and how to find patterns • simplification—what is it? • inverse operations—mult./div.	Fraction Bars and Number Lines
3/1	• multiplying whole numbers and fractions • definition of fraction • equivalent fractions • use of models/stories to build argument or make sense • area of rectangles • division—partitioning • multiplication as repeated addition	
3/2	• relative magnitude of fractions and whole numbers; their location on a number line • measurement • division • fractions greater than and less than 1 • measurement with meter stick to mark sections on the number line	Fraction Bars and Number Lines
3/8	• ordering fractions • improper fractions (relationship in fractions: if you divide the numerator by the denominator you get the whole number) • mixed numbers • fractions: addition and subtraction with like denominators • estimation • multiplication facts	Fraction Bars and Number Lines

Date	Lesson Topics Identified by the Observer	Problem Context
3/8 (cont)	• division • division with remainders ($\frac{100}{8} = 12$ r4 $= 12\frac{1}{2}$) • decimals • adding decimals	
3/15	• decimals • mixed numbers-whole numbers and fractions as they relate to dollars and cents • equivalent fractions • relationship between multiplication and fractions • units—what does the whole stand for, what does the fraction mean	Fraction Bars and Number Lines
4/6	• functions, function rules • even and odd number patterns • the unit in fractions (a fraction as a fraction of something) • multiplication and division	Functions and Graphing
4/11	• functions • function rules • number patterns • division, multiplication • subtraction of positive and negative numbers (and the relationship to distance on a number line) • multiplicative and additive identities • fractions	Functions and Graphing
4/20	• variables • looking for patterns—the way the data is organized helps • how do the operations change the outcomes—keep the number the same	Functions and Graphing

Date	Lesson Topics Identified by the Observer	Problem Context
4/20 (cont)	• relationship between multiplication, division and fractions (⅓ of 15 = 5, when you take a third, you divide by 3) • inverse functions	
5/22	• function rules more complex rule—involving both multiplication and addition • vocabulary: composite function • finding pattern to determine function rule • inverse operations • fractions • division with remainders	Functions and Graphing

Functions and Graphing Quiz

Name_____

Date_____

1. Graph these ordered pairs on the black and white grid. Put the letter for each pair next to the point.

   A   (3, 5)
   B   (7, 2)
   C   (–3, 5)
   D   (0,0)
   E   (4, –2)
   F   (–3, –5)

   What is the point (0,0) called? _____

2. Fill in the missing values in these function charts:

X	Y
10	
15	
20	
25	
20	

X	Y
7	
	81
	36
	18
100	

X	Y
14	
24	
	36
	3
	5

3. On one piece of blue lined graph paper, make a grid and graph the function y = 2x – 3.

   First find at least five ordered pairs that fit the function rule:

X	Y

Name_____

4. On another piece of blue lined graph paper, graph all of these functions on the same grid:

$$y = x + 2 \qquad y = x - 2 \qquad y = 2x \qquad y = \frac{1}{2}x$$

Describe the relationship among the graphs.

Why do you think the graphs turn out the way they do?

5. What is the most interesting thing you have learned about functions and graphing?

1 Understanding Teaching: Why Is It So Hard?

1. What I mean by "problems" here is not the kind of "word problems" we all faced in high school algebra. What I am calling problems, others have called projects, research projects, inquiries, or investigations. What is implied is the close, sustained examination of phenomena and the ways we understand them. For analyses of what makes a classroom problem "problematic," see Guy Brousseau, "Epistemological Obstacles, Problems, and Didactical Engineering," in *Didactique des Mathématiques, 1970–1990 (Theory of Didactical Situations in Mathematics, 1970–1990)*, ed. and trans. Nicolas Balachef et al., (Dordrecht, The Netherlands: Kluwer, 1997), 79–118; and Magdalene Lampert, "When the Problem Is Not the Question and the Solution Is Not the Answer: Mathematical Knowing and Teaching," *American Educational Research Journal 27*, 1 (1990): 29–64.

2. A subset of teachers accomplished in this way, whose accomplishments have been documented and certified, are the hundreds of National Board Certified Teachers. See *What Teachers Should Know and Be Able to Do* (Detroit: National Board for Professional Teaching Standards, 1994) for an overview of what constitutes "accomplished teaching" and *Middle Childhood/Generalist Standards for National Board Certification* (Detroit: National Board for Professional Teaching Standards, 2000) for an example of the Standards that must be met to achieve Board certification at a particular level. The QUASAR Project provides a different kind of evidence for this kind of teaching, suggesting that it can happen in low-income and urban schools and that students can learn from it. For examples of this work, see Edward A. Silver, ed., *Teaching Mathematics for a Change: Evidence from the QUASAR Project Regarding the Challenges and Possibilities for Instructional Reform in Urban Middle Schools* (1999, manuscript in preparation); and Edward A. Silver, Margaret S. Smith, and Barbara S. Nelson, "The QUASAR Project: Equity Concerns Meeting Mathematics Education Reform in the Middle School," in *New Directions for Equity in Mathematics Education*, ed. Walter G. Secada, Elizabeth Fennema, and Lisa B. Adajian (New York: Cambridge University Press, 1995), 476–521.

3. This need was recognized in the June 1999 report of the National Education Research Policy and Priorities Board of the U.S. Department of Education. See "Investing in Learning: A Policy Statement with Recommendations on Research in Education by the National Education Research Policy and Priorities Board" (http://www.ed.gov/offices/OERI/NERPPB/).

4. The kind of mathematical learning I was able to do with my father was also the subject of a major research program in cognitive psychology conducted with dairy workers to investigate their use of mathematics on the job. See Sylvia Scribner, "Mind in Action: A Functional Approach to Thinking," in *Mind and Social Practice: Selected Writings of Sylvia Scribner*, ed. Ethel Tobach et al. (New York: Cambridge University Press, 1997), 296–307.

5. Stephan Körner, *The Philosophy of Mathematics* (New York: Harper Torchbooks, 1962).

6. The idea that one could accomplish these learning goals by having students work on problems, representing the given conditions in terms of mathematical relationships, and talking about their strategy choices is not a unique result of my intellectual genealogy. It follows in a long tradition of mathematical pedagogy. Along the way, my goals as a teacher were inspired by mathematicians and educators like H. P. Fawcett, William A. Brownell, Z. P. Dienes, Imre Lakatos, Hans Freudenthal, Georg Polya, Peter Hilton, David Hawkins, Stephen Krulik, Marion Walter, Robert Davis, Leen Streefland, and Henry Pollak. Each of these people viewed mathematics as an integrated whole, encompassing both the body of knowledge produced by those who developed the field and the processes whereby one takes a mathematical stance toward finding the unknown. Some of them thought about how to put learners together with mathematics in classroom settings by engaging them in working on mathematics problems. Some even taught lessons in schools as a means of developing pedagogical designs. But even though the work of these mathematicians and educators has informed and inspired several waves of reform of public school curriculum and instruction, we still know little about the work that is entailed for teachers and students to make it possible to learn mathematics through work on problems.

7. The school in which I was teaching during the year described in this book was a K–5 school with an average of about two hundred students enrolled each year. The current per-pupil expenditures at the school are about $5,700 per year, and the pupil/ teacher ratio averages about 20:1. Between 50 and 60 percent of the students receive free and reduced lunch. Student scores on the Michigan Educational Assessment Program (MEAP) tests administered in the fourth grade ranged between 71.4 and 94.4 percent satisfactory in mathematics and between 60.7 and 72.2 percent satisfactory in reading for 1996–99. *Michigan School Report* (http://www.state.mi.us/mde/reports/msr99/rptdef.htm).

2 *An Instance of Teaching Practice*

1. For example: Joan Krater, Jane Zeni, and Nancy Devlin Cason, *Mirror Images: Teaching Writing in Black and White* (Portsmouth, N.H.: Heinemann, 1994); Karen Gallas, *Talking Their Way into Science: Hearing Children's Questions and Theories and Responding with Curricula* (New York: Teachers College Press, 1995); and Gallas, *Sometimes I Can be Anything: Power, Gender, and Identity in a Primary Classroom* (New York: Teachers College Press, 1998); Daniel Meier, *Learning in Small Moments: Life in an Urban Classroom* (New York: Teachers College Press, 1997); Vivian Paley, *Wally's Stories: Conversations in the Kindergarten* (Cambridge: Harvard University Press, 1981).

2. Cathy Fleischer, *Composing Teacher Research: Prosaic History* (Albany, N.Y.: SUNY Press, 1995); D. Jean Clandinin and F. Michael Connelly, "Teachers' Professional Knowledge Landscapes: Teacher Stories—Stories of Teachers—School Stories—Stories of Schools," *Educational Researcher* 25(3): 24–30 (1996); Kathy Carter, "The Place of Story in the Study of Teaching and Teacher Education," *Educational Researcher* 22(1): 5–12, 18 (1993).

3. An effort to create such a hybrid has been initiated by teacher-scholars. For example, Daniel Chazan's recent book, *Beyond Formulas in Mathematics and Teaching: Dynamics of the High School Algebra Classroom* (New York: Teachers College Press, 2000), is a teacher narrative and scholarly investigation of practice that investigates the problems that arise in the overlap between the social and intellectual "dynamics" in the classroom. See also Suzanne M. Wilson, "Mastodons, Maps, and Michigan: Exploring Uncharted Territory While Teaching Elementary School Social Studies," in *Elementary Subjects Center,* series no. 24. Presented at the Annual Meeting of the American Educational Research Association (Boston, Mass., 1990); Deborah Lowenberg Ball, "With an Eye on the Mathematical Horizon: Dilemmas of Teaching Elementary School Mathematics," *Elementary School Journal* 93(4): 373–97 (1993); Ball and Wilson, "Integrity in Teaching: Recognizing the Fusion of the Moral and Intellectual," *American Educational Research Journal* 33(1): 155–192 (1996); Karen Hale Hankins, "Cacophony to Symphony: Memoirs in Teacher Research," Harvard Educational Review 68(1): 80–95 (1998); Timothy Lensmeir, *When Children Write: Critical Re-Visions of the Writing Workshop* (New York: Teachers College Press, 1994). The analytic language of these boundary crossers is not found in most teachers' professional writing.

4. Gary Fenstermacher, "The Knower and the Known: The Nature of Knowledge in Research on Teaching," *Review of Research in Education*, 20: 3–56 (1994); Gary Anderson and Kathryn Herr, "The New Paradigm Wars: Is There Room for Rigorous Practitioner Knowledge in Schools and Universities?" *Educational Researcher* 28(5): 12–21, 40 (1999); Michael Huberman, "Focus on Research—Moving Mainstream: Taking a Closer Look at Teacher Research," *Language Arts* 73: 124–40 (1996); Harriet Bjerrum Nielsen, "Seductive Texts with Serious Intentions," *Educational Researcher* 24(1): 4–12 (1995); and Dennis Phillips, "Telling It Straight: Issues in Assessing Narrative Research," *Educational Psychologist* 29(1): 13–21 (1994).

3 Why I Wrote This Book—and How

1. In "Leadership of Large-Scale Improvement in American Education" (paper prepared for the Albert Shanker Institute, September 1999), Richard Elmore explains this tendency toward isolation in terms of the institutional structure of school leadership. For studies of isolation in the professional culture of teaching, see Brian Lord, "Teachers' Professional Development: Critical Colleagueship and the Role of Professional Communities," in *The Future of Education: Perspectives on National Standards in America*, ed. N. Cobb (Princeton, N.J.: The College Board, 1994), 175–204; Judith Warren Little, "The Persistence of Privacy: Autonomy and Initiative in Teachers' Professional Relations," *Teachers College Record* 91(4): 509–36 (1990); Susan J. Rosenholtz, *Teachers' Workplace: The Social Organization of Schools* (New York: Teachers College Press, 1989); Joan E. Talbert and Milbrey M. McLaughlin, "Teacher Professionalism in Local School Contexts," *American Journal of Education* 102: 123–53 (1994).

2. The possibility of teacher collaboration on the problems of practice is well articulated in James Stigler and James Hiebert, *The Teaching Gap: Best Ideas from the World's Teachers for Improving Education in the Classroom* (New York: Free Press, 1999), as they

compare American professional collaboration in teaching with what has been observed in Japan. Richard Elmore presents an American example and argues for its role in improving instruction in "Leadership of Large-Scale Improvement."

3. David Cohen, Stephen Raudenbusch, and Deborah Ball make this argument in "Resources, Instruction, and Research," in *Education, Evaluation, and Randomized Trials*, ed. Robert Baruch and Fredrick Mosteller, Washington, D.C.: Brookings Institute (in press).

4. Classroom teaching is a special form of communication and communication always involves a transaction between two or more people interpreting some content. My thinking about teaching as communication among teacher, students, and content is built on developments in the philosophy of language in the 1920s. At that time in Russian social psychology, Bakhtin and Vygotsky built on Saussere's distinction between the objective structure of language and the subjective character of the utterance in everyday speech. Many of the same self/other issues that concerned Bakhtin and Vygotsky were taken up in the United States by George Herbert Mead as he attempted to define a language-based social psychology (Chicago: University of Chicago Press, 1986): 1–40; H. Blumer, "Sociological Implications of the Thought of George Herbert Mead," in *School and Society: A Sociological Reader*, ed. B. Cosin (London: Routledge and Kegan Paul, 1971): 16–22. See Lev S. Vygotsky, *Thought and Language* (Cambridge: M.I.T. Press, 1962); Mikhail M. Bakhtin, *Speech Genres and Other Late Essays*, trans. Vern W. McGee, ed. Caryl Emerson and Michael Holquist (Austin, Tex.: University of Texas Press, 1986); Gary S. Morson, "Who Speaks for Bakhtin?" in *Bakhtin: Essays and Dialogues on His Work*, ed. Morton. Like nursing and personnel management, teaching might be thought of as a *relational* practice. Jean Baker Miller, Joyce Fletcher, Kenneth Gergen, and Mary Gergen, "Relational Practice and Organizations," Interdisciplinary Committee on Organizational Studies Colloquium, October 29, 1999.

5. David K. Cohen, "Teaching Practice: Plus ça Change…" Issue paper 88–3 (East Lansing, Mich.: The National Center for Research on Teacher Education, 1988). Also published in *Contributing to Educational Change: Perspectives on Research and Practice*, National Society for the Study of Education Series, ed. Philip W. Jackson (Berkeley, Calif.: McCutchan, 1988).

6. The kind of practical knowledge associated with this aspect of the work of teaching was elaborated by Lee Shulman and his research group at Stanford University. Lee S. Shulman, "Knowledge and Teaching: Foundations of the New Reform," *Harvard Educational Review* 57(1): 1–22.

7. In several other languages, there is one word meaning both "to learn" and "to teach" that is defined to be the process whereby knowledge is acquired. For example, *obuchenie* in Russian, *lehren* in Dutch, etc. Even the dictionary of American English acknowledges a "nonstandard" definition of "to learn" as: "to cause to acquire knowledge; to teach." The *American Heritage Dictionary of the English Language*, 3d ed., electronic version, s.v. "learn" (Boston, Mass.: Houghton Mifflin, licensed from INSO Corporation, 1992). See also Fenstermacher in "Philosophy of Research on Teaching: Three Aspects," in *Handbook of Research on Teaching*, 3d Edition, ed. Merlin C. Wittrock (New York: Macmillan, 1986): 37–49; and Cohen, "Teaching Practice."

8. Claire E. Weinstein and Richard E. Mayer, "The Teaching of Learning Strategies," *Handbook of Research on Teaching*, 3d ed., Merlin Wittrock ed., pp. 315-27.

9. What I am calling "studying" here resembles what Bereiter and Scardamalia call "intentional learning." See Carl Bereiter and Marlene Scardamalia, "Intentional Learning as a Goal of Instruction," *Knowing, Learning, and Instruction: Essays in Honor of Robert Glaser*, Lauren Resnick, ed. (Hillsdale, N.J.; Lawrence Erlbaum Associates, 1989), pp. 361–92.

10. Ibid., s.v. "study."

11. Gloria Ladson-Billings describes the practice of teachers whom she has found to be successful in this kind of work with African American students in *The Dreamkeepers: Successful Teachers of African American Children* (San Francisco: Jossey-Bass, 1994).

12. For other work on the triadic nature of the relationships in teaching practice, see David Hawkins, "I, Thou, and It," in *The Informed Vision: Essays on Learning and Human Nature* (New York: Agathon, 1974): 48–62, and the theory of instruction currently being developed by David Cohen and Deborah Ball in *Instruction, Capacity, and Improvement*, CPRE Research Report No. RR-043 (Philadelphia: University of Pennsylvania, Consortium for Policy Research in Education, 1999); *Challenges of Improving Instruction: A View from the Classroom* (Washington, D.C.: Council of Basic Education, 2000); and *Instructional Innovation: Reconsidering the Story* (Ann Arbor, Michigan: University of Michigan, manuscript in preparation). The triadic model has interesting intellectual roots in the European tradition of Didaktik/Didactique and the relational theories of philosophers like Martin Buber and Wilhelm Dilthey. See Brousseau, *Didactique des Mathématiques, 1970–1990* (*Theory of Didactical Situations in Mathematics, 1970–1990*), ed. and trans. Nicolas Balachef et al. (Dordrecht, the Netherlands: Kluwer, 1997), and *Teaching as a Reflective Practice: The German Didaktik Tradition*, ed. Ian Westbury, Stephan Hopmann, and Kurt Riquarts (Mahwah, N.J.: Lawrence Erlbaum Associates, 2000).

13. A version of this transaction is described by Martin Simon in "Reconstructing Mathematics Pedagogy from a Constructivist Perspective," *Journal for Research in Mathematics Teaching*, 26: 2, 114–45 (March 1995). Of particular interest is Simon's speculation about the ways in which assessment of student knowledge leads to an improvement of the teacher's knowledge of mathematical activities and representations.

14. For examples, see Derek Edwards and Neil Mercer, *Common Knowledge: The Development of Understanding in the Classroom* (Routledge, 1989); Magdalene Lampert and Merrie Blunk, eds., *Talking Mathematics: Studies of Teaching and Learning in School* (New York: Cambridge University Press, 1998); Lesley A. Rex, Judith L. Green, and Carol Dixon, "Making a Case from Evidence: Constructing Opportunities for Learning Academic Literacy Practices," *Interpretations* 30(2): 78–104 (1997); Sabrina Tuyay, Louise Jennings, and Carol Dixon, "Classroom Discourse and Opportunities to Learn: An Ethnographic Study of Knowledge Construction in a Bilingual Third-Grade Classroom," *Discourse Processes* 19: 75–110 (1995).

15. Hugh Mehan, "The Structure of Classroom Lessons," in *Learning Lessons* (Cambridge, Mass.: Harvard University Press, 1979); Miriam Ben-Peretz and Rainer Bromme, eds., *The Nature of Time in Schools: Theoretical Concepts, Practitioner Perceptions* (New York: Teachers College Press, 1990); and James Stigler et al., *The TIMSS Videotape*

Classroom Study: Methods and Findings from an Exploratory Research Project on Eighth-Grade Mathematics Instruction in Germany, Japan, and the United States (Washington D.C.: U.S. Department of Education and OERI 1999): 133–34.

16. Frederick Erickson (with David Boersema, Margaret Brown, Becky Kirschner, Brenda Lazarus, Catherine Pelissier, and Daisy Thomas), "Teachers' Practical Ways of Seeing and Making Sense: A Final Report." Michigan State University: Institute for Research on Teaching, Sept. 30, 1986. (United States Department of Education, Office of Educational Research and Improvement, Contract No. 400-81-0014).

17. Rogers Hall and Andee Rubin, "…There's Five Little Notches in Here: Dilemmas in Teaching and Learning the Conventional Structure of Rate," in *Thinking Practices in Mathematics and Science Learning*, ed. James Greeno and Shelley V. Goldman (Mahwah, N.J.: Lawrence Erlbaum Associates, 1998), 189–236.

18. This orientation toward recordkeeping and documentation in teaching is not unique to me nor is it simply a "research" practice. It was something I had learned to do in my elementary teacher preparation and certification program at The Prospect School in 1975 and made a regular part of my practice as a teacher thereafter. For a description of this practice and its use in teaching, see Patricia F. Carini, *The Art of Seeing and the Visibility of the Person* (Grand Forks, N.D.: North Dakota Study Group on Evaluation, February, 1979).

19. Susan Florio-Ruane, Gaea Leinhardt, Ricki-Goldman Siegal, Kristina Hooper, and Mark Rosenberg, and of course Deborah Ball all had major influence on my thinking at the time about how the potential of new technologies could be harnessed to study and represent teaching.

20. The fundamental purpose of the collection of these records was for a pilot study of their use in teacher preparation. See Lampert and Ball, *Teaching, Multimedia, and Mathematics: Investigations of Real Practice* (New York: Teacher's College Press, 1998), for a complete description of this project. See Ball and Lampert, "Multiples of Evidence, Time, Perspective: Revising the Study of Teaching and Learning," in *Issues in Education Research: Problems and Possibilities*, ed. Ellen C. Lagemann and Lee S. Shulman (San Francisco: Jossey-Bass, 1999): 371–98, for a description of the research rationale for our work.

21. See S. Feld & C. Williams, "Toward Researchable Film Language," in S*tudies in the Anthropology of Visual Communication* 2(1): 25–32 (1975), for an argument supporting this approach.

22. As in the film *High School*, directed and edited by Frederick Wiseman, photography by Richard Leiterman (published by Frederick Wiseman, released by Zipporah Films, 1969).

23. As in the lesson data collected in the TIMSS teaching study, Stigler et al., TIMSS Videotape Classroom Study, 15–20.

24. The fifth-grade class was large and the classroom in which it met was small, which often made getting good sound difficult, given the sort of technical equipment we had to work with. During a portion of the year, one small group met in an anteroom to the main classroom within view of the teacher and other students so that their conversation could be more clearly recorded. We audiotaped conversation in a different small group than the one that was being videotaped to expand the regions of the classroom that were recorded.

The daily audiotapes were used to produce "first pass" transcripts of each lesson. These transcripts were then "enhanced" by a member of the observation team using video records to supplement the information available on audio.

25. The supplementary documentation of teaching and learning in my classroom was produced by a research team of graduate students in Teaching and Teacher Education that included Ruth Heaton, an experienced elementary teacher; Nan Jackson, a secondary school teacher with a master's degree in mathematics; and Virginia Keen, an experienced staff developer for mathematics educators. These same three documenters, with their different perspectives on what was happening, were in the classroom every day of the school year and rotated through periods of producing the field notes and taping the lessons. To guide this work we drew heavily on Frederick Erickson and Jan Wilson, *Sights and Sounds of Life in Schools: A Resource Guide to Film and Videotape for Research and Education*, Research Series No. 125 (East Lansing, Mich.: Institute for Research on Teaching, 1982), pp. 39–47.

26. The production of this database, entitled "Records of Practice," was the work of Jim Merz. The University of Michigan, the National Science Foundation, and the MacArthur Foundation funded it. Merz was assisted by continuous interaction with users of the records including Merrie Blunk, Peri Weingrad, Alice Horton Merz, Mike Goldenberg, and myself, and by a pilot study of the use of the records in electronic form by a group of teacher educators selected from around the United States. An earlier version of the database was developed by Mark Rosenberg at Michigan State University.

27. Miriam Sherin, "Developing a Professional Vision of Classroom Events," in *Beyond Classical Pedagogy: Teaching Elementary School Mathematics*, ed. Terry Wood, Barbara S. Nelson and J. Warfield (Hillsdale, N.J.: Lawrence Erlbaum Associates, 2001); Deidre LeFevre, "What Possibilities Do Video Records of Practice Afford as a Tool for Learning the Practice of Teaching?'" (unpublished manuscript, University of Michigan, 2000); Nanette Seago and Judy Mumme, *Videocases for Mathematics Professional Development: A New Tool for Teacher Learning* (unpublished manuscript, San Diego State Foundation, 2000); Francois Victor Tochon, *Video Study Groups for Education, Professional Development and Change* (Madison, Wisc.: Atwood, 1999); D. A. Smith, *A Primer for Using Video in the Classroom* (Portsmouth, N.H.: Heinemann, 1996); Mary DiSchino, "Why Do Bees Sting and Why Do They Die Afterward?" in *Boats, Balloons, and Classroom Video*, ed. Ann S. Rosebery and Beth Warren (Portsmouth, N.H.: Heinemann, 1998), 109–33; J. A. Eckart and S. L. Gibson, "Using Camcorders to Improve Teaching," *The Clearing House* 66(5): 288–92 (1993); Barbara Jaworski, *Using Classroom Videotape to Develop Your Teaching*, (Cambridge, England: The Open University, Center for Mathematics Education, 1989).

28. Jorge Luis Borges, *A Universal History of Infamy* (New York: Dutton, 1972); see also Umberto Eco, "Map of the Empire," *Literary Review* 28 (2): 233–38 (1985).

29. Although earlier mapmakers considered it their challenge to reduce fear of the unknown and open up the imagination, we now recognize that they accomplished their goal not through accurate portrayals but through usable symbol systems. Dennis Wood, *The Power of Maps* (New York: The Guilford Press, 1992); Nigel Holmes, *Pictoral Maps* (New York: Watson-Guptill, 1991). Many current theories of geographical representation point to the fact that a map is not an accurate representation, but a filter for information.

Drawing on a wide range of historical and anthropological information about mapmaking, cartographers assert that the measure of a map's accuracy is its "workability," i.e., how successful it is in achieving the aims for which it is drawn and its range of application. Through the decisions that are made in map making about inclusion and exclusion, what is actually represented is a perspective on the terrain within which we can locate ourselves and make decisions about which way to go. See Ronit Eisenbach, "The Map and the Madeline," in *Architecture Studio, Cranbrook Academy of Art, 1986–1993*, ed. Dan Hoffman (New York: Rizzoli, 1994), 206–13.

30. Eisenbach, ibid.; Wood, ibid.

31. The image presented here is borrowed from the film and book by Philip Morrison, Phyllis Morrison, and the office of Charles and Ray Eames, *Powers of Ten: About the Relative Size of Things in the Universe and the Effect of Adding Another Zero* (New York: Scientific American Books, 1982). In this representation of exponential relationships, the first picture we see is life-sized, of a couple picnicking on the beach in Chicago. The camera pulls away by powers of ten, first viewing them from 10 meters above, then from 100 meters, then from 1,000 meters and so on until we are 10 to the 25th power away, outside of our galaxy. The camera quickly zooms in, and we are back at life-sized people on a beach. Now we focus on the man's hand, enlarging the image by a power of ten. The image is enlarged again to 100 times life size and we see deep crevices, which are the creases in the skin of his hand. We move in closer and closer, until the image has been enlarged such that what we see is the inner structure of the proton, a level which, when the Morrisons were writing, physicists were just beginning to comprehend.

32. The problem of misapprehension that comes of looking at a complex phenomenon at only one level of magnification is well illustrated in *Zoom* by Istvan Banyai (New York: Puffin Books, 1995).

33. Morrison, Morrison, and Eames, p. vii.

34. In 1998, I worked with Raven Wallace and George Furness on a prototype of this idea in the School of Information at the University of Michigan using Pad++ software. See B. B. Bederson and J. D. Hollan, "Pad++: A Zooming Graphical Interface for Exploring Alternate Interface Physics," in *Proceedings of ACM UIST '94* (New York: ACM Press, 1994), 17–26; K. Perlin and D. Fox, "Pad: An Alternative Approach to the Computer Interface," in *Proceedings of ACM SigGraph '93* (New York: ACM Press, 1993), 57–64.

4   *Teaching to Establish a Classroom Culture*

1. For the radical constructivist, this assertion is controversial, for the assumption within this tradition is that doing alone is educative. See Ernst von Glasersfeld, ed. *Radical Constructivism in Mathematics Education* (Dordrecht, The Netherlands: Kluwer, 1991); and Leslie P. Steffe and Patrick W. Thompson, eds., *Radical Constructivism in Action: Building on the Pioneering Work of Ernst Von Glasersfeld* (New York: Falmer, 2000). Mathematics educators have been stymied for many years by the lack of learning associated with teachers and students simply doing the "activities" that are described in teacher guides and articles.

2. Walter Doyle's review of his own and others' research on classroom organization and management richly captures the possible variations in the teacher's role in establishing the

meaning of tasks and interactions in the classroom culture. See "Classroom Organization and Management," in *Handbook of Research on Teaching*, 3d ed., ed. Merlin Wittrock (New York.: Macmillan, 1986), 392–431.

3. The importance of such deliberate teaching of how to "do school" is argued by scholars concerned with equal access for all children. See for example, Lisa Delpit, "The Silenced Dialogue: Power and Pedagogy in Teaching Other People's Children," *Harvard Educational Review*, 58, 280–98 (1988).

4. Peggy Rittenhouse carried out a more detailed analysis of this event as part of a study of the teacher's role in discourse in this kind of teaching. See Peggy Rittenhouse, "The Teacher's Role in Mathematical Conversation: Stepping In and Stepping Out," in *Talking Mathematics*, ed. Lampert and Blunk (New York: Cambridge University Press, 1998): 163–89.

5. The term "conjecture" as I use it here is not strictly parallel to the way it is used by mathematicians, rather it is an adaptation of the process to the classroom culture.

6. The first Problem of the Day in a series functions as a "generative problem" that is then used as the basis for several related lessons. The choice and use of generative problems will be examined in chapter 5 and chapter 8.

7. The symbol $\overset{\wedge}{9}$ means "negative nine." This way of indicating negative value was introduced when students used the Comprehensive School Mathematics Program curriculum (CSMP) in earlier grades to avoid the confusion between negativity and subtraction. *CSMP Mathematics for the Intermediate Grades* (St. Louis, Mo.: CEMREL, 1976).

8. This representation is also found in the *CSMP* curriculum (ibid.). Dots in the lower right section are worth 1, in the lower left, they are worth 2, in the upper right they are worth 4, and in the upper left they are worth 8. So this representation means $(1 \times 1) + (1 \times 2) + (0 \times 4) + (6 \times 8) = 1 + 2 + 48 = 51$.

9. The "minuend" is the number being subtracted from. The subtrahend is the number symbolizing the quantity being taken away from the minuend. In discussing their conjectures, these somewhat obscure terms actually became useful to students as they tried to communicate their thinking to me and to their peers.

10. These counts were obtained from a search of transcribed lessons. All of the lessons across the year were transcribed, but the quality of the sound recorded during small-group discussion varied greatly as we were experimenting with a variety of microphone arrangements. The counts reported thus do not include the use of these words in most of the talk that went on outside of whole-class discussions.

11. Carol Meyer and Tom Salle, *Make it Simpler: A Practical Guide to Problem Solving in Mathematics* (Palo Alto, Calif.: Addison-Wesley, 1983).

12. For an analysis of the specific teaching practices used in my classroom to establish and maintain norms of small group work, see Blunk, "Teacher Talk About How to Talk in Small Groups," in *Talking Mathematics*, ed. Lampert and Blunk: *Studies of Teaching and Learning in School* (New York: Cambridge University Press, 1998), 190–212.

13. Like all organizations, school classes have three basic components: members, tools, and tasks. These components interact in patterned networks of activity in such a way as to regularize the division of labor (who does which tasks when), the use of tools (who uses what when), and the application of tools to the work to be done (who uses what for what).

Linda Argotte and Paul Ingram, "Knowledge Transfer: A Basis for Competitive Advantage in Firms," paper delivered at the Interdisciplinary Committee in Organizational Studies Seminar, University of Michigan, Ann Arbor, Michigan, January 21, 2000. R. L. Moreland, Linda Argotte, and R. Krishnan, "Training People to Work in Groups," in *Applications of Theory and Research on Groups to Social Issues*, ed. R. S. Tindale et al. (New York: Plenum, 1998): 37–60.

14. It is important to note that "culture" is something that belongs to a group, not an individual. Issues about what transfers from learning to participate in the kind of classroom culture I have described here as individuals move from one setting to another are important as we begin to think about measuring the more elusive aspects of knowledge acquired in classrooms, See Scott D. N. Cook and Dvora Yanow, "Culture and Organizational Learning," *Journal of Management Inquiry* 2(4), 373–90 (1993), for an explication of organizational learning as a social accomplishment rather than an individual one.

15. Jean Lave and Etienne Wenger, *Situated Learning: Legitimate Peripheral Participation* (Cambridge: Cambridge University Press, 1991); Barbara Rogoff, *Apprenticeship in Thinking: Cognitive Development in Social Context* (New York: Oxford University Press, 1990).

16. The fact that my students are socially and intellectually diverse and that I have them working variously on different activities entailed in solving problems means that my class is a more complex organization than one in which students all work on the same set of well-defined exercises and/or one in which the students are more socially and intellectually homogeneous. This complexity makes it harder to align activity with the accomplishment of goals. In such a complex organization, the members of the organization take on multiple roles. In the midst of this multiplicity, the teacher must manage the class's general direction without directing or observing many of the details of individual students' activities. Keeping the work of studying prominent in such a complex organization is made possible by the establishment of routines to coordinate everyone's activity toward the goal of student learning. All classrooms have routines, but with a diversity of students and activities, routines matter more in maintaining focus and coherence in learning-directed activities. In organizational theory, such routines have been conceived as "organizational knowledge." In contrast to the skills and knowledge that are acquired and used by individuals, organizational knowledge resides in the group and is remembered as it is used in social encounters. See Richard R. Nelson and Sidney G. Winter, *An Evolutionary Theory of Economic Change* (Cambridge, Mass.: The Belknap Press of Harvard University Press, 1982), esp. chapter 5, "Organizational Capabilities and Behavior," 96–138.

17. *The American Heritage Dictionary.* I am using standard definitions here rather than a psychological investigation of the process of acquiring knowledge and relying on common understandings rather than entering the debate within psychology about the nature of cognition. For an interesting set of exchanges on this debate see John R. Anderson, Lynne M. Reder, and Herbert A. Simon, "Situated Learning and Education," *Educational Researcher* 25(4): 5–11 (1996), and James Greeno, "On Claims That Answer the Wrong Questions," *Educational Researcher* 26(1): 5–17 (1997).

18. Greeno, "The Situativity of Knowing, Learning, and Research." *American Psychologist* 53(1): 5–26 (1998).

19. See Nelson and Winter, *An Evolutionary Theory*: 110–11, on enforcement mechanisms in organizations, and how they function in relation to routines and as routines.

5 Teaching While Preparing for a Lesson

1. This is Bob Yinger's term, and the focus of much of his research on teaching. He makes a useful distinction between "preparation" and "planning." See "The Conversation of Practice," in *Reflection in Teacher Education* (New York: Teachers College Press, 1988), pp. 73–94; "Learning the Language of Practice," in *Curriculum Inquiry* 17(3): 293–318 (1987); and "By the Seat of Your Pants: An Inquiry into Improvisation and Teaching," paper presented at the 1987 annual meeting of the American Educational Research Association, Washington, D.C. What Yinger and I mean by "preparation" is similar to what Japanese teachers do collaboratively when they do "lesson study." It is not lesson planning or curriculum design in the traditional sense, although it encompasses elements of both of those kinds of work. As Catherine Lewis has observed, it is "about learning how children are learning." See "Lesson Study: Japanese Method Benefits all Teachers," by Joan Richardson, *Results* (Washington, D.C.: National Staff Development Council, 2000), p. 1.

2. Besides writing in my journal to prepare, I did this kind of work while driving to school, eating lunch with other teachers, and talking with the teachers in our district's weekly math study group.

3. My work on this problem is represented here by my journal entries. I also did this kind of work in a less formal way, but that was not documented.

4. Japanese lesson study by teachers provides strong evidence for the need for this kind of work even when the curriculum is highly standardized.

6 Teaching While Students Work Independently

1. Guy Brousseau, "The Didactical Contract: The Teacher, the Student, and the Milieu," *Didactique des Mathématiques, 1970–1990* (*Theory of Didactical Situations in Mathematics, 1970–1990*), ed. and trans. Nicolas Balachef et al. (Dordrecht, The Netherlands: Kluwer, 1997), 227–50.

2. In formal mathematical terms, what she was doing would be called "decomposition" and "recomposition." These are commonly used strategies for doing computations with mixed numbers or numbers larger than ten.

3. This sample was chosen by listing the students in alphabetical order and choosing the notebook page of every fifth student for the day of the lesson under examination.

7 Teaching While Leading a Whole-Class Discussion

1. The kind of work I was doing here, connecting symbols, words, and representations, is also described in Kay McClain and Paul Cobb in "The Role of Imagery and Discourse in Supporting Students' Mathematical Development," in *Talking Mathematics: Studies of Teaching and Learning in School* (New York: Cambridge University Press, 1998), 56–82; Paul Cobb, "From Representing to Symbolizing: Introductory Comments on Semiotics and Mathematical Learning," in *Symbolizing and Communicating in Mathematics Classrooms: Perspectives on Discourse, Tools, and Instructional Design*, ed. Erna Yackel, Paul Cobb, and Kay McClain (Mahwah, N.J.: Lawrence Erlbaum Associates, 2000), 17–36; and Anna

Sfaard, "Symbolizing Mathematical Reality into Being—or How Mathematical Objects Create Each Other," in *Symbolizing and Communicating in Mathematics Classrooms: Perspectives on Discourse, Tools, and Instructional Design*, ed. Erna Yackel, Paul Cobb, and Kay McClain (Mahwah, N.J.: Lawrence Erlbaum Associates, 2000), 37–98.

2. This elegant phrase describing an important element of teacher's work in classrooms organized around work on problems comes from David Hawkins. In his essay "Nature, Man, and Mathematics," he describes eight- to ten-year-olds working with an Archimedian balance. He asserts here that, even if students initial investigations are limited, "Where a teacher can support and provide, can *dignify with pertinent curiosity*, children will sometimes reach the law of moments empirically, and less easily, a simpler fact underlying the famous theorem of Archimedes: the invariance of balance to any pairwise symmetrical displacement of equal weights—the law of the equal arm balance." In *The Informed Vision: Essays on Learning and Human Nature* (New York: Agathon, 1974), p. 117, emphasis mine.

3. Based on an "n" of two here, the reader might conclude that when the answer a student gives is "wrong" by conventional standards, I ask for an explanation, and when it is "right" I ask for other students to comment. This generalization is not borne out in a further study of the data.

8 *Teaching to Deliberately Connect Content Across Lessons*

1. The lesson described in chapter 2 occurred in the latter part of this unit.

2. Bank Street College Project in Science and Math, *The Voyage of the Mimi: A Teacher's Guide* (New York: Holt Reinhart, 1985).

3. A study of this kind of problem-solving can be found in Edward Hutchins, "Learning to Navigate," in *Understanding Practice*, ed. Seth Chaiklin and Jean Lave (New York: Cambridge University Press, 1993), pp. 35–64.

4. See Lampert, "Mathematics Learning in Context: 'The Voyage of the *Mimi.*'" *The Journal of Mathematical Behavior* 4: 157–68 (1985), for a detailed description of this problem.

5. The journey line evolved into the representation we saw in chapter 2, once we switched from ship travel to car travel.

6. Ten minutes is one-sixth of an hour, so in that time, a car traveling at a constant speed of 50 mph would travel one-sixth of fifty miles. Finding one-sixth of fifty involves a division with a remainder that might be expressed as a repeating decimal: 8.3333....

7. In Judah Schwartz's terms, speed is an "extensive" quantity, composed of two other "intensive" quantities. See "Intensive Quantity and Referent Transforming Arithmetic Operations," in *Number Concepts and Operations in the Middle Grades*, volume 2, in the Research Agenda for Mathematics Education Series, ed. James Hiebert and Merlyn Behr (Reston, Va.: National Council of Teachers of Mathematics, 1988), pp. 41–52.

8. The idea that mathematicians have developed to refer to this phenomenon is closure. Because I can add any two whole numbers and get another whole number, or multiply any two whole numbers and get a whole number, the set of all whole numbers is said to be "closed" under addition and multiplication. It is not, however, closed under subtraction

and division, because subtraction can produce a negative number (as in taking ten away from seven) and division can produce a fraction (as in dividing one by seven).

9. It could also be interpreted as a "scaffold" in the Vygotskian sense. See *The Collected Works of L. S. Vygotsky: Problems of General Psychology*, vol. 1, ed. R. W. Rieber and A. S. Carlton, trans. Norris Minick (New York: Plenum, 1987).

10. Other examples of this kind of improvisational teaching work can be found in Ruth Heaton, *Teaching Mathematics to the New Standards: Relearning the Dance* (New York: Teachers College Press, 2000).

11. See Hans Freudenthal, *Didactical Phenomenology of Mathematical Structures* (Dordrecht, The Netherlands: D. Reidel, 1983).

12. This term was coined by Deborah Ball, "With an Eye on the Mathematical Horizon," *Elementary School Journal* 93(4): 373–97 (1993).

13. It is tempting to avoid this teaching problem altogether and assert that Charlotte never should have been taught the conventional algorithm or at least that she should not be introduced to it until she has a strong grasp on the meaning of division as it relates to the leftovers. Proponents of Realistic Mathematics Education, for example, might say that this problem (of how to give meaning to the "R.4") would not arise if I had designed the learning environment so that Charlotte would build up to the level of mathematizing the time-speed-distance relationship herself from the concrete reality of the situation. (See Koeno Gravemeyer, *Developing Realistic Mathematics Education* [Utrecht, The Netherlands: Freudenthal Institute, 1994].) This may be true, and it is relevant to the problem of curriculum design, but since I enter the students' mathematical career when they are ten years old and they have already had many formal and informal mathematics experiences, I do not control what "tools" they bring to problem solving. If I allow them to be mathematical "bricolleurs" then they will present me with the kind of didactical problem that Charlotte presents here—how to teach her *not* to use mathematical formalisms that do not make sense.

14. This may be interpreted as making a link across ethnomathematical knowledge, intuitive knowledge, and technical symbolic knowledge as Thomas Kieran uses these terms in "Personal Knowledge of Rational Numbers," in *Number Concepts and Operations in the Middle Grades,* ed. James Hiebert and Merlyn Behr (Reston, Va.: National Council of Teachers of Mathematics, 1988), 162–80.

15. In later chapters, I take up the same "big idea" in terms of what counts as "the whole" when working with fractions.

16. I do not mean to suggest that this "trying out" need be the work of every individual teacher. Although each teacher does lesson work as the lone adult in a classroom, work that occurs between and across lessons can be done in collaboration with other adults. In Japan, for example, it is done as collective professional work by groups of teachers. See Stigler and Hiebert, *The Teaching Gap: Best Ideas from the World's Teachers for Improving Education in the Classroom* (New York: Free Press, 1999); Catherine Lewis and Ineko Tsuchida, "A Lesson Is Like a Swiftly Flowing River," *American Educator* 22(4): 12–17, 50–51 (1998).

9   Teaching to Cover the Curriculum

1. *Michigan Essential Goals and Objectives for Mathematics Education* (Lansing, Mich.: Michigan State Board of Education, 1988).

2. *CSMP Mathematics for the Intermediate Grades* (St Louis, Mo.: CEMREL, 1976) and L. Carey Bolster et al., *Mathematics Around Us: Skills and Applications* (Glenview, Ill.: Scott, Foresman and Company, 1978).

3. Bolster, *Mathematics Around Us.*

4. This research was reported earlier in M. Lampert, "The Collaborative Construction of the Mathematics Curriculum Using Teacher-Constructed Problems." Plenary Address, 7th International Congress on Mathematics Education, Quebec, Canada, August 22, 1992. My research assistants on this project were Sarah Theule-Lubienski and Ruth Heaton.

5. I do not claim that these lessons are a "representative sample" in the sense that this term is used in quantitative investigations. The question of what a representative sample of classroom discourse might be is a knotty one (Mary Catherine O'Connor, personal communication).

6. See *Curriculum Standards* (Reston, Va.: National Council of Teachers of Mathematics, 1989) and our state's curriculum guidelines cited above. Although we settled on the list that appears in the tables, we argued considerably about where one topic ended and another began. One of my research assistants had a strong mathematics education through the master's degree level (Theule-Lubienski), and the other had been an elementary school teacher for ten years (Heaton). Their different frames of reference were accommodated in our negotiations about labeling the content and processes on the list.

7. We also argued about when a student could be said to be "working on" something in such a way as to fit the definition of studying as "applying one's mind to the acquisition of knowledge." We knew from reflecting on our own mental habits that it is possible to be working (hard) on an idea and even to be acquiring some knowledge, and not produce any visible evidence of engagement or records of the work. But we decided to be conservative and only count direct observations or records of engagement. Because the nature of the students' work was so varied across students, we faced a further problem in linking instances of students' work to the list of content and process topics.

8. The expression of the remainder in division is as example that is often used to illustrate this point. Students need to be taught that the leftovers are treated differently if people are being assigned to buses, if bags of pieces of candy are being distributed to people, or if distance is being distributed over time. See Edward A. Silver, "Knowledge Organization and Mathematical Problem Solving," in *Mathematical Problem Solving: Issues in Research,* ed. Frank Lester (Philadelphia: Franklin Institute Press, 1982).

9. Judah Schwartz, "Intensive Quantity and Referent Transforming Arithmetic Operations," in *Number Concepts and Operations in the Middle Grades,* ed. James Hiebert and Merlyn Behr (Reston, Va.: National Council of Teachers of Mathematics, 1988), 41–52.

10. See Gerard Vergnaud, "Multiplicative Structures," in *Number Concepts in the Middle Grades,* ed. James Hiebert and Merlyn Behr, 141–61. See also Lampert, "Teaching and Learning Long Division for Understanding in School," in *Disseminating New Knowledge About Mathematics Instruction,* ed. Gaea Leinhardt, Ralph Putnam, and R. Hattrup (Hillsdale, N.J.: Lawrence Erlbaum Associates, 1992).

11. Vergnaud, "Multiplicative Structures," p. 141.

12. Ibid., p. 142. Note that the question of "transfer" of knowledge among situations is one of the central debates in cognitive psychology. See John R. Anderson, Lynne M. Reder, and Herbert Simon, "Situated Learning and Education," *Educational Researcher* 25(4): 5–11 (1996), and James Greeno, "On Claims That Answer the Wrong Questions," *Educational Researcher* 26(1): 5–17 (1997).

13. Mary Catherine O'Connor, "Language Socialization in the Mathematics Classroom," in *Talking Mathematics: Studies of Teaching and Learning in School* (New York: Cambridge University Press, 1998), 17–55.

14. A third case of work on this problem can be found in chapter 10 within the section entitled "Integrating Academic Character into Preadolescent Social Life: Teaching Saundra to Think and Reason." In the analysis of my teaching Saundra, I also describe a third problem context in which I taught the mathematics of multiplicative structures while teaching conventional fifth-grade topics.

15. The algorithm for doing "long" division has many steps, and remembering to do all of them in order is challenging. This is not to say students should not learn to do long division by some mechanical procedure, but that they need some sort of conceptual frame to hang it on if they are to use it sensibly. See Lampert, "Teaching and Learning Long Division."

16. If I had continued to extend the conventional long division procedure to distribute these leftovers, I would obtain the same kind of answer as Ivan was puzzling over the day before, having used the calculator:

$$
\begin{array}{r}
4.625 \\
24{\overline{)}\,111.000} \\
-\underline{96} \\
150 \\
-\underline{144} \\
60 \\
-\underline{48} \\
120 \\
-\underline{120}
\end{array}
$$

This would have had me talking about distributing absurdly small pieces of cake, so I concluded that this problem context would not be good for teaching this way of working with remainders.

17. With hours and minutes or miles and feet, any fraction can be dealt with by trading it for another, smaller unit (e.g., three half-hours is equal to ninety minutes, one and one-fourth minutes is seventy-five seconds, and so on). Doing this trading avoids having to confront its meaning directly in terms of parts *and* wholes.

18. Linguists might refer to the different ways the students and I are talking about these numbers as different "registers." The invariants that characterize the relationships between ideas in conceptual fields across the situations in which we use those ideas are what Anna Sfaard calls "mathematical objects." See "Symbolizing Mathematical Reality into Being— Or How Mathematical Discourse and Mathematical Objects Create Each Other," in *Symbolizing and Communicating in Mathematics Classrooms: Perspectives on Discourse,*

Tools, and Instructional Design, ed. Erna Yackel, Paul Cobb, and Kay McClain (Mahwah, N.J.: Lawrence Erlbaum Associates, 2000), 37–98.

19. O'Connor, "Language Socialization." It is odd that the United States has never accepted the metric system for measure, which would have length, weight, and other measures using the structure of decimal system as well.

20. "Thoughts on Teaching Mechanics: Didactical Phenomenology of the Concept of Force" in *Educational Studies in Mathematics*, 25: 71–87 (1993). See p. 72.

21. The nature and usefulness of mathematical abstractions has been debated throughout the history of the discipline. See, for example, Philip Davis and Reuben Hersh, *Descartes' Dream: The World According to Mathematics* (San Diego: Harcourt Brace Jovanovich, 1986); Morris Kline, *Mathematics and the Search for Knowledge* (New York: Oxford University Press, 1985); Horace Freeland Judson, *The Search for Solutions* (Baltimore, Md.: Johns Hopkins University Press, 1987).

22. *The American Heritage Dictionary of the English Language, Third Edition*, copyright © 1992 by Houghton Mifflin Company. Electronic version licensed from INSO Corporation. All rights reserved.

23. I attribute my thinking about aspects of practice in teaching as "invisible work" to Leigh Star, "Layers of Silence, Arenas of Voice: The Ecology of Visible and Invisible Work," Colloquium for the Interdisciplinary Committee on Organizational Studies, University of Michigan, February 5, 1999.

24. Parents, too, would have used this as a framework for identifying whether their children were progressing as they should be in any particular class. When they moved on to sixth grade, my fifth-grade students would return to a setting that was organized according to this framework of units and lessons, with the assumption that they had "covered" all the previous content, topic by topic, in the fifth-grade book. In my school, it had been common practice to instruct the students who were thought to be more talented mathematically by allowing them to work quickly and independently through the textbook units. A mark of success was being able to say you were in the fourth-grade book while still in third grade, or the in the fifth-grade book in fourth grade. This measurement of accomplishment was not a mere brag fest—those students who proceeded accordingly were able to take calculus in their senior year in high school rather than wait until they got to college, and it was believed they would get into "better" colleges if they did.

25. TIMSS data (1997) shows that this is the way instruction in many American mathematics classrooms is organized.

26. Scott, Foresman, *Mathematics*, Teachers Edition, P.T.A., page T19.

27. Ralph Putnam, "Structuring and Adjusting Content for Students: A Study of Live and Simulated Tutoring of Addition," *American Educational Research Journal* 24(1): 13–48 (1987).

28. 1989, National Council of Teachers of Mathematics, p. 3.

10 Teaching Students to Be People Who Study in School

1. The analyses of Bereiter and Scardamalia suggest that students in the United States. and Canada do not come to school already prepared to be "intentional learners." See Marlene Scardamalia and Carl Bereiter, "Adaptation and Understanding: A Case for New

Cultures of Schooling," in *International Perspectives on the Design of Technology-Supported Learning Environments*, ed. S. Vosniadou et al. (Mahwah, N.J.: Lawrence Erlbaum Associates, 1996), 149–64. In contrast, students in other cultures like Japan and China share cultural norms and agreement on the purposes of schooling that dispose them toward studying. See James W. Stigler and Michelle Perry, "Mathematics Learning in Japanese, Chinese, and American Classrooms," in *Cultural Psychology: Essays on Comparative Human Development*, ed. James W. Stigler, Richard A. Schweder, and Gilbert Herdt (New York: Cambridge University Press, 1990), 328–56. I also draw here on two studies of adolescents in school, one of which (Chazan) is focused directly on the problems entailed in teaching them in a social setting where academic work is not valued. See Dan Chazan, *Beyond Formulas in Mathematics and Teaching: Dynamics of the High School Algebra Classroom* (New York: Teachers College Press, 2000), and Penelope Eckert, *Jocks and Burnouts: Social Categories and Identity in the High School* (New York: Teachers College Press, 1989).

2. The work of Annemarie Palincsar and Ann Brown on "reciprocal teaching" is informative in this regard. See Palincsar and Brown, "Reciprocal Teaching of Comprehension-Fostering and Monitoring Activities," *Cognition and Instruction* 1(2): 117–75 (1984); Brown and Palincsar, "Guided Cooperative Learning and Individual Knowledge Acquisition," in *Knowing, Learning, and Instruction: Essays in Honor of Robert Glaser*, ed. Lauren Resnick (Hillsdale, N.J.: Lawrence Erlbaum Associates, 1989), 393–451.

3. *Teaching Children Mathematics*, the monthly magazine for teachers published by the National Council of Teachers of Mathematics, recently featured on its cover two children standing on the beach wearing tee shirts with the message "It's okay to like math" emblazoned across the back (vol. 6, no. 9, May 2000). A letter from a teacher concerned about adults with "bad experiences" passing on "an unspoken message that mathematics is not important and definitely not fun" inspired this cover (p. 2).

4. The problematic relationship between developing academic competence and acquiring practical skills and knowledge is not to be ignored, but this is not the place to take up that argument. See Greeno and Goldman (eds.), *Thinking Practices in Mathematics and Science Learning* (Mahwah, N.J.: Lawrence Erlbaum Associates, 1998), and Reed Stevens and Rogers Hall, "Disciplined Perception: Learning to See in Technoscience" in Lampert and Blunk, eds. *Talking Mathematics: Studies of Teaching and Learning in School* (New York: Cambridge University Press, 1998), 107–50.

5. George Herbert Mead in his "I-me" theory of the self perhaps best elucidated this tenet of social psychology. See *Mind, Self, and Society*, ed. Charles W. Morris (Chicago: University of Chicago Press, 1934).

6. Willard Waller was the first sociologist to call attention to the interpersonal aspects of teaching as they play out in classrooms and their effects on identity formation. Cf. Waller, *The Sociology of Teaching* (Chicago: University of Chicago Press, 1932). In more recent years, except for a few studies, the sociology of education has turned to the place of schools in society or the relationship between curriculum and social reproduction, and neglected the conduct of society among persons in the classroom. These phenomena are certainly related, as the ways in which a culture defines the purposes of schooling and the

extent to which there is cultural agreement on those purposes will shape the extent of the interpersonal work a teacher needs to do to bring students along in the work of studying.

7. In *Life in Classrooms* (New York: Holt, Reinhart, and Winston, 1968). Philip Jackson speaks of "crowds, praise, and power" as central features of social relationships in classrooms, but he does not attend to the academic implications or contexts of these social challenges.

8. Chazan, *Beyond Formulas*. See also Penelope Eckert, *Jocks and Burnouts*, Laurence Steinberg, *Beyond the Classroom: Why School Reform Has Failed and What Parents Need to Do* (New York: Simon & Schuster, 1996), and Mary Haywood Metz, "Teachers' Ultimate Dependence on Their Students," in *Teachers' Work: Individuals, Colleagues, and Contexts,* ed. Little and McLaughlin (New York: Teachers College Press, 1993), 104–36.

9. George Polya, *Induction and Analogy in Mathematics* (Princeton, N.J.: Princeton University Press, 1954), 7–8.

10. Among other indications of her social orientation, Saundra included drawings of flowers and the words to this popular song by Madonna in her math notebook: Madonna, "Vogue" (1990, Warner Brothers).

11. Deborah Ball describes a similar problem in a case of her teaching in D. L. Ball and S. W. Wilson, "Integrity in Teaching: Recognizing the Fusion of the Moral and Intellectual," *American Educational Research Journal* 33(1): 155–92 (1993).

12. Fraction Bars were designed by Albert B. Bennett in 1989 (www.24hours7days.com /Education1/FB.html). There are many commercially available materials that teachers and students can use to represent and study fractions. From my point of view as a teacher, what is distinctive about the Fraction Bars as a tool for investigating the mathematics of fractions is:

- They are all the same size, making "the whole" of which a fractional part is emphasized the same in every case.
- They represent the most commonly used fractions.
- They use both color and shape to represent mathematical elements.
- They are easy to move around and compare with one another in the amount of space a student commonly has available on his or her desktop, and their movement does not add extraneous noise to the classroom.
- They do not require a knowledge of symbols or terms in order to represent fundamental ideas and operations.
- They do not look like "toys."
- They are inexpensive and so multiple sets can be provided to a class.
- They are easy to keep track of and clean up.

These mathematical and practical characteristics of the materials contributed to my choosing to use them with my class.

13. The mathematical content of these lessons was again, multiplicative structures. The teaching in the Fraction Bars lessons displays another example of the kind of work described in chapter 9.

14. Deborah Ball, "Magical Hopes: Manipulatives and the Reform of Mathematics Education," *American Educator*, 16(2), 14–18, 46–47 (1992).

15. Albert B. Bennett, Jr., and Patricia S. Davidson, *Fraction Bars: Step by Step Workbook* (Fort Collins, Colo.: Scott Resources, n.d.).

16. This strategy does not work with units of different areas, for example a medium and a large pizza. The unit area is deliberately held constant in Fraction Bars to highlight the difference between counting the number of pieces and considering the area "colored in."

17. This was a conclusion we had come to through whole-class discussions some days before. We considered other ways of identifying the larger number represented by a Fraction Bar and decided this one made the most sense in this context.

18. The arrows at either end of the line indicate that this segment is part of a longer line that goes on infinitely in both directions. The class had done some work with the number line in previous years to represent addition and multiplication of whole numbers, but I knew they did not have much experience with thinking about the portion of the line that represents the numbers between 0 and 1. The numbers represented in that part of the line were also the numbers represented by the Fraction Bars.

19. In this work, Ellie and the other students are having another opportunity to study the "big idea" that was the theme of chapter 9. The nature of "the whole" in their talk changes and the assumptions they make about it are crucial to making comparisons among numbers written as fractions.

20. There are fundamental implications here for constructing ethnically, racially, and gender-appropriate teaching. See Carol Lee's work on the teaching of English to

African American high school students in "A Culturally Based Cognitive Apprenticeship: Teaching African American High School Students Skills in Literacy Interpretation," *Reading Research Quarterly* 30(4), 608–30 (1995), and Gloria Ladson Billings in *The Dreamkeepers: Successful Teachers of African American Children* (San Francisco, Calif.: Jossey-Bass, 1994).

21. The stress on students is written about more commonly than the stress on teachers. We can understand the latter from cross-cultural comparisons like the research conducted by Stigler and Stevenson in China and Japan. This work highlights the differences between what teachers have to work with in the way of cultural assumptions about learning and schooling in different cultures. See James Stigler and James Hiebert, *The Teaching Gap: Best Ideas from the World's Teachers for Improving Education in the Classroom* (New York: Free Press, 1999), and Harold W. Stevenson and James Stigler, *The Learning Gap: Why Our Schools Are Failing and What We Can Learn from Japanese and Chinese Education* (New York: Summit Books, 1992).

22. David K. Cohen, "Teaching Practice: Plus ça Change..." Issue paper 88-3 (East Lansing, Mich.: The National Center for Research on Teacher Education, 1988).

11 Teaching the Nature of Accomplishment

1. Gavriel Salomon and R. E. Clark, "Reexamining the Methodology of Research on Media and Technology in Education," *Review of Educational Research* 47: 99–120 (1977).

2. In the classic work *Life in Classrooms*, Philip Jackson reports both empirical and conceptual studies of this phenomenon (New York: Holt, Rinehart and Winston, 1968).

3. This is a particular problem for teaching in school. If a teacher worked as an academic tutor with individual students or as a master with a group of apprentices in producing goods or services, some of these problems would still remain to be solved, but their combined effect on practice would be less complex. A single student working with a teacher is not subject to the judgments of peers, or to a comparison with their progress. In producing goods or services, the visible outcomes of one's work stand beside social judgments about accomplishment, making the influence of peers in defining one's progress somewhat weaker.

4. What happens to students' opportunities to learn when having new knowledge is not valued by their classmates is taken up in Chazan, *Beyond Formulas in Mathematics and Teaching: Dynamics of the High School Algebra Classroom* (New York: Teachers College Press, 2000).

5. I use this convoluted language here and I put quotation marks around the fractions written by students in the form of numbers because I do not know whether Ivan and others would necessarily make the connection that "⅜" means two parts out of eight.

6. In mathematics, "conventional" meanings and rules for doing arithmetic are partly a matter of social agreements but most often they also have a component of logical necessity. For example, the logical implications of adding denominators in fractions would lead to a contradiction both in the possible uses of addition and in the way in which the fractional sum could be used in a problem setting.

7. In a society where failure is an incentive to try harder, this would not be a teaching problem. In the United States, however, mathematical failure is accepted as something like

a personality trait, which cannot be overcome with effort. See Carol Dweck, "Children's Theories of Intelligence," in *Learning and Motivation in the Classroom*, ed. S. G. Paris, G. M. Olson, and H. W. Stevenson (Hillsdale, N.J.: Lawrence Erlbaum Associates, 1983), and *Self-Theories: Their Role in Motivation, Personality, and Development* (Philadelphia, Penn.: Psychology Press, 1999), and J. Stigler and R. Baranes, "Culture and Mathematics Learning," *Review of Research in Education* 15 (Washington, D.C.: American Educational Research Association, 1989), 253–306.

8. In the district in which I taught, grades were not assigned to students, either in class or on parent reports or permanent record cards, until sixth grade. Both Thom Dye and I did various activities during the year to prepare students for getting grades the following year.

9. During class discussions, I had more degrees of freedom to investigate levels of student understanding. If a student did not volunteer several representations in what they said in a class discussion, I could register that information and then use a prompt to see if I could push them further toward such a performance. In this way I could both assess and teach in the same exchange. But that approach to teaching was not possible within the constraints of the quiz. See Brousseau, "The Didactical Contract," in *Didactique des Mathématiques, 1970–1990* (*Theory of Didactical Situations in Mathematics, 1970–1990*) ed. and trans. Nicolas Balachef et al., (Dordrecht, The Netherlands: Kluwer, 1997), 227–50, for an analysis of the subtle form that such prompts take in classrooms, and the problematic implications they have for accurately assessing student competence.

12 Teaching the Whole Class

1. My purpose here is not to advocate this kind of arrangement but to analyze the teaching practices I used to cope with my choice to teach the whole class together.

2. Stephen Willoughby, Carl Bereiter, Peter Hilton, and Joseph Rubenstein, *Real Math*, Level 5 (LaSalle, Ill.: Open Court, 1987). A similar set of lessons which I taught a few years earlier was analyzed more fully by Gaea Leinhardt in "Seeing the Complexity of Standing to the Side: Lampert's Instructional Dialogues," *Cognition and Instruction*, in preparation.

3. Willoughby et al., *Real Math*, p. 20.

4. There is a great deal more to be said about functions, both mathematically and pedagogically. I do not explicate functions in the ways I have explicated other mathematical ideas in the book, but I have tried to say enough to explain why I chose to work on this topic as a way to engage a wide spectrum of students at the close of the school year. I try to explain functions here in a way that will be accessible to all of my readers, and therefore I have left out many of the mathematical subtleties that would be considered important by more mathematically well-educated readers. See Gaea Leinhardt, Orit Zaslavsky, and Mary Kay Stein, "Functions, Graphs, and Graphing: Tasks, Learning, and Teaching," *Review of Educational Research*, 60(1): 1–64 (1990), for a more adequate explication of the elementary mathematics of functions and graphing.

5. Willoughby et al., *Real Math*, p. 147.

6. Mathematicians refer to this as the "identity function." It has many applications in both concrete and abstract problem solving.

7. In this group of five, it is notable that three are girls and two are students of color.

8. In this group, there are five girls and five boys, and there are five students of color.

9. Of the nine students in this group, eight were girls and five were students of color.

13 *Teaching Closure*

1. See Veronica Boix Mansilla and Howard Gardner, "What are the Qualities of Understanding?" in Martha Stone Wiske, *Teaching for Understanding: Linking Research with Practice*, ed. Martha Stone Wiske (San Francisco, Calif.: Jossey-Bass, 1998), 161–96.

2. Although it will not be analyzed, the quiz is included in Appendix C.

3. Robert Baratta-Lorton, *Mathematics: A Way of Thinking* (Menlo Park, Calif.: Addison-Wesley, 1977).

4. This would more formally be called a "Venn Diagram." The term "string picture" comes from the Comprehensive School Mathematics Program materials.

5. Baratta-Lorton, *Mathematics*, p. 277.

6. Santa Barbara Classroom Discourse Group, "Constructing Literacy in Classrooms: Literate Action as Social Accomplishment," in *Redefining Student Learning: Roots of Educational Change*, ed. H. Marshall (Norwood, N.J.: Ablex, 1922), 119–50. James Gee, *What Is Literacy?* (Brookline, Mass.: The Literacies Institute, Educational Development Corporation, 1989). James Gee and Judith Green, "Discourse Analysis, Learning, and Social Practice: A Methodological Study," *Review of Research in Education* 23: 119–69, (1998). Kathryn Au, "Participation Structures in a Reading Lesson with Hawaiian Children: Analysis of a Culturally Appropriate Instructional Event," *Anthropology and Education Quarterly* 11(23), 91–115 (1980). Kathryn Au, "Social Constructivism and the School Literacy Learning of Students of Diverse Cultural Backgrounds," *Journal of Literacy Research* 30(2), 297–319 (1998).

7. Weinstein and Mayer, "The Teaching of Learning Strategies," *Handbook of Research on Teaching*, 3d ed., ed. Merlin Wittrock (New York: Macmillan, 1986), 315–27.

8. See, for example, Samuel S. Wineburg and Suzanne M. Wilson, "Subject-Matter Knowledge in the Teaching of History," *Advances in Research Teaching*, vol. 2, 305–47 (1991); Pamela L. Grossman and Susan S. Stodolsky, "Content as Context: The Role of School Subjects in Secondary School Teaching," *Educational Researcher* 24(8), 5–11 (1995).

9. Because Richard left in the middle of the year, there is not essay from him.

14 *An Elaborated Model of Teaching Practice*

1. Theodore Sizer, *Horace's Compromise* (Boston: Houghton Mifflin, 1984), 151–52.

2. Patricia Benner, Christine A. Tanner, and Catherine A. Chelsa, *Expertise in Nursing Practice: Caring, Clinical Judgment, and Ethics* (New York: Springer, 1996).

3. See Nel Noddings, "Caring and Competence," in *The Education of Teachers*, Yearbook of the National Society for the Study of Education, ed. Gary A. Griffin (Chicago: University of Chicago Press, 1999), 205–20.

4. The term "compound" in chemistry refers to a substance composed of atoms of two or more elements in chemical combination, occurring in fixed, definite proportion and arranged in fixed, definite structures. A compound has unique properties that are distinct from the properties of its elemental constituents and of all other compounds. A com-

pound differs from a mixture in that the components of a mixture retain their own properties and may be present in many different proportions. The components of a mixture are
not chemically combined; they can be separated by physical means.

5. I do not pretend that this is a comprehensive map of the terrain we were investigating. It is meant as a proxy to represent the integrated nature of the subject matter.

6. See Richard Saul Wurman, *Information Architects* (New York: Graphis Publications,
1997), and earlier work by Edward R. Tufte, e.g., *Envisioning Information* (Cheshire, Conn.:
Graphics Press, 1990), for current examples of efforts to solve similar problems in other
fields, with and without computer assistance.

7. As on early Roman coaching maps or the "triptiks" we get from AAA, all of the places
that one is to visit in the domain of mathematics are in a straight line because that is how
they are encountered on the journey. This kind of map does not show relationships among
the parts of a terrain as they might be encountered on a different journey. John Noble
Wilford, *The Mapmakers* (New York: Vintage Books, 1981), p. 48.

8. Although it is not within the scope of this book to take on the question of what
teachers need to know to teach with problems, my analysis suggests that they would have
to have a particular kind of mathematical knowledge to teach mathematics, a kind that is
rarely offered to elementary teachers in their professional preparation. Alternatively, a
holistic perspective on content could be made more available in curriculum materials.
Currently, there are many mathematics curricula that take this perspective, but it is not
made explicit enough for the teacher to learn from it and use it in her interactions with
students.

9. See O'Connor, "Language Socialization in the Mathematics Classroom: Discourse
Practices and Mathematical Thinking," in *Talking Mathematics: Studies of Teaching and
Learning in School* (New York: Cambridge University Press, 1998), 17–55. A provocative
perspective on the relationship between mathematical reasoning and the psychological
construction of knowledge is presented in Philip Kitcher, *The Nature of Mathematical
Knowledge* (New York: Oxford University Press, 1983). See also Ralph Putnam, Magdalene
Lampert, and Penelope Peterson, "Alternative Perspectives on Knowing Mathematics in
Elementary Schools," in *Review of Research in Education*, vol. 16, 57–150 (1990).

10. For a thought-provoking example, see Deborah Ball (1993), "With an Eye on the
Mathematical Horizon: Dilemmas of Teaching Elementary School Mathematics," *Elementary School Journal* 93(4), 373–97.

11. The relationship between students' creation of mathematical knowledge using
mathematical discourse rules in the classroom and the creation of such knowledge in the
discipline has been a complicated one. Cognitive psychology, social psychology, pedagogy,
and epistemology are each domains in which questions about this relationship arise and
for the most part remain unsettled. Deborah Ball and Hyman Bass, "Making Believe: The
Collective Construction of Public Mathematical Knowledge in the Elementary
Classroom," in *Constructivism in Education*, Yearbook of the National Society for the Study
of Education, ed. D. Phillips (Chicago: University of Chicago Press, 2000), 193–224; and
Hans-Georg Steiner, "Two Kinds of Elements and the Dialectic Between Synthetico-
Deductive and Analytic Genetic Approaches in Mathematics," in *For the Learning of
Mathematics* 8(3), 7–15 (1988).

12. Attempts have been made to make it stand still for the purposes of teaching and studying. See Steiner, "Two Kinds of Elements."

13. In *Dreamkeepers: Successful Teachers of African American Children* (San Francisco: Jossey Bass, 1994), Gloria Ladson Billings focuses on the role of will in several cases of teachers working with African American students in urban settings.

14. Carol Dweck has conducted extensive research on how students' theories of talent and studying affect the way they learn. See "Children's Theories of Intelligence," in *Learning and Motivation in the Classroom*, ed. S. G. Paris, G. M. Olson, and H. W. Stevenson (Hillsdale, N.J.: Lawrence Erlbaum Associates, 1983). Also see J. Stigler and R. Baranes, "Culture and Mathematics Learning," *Review of Research in Education*, 15 (Washington, D.C.: American Educational Research Association, 1989), 253–306.

15. See Noddings, "Caring and Competence," as well as Frederick Erickson, "School Reasoning, Literacy, and Civility: An Anthropologist's Perspective," in *Review of Educational Research* 54 (winter), 525–46 (1984).

16. Philip Jackson, *Life in Classrooms* (New York: Holt, Rinehart and Winston, 1968), calls this the "hidden curriculum." See also Heinrich Bauersfeld, "Hidden Dimensions in the So-Called Reality of a Mathematics Classroom," in Richard Lesh and Walter Secada, *Some Theoretical Issues in Mathematics Education: Papers from a Research Presession* (Columbus, Ohio: ERIC Clearinghouse, 1979), and Susan Florio-Ruane, *Learning to Go to School: An Ethnography of Interaction in A Kindergarten/First Grade Classroom.* Unpublished doctoral dissertation, Harvard University, 1978.

17. Walter Doyle, "Classroom Organization and Management," in *Handbook of Research on Teaching,* 3d ed. (New York: Macmillan, 1986), 392–431.

18. I owe my appreciation of this analogy to Chris Clark, who developed it from his experience as a navigator on a Navy submarine.

19. William James, "The Moral Philosopher and the Moral Life," *The Moral Philosophy of William James* (New York: Thomas Y. Crowell, 1891/1969), p. 183.

20. James, "The Moral Philosopher," p. 187.

21. Ruth Heaton, T*eaching Mathematics to the New Standards: Relearning the Dance* (New York: Teachers College Press, 2000); Robert Yinger, "Routines in Teacher Planning, *Theory into Practice* 18, 163–89 (1979); "Learning the Language of Practice," *Curriculum Inquiry* 17(3), 293–318 (1987); "The Conversation of Practice," *Reflection in Teacher Education,* ed. Peter P. Grimmet and Galen L. Erickson (New York: Teachers College Press, 1988), 73–94; Gaea Leinhardt and James Greeno, "The Cognitive Skill of Teaching," *Journal of Educational Psychology* 78 (2), 75–95 (1986).